Critical Essays on

TONI MORRISON'S
Beloved

CRITICAL ESSAYS
ON
AMERICAN LITERATURE

James Nagel, General Editor
University of Georgia, Athens

◆

Critical Essays on
TONI MORRISON'S
Beloved

◆

edited by

BARBARA H. SOLOMON

G. K. Hall & Co.
New York

Prentice Hall International
London   Mexico City   New Delhi   Singapore   Sydney   Toronto

G.K. Hall & Co.
1633 Broadway
New York, NY 10019

Library of Congress Cataloging-in-Publication Data

Critical essays on Toni Morrison's Beloved / edited by Barbara H. Solomon.
    p. cm. — (Critical essays on American literature)
    Includes bibliographical references and index.
    ISBN 0-7838-0049-5 (alk. paper)
    1. Morrison, Toni. Beloved. 2. Historical fiction, American—History and criticism. 3. Afro-American women in literature. 4. Infanticide in literature. 5. Slaves in literature. 6. Ohio—In literature. I. Soloman, Barbara H. II. Series.
PS3563.08749B434 1998
813'.54—dc21   98-26861
                                                                CIP

This paper meets the requirements of ANSI/NISO Z3948-1992 (Permanence of Paper).

10 9 8 7 6 5 4 3

Printed in the United States of America

This book is for
Sybil Jordan Hampton

Contents

◆

ORIGINAL ESSAYS

General Editor's Note

◆

This series seeks to anthologize the most important criticism on a wide variety of topics and writers in American literature. Our readers will find in various volumes not only a generous selection of reprinted articles and reviews but original essays, bibliographies, manuscript selections, and other materials brought to public attention for the first time. This volume, *Critical Essays on Toni Morrison's* Beloved, is the most comprehensive gathering of essays ever published on one of the most important contemporary novels in the United States. It contains both a sizable gathering of early reviews and a broad selection of more recent scholarship. Among the authors of reprinted articles and reviews are Margaret Atwood, Rosellen Brown, Trudier Harris, and Bernard W. Bell, as well as Toni Morrison, discussing the opening of her novel. In addition to a substantial introduction by Barbara H. Solomon, there are also four original essays commissioned specifically for publication in this volume, new studies by Yvonne Atkinson on the black oral tradition in the novel, Jan Furman on Sethe's memories, Lovalerie King on the disruption of formulaic discourse, and Terry Otten on the transfiguration of the novel from melodrama to tragedy. We are confident that this book will make a permanent and significant contribution to the study of American literature.

JAMES NAGEL
University of Georgia

Publisher's Note

◆

Producing a volume that contains both newly commissioned and reprinted material presents the publisher with the challenge of balancing the desire to achieve stylistic consistency with the need to preserve the integrity of works first published elsewhere. In the Critical Essays series, essays commissioned especially for a particular volume are edited to be consistent with G. K. Hall's house style; reprinted essays appear in the style in which they were first published, with only typographical errors corrected. Consequently, shifts in style from one essay to another are the result of our efforts to be faithful to each text as it was originally published.

Acknowledgments

◆

I would like to thank Stanley, my husband, friend, and colleague, for his encouragement and good humor, and Nancy and Jen, who turned out to be my good friends as well as my affectionate daughters. At the Department of English at Iona College, colleagues Helen Bauer and Cedric R. Winslow were particularly helpful. Departmental graduate research assistants Kimberly Hall-Kouril and Liisa Chider cheerfully and energetically pursued and organized numerous materials; and undergraduate student assistants Allison Balcan, Brendan Breen, and Andrea O'Neill also worked diligently on this project. A great deal of assistance was provided at Ryan Library by Adrienne Franco, Melaine Forsburg, Robert Monteleone, and Janet Steins, as well as by Mary A. Bruno, Teresa Alifante, and Alexandra Russell-DelPrincipe of Iona's Information Technology Resource Center. To Iona College, I am indebted for a faculty fellowship during 1996 and 1997 and for the funding of the *Beloved* Research Group (Kimberly Clansy, Clorisa Cook, and Shauné Wallace).

Introduction

BARBARA H. SOLOMON

Within a decade of its 1987 publication, Toni Morrison's *Beloved* has become a classic of American fiction. The novel was briefly the topic of a controversy about racism and literature when 48 black writers and critics published a letter and "Statement" in the *New York Times Book Review* titled "Black Writers in Praise of Toni Morrison." This letter, signed by well-known artists and scholars such as Maya Angelou, Houston A. Baker Jr., Toni Cade Bambara, Henry Louis Gates, Paule Marshall, and Alice Walker, paralleled the lack of recognition and acclaim suffered by James Baldwin in America with *Beloved* being passed over for the 1987 National Book Award for fiction. Describing Baldwin's treatment in terms of "shame" and "national neglect," and reveling "in the posthumous acclamations of his impact and his public glory," the writers (June Jordan and Houston A. Baker Jr.) implied that Toni Morrison had become a similar victim of racism of a white literary establishment since she, like Baldwin, had never received the National Book Award or the Pulitzer Prize.[1] (She had been awarded the Book Critics Circle Award for *Song of Solomon*.)

Referring to "the written wizardry of Toni Morrison" Jordan and Baker summed up both the literary and cultural achievement of the novelist: "Throughout, she [Morrison] has persisted in the task of calling 'her beloved/which was not beloved.' She has insisted on the subjects of her sorrowing concern: 'my people/which were not my people'—black children and women and men variously not themselves, variously not yet free from an inexplicable, mad, impinging hatred that would throttle or derange all village/family/sexual love. And devoutly, she has conjured up alternatives to such a destiny: political and skin-close means to a transcendent self-respect. Today, all the literate world knows Toni Morrison" (36).

New York Times book reviewer Michiko Kakutani discussed the choice of the 1987 National Book Award for fiction committee in her article "Did 'Paco's Story' Deserve Its Award?" The chair of that committee had described

1

the choice of Larry Heinemann's Vietnam novel over *Beloved* as reflecting "an agonizing down-to-the-wire deliberation."[2] But Kakutani described Heinemann's narrative strategy in unfavorable terms, commenting that "by making that voice [the collective voice of Paco's dead buddies] a hip cynical one, he's able to avoid dealing with many of the troubling political and moral ambiguities raised by the war. . . ." (15 C). On the other hand, in analyzing the subject matter of Morrison, the reviewer clearly was far more impressed with this "work of mature imagination—a magisterial and deeply moving meditation not only on the cruelties of a single institution, but on family, history and love. Instead of reconfirming our feelings about tragedies in our nation's past (war is hell, slavery is evil), the novel shakes up all our preconceptions, makes us grapple with the moral chiaroscuro that shades each of the characters' decisions. It does not merely give us a portrait of one individual's loss of innocence, but also reveals the myriad ways in which families and strangers can hurt and redeem one another" (15 C).

Some writers and critics feared that the protest letter and ensuing controversy about whether Morrison was a black writer who had been treated unfairly would have a negative effect on the Pulitzer judges who were meeting during that time. The awarding of the 1988 Pulitzer Prize for fiction to *Beloved* seemed to signal an end to the question of fitting recognition of Morrison's merits. And Toni Morrison's selection as the 1993 winner of the Nobel Prize in literature clearly confirmed her international stature as one of America's leading writers, or, as some would assert, as America's leading writer.

THE REVIEWS

Because of their high regard for Morrison as a preeminent writer of American fiction and because of their respect for her four previous novels, a number of the newspaper and magazine reviewers of *Beloved* wrote detailed discussions of the novel that are analytical, informative, and even somewhat scholarly. As Marilyn Judith Atlas observes in "Toni Morrison's *Beloved* and the Reviewers," most reviewers focused "their attention not so much on whether the novel deserved to be read, but how it fits into the world of modern American literature, how it connects the past with the future and whether or not it was one of Morrison's best novels. Many reviews were actually review essays, trying to analyze as well as describe the nature of Morrison's writing and ideas. Most would agree with Thomas R. Edwards, who wrote in the *New York Review of Books,* 'A novel like Toni Morrison's *Beloved* makes the reviewer's usual stereotypes of praise and grumbling seem shallow.' "[3] As Atlas notes, most of the reviewers explored *Beloved* in the context of the previous work of Morrison, relating it "to an Afro-American intellectual tradition. And they assumed that their job was not to convince others to read her" (47). On the other hand, the job of assessing *Beloved* "was complicated by the novel's subject—the horror of slavery and its fallout—reminding both reviewer and reader not only of the existence of past atrocities, but that these atrocities can never be totally annihilated. Between Morrison's prestige, her race, and her subject, *Beloved* was difficult to evaluate with even a semblance of objectivity" (46–47).

While the number of favorable and laudatory reviews greatly outnumbered the unfavorable ones, several of the critics who disliked the novel clearly articulated their objections to Morrison's subject and style. But, as James Berger observes: "The few negative reviews of *Beloved* emerged from the conservative position and condemned the novel for setting Sethe's infanticide in the context of general social injustice."[4]

Three of the most condemnatory reviews, those written by Carol Iannone, Martha Bayles, and Stanley Crouch, reflected these critics' political or cultural perspectives as much as literary judgments. For example, in "Toni Morrison's Career," Iannone summarizes the novelist's depiction of her characters' experiences:

> [T]he book grows massive and heavy with cumulative and oft-repeated miseries, with new miseries and new dimensions of miseries added in each telling and retelling long after the point has been made and the reader has grown numb. The graphic descriptions of physical humiliation begin to grow sensationalistic, and the gradual unfolding of secret horror has an unmistakably Gothic dimension which soon comes to seem merely lurid, designed to arouse and entertain.[5]

In Iannone's judgment, the novelist "does not display a really sure hand in her treatment of the moral dimensions of Sethe's initial act of child murder," and "the fantastical, sensational elements in her work often come to look like artistic evasions" (63).

In "Special Effects, Special Pleading," Martha Bayles refers to *Beloved* as "two hundred and seventy-five pages of self-indulgent prose" to be plowed through by the reader.[6] She finds Paul D's characterization unrealistic and asserts:

> He's just a list of saintly traits, combined with a longer list of sufferings. Obviously, the clipping from *The American Baptist* was only one item in a bulging file of antebellum atrocities which Morrison decided to cram, willy-nilly, into this novel. Paul D, Sethe, and a few other slaves belonging to the same owner in Kentucky experience a complete catalogue of barbaric practices and ungodly perversions from all over the South, as well as from Brazil and the West Indies. For instance, they are forced to wear a type of iron headgear used to keep starving slaves on vast Caribbean plantations from eating the sugarcane they were cutting. Neither Morrison nor her conscience-stricken admirers bother to ask whether such a device would really have existed on a small farm in tobacco-growing Kentucky. (36)

Bayles concludes that Morrison excuses "Sethe from lasting blame" and that "in Morrison's mind there seems to be only one crime, that of slavery itself, and no person who lives under it has to answer for anything" (40).

In his *New Republic* review, "Aunt Medea," Stanley Crouch asserts that Morrison "lacks a true sense of the tragic" and that in the novel she "only asks that her readers tally up the sins committed against the darker people and feel sorry for them, not experience the horrors of slavery as they do."[7] Crouch refers to *Beloved* as a work of "protest pulp fiction," in which "the world exists in a purple haze of overstatement, of false voices, of strained homilies; nothing very subtle is ever really tried. *Beloved* reads largely like a melodrama lashed to the structural conceits of the miniseries."

Ann Snitow and Judith Thurman are among the reviewers who express significant reservations about *Beloved* while at the same time discussing the novel's strengths and its powerful effect. In "Death Duties: Toni Morrison Looks Back in Sorrow," Snitow describes her reaction to the role of Beloved, whom she considers "a drag on the narrative, a sour mixed with a great deal of dross," adding that "no matter how she kicks and squalls and screams, the ghost is too light to symbolize the static fact of her own death. She is a distraction from those in the flesh who must bear the pain of a dead child's absence. She is dead, which is the only arresting thing about her, and Morrison's prose goes dead when it concerns her."[8] On a positive note, the reviewer declared that even if *Beloved* had not succeeded in its ambitions, "It is still a novel by Toni Morrison, still therefore full of beautiful prose, dialogue as rhythmically satisfying as music, delicious characters with names like Grandma Baby and Stamp Paid, and scenes so clearly etched they're like hallucinations." Snitow likens Morrison to Dickens, both creators of "wild, flamboyant, abstractly symbolic characters who are at the same time not grotesques but sweetly alive, full of deep feeling."

In "A House Divided," Judith Thurman objects to the novelist's use of "melodrama in her big, violent scenes, or weeping in her domestic ones. There is a chorus of stock characters—good neighbors, evil prison guards, a messenger of the gods called Stamp Paid, and even a tree named Brother."[9] In spite of these qualities, the reviewer concludes: "But if you read *Beloved* with a vigilant eye, you should also listen to it with a vigilant ear. There's something great in it: a play of human voices, consciously exalted, perversely stressed, yet holding true. It gets you."

Many of the numerous positive reviewers of *Beloved* praised Morrison as a writer who is also a cultural force. They lauded the publication of the novel with great enthusiasm. Walter Clemons declared, "I think we have a masterpiece on our hands here."[10]

Margaret Atwood begins her review "Haunted by Their Nightmares" by proclaiming that *Beloved* is a triumph: "Indeed, Ms. Morrison's versatility and technical and emotional range appear to know no bounds. If there were any doubts about her stature as a pre-eminent American novelist, of her own or any other generation, *Beloved* will put them to rest."[11] And Thomas R. Edwards, self-conscious of himself as a "white male reader" who is unsure of some of his suppositions about Morrison's goals, concludes his review "Ghost Story" by writing: "What I am sure about is that this book will convince any thoughtful reader, of any sex or color, that Toni Morrison is not just an important contemporary novelist but a major figure of our national literature. She has written a work that brings to the darkest corners of American experience the wisdom, and the courage, to know them as they are."[12]

THE CRITICISM

Narrative Form, Chronology, and Point of View

Many of the topics discussed by the initial reviewers of *Beloved* have been explored in depth by literary critics and scholars who have participated in a lively and provocative dialogue about the novel. Within the first decade of its publication, the sophisticated narrative structure and compelling subjects of the novel have been analyzed and interpreted from a wide range of perspectives. As might be expected, in many of the best critical articles about the novel, scholars have employed a combination of approaches, sometimes combining elements of feminist, psychoanalytical, new historicist, deconstructionist, and reader-response criticism.

Additionally, many of the topics addressed in these articles overlap, as it is often impossible (and undesirable) to focus on a character or theme in isolation from the other characters and themes, from the community as a whole, from the historical background, or from the literary and cultural influences that help to illustrate events and ideas.

A considerable number of critics have addressed Morrison's narrative structure and rhetorical strategies in *Beloved*. The novel's fragmented chronology; elliptical, ambiguous, and repeated descriptions of events; multiplicity of narrative voices; and repeated patterns of images and motifs are central to *Beloved*'s powerful impact. These strategies require the intensive participation of readers who must sort out the characters' relationships, piece together details of setting and time, restructure developing information, relate clusters of images to particular events, rethink those actions in terms of additional details, explanations, and revelations in later sections of the novel, and identify and evaluate the varied narrative perspectives from which events are viewed.

Significantly, the artistic goal of profoundly involving and moving her readers that Morrison realizes through her narrative strategies in *Beloved* had long been one of the novelist's major preoccupations. Commenting on her first novel, *The Bluest Eye* (1970), in an Afterword she supplied in 1993 to the

Plume/Penguin edition, Morrison discusses that novel's structure and the effect she had hoped to achieve: "My solution—break the narrative into parts that had to be reassembled by the reader—seemed to me a good idea, the execution of which does not satisfy me now. Besides, it didn't work: many readers remain touched but not moved."[13]

In "Circularity in Toni Morrison's *Beloved*," Philip Page identifies the circle as the dominating structure of the novel: "The principal narrative strategy is to drop an unexplained fact on the reader, veer away into other matters, then circle back with more information about the initial fact, then veer away again, circle back again, and so on."[14] Page's first example of this technique is the process by which readers discover that 124 is indeed the number of a house, and he notes that the strategy is particularly evident "when the opening words of a chapter introduce a new mysterious detail, often from a point of view that is at first unidentified (examples include 'It was time to lay it all down' [86]; 'She moved him' [119]; and 'That ain't her mouth' [154])." The critic notes that a number of circular patterns of *Beloved*'s content parallel the circular structure of the narrative form: "The telling of the novel replicates Sethe's act of circling her subject in the kitchen with Paul D. Just as she cannot say directly what she did or why, so the narration does not tell the story directly. Just as she says a little, then digresses, then circles back, so does the narration. Just as Paul D only catches fragments, and must wait until she circles closer and closer, so must readers be content with fragments and wait until they are told enough" (35). Page identifies metaphoric circles such as that of the Cincinnati black neighborhood around the house and both the actual and attempted family circles of the characters. The generations of women repeat and dovetail with each other. Baby Suggs, the grandmother, mothers Sethe in the absence of her own children, as Sethe in turn mothers her children. Sethe then replaces Baby Suggs in the mother's role, which is represented by Sethe's replacing Baby Suggs in "the keeping room" (19). In turn, Sethe as mother is replaced by Denver when Denver learns to cope with the world and to provide for the family. Repetition also structures the novel in the duplication of key events. Mr. Bodwin's arrival at the house parallels the earlier arrival of schoolteacher's posse, and Sethe's attack echoes her earlier action. Paul D arrives, leaves, and arrives again. Denver goes twice to Lady Jones and interacts significantly twice with Nelson Lord. The ghost of Beloved haunts Sethe and Denver, is chased away by Paul D, but returns more powerfully, and finally, through the action of Sethe, Denver, and the community, is exorcised for good (34).

In her article "Call and Response as Critical Method: African-American Oral Traditions and *Beloved*," Maggie Sale explores the way in which one of the novel's vivid images functions to describe a central narrative strategy of the novel. Before the Civil War, according to Morrison, 124 was a stop on the Underground Railroad, a house " 'where bits of news soaked like dried beans in spring water—until they were soft enough to digest (65).' The text of *Beloved* functions in a similar way for contemporary readers: as a textual space in which the horrors of slavery and the sometimes equally horrific responses to it by the (formerly) enslaved are not simply denied, or justified, or explained away, but are presented through an empowering use of oral traditions and language so that they become *digestible*."[15] The individual stories in *Beloved,* such as those of Sethe's murder of her child and of Paul D's chain-gang days in Alfred, Georgia, are experiences the characters don't want to remember. Sale notes, as do Page and many other critics, the way in which such events are circled "from a number of different perspectives." She emphasizes the psychological state of the characters as they try to deal with the past: "This process of retelling describes the outermost circling paths of a deepening and narrowing spiral that is the form of the novel. Each of these circling paths is demarcated by the peeling away of emotional defenses to reveal an individual character's remembered story about the infanticide or events leading up to it. The remembered stories come in digestible bits and pieces, emphasizing slightly different or new material depending on the particular perspective, which, when considered together, move chronologically toward the act." Both Morrison's characters and her readers are in need of a mediating narrative structure to make the protagonists' memories more bearable, more digestible.

In "The Ghosts of Slavery: Historical Recovery in Toni Morrison's *Beloved,*" Linda Krumholz observes that Morrison's "indirection also has to do with the nature of memory itself," and is a reflection of the "nature of repression," of an event that "is part of the inarticulate and irrational unconscious."[16] In her view, "[T]he process of the novel corresponds to Sethe's healing ritual, in which the unspoken incident is her most repressed memory, whose recollection and recreation are essential to her recovery" (406). One important effect of "Morrison's fragmented revelation of Sethe's terrible act," notes the critic, is that it "works to postpone the reader's judgment" (406).

Karla F. C. Holloway in "*Beloved:* A Spiritual," emphasizes Morrison's "assurance of her mediative narrative presence"[17] as an important strategy in the novel. She explains that the "narrative structures have been consciously manipulated through a complicated interplay between the implicit orature of recovered and (re)membered events and the explicit structures of literature. The reclamation and revision of history function as both a thematic emphasis and textual methodology. The persistence of this revision is the significant strategic device of the narrative structures of the novel" (516). Holloway describes the distinct voices of Sethe, Denver, and Beloved. For example, she characterizes Sethe's discourse as "vibrant and redolent," noting that "Sethe's discourse is dense—interwoven with dialect and poetry and complicated with the smells and touches and colors that are left to frame her reality" (519). The critic believes that in particular passages Morrison blends and merges the three women's voices "into a tightened poetic chant" in a departure from the Western literary tradition, because "the identity of the speaker is absolutely unclear and singularly irrelevant" (520).

In "One Reader's Response to Toni Morrison's *Beloved*," Sue Park discusses the structuring of the novel through three books or divisions that "begin identically with the numeral '124' followed by the verb 'was':

> 124 was spiteful. (3)
> 124 was loud. (169)
> 124 was quiet. (239)"[18]

Park comments that readers are "struck initially by the peculiarity of a sentence's beginning with numerals, followed by an uncertainty as to the identity of 124" (41), as she examines the relationship between the opening sentence and the section of the novel that each introduces. Additionally, the critic describes and analyzes the three pictures that appear at the beginning of each of the three major divisions of the text. Of the first drawing she comments:

> The novel's title page has what looks like a rubbing in black and white, the stylized head and wings of an angel in a half-circle, above the title, printed in a font suggestive of stone carving. The reader discovers within the first half-dozen pages of the story the appropriateness of the design, for Sethe has used sex to pay for letters chiseled on the gravestone for her dead baby girl. . . .
>
> The title page design, then, becomes for the reader/co-creator a delineation of the tombstone marking the grave of Sethe's baby. Each of the half-title pages for the major divisions bears a variation on this rubbing motif—a black head with black wings, a black-and-white design of intertwined spirals and six-petalled flowers inscribed in circles, and a pair of black wings on a hollow-eyed skull. The starkness of these designs suggests the grim reality of existence under slavery. . . . (40)

Although these markers are "perhaps not technically an element of the written word" (40), they function as structuring devices with thematic relevance.

According to Rafael Pérez-Torres in "Knitting and Knotting the Narrative Thread—*Beloved* as Postmodern Novel," Morrison's novel confronts "a facelessness the dominant culture in America threatens to impose on black experience, [and] forges out of cultural and social absence a voice and identity. *Beloved* creates an aesthetic identity by playing against and through the cultural field of postmodernism."[19] Describing the text as "a story woven of myth that creates a pattern of sophisticated linguistic play" (690), the critic identifies "the motif of absence and presence" as central to the novel (691). He observes that "the action in *Beloved* turns on processes of reinscription and reinterpretation. It intertwines the mythic, folkloric and poetic threads of an oral literature with the rhetorical and discursive trajectories of a postmodern literary landscape" (690). Of considerable significance, he asserts, is Morrison's employment of pastiche as "a liberating technique which frees the signifier from a fixed frame of reference"; it "suggests that each narrative form evoked by the novel—novelistic, modernistic, oral, preliterate, journalistic—becomes a metanarrative at play in the field of the novel" (703).

After summarizing some information about the setting and characters of *Beloved* in "An Apocalypse of Race and Gender: Body Violence and Forming Identity in Toni Morrison's *Beloved*," T. Mark Ledbetter comments that his own "description is somewhat unfair to the novel because it imposes an order on the life of an enslaved people seeking self-identity and order—neat, even romantic."[20] Instead, observes Ledbetter, "*Beloved* has no plot but a series of plottings, stories within stories without respect for conventional time sequences of past, present and future. These isolated stories need not know one another. Alone they lay claim to what it means to be black and/or woman in a white and male world. There is power in the stories' isolation" (80). The stories, according to the critic, "are connected by 'rememory,' the word Sethe uses to describe the 'things that never die' " (81). Ledbetter characterizes and discusses "three types of stories: body disfigured, body violated, and body dismembered, each giving some insight into a moment when black and woman, developing some newfound sense of identity, within the pain, release horror onto the world, a horror born of otherness" (81).

In "Mixed Genres and the Logic of Slavery in Toni Morrison's *Beloved*," Carl D. Malmgren describes *Beloved* as "a novel that straddles generic forms."[21] Labeling the work "as unusually hybridized text—part ghost story, part historical novel, part slave narrative, part love story," he examines the way in which Morrison joins together such disparate forms as a ghost story, which requires the readers' "willing suspension of disbelief in the supernatural," and the historical novel, which "is based on a respect for the reality principle . . . [with] its basic allegiance to the world as it is or as it has been" (96). The critic believes that yet "another narrative form, the slave narrative, holds the key to the narrative's unity. It is the institution of slavery that supplies the logic underwriting the novel, the thematic glue that unifies this multifaceted text" (96). Additionally, as a love story, the novel "mediates upon and mediates between the various forms that love takes" [and, thus] "its dominant theme is the problematics of love, particularly as regards the question of identity" (101). The critic considers the so-called "logic of slavery" as one of the ghosts that Sethe must lay "to rest" in order to have a future (105).

Marilyn Sanders Mobley, in "A Different Remembering: Memory, History, and Meaning in *Beloved*," also emphasizes the connection between *Beloved* and the genre of the slave narrative, suggesting that there is an important "inter-textual relationship" between the two:[22]

> . . . I would like to argue that Morrison uses the trope of memory to revise the genre of the slave narrative and to thereby make the slave experience it inscribes more accessible to contemporary readers. In other words, she uses memory as the metaphorical sign of the interior life to explore and represent dimensions of slave life that the classic slave narrative omitted. By so doing, she seeks to make

slavery accessible to readers for whom slavery is not a memory, but a remote historical fact to be ignored, repressed or forgotten. Thus, just as the slave narratives were a form of narrative intervention designed to disrupt the system of slavery, *Beloved* can be read as a narrative intervention that disrupts the cultural notion that the untold story of the black slave mother is, in the words of the novel, "the past something to leave behind." (357–58)

The critic asserts that Morrison's "narrative poetics operate through memory and history to create meaning" (359) and that her novel depicts "the unsaid of the narratives, the psychic subtexts that lie within and beneath the historical facts" (359).

In "Narrative Control and Subjectivity: Dismantling Safety in Toni Morrison's *Beloved,*" Andrew Schopp discusses the importance of the silences or absences within the novel, the "unspeakable thoughts, unspoken (Morrison, *Beloved,* 245)" of the women who inhabit 124 Bluestone:[23] "Of course, to speak the unspeakable, to articulate the culturally repressed, is to threaten the inherent 'safety' provided by the maintenance of dichotomies such as speakable/unspeakable, known/unknown, etc. To some degree, the house at 124 seems to constitute a 'safe' space within which Sethe, Denver and Beloved can speak what cannot be spoken elsewhere. This would seem incredibly ironic, since the house is also haunted. The house has its parallel in the novel itself, since a horrific history (that much of American culture would like to keep silenced) haunts this text and its characters" (355). Schopp finds the word "suture" particularly useful because the novel "lends itself to an analysis based on recent theories of cinematic suture [especially those of Kaja Silverman] as they have been applied to literary studies" (358). The critic describes Paul D's need to tell Sethe about seeing Halle after she had been "milked" by schoolteacher's nephew and about his inability to speak to Halle because of the bit he was forced to wear. Sethe and Paul D both "*need* to engage in a suturing process because they have effectively been narrated out of the dominant culture" (358). Schopp then explains that the suturing process that takes place within the novel is also the process that *Beloved's* readers experience: "At the core of this process is narrative control, and I would argue that Morrison's novel self-consciously invites and disrupts the suturing process while it also uses 'suture' as a crucial metaphor that exposes narrative's horror and power. In fact, Morrison's own narrative agency enables her to manipulate a series of narratological mechanisms (e.g., shifts in focalization, proairetic sequence, and hermeneutic codes), thereby revealing to the reading subject his/her own subjugation to narrative control. However, it is her manipulation of suture, as both narrative process and metaphor, that constitutes the novel's most significant use of displeasure and horror. In *Beloved,* the suturing process creates a disturbing dual identification between reading subject and textual subject (i.e., characters) and between reading subject and speaking subject (i.e., the processes of narrative control)" (359).

In "Narrative Possibilities at Play in Toni Morrison's *Beloved*," Giulia Scarpa describes the development of the novel "through the variation of a few crucial events that are reiterated over and over by different voices."[24] The critic notes that the arrival of Paul D and Beloved at 124 triggers "two parallel streams of memory that Sethe has been trying to repress": "The fact that she manages to hide her baby's fate from Paul D is the device by which two lines of the story can run parallel and be intertwined without touching one another, except when they finally collide. The reader is progressively made the narrator's accomplice and knows more than some of the characters . . . but there are always surprises even for the well informed reader" (95). Of the novel's failure to provide a linear chronological story, the critic observes that "its fragmented discourse epitomizes the experience of Black Americans since their displacement from Africa" (102). Scarpa considers the wedding gown that Sethe "patched together with stolen pieces of cloth from the Garners' house" as emblematic of the fragmented and anxious slave experience (102).

In "Telling *Beloved*," Andrew Levy comments on Sethe's role as one of the novel's narrative voices: "The story of Sethe's life and her infanticide is the story of *Beloved*, and it is told time and again within *Beloved*, narrated by individual characters, retrieved from press clippings, passed on as abolitionist rhetoric or racist sociology, but mostly told by Sethe herself."[25] Significantly, no single individual is successful in telling the story, and thus "Morrison appears to suggest . . . perhaps the story is meant to be told multivocally, as a fluid amalgamation of many individual perspectives—the community of narrative voices, for instance, that constitutes *Beloved* itself" (115). Characterizing Sethe as an "obsessive" speaker, the critic observes that "[o]nly Beloved herself seems not to be listening; or rather, listening with an uncontrollable intensity" (115), and that she seems unable to comprehend anything except that Sethe abandoned her. In Levy's somewhat atypical view, the scar where Beloved's throat was cut "*intrudes* on the story: the emotional upheaval of past events makes obsessive speakers and obsessive audiences, who, in trying to assuage their grief, only destroy the possibility of creating healing contacts through storytelling" (116).

Barbara Hill Rigney, in " 'Breaking the Back of Words': Language, Silence, and the Politics of Identity in *Beloved*," points out that it is "only through an analysis of her [Morrison's] language that we can reconstruct an idea of the political and artistic revolution she represents."[26] Employing the terms "confrontational" and "unpoliced," Rigney describes the novelist's language as that "of black feminine discourse—semiotic, maternal, informed as much by silence as by dialogue, as much by absence as by presence." According to the critic,

[I]n all of Morrison's fictions what is left unsaid is as important as what is stated and specified, what is felt is as significant as what is experienced, what is dreamed is as valid as what transpires in the world of "fact." And none of these conditions of being is rendered as opposites; there are no polarities between logic and mysticism, between real and fantastic. Rather, experience for Morrison's characters is the acceptance of a continuum, as recognition that the mind is not separate from the body nor the real separate from that which the imagination can conceive.

Prose Style and Language

In a 1987 television interview, Morrison discussed her reverence for and the strength of the black oral tradition in a way that provided some glimpses into her own prose style and artistic aims. She described the African American experience of listening to sermons in storefront churches with their stylized messages and the power of speakers such as Martin Luther King Jr. and Jesse Jackson and commented that such speakers expect "to get a real response." They don't expect the audience, as in the Western tradition, "to listen silently."[27]

Elsewhere, Morrison has emphasized the ongoing challenge she faces in creating a prose style that reflects the African American experience: "My choices of language (speakerly, aural, colloquial), my reliance for full comprehension on codes embedded in black culture, my effort to effect immediate co-conspiracy, and intimacy (without any distancing, explanatory fabric), as well as my attempt to shape a silence while breaking it are attempts to transfigure the complexity and wealth of Black-American culture into a language worthy of the culture" (Morrison, *The Bluest Eye,* 215–16).

Several critics have explored some of the uniquely African American characteristics of Toni Morrison's prose style in *Beloved.* One distinctive trope, the call-and-response pattern that she employs to involve the novel's readers as actively as possible, has been analyzed by Maggie Sale and Yvonne Atkinson, both of whose work appears in this volume.

According to Sale:

> Call-and-response patterns, developed in spirituals and play and work songs, are related to the group or communal nature of art; these patterns both value improvisation and demand that new meanings be created for each particular moment. The valuing of these characteristics suggests that importance lies not only in what is said, but also in how it is said. The assumption is that a story will be repeated and will change with every telling, and that the success of the telling, and so of the particular story, resides not so much in its similarity to the original as in its individual nuances and its ability to involve others.

Although the novelist doesn't "recreate the 'actual' oral traditions of enslaved African Americans," she uses the general principles of those traditions in "her representation of an enslaved and formerly enslaved past." Sale considers

Morrison's description of the prayers of the 30 women in Sethe's yard at the conclusion of the novel as "a familiar antiphonal form," an example of a translation into print of a call-and-response pattern: " 'Denver saw lowered heads, but could not hear the lead prayer—only the earnest syllables of agreement that backed it: Yes, yes, yes, oh yes. Hear me. Hear me. Do it, Maker, do it.' "

In "The Black English Oral Tradition in *Beloved*: 'listen to the spaces,' " Yvonne Atkinson describes the call as "directed by an individual . . . for the specific purpose of eliciting a response."[28] She illustrates Morrison's practice with a description of Baby Suggs's unchurched preaching:

> Baby Suggs Calls the people to the clearing when "she shouted, 'Let the children come' " (87) and they Respond by "open[ing] their mouths and [giving] her the music. Long notes held until the four-part harmony was perfect enough for their deeply loved flesh" (89). Stamp Paid recalls Baby Suggs' "powerful Call (she didn't deliver sermons or preach—insisting she was too ignorant for that—she called and the hearing heard)" (177).

Atkinson identifies and discusses several prose elements from the oral tradition in addition to the call-and-response pattern such as signifying and witnessing and testifying.

Among Morrison's distinctive practices is her use of coined words. Throughout *Beloved,* Morrison combines the adjective describing an individual's race with a noun to create a single word: for example, "coloredpeople" (47), "whitefolks" (48), "blackwoman" (264), "whitegirl" (78), "blackman" (108), and "whitebabies" (200). The effect of these coined words is, perhaps, to suggest the inseparability of race in any basic description. A memorable example of a combined noun in the novel is, of course, the term used to identify Mrs. Garner's brother-in-law: "schoolteacher."

Creating a coined verb from an unlikely noun, Morrison describes Sethe after Paul D has left 124 as "the woman *junkheaped* [emphasis mine] for the third time because she loved her children . . ." (174). Earlier, Paul D wonders whether he is having "house-fits" as he is moved from room to room by Beloved (115).

The most significant of the novel's coined words is, of course, *rememory.* In "Toni Morrison's *Beloved*: History, 'Rememory,' and a 'Clamor for a Kiss,' " Caroline Rody observes that the word functions as a verb as well as a noun. She explains:

> For Sethe a "rememory" (an individual experience) hangs around as a "picture" that can enter another's "rememory" (the part of the brain that "rememories") and complicate consciousness and identity. "Rememory" as trope postulates the interconnectedness of minds, past and present, and thus neatly conjoins the novel's supernatural vision with its aspiration to communal epic, realizing the "collective memory" of which Morrison speaks. For while the prefix "re" (normally used for the act, not the property of consciousness) suggests that

"rememory" is an active, creative mental function, Sethe's explanation describes a natural—or a supernatural—phenomenon. For Sethe as for her author, then, to "rememory is to use one's imaginative power to realize a latent, abiding connection to the past."[29]

In an emotional conversation in *Beloved,* one of Morrison's characters coins a word, and another character seems to both acknowledge the word and the appropriateness of the user's new coinage: an angry Stamp Paid questions Ella about why the members of their community have allowed Paul D "to sleep in a cellar like a dog." Ella's response is " 'Unrile yourself, Stamp.' " Picking up on the word "unrile," he responds: " 'Not me. I'm going to stay riled till somebody gets some sense and leastway act like a Christian' " (186). Here, as throughout *Beloved,* Morrison creates dialogue between characters that distinguishes them as former slaves while dignifying them as moral, caring, and articulate leaders of the community. In "Unspeakable Things Unspoken: The Afro-American Presence in American Literature," the novelist expresses her disgust with the attempts of some white writers to portray the speech of black characters when she ridicules a passage in Edgar Allan Poe's "The Gold Bug" (1848). Morrison characterizes Poe's work as an effort "to render my grandfather's speech to something as close to braying as possible, an effort so intense you can see the perspiration—and the stupidity—when Jupiter says 'I knows,' and Mr. Poe spells the verb 'nose'."[30]

In a very different sort of passage of dialogue, Morrison dramatizes Sixo's reply to schoolteacher's accusation of theft: " 'Sixo plant rye to give the high piece a better chance. Sixo take and feed the soil, give you more crop. Sixo take and feed Sixo give you more work' " (190). Using parallel phrases, Sixo creates an analogy between making the earth more fertile and a worker more productive in a way that suggests English is a second language for him—which it is—as he reveals the clarity, wit, and intelligence behind his reasoning. In "The Disruption of Formulaic Discourse: Writing Resistance and Truth in *Beloved,*" Lovalerie King analyzes this passage of dialogue as part of a formulaic catechism in which Sixo is resisting the slave holder by refusing to supply the answer expected of him.[31] Brian Finney comments that the "double grammatical use to which Sixo puts his own name . . . indicates the contortions to which the slave is put to make the whiteman's language serve his purposes."[32]

Bernard W. Bell, in "*Beloved:* A Womanist Neo-Slave Narrative; or Multivocal Remembrances of Things Past," discusses the novel's "three basic types of represented discourse (direct, simple indirect, and free indirect)" as well as "five different yet related linguistic codes and their concomitant ideologies (i.e., their implicit, related systems of beliefs and values)" as "standard American English, rural black vernacular English, black feminist discourse, black patriarchal discourse, and white male hegemonic discourse. The two dominant voices, however, are in standard American English and black feminist discourse."[33] He describes the novelist as "the implied author, the version of herself that Morrison creates as she creates the narrative" and Sethe as the "dramatized narrator/protagonist." Bell notes that the novelist "employs Denver to voice the manner and degree to which storyteller, story, and primary audience of *Beloved* share a concord of sensibilities in a residually oral culture which sanctions the dynamic coexistence of the spoken and written word, the metaphysical and physical, the mythic and historic." In the critic's view, "Morrison employs a multivocal text and a highly figurative language to probe her characters' double consciousness of their terribly paradoxical circumstances as people and non-people in a social arena of white male hegemony." He observes that the implied author privileges "metaphor and metonym over black dialect to achieve just the right balance between the poetics and polemics of the long black song of the many thousands gone that she skillfully orchestrates to engage our hearts and mind."

Eusebio L. Rodrigues emphasizes the extent to which techniques associated with music are employed in the novel. In "The Telling of *Beloved*," he asserts that the structuring of the novel is "not spatial but musical."[34] Toni Morrison's narrator, according to the critic, "will stage an extended blues performance, controlling the release of . . . memories, syncopating the accompanying stories of Sixo, Stamp Paid and Grandmother Suggs, making rhythms clash, turning beats into offbeats, introducing blue notes of loneliness and injustice and despair, generating at the end, meanings that hit her listeners in the heart, that region below the intellect where knowledge deepens into understanding." In analyzing the novelist's methods, Rodrigues supplies examples of the way "Morrison undermines the heaviness of print by turning word-shapes into word-sounds in order to allow her narrator to chant, to sing, to exploit sound effects. '. . . No. No. Nono. Nonono' (163): these staccato drumbeats—single, double, triple—translate Sethe's fears of the threatening white world into ominous sounds. Word-sounds enact the rhythmic steps of a dance: 'A little two-step, two-step, make-a-new-step, slide, slide and strut on down' (74)."

Morrison frequently uses catalogs of nouns, verbs, or even complete sentences in creating some of her musical or lyrical effects. Among the other writers who have extensively employed the cataloging of objects or actions in order to achieve a powerful effect through accumulated details are Homer, Jonathan Swift, Walt Whitman, and Langston Hughes. For example, Morrison writes of Baby Suggs that she had "decided that, because slave life had 'busted her legs, back, head, eyes, hands, kidneys, womb and tongue,' she had nothing left to make a living with but her heart" (87).

Valerie Smith, interpreting this passage in " 'Circling the Subject': History and Narrative in *Beloved*," notes that "readers may be inclined to read her use of 'heart' metaphorically, to assume that by 'heart' she means compassion, generosity of spirit. But in the context of this litany of broken body parts, one is reminded that the word 'heart' points to an organ as well as to an emotional capacity. In this context it becomes more difficult to make the familiar move from the corporeal referent to the metaphysical: for this erasure of the corporeal might be read as analogous to the expendability of black bodies under slavery."[35]

When Sethe recollects all the intense pleasures and pain of her first 28 days at Baby Suggs's house, Morrison catalogs her losses through a series of parallel thoughts. There would be "no more dancing in the clearing or happy feeds"; "no more discussions . . . about the true meaning of the Fugitive Bill"; "[n]o anxious wait for the *North Star* or news of a beat off"; and "[n]o sighing at a new betrayal or handclapping at a small victory" (173).

Morrison employs two contrasting catalogs to dramatize the idea of loving small in describing Paul D's inhuman life as a prisoner. Alfred is a place where "mist, doves, sunlight, copper dirt, moon—everything belonged to the men who had the guns" (162). Loving small, which was the only way to survive life on the chain gang, meant that Paul D "picked out the tiniest stars out of the sky to own" and added to them "grass blades, salamanders, spiders, woodpeckers, beetles, a kingdom of ants," because "anything bigger wouldn't do" (162). In "Sethe's 'Big, Bad' Love," Chauncey A. Ridley compares Paul D's goal of "loving small" to protect his sanity with Sethe's " 'big' love, a love more uncompromisingly committed, self-sufficient, and autonomous than any other represented in *Beloved*."[36] In his view, the black community in Cincinnati is guilty of "loving small," whereas "Sethe claims a power to protect and rear her children, overreaching the legal prescription that slaves 'love small' " (161).

Among Morrison's most effective catalogs is that which lists the subjects of the songs sung by the 46 prisoners in Alfred in order to get through another day:

> They sang it out and beat it up, garbling the words so they could not be understood; tricking the words so their syllables yielded up other meanings. They sang the women they knew; the children they had been; the animals they had tamed themselves or seen others tame. They sang of bosses and masters and misses; of mules and dogs and the shamelessness of life. They sang lovingly of graveyards and sisters long gone. Of pork in the woods; meal in the pan; fish on the line; cane, rain and rocking chairs.
>
> And they beat. The women for having known them and no more, no more; the children for having been them but never again. They killed a boss so often and so completely they had to bring him back to life to pulp him one more time. Tasting hot mealcake among pine trees, they beat it away. Singing love songs to Mr. Death, they smashed his head. More than the rest, they killed the flirt whom folks called Life for leading them on. (108–9)

After reading a selection from this passage during the *Profile of a Writer* television interview, Morrison paused to characterize her artistic goals and stylistic practices seemingly with that passage in mind: "I wanted my language to be musical, and I know how terrible that must sound, but not to have ornate poetic words, but in fact to write very simply, which I think I do—write very simply." She continued by discussing "the ornate quality or the rich quality" [that] "really comes from simple sentences in which the reader is invited in with his own emotions; therefore, the experience is rich because the reader has provided so much of what he or she takes away from the book." She added that "if you place the sentences in the proper order and leave a certain amount of space, and dust and clean sometimes very old words, you can arrive at a rich effect without having recourse to overwhelming ornate purple prose—so that I would translate these huge problematic, emotionally problematic and intellectually problematic, things into smaller but more precise images."

The sophisticated and varied use Morrison makes of images has been analyzed by a considerable number of critics. Philip Page likens Morrison's depiction of repeated images throughout the novel to the techniques employed "in African folk narratives, which tend to be built on repetition—of words, phrases, and motifs" (35). The critic notes that there are important parallels between *Beloved* and "the typical form of the Xhosa *ntsomi,* or fanciful tale, as described by Harold Scheub" in Scheub's article "The Technique of the Expansible Image in Xhosa *Ntsomi*-Performances" (36). Page explains that Scheub has found "that storytellers rely upon a vast stock of 'core-cliches'—stock images, characters, and episodes that can be varied to suit a particular story, audience, or occasion. Most stories are built upon one or more 'core-images' drawn from the storyteller's repertoire and expanded to form the core of a particular story. The plot is developed through repetition and variation of one or more core-images in overlapping waves, much like the refrain of a song" (36). In analyzing the narrative development of *Beloved,* Page describes "such core-images" as "the beginning lines of its three main sections: '124 was spiteful' (3), '124 was loud' (169), '124 was quiet' (239). The narrative is developed through the overlapping and accumulating descriptions of such images as Amy's velvet, the tree on Sethe's back, the mating turtles, and Paul D's tobacco tin. And it is developed through the iteration and reiteration of such episodes as the milking of Sethe and Sethe's murder of Beloved, and through the spiraling reiteration of larger, mythical acts such as birth, death, rebirth, quest-journeys, and the formation and disintegration of families" (36).

A number of Morrison's vivid and repeated images function as allusions or references to specific motifs and themes, becoming symbols for them throughout the novel. For example, the red ribbon carried by Stamp Paid is introduced as Stamp approaches 124 "fingering a ribbon and smelling skin" (176), a few pages before the novelist has described his discovery of the ribbon and, thus, made clear its significance:

> Tying his flatbed up on the bank of the Licking River, securing it the best he could, he caught sight of something red on its bottom. Reaching for it, he

thought it was a cardinal feather stuck to his boat. He tugged and what came loose in his hand was a red ribbon knotted around a curl of wet woolly hair, clinging still to its bit of scalp. He untied the ribbon and put it in his pocket, dropped the curl in the weeds. (180)

The ribbon, an image that functions as a symbol of the barbarity of white people and the suffering of black people, perhaps particularly of the women and children, reappears twice on the next page of the text. Morrison declares that "he kept the ribbon" [although] "the skin smell nagged him" and that he believes the voices he hears at 124 are those of "the people of the broken necks, of fire-cooked blood and black girls who had lost their ribbons" (181). Among the other images that function as important symbols or motifs are the chokecherry tree on Sethe's back, the hummingbird beaks through her head-cloth, Denver's emerald closet, the clabber on Halle's face, Baby Suggs's quilt, and the cornfield where Sethe and Halle experienced their first sexual union.

Several critics have commented on the positive significance and beauty of the corn imagery connected to the "wedding" day of Sethe and Halle. According to David Lawrence in "Fleshly Ghosts and Ghostly Flesh: The Word and the Body in *Beloved*,"

> Morrison's narrator creates seamless transitions between their [Sethe's and Paul D's] separate but simultaneous memories of Sethe and Halle's first lovemaking in the cornfield. The recollection culminates in the shared trope for sexual arousal and fulfillment expressed in the husked corn: "How loose the silk. How quick the jailed-up flavor ran free" (27). This convergence of sexuality, memory, and poetic figure beautifully illustrates the intimate communion of linguistic and bodily experience enacted in the novel.[37]

In her analysis of those images, Maggie Sale emphasizes the connection between Morrison's prose style and the composition of music: "[A]n example of repetition that involves improvisation comes when Sethe and Halle make love for the first time in the corn field: 'How loose the silk. How jailed down the juice.... How loose the silk. How quick the jailed-up flavor ran free.... How loose the silk. How fine and loose and free' (27). This kind of progression is characteristic of the blues and is a simple form of improvisation."

Eusebio L. Rodrigues also emphasizes the musical elements of this scene: "Sad, but full of admiration and affection for Sethe, the narrator herself turns celebrant, the music of her language transforming the mating into a unique fertility rite in a tiny cornfield, witnessed by their friends who partake of the young corn. Fourteen-year-old Sethe's virgin surrender to Halle, her moments of pain and joy, have as accompaniments the dance of the corn-stalks, the husk, the cornsilk hair, the pulling down of the tight sheath, the ripping sound, the juice, the loose silk, the jailed-up flavor running free, the joy (27). Light monosyllabic sounds bring this epithalamium to a close: 'How loose the silk. How fine and loose and free.' "

In contrast, Wendy Harding and Jacky Martin in "Reading at the Cultural Interface: The Corn Symbolism of *Beloved*," find the corn images much more problematic and complex than do most other critics. They supply an extensive analysis of the "nuptial" and related cornfield images including that of the ears of corn eaten by Sethe's four rejected suitors (Sixo, Paul A, Paul D, and Paul F) on the night after they watched the rippling corn tops over Sethe and Halle's heads. According to these critics, Morrison employs corn to symbolize complicated and ambivalent ideas of "freedom and confinement" as well as sexuality. Harding and Martin also discuss other scenes associated with corn, such as the field in which the Sweet Home slaves plan to meet to begin their journey to freedom, as well as the ripening ears of corn growing in the yard at 124 Bluestone Road as schoolteacher pursues the young woman and children he considers his property.[38]

Another image that has generated diverse critical analyses is that depicting the arrival of schoolteacher in Baby Suggs's yard. In "Ghosts of Liberalism: Morrison's *Beloved* and the Moynihan Report," James Berger points out, "Morrison frames this event . . . in the language of apocalypse. 'When the four horsemen came . . . ,' the beginning of the chapter in which the infanticide occurs, signals the approach of a world-ending catastrophe. The reference to the book of Revelation makes the slave hunters' entrance into Baby Suggs's yard a sign and portent that transcends history, rends it apart, restructures its movement, and perhaps brings it to an end. The apocalyptic event constitutes a pivotal moment that separates what came before from what comes after" (409). Susan Bowers, in "*Beloved* and the New Apocalypse," T. Mark Ledbetter in "An Apocalypse of Race and Gender: Body Violence and Forming Identity in Toni Morrison's *Beloved*," and Josef Pesch in "*Beloved:* Toni Morrison's Post-Apocalyptic Novel," have commented on this allusive image and theme, particularly as it applies to the African American experience.[39]

Mary G. Basson, Trudier Harris, and Howard W. Fulweiler identify several different patterns of imagery in the novel. In "Unburdening Down by the Riverside: The Imagery of Water as a Precursor to Peace in Toni Morrison's *Beloved*," Basson asserts that "Sethe's escape from her physical bonds and the resolution of her psychological enslavement are associated with water. Water signals episodes which suggest the power of self-knowledge, bringing peace and serenity to the afflicted."[40] Among the water-related images that Basson discusses are Sethe's washing of her legs at the pump, her offering to Paul D of a basin of water for soaking his feet, and Beloved's final disappearance at the stream. The critic also notes that river images appear in several pre–Civil War spirituals such as "Michael, Row the Boat Ashore," "Deep River," "Down by the Riverside," and "One More River," and that early in the novel Paul D sings "Storm upon the Waters" (7).

In "Escaping Slavery but Not Its Images," Harris suggests that Morrison focuses attention on "the buying and selling of human beings by inserting images of monetary units to describe physical features and to convey states such as frustration and remorse."[41] According to the critic, the novelist employs these images of money to "suggest that *some* black people may have modeled their behavior too closely on that of their masters" (333). Harris finds that these images "also become the language of desire in the novel, as characters express their greatest wants in financial terms" (333). She catalogs numerous examples of images dealing with pennies, a silver dollar, coins, prices, and payments and describes the stereotypical Sambo figure on the Bodwins' shelf with his distorted and gaping mouth filled with coins to be used for tips. Even the abolitionist Bodwins are oblivious of the meaning conveyed by the caricatured black boy figure as an obsequious servant.

In "Belonging and Freedom in Morrison's *Beloved:* Slavery, Sentimentality, and the Evolution of Consciousness," Howard W. Fulweiler describes biblical patterns of action, images, and allusions throughout *Beloved.* He notes that a recurring New Testament image "is that of washing or massaging feet: Amy Denver massages Sethe's swollen feet (35); Sethe offers to soak Paul D's feet after his travels (8); Baby Suggs washes Sethe's feet (93); Paul D returns to the isolated Sethe at the end of the novel and asks permission to heat up water to 'rub your feet' (272). These reciprocal acts of humility and service are related to Christ's washing the feet of the disciples at the Last Supper: 'If I then, your Lord and Teacher, have washed your feet, you also ought to wash one another's feet' (John 13:14)."[42] Another scriptural image analyzed by the critic is Sethe's escape across the Ohio River, a trip made possible by the appearance, at a crucial moment, "by a wise boatman named Stamp Paid, a name suggesting independence and responsibility" (343). Noting that Stamp Paid was originally named Joshua, Fulweiler comments that "like Joshua he is not only a type of Christ allegorically, but he in fact tries to be a 'high-minded Soldier of Christ,' despite his self-doubt" (343).

Deborah Guth also finds a significant pattern of religious images, allusions, and references throughout the novel. In " 'Wonder what God had in mind': *Beloved*'s Dialogue with Christianity," she focuses on the "Christian belief and symbolism whose repeated appearance in outlines, displaced, and inverted form throughout the narrative creates a far-reaching tension between the unfolding drama of Beloved's resurrection within the text and the extratextual Biblical model story of suffering and redemption that it refracts and challenges."[43] According to Guth:

> Four major images and motifs mediate the dialogue between the personal experience unfolding through the narrative and the paradigms of Christianity: the words "Dearly Beloved" that are best known as the opening phrase of the marriage service, the symbol of the Cross in a circle burned onto Sethe's mother's body, the Tree of Life grotesquely scarred on Sethe's own back, and the motif of the sacrificial lamb resurrected from the dead—originally Jesus, here Beloved. These and other elements deriving from Scripture and liturgy enter into complex dialogic relations—mainly parodic and tragi-grotesque—

with immediately surrounding elements in the text, with more distant motifs and images, and ultimately with the basic tenets and symbols of the Christian faith itself. At times, in fact, the fragmented and disjunctive way these motifs are refracted suggests not only parody but an almost ritual dismembering of the message of hope. (85)

In "The Bonds of Love and the Boundaries of Self in Toni Morrison's *Beloved*," Barbara Schapiro identifies "a preponderance of oral imagery [that] characterizes Morrison's novel."[44] Approaching *Beloved* from a psychoanalytic perspective, the critic observes:

Beloved, in her fantasies, repeatedly states that Sethe "chews and swallows me" (213), while the metaphor of Beloved chewing and swallowing Sethe is almost literal: "Beloved ate up her life, took it, swelled up with it, grew taller on it" (250). Denver's problems of identity and self-cohesion, too, are often imaged in oral terms: leaving the house means being prepared to "be swallowed up in the world beyond the edge of the porch" (243). When Denver temporarily loses sight of Beloved in the shed, she experiences a dissolution of self . . . and feels she is being "eaten alive by the dark" (123). Beloved, in the second part of the novel, is said to have two dreams: "exploding, and being swallowed" (133). Everywhere in the novel, the fantasy of annihilation is figured orally; the love hunger, the boundless greed, that so determines the life of the characters also threatens to destroy them. (198)

Schapiro also comments that numerous "images of eyes and seeing" are closely connected to the oral imagery, as in the description of Sethe "as being 'licked, tasted, eaten by Beloved's eyes' (57)" (200).

Jean Wyatt, another critic who employs a psychoanalytic approach, begins her essay "Giving Body to the Word: The Maternal Symbolic in Toni Morrison's *Beloved*" by noting that the novelist is depicting three kinds of experiences that are not generally represented in Western literature: "childbirth and nursing from a mother's perspective; the desires of a preverbal infant; and the sufferings of those destroyed by slavery, including the Africans who died on the slave ships. The project of incorporating into a text subjects previously excluded from language causes a breakdown and restructuring of linguistic forms; to make room for the articulation of alternative desires, Morrison's textual practice flouts basic rules of normative discourse."[45] The critic observes that the 19-year-old Beloved is articulating the feelings and needs of an infant "that ordinarily remain unspoken. Her desire to regain the maternal closeness of a nursing baby powers a dialogue that fuses pronoun positions and abolishes punctuation, undoing all the marks of separation that usually stabilize language." Because she "also has a collective identity" as the incarnation or representation of people obliterated by slavery, the "sixty million and more" of the novel's epigraph, Beloved "describes conditions on the slave ships in fragmented images without connective syntax or punctuation," reflecting the bewilderment and loss of identity of the transported captives.

Throughout the novel, according to Wyatt, Morrison "literalizes" metaphors that at first appear to be symbolic or abstract. Among the critic's examples of this practice are several descriptions relating to Paul D's arrival and move into 124: his question of whether "there was some space" (45) for him, Sethe's thought that "the responsibility for her breasts, at last, was in somebody else's hands" (18), and the statement that "She [Beloved] moved him" (114). Wyatt explains the parallel between this prose technique and a central theme of the novel: "What at first appears symbolic becomes actual in a characteristic collapse of metaphor into literal reality—a slippage that accompanies the central materialization of the novel, Beloved's embodiment."

While Wyatt emphasizes the literal level of meaning of seemingly abstract statements, Carolyn Mitchell analyzes the spiritual and symbolic meaning of a repeated and seemingly literal—even prosaic—statement by a character in the novel. In " 'I Love to Tell the Story': Biblical Revisions in *Beloved*," Mitchell discusses Amy Denver's repeated assertions that she is going to Boston to buy crimson velvet as "a trope for female adventure, for the rite of passage, for the realization of larger aspirations."[46] The critic considers Amy's fixation with velvet to represent her goal of achieving freedom and suggests that although her chatter may seem superficial, her behavior with Sethe reflects a "commonality" between the two that is reflected in Morrison's "lyrical" description of Denver's birth.

Beloved's Identity

Quite naturally, a central topic for approaching the novel is the question of the origin and identity of Beloved and the nature of her relationships with Sethe, Paul D, and Denver. Numerous critics have supplied a range of interpretations of her character and role, but a significant element in the controversy—or more accurately the dialogue—about the subject has been the willingness of scholars to entertain multiple and overlapping views of Beloved. Rather than arguing for the exclusivity of their own readings, many critics catalog the varied analyses of Beloved and frequently acknowledge the value of widely differing perceptions.

Robert L. Broad believes that "Morrison's tortured crafting of Beloved's identities can teach us a great deal not just about ghosts, or ancestors, but also about us, the novel's living and breathing readers."[47] In "Giving Blood to the Scraps: Haints, History, and Hosea in *Beloved*," he concludes that Sethe and Denver misinterpret the clues about Beloved to mean that she is "a good, old-fashioned, unified spectral identity" (190). Instead, he finds that Beloved's interior monologue and her confusing questions and complaints about Sethe "are far easier to comprehend if Beloved's anger stems from a trauma completely different in time, place, and nature from the expected one" (191)—her murder at Sethe's hands. In the critic's judgment, "Sethe and Denver don't just get their daughter and sister back; they get a puzzled and puzzling poly-generational, mnemonically tortured, uncertain spirit whose resurrection brings wildly unpredictable results, such as making a whole woman of the spoiled child Denver, and shattering the woman of iron, Sethe. Go looking for a lost ancestor, suggests Morrison, and you don't get a polite, manageable ghost, you get '*Sixty Million and more*' (v) of the 'disremembered and unaccounted for' (274). You get trouble" (192).

In "Nameless Ghosts: Possession and Dispossession in *Beloved*," Deborah Horvitz summarizes the identities of Beloved that are based on an acceptance of her as a symbolic figure with supernatural origins:

> The powerful corporeal ghost who creates matrilineal connection between Africa and America, Beloved stands for every African woman whose story will never be told. She is the haunting symbol of the many Beloveds—generations of mothers and daughters—hunted down and stolen from Africa; as such, she is, unlike mortals, invulnerable to barriers of time, space, and place. She moves with the freedom of an omnipresent and omnipotent spirit who weaves in and out of different generations within the matrilineal chain. Yet, Morrison is cautious not to use Beloved as a symbol in a way that either traps the reader in polemics or detaches one from the character who is at different times a caring mother and a lonely girl. Nor is Beloved so universalized that her many meanings lose specificity. She is rooted in a particular story and is the embodiment of specific members of Sethe's family. At the same time she represents the spirit of all the women dragged onto slave ships in Africa and also all Black women in America trying to trace their ancestry back to the mother on the ship attached to them. Beloved is the haunting presence who becomes the spirit of the women from "the other side." As Sethe's mother she comes from the geographic other side of the world, Africa; as Sethe's daughter, she comes from the physical other side of life, death.[48]

Horvitz concludes that the woman who jumped into the sea is certainly Sethe's grandmother and that Morrison has created "a fluidity of identity among Sethe's mother, Sethe's grandmother, and the murdered two-year-old, so that Beloved is both an individual and a collective being."

In "Toni Morrison's *Beloved*: Re-Membering the Body as Historical Text," Mae G. Henderson, like Horvitz, explores Beloved's symbolic function. She identifies individual women in her description:

> Further, Beloved symbolizes women in both the contemporaneous and historical black communities. Affiliated with the experiences of various women in the novel, Beloved represents the unsuccessfully repressed "other" of Sethe as well as other women in and associated with the community—including Ella, whose "puberty was spent in a house where she was abused by a father and son"; Vashti . . . , who was concubined by her young master, and the girl who (as rumor had it) was locked up by a "whiteman" who had used her to his own pur-

pose. . . . Beyond this, however, Beloved is associated with her maternal and paternal grandmothers and the generation of slave women who failed to survive the "middle passage." As trace of "the disremembered and unaccounted for," Beloved's symbolic function of otherness connects the individual to repressed aspects of the self, as well as to contemporaneous and historical others.[49]

In Henderson's opinion, Beloved is also a symbol of Sethe's past, a past that Sethe must "conjure up" and confront "as an antagonist" if she is "to work through" the "dis-ease" that traps her (74).

Sharon Jessee discusses Beloved's identity in terms of West African religious and cultural beliefs about death and the afterlife. In " 'Tell me your earrings': Time and the Marvelous in Toni Morrison's *Beloved*," she describes Beloved in terms of attitudes toward time and ancestral relationships between the living and the dead. "In her most comprehensive context within the narrative, Beloved stands for all the ancestors lost in the Diaspora, demanding restoration to a temporal continuum in which 'present' time encompasses much of the immediate past, including several generations of the dead."[50] Jessee explains the Swahili concept of *sasa* time during which four or five generations of deceased await their entrance into a final resting place or "storehouse of time" (199). The dead who exist in *sasa* time can appear to relatives and should be recognized and identified by name. According to the critic: "From such African viewpoints, then, cutting off individuals from their earthly relations through slavery and violent death in *Beloved* caused them insufferable isolation and a seemingly irreparable tear in the cohesion of their world" (201).

Dana Heller, in "Reconstructing Kin: Family History and Narrative in Toni Morrison's *Beloved*," believes that "Beloved is perhaps best understood as an embodiment of history held aloft by a foundation we call memory, a foundation that is shown to be partial and fragmentary."[51] In Heller's opinion, "Beloved represents the family as well as the familial. She is as much the family Sethe, Denver, and Paul D have lost as she is all the families separated and dismembered under the slavery system. And the reason she comes back is the same as the reason that this novel had to be written: in order to understand" (107).

Caroline Rody observes that "in imagining the longing of the murdered child for the mother, Morrison reverses the usual direction of grief, in which the living mourn the dead, the child or descendent mourns the mother or ancestor" (104). The critic believes that "to write history as a ghost story, to cast the past as longing for *us,* instead of the other way around, is to inscribe a reversal of desire that informs this text's structure—and the structure of all ghost tales—on a deep level" (104).

Focusing on the genre of the ghost story in "The Haunting of 124," Carol E. Schmudde refers to the 19-year-old haunting that has gone on at Sethe's house. She catalogs a number of Beloved's supernatural traits: "Beloved is much more complexly characterized than most fictional ghosts, but she shares many features of traditional manifestations of phantoms in human form who inhabit haunted houses. She has 'new skin, lineless and smooth' (50), except for the telltale scars of her violent death. She knows things no human being could know. She has supernatural strength and the ability to change shape and to appear and disappear at will. She puts a spell on Paul D which moves him out of the house, and she is finally exorcised by a ritual act of prayers and chanting."[52] The critic examines the description and history of 124 Bluestone Road as a haunted house that is "a necessary condition of Beloved's appearance" as well as "a condition of her interaction with the other characters of the novel" (412). She considers the house "a point of intersection for powerful antithetical forces: North and South, black and white, past and present, this world and the other" (410).

On the other hand, asserting a highly atypical view, Elizabeth B. House believes that "evidence throughout the book suggests that the girl is not a supernatural being of any kind but simply a young woman who has herself suffered the horrors of slavery."[53] In "Toni Morrison's Ghost: The Beloved Who Is Not Beloved," the critic creates a chronological narrative of Beloved's experience that begins with Beloved as a young child in Africa, chronicles her voyage on a slave ship to America, conjectures that she was imprisoned and sexually abused by a white man, and concludes that both Sethe and Beloved mistakenly believe that they are related to one another. According to House, many details that generally have been interpreted to prove that Beloved is a ghost should be considered as realistic descriptions of a young woman whose appearance and behavior reflect her life as an isolated and bewildered escaped captive.

In contrast to House's view, Denise Heinze, in "Beloved and the Tyranny of the Double," characterizes Beloved as "Morrison's most unambiguous endorsement of the supernatural; so rife is the novel with the physical and spiritual presence of ghostly energy that a better term than supernatural would be uncanny. . . ."[54] Emphasizing a psychological approach in interpreting Beloved's role in the novel, the critic describes her as "a memory come to life," as "Sethe's hair shirt," and as "Sethe's alter ego," and believes that Beloved serves "a confrontational function" to act "as Sethe's double." In Heinze's judgment, "for Sethe, Beloved represents more of a psychological than a supernatural phenomenon."

Trudier Harris, in "Beloved: 'Woman, Thy Name Is Demon'," analyzes Beloved in the context of highly negative, patriarchal cultural attitudes and stereotypes of females as the fearful "Other."[55] Labeling Beloved "parasitic," "vampire"-like, and "humanoid," Harris asserts: "The nature of evil—the demonic, the satanic—those are the features of the female body as written by Toni Morrison in Beloved. We can describe the title character as a witch, a ghost, a devil, or a succubus; in her manipulation of those around her, she exerts a power not of this world. In her absence of the tempering emotions that we usually identify with humankind, such as mercy, she is inhumanly vengeful in setting out to repay the one upon whom she places the blame for her too-early demise."

On the other hand, in "To Embrace Dead Strangers: Toni Morrison's *Beloved*," Karen E. Fields emphasizes that Beloved ultimately has highly positive as well as negative effects on Paul D, Denver, and Sethe. The critic describes Beloved as an "apparition [who] is a strange-looking girl of about twenty. . . . She may or may not be a ghost and may or may not be the ghost of Sethe's child. Who or whatever she is, she takes up residence in the lives of Sethe, Paul D, and Denver, Sethe's bottomlessly lonely daughter. She resides with them as Need itself—need for human connection, for warmth, for identity, for stories and on ad infinitum through all the things one human can willingly give to another, and more than that."[56] In Fields's view, however, "there is also reciprocity with this ghost—or—girl. In giving to this being of unbounded demand, the three also receive. Beloved gives by taking" (160). For example, "[T]o Paul D she is a terrifying seductress who compromises his loyalty to Sethe, but from whom he at the same time gets back parts of his living self long shut away" (160). And to Sethe, "she is a compensation and a retribution" (160).

In "Is Morrison Also Among the Prophets?: 'Psychoanalytic' Strategies in *Beloved*," Iyunolu Osagie argues that the novel's contradictory descriptions of Beloved are actually complementary interpretations. In the critic's opinion, Morrison's basic narrative strategy is to displace "the 'comfortable' historical positions we might take on the matter of American slavery."[57] Osagie summarizes the views of Beloved as Sethe's murdered daughter as well as of Beloved as a sexually abused captive who mistakenly thinks Sethe is the mother with whom she made the voyage on a slave ship, concluding that *Beloved* presents "a narrative emplotment that begs to be comprehended on contradictory levels at the same time" (435). Morrison employs a "rhetorical sleight-of-hand" that seduces readers to accept multiple readings of Beloved's origins (435). According to the critic, "[T]he multiple readings of *Beloved* echo the elusive nature of psychoanalysis and its tendency to recover itself constantly; this tendency makes psychoanalysis an uncanny representation of literature" (435). The kind of analysis that she refers to, however, is African rather than Freudian: "African psychoanalysis has its roots in the social and cultural setting of its peoples—in their beliefs in concepts such as nature, the supernatural realm, reincarnation, and retribution. Psychic trauma in the African world usually stems from the immediate historical, social, and political environment, and is responded to in various ways. It can be resisted through the oral transfer of (historical) information, through storytelling, dancing, and exorcism to name a few examples" (424).

Sethe

A substantial body of criticism about Sethe employs a psychoanalytic approach to the novel that is sometimes linked with a feminist critical perspective as well. These approaches are helpful because the central actions and themes of *Beloved* revolve around the trauma of enslavement or escaping slavery, the infanticide, and the process of not merely surviving these experiences but of healing the wounds, recreating family and community relationships, and looking forward to the future. In essence, the institution of slavery is a pathology from which Sethe and those who surround her must attempt to recover.

Barbara Schapiro discusses "the unconscious emotional and psychic consequences of slavery," particularly the way in which "the denial of one's status as a human subject has deep repercussions in the individual's internal world" (194). She believes that the relationships between Sethe, Beloved, and Denver as reflected in their monologues "suggest something more extreme and dangerous than mere fluidity of boundaries: the monologues reveal an utter breakdown of the borders between self and other, a collapse that is bound up with incorporative fantasies" (202). Moreover, the critic notes that after Beloved's return, Sethe "retreats from external reality and succumbs to her destructive, narcissistic fantasies, to her murderously enraged child-self as well as her insatiable need to make reparation for her murderous love" (204).

Jennifer FitzGerald in "Selfhood and Community: Psychoanalysis and Discourse in *Beloved*" contends that Western or classic Freudian psychoanalysis is not an appropriate methodology for interpreting *Beloved* because it tends to isolate "psychic experience from the diversities of ethnicity and class; furthermore, it focuses intensively on the interaction of infant and mother as if this existed as a free-standing relation, independent of the economic, political or social conditions which affect the circumstances of parenting."[58] She finds that one school of psychoanalytic thought, "objects relations theory," is particularly useful in analyzing *Beloved* because of its emphasis on the process by which "social, cultural and political forces become internalized" (670). FitzGerald establishes five categories of discourse as the basis of her methodology because "[l]iterary criticism examines texts, not people; it analyzes discourse, not psyches" (670). The categories she employs are "the dominant discourse of slavery," "the discourse of the good mother," "the discourse of masculinity," "the discourse of black solidarity," and "the pre-Oedipal discourse of objects relations psychoanalysis" (671–72).

Stephanie Demetrakopoulos is one of a number of critics who combine psychoanalytic and feminist perspectives. In "Maternal Bonds as Devourers of Women's Individuation in Toni Morrison's *Beloved*," she explores the "dark and painful side of mothering, the fact that mothering can extinguish the developing self of the mother, sometimes even before that individuation can really begin. . . ."[59] Sethe has gloried in her determination, strength, and resilience as attributes of a mother who needs these characteristics to enable her children to survive, but the critic adds that Sethe's "idea that her children are her best parts, her best self (ultimately her only self)" reflects a destructive "pathological and painfully protracted mothering" from which she must be released in order to have a future (54). According to Demetrakopoulos, "Morrison deliberately creates a character whose strength will not break under the weight of the atrocities that push her maternal bonds in such isolation—away from her community, out of history itself, so far from the rest of life that they can be scrutinized as almost the sole forces in Sethe's life" (53). Moreover, the critic describes the process by which Denver must free herself and help free her mother so that they can become fully adult individuals, escaping the damaging kind of daughter/mother relationship in which they have been entrapped. Denver must recover "from some terrifying clinical symptoms, such as the deafness that follows her hearing the horror of Beloved's death, to carry her mother's soul into the future, into history" (56).

Rebecca Ferguson also combines psychoanalytic and feminist perspectives in "History, Memory and Language in Toni Morrison's *Beloved*," as she discusses the destructive elements in the reuniting of Sethe and Beloved. Examining the deep pre-Oedipal bond between daughter and mother, the critic observes: "[T]here is also a sad irony in that the nearest Beloved comes to seeing herself as 'separate' is when she is lost into death. Dissolution is forced on her at the very point when a fragile process of individuation might begin, in the midst of becoming, and Beloved finds that she is 'going to be in pieces' just when she was striving to join. . . . Beloved's will to return again is to *exist*, to 'find a place to be,' to identify 'the face that left me' so that finally when this is achieved, 'Sethe sees me see her and I see the smile' (p. 213)."[60] Since, according to the critic, Beloved exists in two worlds, she is always "strenuously holding herself together, defending herself from being engulfed or exploding . . ." (114). Additionally, "being in both realms, she seems to exist fully in neither. Likewise, although being swallowed and exploding appear perhaps as opposite figures, both express the same physical instability, the potential for fragmentation and dissolution that the text so often invokes" (114–15). Although both Sethe and Beloved desperately want to create connections—and reconnections—their relationship is marked instead by regression and destructive possession.

In "Pain and the Unmaking of Self in Toni Morrison's *Beloved*," Kristin Boudreau asserts that "[t]he novel . . . takes to task a tradition of romantic suffering, a tradition that valorizes suffering as the pivotal experience whereby an individual becomes fully human."[61] She explores the differences between Wordsworthian, that is, the private, treatment of pain and that of African American writers and blues composers that transfers the articulation of private suffering into the public realm where the group experience of the cultural reality forms a context for an individual's experience. Boudreau carefully defines the goal and method of torture because she believes that "*Beloved* returns repeatedly to sites of physical, psychological, and sexual victimization, suggesting that these characters, scarred in an unfolding variety of ways, represent the product of a system of torture. . . . Their language, their reasoning powers, even their sense of self have been dismantled by the process of torture" (453). After describing Sethe's experiences with pain, such as her mother's lynching and burning and her own lashing with cowhide, Boudreau asserts that "*Beloved* challenges the romantic notion of beautiful, communicable, and humanizing pain by calling attention to the role of pain in unmaking language—not just the language of pain, but any language whatsoever" (456). In examining the problems of identity of a number of the novel's characters, Boudreau concludes that "*Beloved* persistently asks its readers where selfhood is located and seems to imply that language and memory, already dissolved by pain, bear responsibility for constructions of self" (457).

In a highly personal essay, "Spitting Out the Seed: Ownership of Mother, Child, Breasts, Milk and Voice in Toni Morrison's *Beloved*," Michele Mock intersperses descriptions of her own experiences as a nursing mother with descriptions of Sethe's experiences as an enslaved mother. Mock asserts that "slavery has many horrors," but as a mother she finds "the avulsion of the mother child circle the most appalling horror of all."[62] She describes breast-feeding as "the ultimate expression of maternal love" (117) and emphasizes the psychological bonding that occurs between the nursing mother and the needy infant. The critic notes that Sethe was deprived of both an emotional connection and sufficient mother's milk when her mother was separated from her to return to the fields. Moreover, from Sethe's perspective her greatest suffering at the hands of the nephews was the taking of her milk and not the brutal beating that followed: "The theft of her milk, psychologically abhorrent to Sethe, leaves her feeling hatred and revulsion for the men who stole her milk and power. She must also feel shame and guilt for her forced compliance, a biological response. Sethe mentally recalls 'mossy teeth' (86). As a maternal reader, I am forced to re-enact the horror of scum-covered teeth scraping against her nipple, acutely sensitive as a result of repeated nursing and engorgement" (120). Mock describes her own sense of responsibility and vulnerability as a gloss on Morrison's text.

Mae G. Henderson analyzes the novel "in the context of some contemporary historical theory on discourse and narrativity, suggesting . . . a reading that links historiography and psychoanalysis" (66). Both Morrison and Sethe are engaged in the process of transforming "residual images ('rememories') of her [Sethe's] past into a historical discourse shaped by narrativity" (66). The novelist and the former slave need "to discover a way of organizing memory, of contriving a narrative configuration in the absence of written records" (66–67), the former to create a compelling work of fiction, the latter to heal herself of the wounds and alleviate the guilt and horrors that possess her. According to Henderson, "Sethe has only been able to read herself through the gaze of others. The challenge for Sethe is to learn to read herself—that is, to configure the history of her body's text" (69). Among those who have read Sethe according to their own perspectives, biases, and needs are schoolteacher, Paul D, and Stamp Paid. The critic concludes that "like Sethe, Morrison herself seeks to achieve some mediation between 'resurrecting' the past and 'burying' it" (82). Thus, the novel depicts the "process which enables Sethe to achieve redemption through the creation of a cohesive psychoanalytical and historical narrative" (82).

A number of essays that use the words "history" or "historical" in their titles are mainly about personal histories, about the events that were generally excluded from both slave narratives and the narratives of the slaveholding establishment. They emphasize the significance of absent voices and discuss the need that Morrison has often articulated: for a people to mourn the dead who are nameless to them.

CONCLUSION

It seems fitting to conclude a discussion of criticism about the form and subject of *Beloved* by describing two very different published sources that influenced Toni Morrison in the writing of the novel. The first is an 1856 news article republished by Random House in a modern anthology titled *The Black Book,* compiled by Middleton A. Harris and others. The second is a photograph and brief description of a murder published in *The Harlem Book of the Dead* in 1978.

As a Random House editor in the 1970s, Toni Morrison worked with Middleton A. Harris, Morris Levitt, Roger Furman, and Ernest Smith on a groundbreaking collection of documents and photographs about the lives of black people in America. As the publisher's in-house editor of the book, she was extensively involved in the project and arranged for her parents to contribute materials to the volume. One item published in *The Black Book* is a news account titled "A Visit to the Slave Mother Who Killed Her Child." The mother referred to was Margaret Garner, an enslaved woman who had escaped and who later cut the throat of her young daughter, Mary Garner, when the family was about to be recaptured in Cincinnati and returned to Kentucky. Eight relatives—Margaret, the man she considered her husband (although, under American chattel slavery, marriages between slaves had no legal status), their four children, and her "husband's" parents—had been discovered sheltering in the house of a free black man in Ohio and were besieged by a posse pursuing them.

The historical incidents surrounding Margaret Garner's escape, capture, and subsequent trial are examined in detail by Cynthia Griffin Wolff in " 'Margaret Garner': A Cincinnati Story." Employing materials from the Cincinnati newspapers of the day and of the *Reminiscences of Levi Coffin,* published in 1898, Wolff quotes descriptions of Garner's attempt to kill all four of her children rather than to see them returned to lives as slaves. As Wolff explains, Margaret's fate thereafter is known only through rumors because she was removed from Ohio and returned to the slave system.[63] Although drawn to this story of an escape and a mother's desperate action, Morrison does not attempt to portray Garner's trial or subsequent treatment.

According to Ashraf H. A. Rushdy in "Daughters Signifyin(g) History: The Example of Toni Morrison's *Beloved*," Margaret Garner's story was illuminated for Morrison by a photograph and brief text in Camille Billops's *The Harlem Book of the Dead*, published in 1978. In this collection of photographs of Harlem funerals taken by James Van Der Zee, Morrison saw a photograph of an 18-year-old girl in her coffin along with a brief explanation of her murder and a poem about her by Owen Dodson. Although the dying girl knew who had shot her at a crowded party, she would only say " 'I'll tell you tomorrow' " to those questioning her, because she wanted the person who had wounded her to have a chance to escape. In an interview quoted by Rushdy, Morrison described her reaction to Garner and the Harlem girl's stories: " 'Now what made those stories connect, I can't explain, but I do know that in both instances, something seemed clear to me. A woman loved something other than herself so much. She had placed all of the value of her life in something outside herself.' "[64] The critic emphasizes that Morrison's depiction of Beloved is not dependent on detailed historical research about the Garner family. Instead, he observes, "By taking a historical personage—a daughter of a faintly famous African American victim of racist ideology—and constructing her as a hopeful presence in a contemporary setting, Morrison offers an introjection into the fields of revisionist historiography and fiction. She makes articulate a victim of a patriarchal order in order to criticize that order. Yet she portrays an unrelenting hopefulness in that critique" (568). Thus, he considers the novel as "a requiem that is a resurrection" (571).

The impact of these two accounts and Morrison's plans for using them are described by Jan Furman in *Toni Morrison's Fiction*. She recounts Morrison's bewildering conclusion that she would give up writing novels, made after completing her fourth novel, *Tar Baby*, in 1991. "Ironically, in this milieu of productivity and creative possibility, Morrison decided not to write anymore, feeling relieved perhaps of the responsibility to shape her special vision of black culture since her subject matter, heretofore sporadically explored, was being confidently, sensitively, and consistently mined by her contemporaries. Morrison could rest, so to speak."[65] Yet somehow the novelist found herself obsessed by fragments of two stories, those of Margaret Garner and a Harlem girl. Morrison planned, according to Furman, "to cement the two stories with a single donnée. Margaret Garner's story would be refracted by the Harlem girl's story when Garner's dead daughter is reincarnated in this life, perhaps as the eighteen-year-old" (68). The novelist's idea for combining elements of each story proved unsuitable in the emerging *Beloved*, and the murdered girl became the subject of Morrison's sixth novel, *Jazz*, published in 1992.

Beloved has now challenged and moved a large audience in extraordinary ways for more than a decade. The novel has illuminated the theme of absence, making readers aware of a void that was unimaginable before its publication. It is a fitting tribute to the richness and power of *Beloved* that so many diverse and thoughtful scholars continue to interpret and discuss this work of art, a work that has signaled the beginning of the recovery of a people's historical experience in America.

Notes

1. June Jordon and Houston A. Baker Jr., et al., "Black Writers in Praise of Toni Morrison," *New York Times Book Review,* 24 January 1988, 36.

2. Michiko Kakutani, "Did 'Paco's Story' Deserve Its Award?" *New York Times,* 16 November 1987, 15 C.

3. Marilyn Judith Atlas, "Toni Morrison's *Beloved* and the Reviewers," *Midwestern Miscellany* 18 (1990): 45–57; 48. The Edwards article from which Atlas quotes is reprinted in this volume.

4. James Berger, "Ghosts of Liberalism: Morrison's *Beloved* and the Moynihan Report," *PMLA: Publications of the Modern Language Association of America* 111, no. 3 (May 1996): 408–420; 411. Hereafter cited in the text.

5. Carol Iannone, "Toni Morrison's Career," *Commentary* 84, no. 6 (December 1987): 59–63; 63.

6. Martha Bayles, "Special Effects, Special Pleading," *New Criterion* 6, no. 5 (January 1988): 34–40; 36.

7. Stanley Crouch, "Aunt Medea," *New Republic* 197, no. 16 (19 October 1987): 38–43. Reprinted in this volume.

8. Ann Snitow, "Death Duties: Toni Morrison Looks Back in Sorrow," *Village Voice Literary Supplement* 58 (September 1987): 25–26. Reprinted in this volume.

9. Judith Thurman, "A House Divided," *New Yorker,* 2 November 1987, 175–80. Reprinted in this volume.

10. Walter Clemons, "A Gravestone of Memories," *Newsweek,* 28 September 1987, 74–75; 75. Reprinted in this volume.

11. Margaret Atwood, "Haunted by Their Nightmares," *New York Times Book Review,* 13 September 1987, 49–50. Reprinted in this volume.

12. Thomas R. Edwards, "Ghost Story," *New York Review of Books* 34 (5 November 1987): 18. Reprinted in this volume.

13. Toni Morrison, *The Bluest Eye* (New York: Plume, 1993), 211. Hereafter cited in the text.

14. Philip Page, "Circularity in Toni Morrison's *Beloved,*" *African American Review* 26, no. 1 (Spring 1992): 31–39; 35.

15. Maggie Sale, "Call and Response as Critical Method: African-American Oral Traditions and *Beloved,*" *African American Review* 26, no. 1 (Spring 1992): 41–50. Reprinted in this volume.

16. Linda Krumholz, "The Ghosts of Slavery: Historical Recovery in Toni Morrison's *Beloved,*" *African American Review* 26 (1992): 395–408; 406.

17. Karla F. C. Holloway, "*Beloved:* A Spiritual," *Callaloo* 13, no. 3 (Summer 1990): 516–22; 525.

18. Sue Park, "One Reader's Response to Toni Morrison's *Beloved,*" *Conference of College Teachers of English Studies* 56 (September 1991): 39–46; 41.

19. Rafael Pérez-Torres, "Knitting and Knotting the Narrative Thread—*Beloved* as Postmodern Novel," *Modern Fiction Studies* 39 nos. 3–4 (Fall–Winter 1993): 689–707; 689.

20.   T. Mark Ledbetter, "An Apocalypse of Race and Gender: Body Violence and Forming Identity in Toni Morrison's *Beloved*," in *Postmodernism, Literature and the Future of Theology*, ed. David Jasper (New York: St. Martin's Press, 1993), 78–90; 80.

21.   Carl D. Malmgren, "Mixed Genres and the Logic of Slavery in Toni Morrison's *Beloved*," *Critique: Studies in Contemporary Fiction* 36, no. 2 (Winter 1995): 96–106; 97.

22.   Marilyn Sanders Mobley, "A Different Remembering: Memory, History and Meaning in *Beloved*," in *Toni Morrison: Critical Perspectives Past and Present*, eds. Henry Louis Gates Jr. and K. A. Appiah (New York: Amistad, 1993), 356–65.

23.   Andrew Schopp, "Narrative Control and Subjectivity: Dismantling Safety in Toni Morrison's *Beloved*," *The Centennial Review* 39, no. 2 (Spring 1995): 355–79; 355.

24.   Giulia Scarpa, "Narrative Possibilities at Play in Toni Morrison's *Beloved*," *MELUS: The Journal of the Society for Study of the Multi-Ethnic Literature of the United States* 17, no. 4 (Winter 1991–1992): 91–103; 95.

25.   Andrew Levy, "Telling *Beloved*," *Texas Studies in Literature and Language* 33, no. 1 (Spring 1991): 114–23; 114.

26.   Barbara Hill Rigney, "'Breaking the Back of Words': Language, Silence, and the Politics of Identity in *Beloved*," in *The Voices of Toni Morrison*, by Barbara Hill Rigney (Columbus: Ohio State University Press, 1991). Reprinted in this volume.

27.   Toni Morrison, interview by Melvyn Bragg, *Profile of a Writer: Toni Morrison*, London Weekend Television, 1987. Hereafter cited in the text.

28.   Yvonne Atkinson, "The Black English Oral Tradition in *Beloved*: 'listen to the spaces.'" An original essay in this volume.

29.   Caroline Rody, "Toni Morrison's *Beloved*: History, 'Rememory,' and a 'Clamor for a Kiss,'" *American Literary History* 7, no. 1 (Spring 1995): 92–119. Hereafter cited in the text.

30.   Toni Morrison, "Unspeakable Things Unspoken: The Afro-American Presence in American Literature," *Michigan Quarterly Review* 28, no. 1 (Winter 1989): 31–33; 31.

31.   Lovalerie King, "The Disruption of Formulaic Discourse: Writing Resistance and Truth in *Beloved*." An original essay in this volume.

32.   Brian Finney, "Temporal Defamiliarization in Toni Morrison's *Beloved*," *Obsidian II* 5, no. 1 (1990): 20–36. Reprinted in this volume.

33.   Bernard W. Bell, "*Beloved*: A Womanist Neo-Slave Narrative; or Multivocal Remembrances of Things Past," *African American Review* 26 no. 1 (1992): 7–15; 12–13.

34.   Eusebio L. Rodrigues, "The Telling of *Beloved*," *Journal of Narrative Technique* 21, no. 2, (Spring 1991): 153–69. Reprinted in this volume.

35.   Valerie Smith, "'Circling the Subject': History and Narrative in *Beloved*," in *Toni Morrison: Critical Perspectives Past and Present*, ed. Henry Louis Gates Jr. and K. A. Appiah (New York: Amistad, 1993), 342–55; 346.

36.   Chauncey A. Ridley, "Sethe's 'Big, Bad' Love," in *Understanding Others: Cultural and Cross-Cultural Studies and the Teaching of Literature*, ed. Joseph Trimmer and Tilly Warnock (Urbana, Ill.: National Council of Teachers of English, 1992), 153–64.

37.   David Lawrence, "Fleshly Ghosts and Ghostly Flesh: The Word and the Body in *Beloved*," *Studies in American Fiction* 19, no. 2 (Autumn 1991): 189–201.

38.   Wendy Harding and Jacky Martin, "Reading at the Cultural Interface: The Corn Symbolism of *Beloved*," *MELUS: The Journal of the Society for the Study of the Multi-Ethnic Literature of the United States* 19, no. 2 (Summer 1994): 85–97. Reprinted in this volume.

39.   Susan Bowers, "*Beloved* and the New Apocalypse," *The Journal of Ethnic Studies* 18, no. 1 (Spring 1990): 59–77; T. Mark Ledbetter, "An Apocalypse of Race and Gender"; Josef Pesch, "*Beloved*: Toni Morrison's Post-Apocalyptic Novel," *Canadian Review of Comparative Literature–Revue Canadienne de Littérature Comparée* 20, nos. 3–4 (September–December 1993): 397–408.

40.   Mary G. Basson, "Unburdening Down by the Riverside: The Imagery of Water as a Precursor to Peace in Toni Morrison's *Beloved*," in *Literary Analyses by A P English Teachers: A*

Collection of Ten Essays, ed. Robert J. Jones et al. (College Entrance Examination Board and Educational Testing Service, 1996), 4–9; 5.

41. Trudier Harris, "Escaping Slavery but Not Its Images," in *Toni Morrison: Critical Perspectives Past and Present,* eds. Henry Louis Gates Jr. and K. A. Appiah (New York: Amistad, 1993), 330–41; 333.

42. Howard W. Fulweiler, "Belonging and Freedom in Morrison's *Beloved:* Slavery, Sentimentality, and the Evolution of Consciousness," *The Centennial Review* 40, no. 2 (September 1996): 331–58; 343.

43. Deborah Guth, " 'Wonder what God had in mind': *Beloved*'s Dialogue with Christianity," *Journal of Narrative Technique* 24, no. 2 (Spring 1994): 83–97; 84.

44. Barbara Schapiro, "The Bonds of Love and the Boundaries of Self in Toni Morrison's *Beloved,*" *Contemporary Literature* 32 (1991): 194–210; 198. Hereafter cited in the text.

45. Jean Wyatt, "Giving Body to the Word: The Maternal Symbolic in Toni Morrison's *Beloved,*" *PMLA: Publications of the Modern Language Association of America* 108, no. 3 (May 1993): 474–88. Reprinted in this volume.

46. Carolyn A. Mitchell, " 'I love to Tell the Story': Biblical Revisions in *Beloved,*" *Religion and Literature* 23, no. 3 (Autumn 1991): 27–42; 34.

47. Robert L. Broad, "Giving Blood to the Scraps: Haints, History, and Hosea in *Beloved,*" *African American Review* 28, no. 2 (Summer 1994): 189–96; 190.

48. Deborah Horvitz, "Nameless Ghosts: Possession and Dispossession in *Beloved,*" *Studies in American Fiction* 17, no. 2 (Autumn 1989): 157–67. Reprinted in this volume.

49. Mae G. Henderson, "Toni Morrison's *Beloved:* Re-Membering the Body as Historical Text," in *Comparative American Identities: Race, Sex, and Nationality in the Modern Text,* ed. Hortense J. Spillers (New York: Routledge, 1991), 62–86; 75. Hereafter cited in the text.

50. Sharon Jessee, " 'Tell me your earrings': Time and the Marvelous in Toni Morrison's *Beloved,*" in *Memory, Narrative, and Identity: New Essays in Ethnic American Literatures,* ed. Amritjit Singh, Joseph T. Skerrett Jr., and Robert E. Hogan (Boston: Northeastern University Press, 1994): 198–211; 199.

51. Dana Heller, "Reconstructing Kin: Family, History and Narrative in Toni Morrison's *Beloved,*" *College Literature* 21, no. 2 (June 1994): 105–12; 107.

52. Carol E. Schmudde, "The Haunting of 124," *African American Review* 26, no. 3 (Fall 1992): 409–16; 409.

53. Elizabeth B. House, "Toni Morrison's Ghost: The Beloved Who Is Not Beloved," *Studies in American Fiction* 18, no. 1 (Spring 1990): 17–26. Reprinted in this volume.

54. Denise Heinze, "*Beloved* and the Tyranny of the Double," in *The Dilemma of "Double Consciousness": Toni Morrison's Novels,* by Denise Heinze (Athens: University of Georgia Press, 1993), 174–81. Reprinted in this volume.

55. Trudier Harris, "*Beloved:* 'Woman, Thy Name is Demon,' " in *Fiction and Folklore: The Novels of Toni Morrison* (Knoxville: University of Tennessee Press, 1991), 151–64. Reprinted in this volume.

56. Karen E. Fields, "To Embrace Dead Strangers: Toni Morrison's *Beloved,*" in *Mother Puzzles: Daughters and Mothers in Contemporary American Literature,* ed. Mickey Pearlman (Westport, Conn.: Greenwood, 1989), 159–69; 160.

57. Iyunolu Osagie, "Is Morrison Also Among the Prophets?: 'Psychoanalytic' Strategies in *Beloved,*" *African American Review* 28, no. 3 (Fall 1994): 423–40; 423.

58. Jennifer FitzGerald, "Selfhood and Community: Psychoanalysis and Discourse in *Beloved,*" *Modern Fiction Studies* 39, nos. 3–4 (Fall–Winter 1993): 669–87; 669.

59. Stephanie A. Demetrakopoulos, "Maternal Bonds as Devourers of Women's Individuation in Toni Morrison's *Beloved,*" *African American Review* 26, no. 1 (Spring 1992): 51–59; 51.

60. Rebecca Ferguson, "History, Memory and Language in Toni Morrison's *Beloved,*" in *Feminist Criticism: Theory and Practice,* ed. Susan Sellers, Linda Hutcheon, and Paul Perron (Toronto: University of Toronto Press, 1991), 109–27; 118.

61. Kristin Boudreau, "Pain and the Unmaking of Self in Toni Morrison's *Beloved*," *Contemporary Literature* 36, no. 3 (Fall 1995): 447–65; 447.

62. Michele Mock, "Spitting Out the Seed: Ownership of Mother, Child, Breasts, Milk and Voice in Toni Morrison's *Beloved*. ([De]Colonizing Reading/[Dis]Covering the Other)," *College Literature* 23, no. 3 (October 1996): 117–27; 117.

63. Cynthia Griffin Wolff, " 'Margaret Garner': A Cincinnati Story," *Massachusetts Review* 32 (1991): 417–40.

64. Ashraf H. A. Rushdy, "Daughters Signifyin(g) History: The Example of Toni Morrison's *Beloved*," *American Literature: A Journal of Literary History, Criticism, and Bibliography* 64, no. 3 (September 1992): 567–97; 570.

65. Jan Furman, *Toni Morrison's Fiction* (Columbia: University of South Carolina Press, 1996), 67.

REVIEWS
◆

Haunted by Their Nightmares

MARGARET ATWOOD

Beloved is Toni Morrison's fifth novel, and another triumph. Indeed, Ms. Morrison's versatility and technical and emotional range appear to know no bounds. If there were any doubts about her stature as a pre-eminent American novelist, of her own or any other generation, *Beloved* will put them to rest. In three words or less, it's a hair-raiser.

In *Beloved,* Ms. Morrison turns away from the contemporary scene that has been her concern of late. This new novel is set after the end of the Civil War, during the period of so-called Reconstruction, when a great deal of random violence was let loose upon blacks, both the slaves freed by Emancipation and others who had been given or had bought their freedom earlier. But there are flashbacks to a more distant period, when slavery was still a going concern in the South and the seeds for the bizarre and calamitous events of the novel were sown. The setting is similarly divided: the countryside near Cincinnati, where the central characters have ended up, and a slave-holding plantation in Kentucky, ironically named Sweet Home, from which they fled 18 years before the novel opens.

There are many stories and voices in this novel, but the central one belongs to Sethe, a woman in her mid-30's, who is living in an Ohio farmhouse with her daughter, Denver, and her mother-in-law Baby Suggs. *Beloved* is such a unified novel that it's difficult to discuss it without giving away the plot, but it must be said at the outset that it is, among other things, a ghost story, for the farmhouse is also home to a sad, malicious and angry ghost, the spirit of Sethe's baby daughter, who had her throat cut under appalling circumstances eighteen years before, when she was two. We never know this child's full name, but we—and Sethe—think of her as Beloved, because that is what is on her tombstone. Sethe wanted "Dearly Beloved," from the funeral service, but had only enough strength to pay for one word. Payment was ten minutes of sex with the tombstone engraver. This act, which is recounted early in the novel, is a keynote for the whole book: in the world of

Reprinted from *The New York Times Book Review,* 13 September 1987, 1, 49, 50. © 1987 by The New York Times Company. Reprinted by permission.

slavery and poverty, where human beings are merchandise, everything has its price and price is tyrannical.

"Who would have thought that a little old baby could harbor so much rage?" Sethe thinks, but it does; breaking mirrors, making tiny handprints in cake icing, smashing dishes and manifesting itself in pools of blood-red light. As the novel opens, the ghost is in full possession of the house, having driven away Sethe's two young sons. Old Baby Suggs, after a lifetime of slavery and a brief respite of freedom—purchased for her by the Sunday labor of her son Halle, Sethe's husband—has given up and died. Sethe lives with her memories, almost all of them bad. Denver, her teen-age daughter, courts the baby ghost because, since her family has been ostracized by the neighbors, she doesn't have anyone else to play with.

The supernatural element is treated, not in an "Amityville Horror," watch-me-make-your-flesh-creep mode, but with magnificent practicality, like the ghost of Catherine Earnshaw in *Wuthering Heights*. All the main characters in the book believe in ghosts, so it's merely natural for this one to be there. As Baby Suggs says, "Not a house in the country ain't packed to its rafters with some dead Negro's grief. We lucky this ghost is a baby. My husband's spirit was to come back in here? or yours? Don't talk to me. You lucky." In fact, Sethe would rather have the ghost there than not there. It is, after all, her adored child, and any sign of it is better, for her, than nothing.

This grotesque domestic equilibrium is disturbed by the arrival of Paul D, one of the "Sweet Home men" from Sethe's past. The Sweet Home men were the male slaves of the establishment. Their owner, Mr. Garner, is no Simon Legree; instead he's a best-case slave-holder, treating his "property" well, trusting them, allowing them choice in the running of his small plantation, and calling them "men" in defiance of the neighbors, who want all male blacks to be called "boys." But Mr. Garner dies, and weak, sickly Mrs. Garner brings in her handiest male relative, who is known as "the schoolteacher." This Goebbels-like paragon combines viciousness with intellectual pretensions; he's a sort of master-race proponent who measures the heads of the slaves and tabulates the results to demonstrate that they are more like animals than people. Accompanying him are his two sadistic and repulsive nephews. From there it's all downhill at Sweet Home, as the slaves try to escape, go crazy or are murdered. Sethe, in a trek that makes the ice-floe scene in *Uncle Tom's Cabin* look like a stroll around the block, gets out, just barely; her husband, Halle, doesn't. Paul D does, but has some very unpleasant adventures along the way, including a literally nauseating sojourn in a nineteenth-century Georgia chain gang.

Through the different voices and memories of the book, including that of Sethe's mother, a survivor of the infamous slave-ship crossing, we experience American slavery as it was lived by those who were its objects of exchange, both at its best—which wasn't very good—and at its worst, which was as bad as can be imagined. Above all, it is seen as one of the most viciously antifamily institutions human beings have ever devised. The slaves are motherless, fatherless, deprived of their mates, their children, their kin. It is a world in which people suddenly vanish and are never seen again, not through accident or covert operation or terrorism, but as a matter of everyday legal policy.

Slavery is also presented to us as a paradigm of how most people behave when they are given absolute power over other people. The first effect, of course, is that they start believing in their own superiority and justifying their actions by it. The second effect is that they make a cult of the inferiority of those they subjugate. It's no coincidence that the first of the deadly sins, from which all the others were supposed to stem, is Pride, a sin of which Sethe is, incidentally, also accused.

In a novel that abounds in black bodies—headless, hanging from trees, frying to a crisp, locked in woodsheds for purposes of rape, or floating downstream drowned—it isn't surprising that the "whitepeople," especially the men, don't come off too well. Horrified black children see whites as men "without skin." Sethe thinks of them as having "mossy teeth" and is ready, if necessary, to bite off their faces, and worse, to avoid further mossy-toothed outrages. There are a few whites who behave with something approaching decency. There's Amy, the young runaway indentured servant who helps Sethe in childbirth during her flight to freedom, and incidentally reminds the reader that the nineteenth century, with its child labor, wage slavery and widespread and accepted domestic violence, wasn't tough only for blacks, but for all but the most privileged whites as well. There are also the abolitionists who help Baby Suggs find a house and a job after she is freed. But even the decency of these "good" whitepeople has a grudging side to it, and even they have trouble seeing the people they are helping as full-fledged people, though to show them as totally free of their xenophobia and sense of superiority might well have been anachronistic.

Toni Morrison is careful not to make all the whites awful and all the blacks wonderful. Sethe's black neighbors, for instance, have their own envy and scapegoating tendencies to answer for, and Paul D, though much kinder than, for instance, the woman-bashers of Alice Walker's novel *The Color Purple,* has his own limitations and flaws. But then, considering what he's been through, it's a wonder he isn't a mass murderer. If anything, he's a little too huggable, under the circumstances.

Back in the present tense, in chapter one, Paul D and Sethe make an attempt to establish a "real" family, whereupon the baby ghost, feeling excluded, goes berserk, but is driven out by Paul D's stronger will. So it appears. But then, along comes a strange, beautiful, real flesh-and-blood young woman, about twenty years old, who can't seem to remember where she comes from, who talks like a young child, who has an odd, raspy voice and no lines on her hands, who takes an intense, devouring interest in Sethe, and who says her name is Beloved.

Students of the supernatural will admire the way this twist is handled. Ms. Morrison blends a knowledge of folklore—for instance, in many traditions, the dead cannot return from the grave unless called, and it's the passions of the living that keep them alive—with a highly original treatment. The reader is kept guessing; there's a lot more to Beloved than any one character can see, and she manages to be many things to several people. She is a catalyst for revelations as well as self-revelations; through her we come to know not only how, but why, the original child Beloved was killed. And through her also Sethe achieves, finally, her own form of self-exorcism, her own self-accepting peace.

Beloved is written in an antiminimalist prose that is by turns rich, graceful, eccentric, rough, lyrical, sinuous, colloquial and very much to the point. Here, for instance, is Sethe remembering Sweet Home:

> . . . suddenly there was Sweet Home rolling, rolling, rolling out before her eyes, and although there was not a leaf on that farm that did not want to make her scream, it rolled itself out before her in shameless beauty. It never looked as terrible as it was and it made her wonder if hell was a pretty place too. Fire and brimstone all right, but hidden in lacy groves. Boys hanging from the most beautiful sycamores in the world. It shamed her—remembering the wonderful soughing trees rather than the boys. Try as she might to make it otherwise, the sycamores beat out the children every time and she could not forgive her memory for that.

In this book, the other world exists and magic works, and the prose is up to it. If you can believe page one—and Ms. Morrison's verbal authority compels belief—you're hooked on the rest of the book.

The epigraph to *Beloved* is from the Bible, Romans 9:25: "I will call them my people, which were not my people; and her beloved, which was not beloved." Taken by itself, this might seem to favor doubt about, for instance, the extent to which Beloved was really loved, or the extent to which Sethe herself was rejected by her own community. But there is more to it than that. The passage is from a chapter in which the Apostle Paul ponders, Job-like, the ways of God toward humanity, in particular the evils and inequities visible everywhere on the earth. Paul goes on to talk about the fact that the Gentiles, hitherto despised and outcast, have now been redefined as acceptable. The passage proclaims, not rejection, but reconciliation and hope. It continues: "And it shall come to pass, that in the place where it was said unto them, Ye are not my people; there shall they be called the children of the living God."

Toni Morrison is too smart, and too much of a writer, not to have intended this context. Here, if anywhere, is her own comment on the goings-on in her novel, her final response to the measuring and dividing and excluding "schoolteachers" of this world. An epigraph to a book is like a key signature in music, and *Beloved* is written in major.

A Gravestone of Memories

WALTER CLEMONS

In 1855 a runaway slave from Kentucky named Margaret Garner was tracked by her owner to Cincinnati, where she had taken refuge with her freed mother-in-law. Cornered, she tried to kill her four children. Afterward, she was quite serene about what she had done. A newspaper account of this stark event taken from a documentary sourcebook stayed in Toni Morrison's mind over the years. Now it has become the germ of a magnificent novel.

In a lecture last year, Morrison spoke about omissions in slave narratives written for abolitionist readers during the 19th century. Addressing sympathetic whites, blacks tactfully suppressed feelings of outrage that might offend their hearers. They mentioned "proceedings too terrible to relate" only in formulaic euphemism. They "forgot" many things. "Most importantly—at least for me," Morrison said, "—there was no mention of their interior life."

In *Beloved (275 pages. Knopf. $18.95),* this interior life is re-created with a moving intensity no novelist has even approached before. Morrison has been able to imagine an existence of almost unimaginable precariousness, in which it was illegal for slaves to be taught to read or write, to love and marry with any expectation of permanence, to become parents with any hope of living with their children to maturity.

Through Morrison's bold imagination, the historical Margaret Garner has become Sethe, a stoic outcast; she lives with one daughter in the house outside Cincinnati given to her mother-in-law by a kindly abolitionist. Eighteen years have passed; it's 1873. Sethe's mother-in-law—an eloquent preacher known as Baby Suggs—has died and her two sons have run away, frightened by their mother and by the capricious ghost that shakes the house—the malicious spirit, apparently, of the baby daughter Sethe succeeded in killing before she was prevented from killing the others.

To this house comes Paul D, a former slave on the plantation in Kentucky from which Sethe escaped. Soon there's another arrival—a mysterious, blank-eyed young woman from nowhere, whom Sethe's daughter Denver at once accepts as her murdered sister, grown up and come back from the dead.

This is Beloved, who takes her name from the word chiseled on the grave-stone of Sethe's dead child.

RIGHTFUL OWNERSHIP

To outline this story is to invite the very resistance I felt on first reading it. A specter returned to bedevil the living? A Gothic historical romance from Toni Morrison? But with magisterial confidence Morrison has employed a monstrous anecdote as entrance key to the monstrosity of slavery. The Emancipation Proclamation was issued exactly a decade before this novel begins. Though technically "freed," the book's black characters have stumbled into post-Civil War existence unable to free themselves from memories of a system in which they had no rightful ownership of a Self. Memory is so oppressive for the novel's characters that stifling it is a means of survival. The splintered, piecemeal revelation of the past is one of the technical wonders of Morrison's narrative. We gradually understand that this isn't tricky storytelling but the intricate exploration of trauma.

Under a system in which "men and women were moved around like checkers," Sethe's murderous act was a distorted exertion of her balked maternal instinct. "She ain't crazy. She love those children," says a black man who was at the scene. "She was trying to outhurt the hurter." "My children my best thing," Sethe says, her sense of her own value having been maimed. She wanted to rescue her children from the life she'd fled, and killing them to prevent their return to slavery was the expedient that occurred to her. She welcomes the arrival of the spectral Beloved as a chance to explain herself. Sethe's arrogance has made the black community of Cincinnati shun her, and Paul D, who has not heard of her bloody past during his own 18 years of wandering, deserts her when he learns of it. Her isolation binds her in an unholy relation with Beloved.

At the heart of this astounding book, prose narrative dissolves into a hypnotic, poetic conversation among Sethe, Denver and the otherworldly Beloved. The broken speech of Beloved reveals that she's something other than the ghost of Sethe's murdered baby. "You think she sure 'nough your sister?" Paul D asks Denver. Denver replies: "At times I think she was—more." In Beloved's monologue we can grasp that this something "more" is that she remembers passage on a slave ship, which Sethe's murdered baby couldn't have. Though Sethe and Denver have accepted Beloved as the reincarnation of the dead baby, grown up into a young woman with a baby's insatiable demands—and Sethe never learns otherwise—Beloved is also a ghost from the slave ships of Sethe's ancestry. Beloved rose from water in a nearby river to come to Sethe's doorstep. Sethe invited the invasion, wanting to justify herself, but the Beloved who materialized has an anterior life deeper than the ghostly role she fulfills in the Cincinnati household she visits.

EXACT ATTENTION

Morrison casts a formidable spell. The incantatory, intimate narrative voice disarms our reluctance to enter Sethe's haunted house. We are reassured by feeling that the eerie story is reinforced by exact attention to verifiable detail about the lives of postwar Cincinnati blacks and the inferno from which they emerged. When Sethe's Cincinnati neighbors come to her rescue, and the incubus child who nearly consumed her life has vanished, the flood of daylight that ends the book is overpowering. I think we have a masterpiece on our hands here: difficult, sometimes lushly overwritten, but profoundly imagined and carried out with burning fervor.

The Ghosts of "Sixty Million and More"

WALTER CLEMONS

"You haven't asked about the 60 million," says Toni Morrison at midafternoon in her converted boathouse on the Hudson less than an hour from New York. *Beloved* bears a dedication: "Sixty million and more." She explains that the figure is the best educated guess at the number of black Africans who never even made it into slavery—those who died either as captives in Africa or on slave ships. She says: "One account describes the Congo as so clogged with bodies that the boat couldn't pass. That's a river broader than that one out there." She points to the wide Hudson outside. "They packed 800 into a ship if they'd promised to deliver 400. They assumed that half would die. And half did."

"A few people in my novel remember it," she adds. "Baby Suggs came here out of one of those ships. But mostly it's not remembered at all. I did a lot of hunting in folklore and songs, but it's a big blank. What is this amnesia? I started out wanting to write a story about the feeling of Self. Women feel themselves best through nurturing. The clipping about Margaret Garner stuck in my head. I had to deal with this nurturing instinct that expressed itself in murder."

She did an enormous amount of research for *Beloved;* digested, it lies concealed in the text. "When Paul D, without a compass, travels north by spotting the blossoms on trees, I had to call the hor-ti-cultural so-cie-ties"—her voice deepens comically—to learn what bloomed, when. "I had to take out trees I'd put in because I liked their names. I went to slave museums, but they weren't much help: little handcraft things slaves had made. No chains or restraining devices. In Brazil, though, they've kept *everything*. I got a lot of help down there."

"**White readers:**" Morrison tries to clear up a misunderstanding. She has been quoted as saying she writes for a black audience. Does this mean that whites can't adequately respond to *Beloved?* "I meant something else," she says. "When I write, I don't try to translate for white readers. I imagine Sethe in the room. If I read to her what I've written, will she say I'm telling the truth? Dostoevski wrote for a Russian audience, but we're able to read him. If I'm specific, and I don't overexplain, then anybody can overhear me."

Death Duties:
Toni Morrison Looks Back in Sorrow

ANN SNITOW

The subject of Toni Morrison's new novel, *Beloved,* is slavery, and the book staggers under the terror of its material—as so much holocaust writing does and must. Morrison's other novels teem with people, but in *Beloved* half the important characters are dead in the novel's present, 1873. Though they appear in memory, they have no future. Slavery, says one character, "ain't a battle; it's a rout"—with hardly any of what one could confidently call survivors. The mood is woe, depression, horror, a sense of unbearable loss. Still, those who remain must exorcise the deadly past from their hearts or die themselves; *Beloved* is the tale of such an exorcism.

In complex narrative loops, *Beloved* circles around and hints at the different fates of a group of slaves who once lived on a plantation in Kentucky, "Sweet Home"—of course neither "sweet" nor "home": an old woman called Baby Suggs, her son Halle, Paul A, Paul D, Paul F, Sixo, and the one young woman among them, Sethe. (Here as everywhere in the novel names raise baleful questions. Slaves have a tragically tenuous hold on names, and it is only in their final destinies that the three Pauls are allowed separate lives.)

Halle strikes a bargain with his master to sell his few free hours and use the money to buy his mother's freedom. Baby Suggs wonders why he bothers. What can a crippled old woman do with freedom? But when she stands on the northern side of the Ohio River and walks through the streets of Cincinnati, "she could not believe that Halle knew what she didn't; that Halle, who had never drawn one free breath, knew that there was nothing like it in this world."

Back at Sweet Home the decent master dies. (In slavery, a good master is merely a chance episode, any feeling of autonomy merely a fool's illusion.) The new boss, "schoolteacher," beats his slaves and measures them with rulers, keeping pseudoscholarly lists of their "human and animal characteristics." He demonstrates that any time the whites want to, they can knock you

Reprinted from *The Village Voice Literary Supplement* 58, September 1987, 25–26. Reprinted by permission of the author.

into the middle of next week, or back into the dependency of childhood. But Sethe now has three babies by the generous-spirited Halle, and the idea that she might never see them grow (like Baby Suggs, who saw seven of her children sold), or that they will grow only into schoolteacher's eternal children, strengthens her resolve to join the Sweet Home slaves who plan to run, taking a "train" north. Paul F is long gone—sold, who knows where. During the escape, Paul A gets caught and hanged. Sixo gets caught and burned alive. Paul D gets caught and sold in chains with a bit in his mouth. Sethe manages to get her three children on the train, but is caught herself, assaulted, beaten. Halle fails to appear at their rendezvous—lost, mysteriously lost, and never to be found again. Sethe runs anyway, because she can't forget that hungry baby who's gone on ahead, and because a new one is waiting to be born.

Half dead, and saved only by the help of a young white girl, trash almost as exiled as herself, Sethe gives birth to her baby girl, Denver, on the banks of the Ohio and manages to get them both across and truly home, to Baby Suggs's door.

Told flat, the plot of *Beloved* is the stuff of melodrama, recalling *Uncle Tom's Cabin*. But Morrison doesn't really *tell* these incidents. Bits and pieces of them leak out between the closed eyelids of her characters, or between their clenched fingers. She twists and tortures and fractures events until they are little slivers that cut. She moves the lurid material of melodrama into the minds of her people, where it gets sifted and sorted, lived and relived, until it acquires the enlarging outlines of myth and trauma, dream and obsession.

In fact, the intense past hardly manages to emerge at all. It is repressed, just as the facts of slavery are. Instead, in the foreground of the novel, Morrison places a few lonely minds in torment: Sethe, Denver, Paul D. All the drama of past desire and escape has fled to the margins of their consciousness, while Morrison's survivors are living in one extended moment of grief. Slowly, painfully, we learn that in order to keep schoolteacher from recapturing her children, Sethe tried to kill them all, succeeding with the third, a baby girl Morrison leaves nameless. This act lies at the center of the book: incontrovertible, enormous. Sethe explains that she killed the baby because "if I hadn't killed her she would have died." Morrison makes us believe in this logic down to the ground.

By 1873, 18 years after Sethe's fatal act of resistance, slavery is technically over, whether or not the former slaves feel finished with it. Sethe's eldest two boys have run off, perhaps overfull of the mother love that almost killed them as children. Baby Suggs's house has become the entire world to Sethe and Denver—now 18. They live there ostracized, proud, and alone—except for the active ghost of the murdered two-year-old.

This awkward spirit shakes the furniture, puts tiny handprints on the cakes, shatters mirrors, while Sethe and Denver live stolidly in the chaos, emotionally frozen. Into this landscape of regret walks Paul D, one of the dear lost comrades from Sweet Home. He has been tramping for these 18 years, and now comes to rest on Sethe's front porch. Innocent of the secret of the baby's death, he seems to exorcise her ghost with nothing much more than his warm presence. As it turns out, she is not that easy to dismiss. The bulk of the novel dwells on the ghost's desperate return as a grown woman who calls herself "Beloved," the one word she has found on her tombstone.

At first, Beloved seems benign in her new avatar, and Sethe is ecstatic to have her daughter back. But gradually the strange visitor in elegant clothes and mysteriously unscuffed shoes turns into a fearsome figure, seducing Paul D in order to drag him into the wrong and send him packing, eating all the best food until Sethe and Denver begin to starve, ruling the demented household. The whole center of the novel is a projection of Sethe's longing; Beloved is a snare to catch her anguished, hungry mother's heart and keep her in the prison of guilt forever. She is also memory, the return of the dreadful past. In her, the breathtaking horror of the breakup of Sweet Home lives, sucking up all the air.

And so Toni Morrison has written a novel that's airless. How could this happen to a writer this skillful, working with material this full and important? In the reading, the novel's accomplishments seem driven to the periphery by Morrison's key decision to be literal about her metaphor, to make the dead baby a character whose flesh-and-bone existence takes up a great deal of narrative space. Even Sethe and Denver complain at times about the irritating presence of their ghost. And when she returns as a woman, she is a zombie, animated by abstract ideas. Later those who loved her "realized they couldn't remember or repeat a single thing she said, and began to believe that, other than what they themselves were thinking, she hadn't said anything at all."

Symbolic thinking is one thing, magical thinking quite another. Morrison blurs the distinction in *Beloved,* stripping the real magic of its potency and the symbols of their poetry. Her undigested insistence on the magical keeps bringing this often beautiful novel to earth. Morrison's last two strange and original books, *Song of Solomon* and *Tar Baby,* had some of this unconvincing reliance on the supernatural, too. By contrast, *The Bluest Eye,* her first, was bitten and dry-eyed; the little girl in that novel who thinks she can get blue eyes by magic sinks into the psychosis of wishing. Morrison's best magic was in *Sula,* the novel where it is most elusive, making no more solid a claim for the Unseen than the human spiritual power to move mountains.

This isn't to say ghosts can't or shouldn't be the stuff of fiction. The present generation of South American gothicists often convince us of the living power of ghosts in the worlds they describe. And the literature of disaster is haunted by the noisy dead, clamoring to be remembered as active presences, not cut off from a continuing story. Morrison is working in these traditions when she tries to animate the resistant weight of the slave experience by pouring on magic, lurid visions, fantasies of reconciliation. And why not? In one way, she comes by her magic honestly. It is the lore of the folk she loves, a visionary inheritance that makes her people superior to those—black or white—who don't have any talent for noticing the unseen. She wants to show how the slave past lives on, raising havoc, and to give Sethe, her treasured heroine, a chance to fight it out with the demon of grief. If Beloved is a drag on the narrative, a sour mixed with a great deal of dross, well so be it, Morrison seems to say. When strong, loving women would rather kill their babies than see them hauled back into slavery, the damage to every black who inherits that moment is a literal damage and no metaphor. The novel is meant to give grief body, to make it palpable.

But I suspect Morrison knows she's in some trouble here, since she harps so on the presence of Beloved, sometimes neglecting the mental life of her other characters. Their vitality is sacrificed to the inert ghost until the very end—a structure that makes thematic sense but leaves the novel hollow in the middle. Beloved is, of course, what's heavy in all their hearts, but can the ghost of a tragically murdered two-year-old bear this weight of meaning? No matter how she kicks and squalls and screams, the ghost is too light to symbolize the static fact of her own death. She is a distraction from those in the flesh, who must bear the pain of a dead child's absence. She is dead, which is the only arresting thing about her, and Morrison's prose goes dead when it concerns her.

If *Beloved* fails in its ambitions, it is still a novel by Toni Morrison, still therefore full of beautiful prose, dialogue as rhythmically satisfying as music, delicious characters with names like Grandma Baby and Stamp Paid, and scenes so clearly etched they're like hallucinations. Morrison is one of the great, serious writers we have. Who else tries to do what Dickens did: create wild, flamboyant, abstractly symbolic characters who are at the same time not grotesques but sweetly alive, full of deep feeling? Usually in contemporary fiction, the grotesque is mixed with irony or zaniness, not with passion and romance. Morrison rejects irony, a choice that immediately sets her apart. Like Alice Walker (there are several small, friendly allusions to *The Color Purple* in *Beloved*), she wants to tend the imagination, search for an expansion of the possible, nurture a spiritual richness in the black tradition even after 300 years in the white desert.

From book to book, Morrison's larger project grows clear. First, she insists that every character bear the weight of responsibility for his or her own life. After she's measured out each one's private pain, she adds on to that the shared burden of what the whites did. Then, at last, she tries to find the place where her stories can lighten her readers' load, lift them up from their own and others' guilt, carry them to glory.

In her greatest novel so far, *Sula,* she succeeded amazingly at making this crucial shift in atmosphere. Her characters suffer—from their own limitations and the world's—but their inner life miraculously expands beyond the narrow law of cause and effect. In *Sula,* Morrison found a way to offer her people an insight and sense of recovered self so dignified and glowing that no worldly pain could dull the final light. The novel ends with a song which soars over the top of its own last word, "sorrow":

> And the loss pressed down on her chest: and came up into her throat. "We was girls together," she said as though explaining something. "O Lord, Sula," she cried, "girl, girl, girlgirlgirl."
> It was a fine cry—loud and long—but it had no bottom and it had no top, just circles and circles of sorrow.

Song of Solomon and *Tar Baby,* and now *Beloved,* have writing as beautiful as this, but they are less in control of that delicate turn from fact to wish.

Even at her best, Morrison's techniques are risky, and sometimes, in *Beloved,* she loses her gamble. Slavery resists her impulse towards the grand summation of romance. The novel revolves and searches, searches and revolves, never getting any closer to these people numbed by their overwhelming grief. *Why* could they not save those they loved? Nothing moves here; everything is static and in pieces. The fragmentary, the unresolvable are in order in a story about slavery. When Morrison embraces this hideous fact, the book is dire and powerful: Halle is never found. Baby Suggs never reassembles her scattered children, whose names and faces are now those of strangers. Sethe has collapsed inside, unable to bear what has happened to them all.

Still, for Morrison, it is romance and not the fractured narrative of modernism that is the vehicle of her greatest feeling for her people. Though in their sorrow they resist her, she keeps inviting them to rise up on wings. She can't bear for them to be lost, finished, routed. The romantic in her longs to fuse what's broken, to give us something framed, at least one polychromatic image from above. When this works, it's glorious. And even when it doesn't, it's a magnificent intention. But there are moments in Morrison's recent novels when the brilliant, rich, and evocative image seems a stylistic tic, a shortcut to intensity. Romance can be a temptation. At the end of *Beloved* Morrison joins Sethe and Paul D together for good. Their happy union is a device laid on them from without by a solicitous author. It *should* be possible—why should pain breed only more pain?—but Morrison doesn't manage to maintain a necessary tension between what she knows and what she desires. She wishes too hard. Something in the novel goes slack.

Because Morrison is always a tiger storyteller, she struggles against her novel's tendencies to be at war with itself. She keeps writing gorgeous scenes, inventing characters so compelling and clear they carry us with them, back into a novel that seems determined to expel us. The ending in particular pushes *Beloved* beyond where it seemed capable of going.

> Everybody knew what she was called, but nobody anywhere knew her name. Disremembered and unaccounted for, she cannot be lost because no one is

looking for her, and even if they were, how can they call her if they don't know her name? Although she has claim, she is not claimed. In the place where the long grass opens, the girl who waited to be loved and cry shame erupts into her separate parts, to make it easy for the chewing laughter to swallow her all away.

It was not a story to pass on . . .

By and by all trace is gone. . . . The rest is weather. Not the breath of the disremembered and unaccounted for, but wind in the eaves, or spring ice thawing too quickly. Just weather. Certainly no clamor for a kiss.

Beloved.

"Disremembered and unaccounted for." The Dead may roar, but they are impotent. It is a brave and radical project to center a novel on a dead child ignored by history, cruelly forgotten along with so much else that happened to black people in slavery. A slave baby murdered by its own mother is "not a story to pass on." Even the slaves who know Sethe's reasons find them hard to accept. Paul D is so horrified when he finally learns about her crime that he leaves her for a time, telling her she has two legs not four. It is beastly to kill a baby, and yet Sethe asks, who was the beast? To keep Beloved out of the hands of an owner who would see her only as an animal, Sethe would rather be wild herself, do her own subduing of the human spirit, if killed it must be. As always in the last pages of her novels, Morrison gathers herself together and sings, here of those who didn't even leave their names, who died before they had the chance to become the sort of people about whom you could tell real stories.

There are the novelists who try something new in each book (Doris Lessing, say, or Joanna Russ, Kurt Vonnegut, Alice Walker) and the novelists who keep on worrying the same material (Saul Bellow, Robert Stone, Philip Roth, and Morrison herself). The first group has all the advantage of surprise, offering the thrill of new territory. Some of these trips come out better than others, but the overall effect is of travel. The second group has a different task, to find the same small door into the same necessary world, to wander the same maze trying to find the way home. Each novel in this group says to its readers, here I am again; do you feel what I always feel—as fully as I want you to? Well, not this time. But Morrison is great even in pieces, and worth waiting for, however long it takes.

This novel deserves to be read as much for what it cannot say as for what it can. It is a book of revelations about slavery, and its seriousness ensures that it is just a matter of time before Morrison shakes that brilliant kaleidoscope of hers again and the story of pain, endurance, poetry, and power she is born to tell comes out right.

Toni Morrison's *Beloved* Country:
The Writer and Her Haunting Tale of Slavery

ELIZABETH KASTOR

She remembers the '50s when she and her friends, students at Howard University, came to the Willard knowing the hotel was so tired, so decrepit, even they were welcome. The Mayflower too—there will always be a warm spot in her heart for the Mayflower and its bathroom that anyone, including a young black woman, could use.

Now she is shown to a table at the new Willard and, when offered a seat, sinks into the neo-Victorian red plush couch with an exaggerated delight. A waiter, determined to serve, brings food and yearned-for cigarettes. For breakfast, she plays with a muffin, denudes the croissants of their sugared almonds and sips on bitter grapefruit juice with sugar stirred through it.

"I have reverted to every bad habit I've ever had in my whole life on this tour," says novelist Toni Morrison, 56, the Howard student now grown, as she lights up.

For a week she has been away from her home in Grand-View-on-Hudson, N.Y., talking and answering questions and reading from her work. "124 was spiteful. Full of a baby's venom," she begins, her voice soft as a whisper, introducing the first two sentences of her new book, *Beloved.* The novel, Morrison's fifth, has received almost exclusively exuberant reviews and as of yesterday had risen to the No. 2 spot on the *Washington Post* best-seller list. At a Smithsonian signing, readers—most of them women—hold the volume close to their chests like a treasured object. One fan tells her *Beloved* is so powerful she could not read it alone; the house had to be filled with people, with comforting presences, a comment that reminds the author of her own trepidations.

"I had forgotten that when I started the book, I was very frightened," Morrison says. "It was an unwillingness and a terror of going into an area for which you have no preparation. It's a commitment of three or four years to living inside—because you do try to enter that life."

And the life was a terrible one even to glance at, let alone invite into your mind and house. A Kentucky plantation of the 1850s where the master

Reprinted from the *Washington Post,* 5 October 1987, 1, 12. © 1987, *The Washington Post*. Reprinted with permission.

charts his slaves' "animal characteristics." Families separated, runaways burned to death. Chain gangs, whippings, hangings, guilt, ghosts. And at the center of it all, infanticide: a mother who slits her daughter's throat with a handsaw and is about to kill her three other children, this to "save" them from the slavery she has just managed to escape.

But the true story at the heart of the book, the story of Margaret Garner, who escaped to Cincinnati and succeeded in killing only one daughter before they stopped her, had stayed with Morrison for 10 years after she first read contemporary accounts of the woman's trial for murder.

"I thought at first it couldn't be written," Morrison says, "but I was annoyed and worried that such a story was inaccessible to art. If I couldn't do it, I felt really sold. In the end, I had to rely on the resilience and power of the characters—if they could live it all of their lives, I could write it.

"I recognize something is significant in a variety of ways, one of which is resistance. You stiffen," she says, pulling back in illustration, her full body growing hard and taut. "When you stiffen, you know that whatever you stiffen about is very important. The stuff is important, the fear itself is information. I don't mean I was frightened of some thing. I was frightened of an unknown."

As she explored the unknown, she came to think the story could be told *only* in fiction, in art.

"Historians can't do it—they can't speculate," she says. "They've got to decide that they're going to talk about 'ages' and 'issues' and 'great men' and 'forces.' These people didn't know they were living in 'the age of . . .' They just thought, 'What about tomorrow?' So history can't get the perspective. Also, it's very large. The cruelty was inventive; it was creative cruelty. To deal with the sort of surrounding pathological *whatever*—historians may say 'historical this' and 'precedent for that,' they have rationales that are clear, but an artist can cut it down to size and see what these human beings were doing."

Howard University English professor Claudia Tate, who is currently on leave, thinks Morrison's book is another example of ways in which black artists are creating what she calls "reclamations of slavery."

"Slavery for so long was a dreaded topic, which you only talked about with familiar people, or which you only probed to a limited level," says Tate. "There's a lot of serious pain—you can say, 'Oh yes, that was terrible,' but when you start reliving it as empathy, it's very painful. . . . It seems the only way we can go forward is to go back far enough to establish a legacy of heroism and survival. It's as if the past has a text which we have to learn how to read, and the only way you can read it is to write it for yourself."

About her heroine, Morrison writes:

> She could never close in, pin it down for anybody who had to ask . . .
> If they didn't get it right off—she could never explain. Because the truth was simple, not a long-drawn-out record of flowered shifts, tree cages, selfishness, ankle ropes and wells. Simple: she was squatting in the garden and when she saw them coming and recognized schoolteacher's hat, she heard wings. Lit-

tle hummingbirds stuck their needle beaks right through her headcloth into her hair and beat their wings. And if she thought anything, it was No. No. Nono. Nonono. Simple. She just flew. Collected every bit of life she had made, all the parts of her that were precious and fine and beautiful, and carried, pushed, dragged them through the veil, out, away, over there where no one could hurt them. Over there. Outside this place, where they would be safe. And the hummingbird wings beat on . . . (from *Beloved*)

Before Morrison began the story of the woman who soon ceased to be Margaret Garner and became Sethe ("I listen to the characters and ask what their names are. It's a process that is very respectful"), she had been preoccupied with "the ways in which women are able to love extremely well, nurture extremely well, and the ways that sometimes also destroys something."

> I was thinking about that in really very contemporary terms. And that led me to think about the ways in which we displace the individual self into the beloved. Sometimes it's children, sometimes it's husbands, sometimes it's careers or what have you. And we let the best part of us flourish in something other than ourselves and get completely erased. But no one would want to take that away, so that you're negotiating the tension.
>
> Margaret Garner had a very fierce and insistent love for her children when they were the best part of her, when they were the real part of her. She was not permitted to be a mother, and that is such an elemental desire. Mother hunger. You can understand those people who kidnap babies from supermarkets. It's a real hunger. She was saying, 'I claim my children's lives and I will decide for them whether they live or die.'
>
> I understood and empathized. I'm not sure how much of that I would have been able to do myself, and I realized the only person who is in a position to ask those questions and judge her was the dead child—because you knew a woman like that would be haunted by what she had done.

Once Sethe has been released from jail, thanks to the influence of some white abolitionists, and has placed a stone over her daughter's grave carved with the word "Beloved," she settles with her three remaining children in the home of her mother-in-law on 124 Bluestone Rd. outside of Cincinnati. But 124 is spiteful; furniture flies and sad light plays across the floor and baby hand prints appear in cakes. Eighteen years after the act of maternal love and violence, Sethe and her family are still haunted by the 2-year-old girl whose throat she slit. When Paul D, a former slave from the same Kentucky farm, appears and exorcises the baby ghost, another presence takes her place, a 20-year-old woman with a raspy voice and a scar on her throat. She can not explain where she comes from, and she calls herself Beloved.

Sethe and her living daughter Denver know who this girl is. The black women of the town know, too. "I decided she would be two things," says Morrison. "For the characters in the book, she would indeed be the character returned. I decided for the reader she would be a real person, a real character with a life elsewhere. But their desires mesh. Her needs blend with theirs." Morrison never explains fully why those desires mesh so perfectly, merely hinting at a past for Beloved that may have included a sadistic imprisonment.

"I never describe characters very much . . . ," Morrison told Claudia Tate for her book, *Black Women Writers at Work.* "My language has to have holes and spaces so the reader can come into it." At one point, the mysterious Beloved speaks, and the holes in Morrison's language are the holes memory cannot bear to fill, the spaces left by suffering and yearning.

> I do not eat   the men without skin bring us their morning water to
> drink   we have none   at night I cannot see the dead man on my
> face   daylight comes through the cracks and I can see his locked eyes
> I am not big   small rats do not wait for us to sleep   someone is
> thrashing but there is no room to do it in   if we had more to drink we
> could make tears   we cannot make sweat or morning water so the men
> without skin bring us theirs   one time they bring us sweet rocks to suck
> we are all trying to leave our bodies behind   the man on my face has done
> it . . . the sun closes my eyes   when I open them I see the face I lost
> Sethe's is the face that left me   Sethe sees me see her and I see the smile
> her smiling face is the place for me   it is the face I lost . . . (from *Beloved*)

She [Morrison] was born Chloe Anthony Wofford in 1931 to parents who had migrated from sharecropping in Georgia and Alabama to Lorain, Ohio, and for whom pain, storytelling and magic were accepted elements of existence. The family lived "marginally," as she puts it. "We moved a lot." In *The Bluest Eye, Sula, Song of Solomon* and *Tar Baby,* Morrison's youthful fascination with her family's tales remains. Butterflies and avocado trees express forceful opinions, a woman is born with no navel, a dead child returns, tales and lives are spun out in long, fluid sentences that move through history and even past the grave.

"There are more parents who tell their children stories now," she says, "who read to them as a way of educating their children. We didn't hear stories that way. The adults weren't telling us stories, they were talking to each other. We overheard. They were not patronizing us. Some people sometimes think listening is a passive, almost involuntary process. Hearing may be, but listening isn't. The attention and intellectual activity and participation that you have when you listen to music—that's very complicated. That is what listening to good literature, or speeches or anything, is. You're really engaged. It's that quality of listening engagement I would like to return to the print world."

After graduating from Howard and receiving an MA from Cornell, she taught at Howard, and it was there she began to write. "I had nothing left but my imagination . . . ," she has said. "I had no will, no judgment, no perspective, no power, no authority, no self—just this brutal sense of irony, melancholy, and a trembling respect for words. I wrote like someone with a dirty habit. Secretly—compulsively—slyly."

Finally, she joined a writers' group, and out of a story for the group grew *The Bluest Eye,* a brief, searing novel about a young black girl's dream of having blue eyes, a story almost encyclopedic in its exploration of anger at whites and hatred of self among blacks in Lorain, Ohio.

I destroyed white baby dolls.

But the dismembering of dolls was not the true horror. The truly horrifying thing was the transference of the same impulses to little white girls. The indifference with which I could have axed them was shaken only by my desire to do so. To discover what eluded me: the secret of the magic they weaved on others. What made people look at them and say. 'Awwwww,' but not for me? The eye slide of black women as they approached them on the street, and the possessive gentleness of their touch as they handled them.

If I pinched them, their eyes—unlike the crazed glint of the baby doll's eyes—would fold in pain, and their cry would not be the sound of an icebox door, but a fascinating cry of pain. When I learned how repulsive this disinterested violence was, that it was repulsive because it was disinterested, my shame floundered about for refuge. The best hiding place was love. Thus the conversion from pristine sadism to fabricated hatred, to fraudulent love. It was a small step to Shirley Temple. I learned much later to worship her, just as I learned to delight in cleanliness, knowing, even as I learned, that the change was adjustment without improvement." (from *The Bluest Eye,* 1970)

In 1974 came *Sula,* a novel about friendship between women; once again Morrison was praised by critics and fellow black women writers not only for her prose but for exploring worlds few others entered in fiction. The 1977 *Song of Solomon* won the National Book Critics Circle Award.

Beloved began as the first part of a trio of tales that Morrison believed would make up a book. "I thought it would be 75 or 80 pages long," she says of what became *Beloved.* When I turned it in to the editor, I said, 'I'm very sorry that I'm two years late, but I'm not going to be able to finish.' " The editor read the "unfinished" 275 pages and recognized it as a whole book, and now Morrison is working on the next story, set in Harlem in the '20s. When she admits to this, she rolls her eyes, exhaling something between a laugh and a sigh, for after *Tar Baby* in 1981 she thought she was done.

"I told myself, 'I'm going to free myself, and if I never write another book, it's all right.' " After *The Bluest Eye,* Morrison learned that books could be written only when she was ready. "The process and act of writing is too important to do it because I have the time. I prefer to do it when I am unable to avoid it." She kept writing because she was unable to avoid *Beloved.*

For years she had worked double, if not triple, time: editing at Random House until 1983, teaching and writing whenever she could find the quiet to do it, all the while raising two sons on her own after her divorce. She now holds the Albert Schweitzer chair at the State University of New York in Albany, nurturing several young writers through two-year fellowships that allow them "to put their writing at the middle of their lives," as she describes it.

"I think she's of particular importance for women readers and for all readers because she's one of the few writers we have now who takes on all levels of issues at once," says Charlotte Nekola, who has just completed a fellowship in Albany. "She doesn't only talk about gender—she talks about gender and race and class all at once."

Morrison made a choice not to know too much about Margaret Garner, so she could invent a Sethe of her own. But she and an assistant did extensive research into slavery, abolitionism, Cincinnati in the 1850s and '60s, how much things cost and where streets were, "so all that would be accurate since I was dealing with the supernatural and some very sensational material and didn't want it to be sensational in the bad sense."

Not all of the information she needed was easy to find. She had heard of masters putting a "bit" on slaves, but could find no artifacts or pictures of the device. "Slave museums here are upbeat. They have quilts and all the 'cute' things slaves did." Brazilian museums, she found, eschew "cute."

"They have the tools, the bits, the masks you would wear so you wouldn't eat the cane when you were harvesting it. There were little holes for you to breathe through," she says, and her hands begin to circle her face, her head, shaping the mask and closing in on her features as her voice gains speed and force like a memory that can't be stopped, "and when you cut cane you sweat and when you take that thing off the skin comes off with it. These were not restraining things, they expected you to work in them. They had huge cages they put around them with metal tongues in them that could be tightened in the back—that was the bit. They cooked in that—*cooked* in it. I looked at diaries of slave owners who were considered benevolent. You look in October, and among all the powerful, senatorial, gubernatorial things they were doing, you would see, 'Put the [bit] on Jenny,' or 'My wife got upset and burned Martha's arm with the iron.' "

She laughs: Disbelief, weariness, amazement are all there.

"Which made me think, the story I had written was actually a happy story," she says. Her Sethe is merely haunted. Margaret Garner was not so lucky. "In reality, they sent her back. After the trial, she was sent back to the man who came to get her."

Morrison doesn't know what happened to Garner after that, but it is not impossible that she fell into the group to whom Morrison dedicated *Beloved*. "Sixty Million and more," it reads.

"I asked some scholars to estimate for me the number of black people who died in 200 years of slavery," she says. "Those 60 million are people who didn't make it from there to here and through. Some people told me 40 million, but I also heard 60 million, and I didn't want to leave anybody out."

The Pleasure of Enchantment

Rosellen Brown

A modest proposal: I would like to suggest a way to review books without spoiling them for their readers, and without indulging in a one-sided conversation about works only critics have had the opportunity to read. Can we not assume that most people interested in new fiction will want to read Toni Morrison's latest book, drawn to it not by rave reviews but by an understanding that she is a gifted novelist who always has something important to say? Let us, then, write a few simple, descriptive paragraphs and include ample quotation to represent style and substance. Six months after the book is published, let us discuss it at length. Then, secrets will not be unfairly revealed, and the reader will be brought into a dialogue about a shared experience, not lectured or caviled at prematurely, unable—let's be honest about it—to evaluate the fairness of the evaluation.

I suggest this as prelude to my own words about Toni Morrison's *Beloved* because, more than many novels, it is intricately constructed to make its revelations exactly when it wishes to and not a moment earlier. To discuss the entire book seems to me to deny the reader the pleasure of the author's careful design. *The New York Times* recently reported that certain London cabdrivers, dissatisfied with the tips of theatergoers arriving at the eternally popular Agatha Christie play *The Mousetrap,* have taken to shouting out the name of the murderer in reprisal. Writing a review of a book like *Beloved* before it's been read feels to me like that kind of casual vengeance.

Beloved is an extraordinary novel. It has certain flaws that attach to its design and occasionally to its long reach for eloquence, and an ending that lacks the power of the tragedy it is meant to resolve. But its originality, the pleasure it takes in a language at the same time loose and tight, colloquial and elevated, is stunning. The rhythm of black speech in Morrison's control is complex and versatile, and with it she makes third person narrative sound as intimate as a back porch conversation, and confidences in the first person sound like a dream.

The novel is set in Cincinnati eight years after the end of the Civil War, but its characters have been so formed and deformed by slavery that time

Reprinted from *The Nation,* 17 October 1987, 418–421. Reprinted with permission from the October 17, 1987 issue of *The Nation* magazine.

alone can never undo its effects. Sethe, who escaped from captivity eighteen years before, has delivered two sons and two daughters to freedom. Now, after one baby's violent death and her two sons' flight from a house haunted by the baby's angry ghost, she lives in isolation with her feisty mother-in-law and her surviving daughter, Denver. The mother-in-law dies; Paul D, one of the men who endured slavery with Sethe on the old farm, Sweet Home, arrives on the doorstep full of impassioned memories. The three of them try to establish a family. But in addition to the ordinary jealousy expressed by the adolescent Denver, a great ruckus is caused by Sethe's baby's ghost, partly in fun and partly in grim earnest. Paul D manages to exorcise her only by main force.

This ghost is presented more matter-of-factly even than the flying off of Solomon and his African children in the final pages of *Song of Solomon,* or the plague of robins that accompanies Sula's return to the Bottom in the novel that bears her name. Haints and spirits routinely walk the roads of the black South; to explain would be to acknowledge that outsiders are listening. This is not exactly "magic realism," as some have called it, citing Gabriel García Márquez and I.B. Singer; that label makes an invented genre out of what is merely an extension of ubiquitous beliefs—if you talk to the right people. Morrison has comfortably walked right into the center of what we call from a distance "folk culture," and used it without so much as a raised eyebrow. (A certain number of exchanges in the early part of the book, however, have a quality of unintended absurdity, as when Paul D defends the angry Denver against her mother's impatience with all the deadpan aplomb of Dr. Joyce Brothers: "Leave off, Sethe. It's hard for a young girl living in a haunted house. That can't be easy.")

But fortunately it's not too many pages before Morrison settles fully into her subject. Just when Paul D seems to have cleared the air in Sethe's house and the three of them have joined hands to begin anew, a mysterious young woman emerges from the water of a stream, dressed, as it were, in "new skin." Certain about some details of her history and of the world, yet strangely innocent of others, she enters their lives as an ordinary, if rather peculiar, visitor. She will not leave until an amazing upheaval and assertion of force and decisiveness on everybody's part drives her back. By this time we have grown to know her better than we'd have imagined possible.

The young woman is named Beloved and her astonishing presence is unlike that of any character in American fiction. Beloved is a ghost and yet she has a body; she has fears, which we see from within. But she also has needs too voracious to be borne: she is there to settle a score, and to do that she will suck the love and concern out of the others as if it were air, no matter how she may suffocate them in the act. In a scene of extraordinary, eerie poignancy, Beloved loses a tooth and suddenly thinks she could just as easily drop an arm, a hand, a toe, could find herself in pieces. This is a ghost who dreams: she is in terror of exploding or being swallowed. We feel about this vulnerable girl, at least at first, as we might about a benign extraterrestrial: in this scene, she sits "holding a small white tooth in the palm of her smooth smooth hand."

Meanwhile, in the course of re-establishing their friendship memory by memory, peeling time away like layers of live flesh, Sethe and Paul D re-experience their years in slavery—when "men and women were moved around like checkers," when anyone could have been "run off or been hanged, got rented out, loaned out, bought up, brought back, stored up, mortgaged, won, stolen or seized," when one's children might be traded for lumber, when men needed "permission for desire," and a man was "something . . . less than a chicken sitting in the sun on a tub." "My firstborn," Sethe's mother-in-law tells her, "all I can remember of her is how she loved the burned bottom of bread."

Others have written about slavery, from within and from without; what Morrison manages is a continual heaving up of images and specific memories like stones, only to have them disappear and resurface again and yet again, each time more deeply embedded in the jagged landscape of relationships. She uses these memories like the recurrent tolling of the end-words in the lines of a sestina, moving them, advancing them in their positions until the entire novel is like that most inventive and obsessive of poetic forms, a tight verbal net from which no feeling can escape unscrutinized. There are recurring, clarifying allusions to stories whose bits and pieces have gone before; there are cryptic images that solidify into circumstances whose very familiarity begins to attest to their truth. Morrison rarely mentions anything once: we seem to travel back and forth across an increasingly familiar psychological field until the whole deadly scene coheres.

Paul D senses from the way Sethe speaks of Denver that she loves her child too well. Years after the end of slavery, its numbing reverberations continue:

> For a used-to-be slave woman to love anything that much was dangerous, especially if it was her children she had settled on to love. The best thing, he knew, was to love just a little bit . . . so when they broke its back, or shoved it in a croaker sack, well, maybe you'd have a little love left over for the next one.

In Sethe's case, her love of her children has driven her much farther than even Paul D can see. She has gone to unimaginable lengths to protect them from a return to slavery, to that life she cannot imagine enduring again. But he has been there too, and in the end no discovery is too shocking for him—both of them have been mortally humiliated in countless ways that we hear about repeatedly, from different angles. Only Beloved, caught in the middle between lives, can forgive nothing. "People who die bad," someone tells Paul D, "don't stay in the ground."

Newly confronting their old wounds, Morrison's characters ask some profound questions: Was their relatively kind treatment by Mr. Garner, their original owner, significantly or only incidentally different from that of "schoolteacher," the cruel and "scientific" relative who succeeded him? "For years Paul D believed schoolteacher broke into children what Garner had raised into men," writes Morrison (a sentence that puts in a sad new context César Vallejo's poem "The anger that breaks man into children"). "He wondered how much difference there really was. . . . Garner called and announced them men—but only on Sweet Home, and by his leave. Was he naming what he saw or creating what he did not? . . . Suppose Garner woke up one morning and changed his mind? Took the world away."

There is a memorable moment in Morrison's first novel, *The Bluest Eye,* in which she patiently anatomizes the hatred a poor man feels for a couch, still new but not yet paid for, which represents for him the sickening taste of his powerlessness. It is impossible to read this scene and fail to understand why so many fine schemes for social renewal and economic optimism are overthrown at the start. Some of Morrison's instances of slavery's annihilation of self and family have the same devastating power. Caught in the wheels of such a system, in which the terms are always someone else's, can parents protect their children from a world of pain? And if they can't? Do children have the right to punish their parents for their actions? "What's fair ain't necessarily right," says one of the community of women always portrayed by Morrison as a wise (though not necessarily kind) chorus.

Beginning with *The Bluest Eye,* Morrison's work has moved along two tracks, sometimes intersecting, sometimes parallel: the imagistic and the didactic. She dares to instruct and analyze, and her angry pronouncements rarely feel intrusive because they come live and full of wit from the mouths of her marvelously animated and self-possessed characters, or punctuate the irresistibly dramatic visual images that provide the organizing principle of the novels. *The Bluest Eye* begins with marigolds that will not bloom the year Pecola has her father's baby; in *Sula,* there is fire and water. Each of the books is a skein of leitmotifs and unforgettably arresting moments in which the complex of character and plot is caught. And in between, unapologetic, are speculations and assertions that hold the whole structure steady.

Beloved may be the most "visualizable" of all Morrison's novels. There are consoling images—Sethe at prayer embraced by a white dress that kneels down beside her, its arm tenderly around her waist—and horrific ones—Paul D driven around Sweet Home like an animal, with a bit in his mouth. Many of these moments are nothing less than overwhelming. But in the end, while this is *Beloved*'s satisfying strength, it is also its weakness. There is a slightly uneven, stepping-stone quality to *Beloved* that seems, at times, to take us from one ugly or poignant or reconciling scene to another, like an opera with a succession of great arias. In some profound way I believe in the beauty and horror of the individual instances more than I do in the story, in which a mother who has felt herself guilty of an atrocity for nearly two decades finally makes peace with herself and begins a "new" life with a man who has never stopped being good, no matter what has happened to undo him. The will to console, to make a positive myth out of unspeakable circumstances, seems to have moved Morrison to wrench her characters nearly free of their ghosts when we might imagine them fighting to a more complex or ambivalent conclusion. "It was not a story to pass on. . . . So [the community] forgot her. Like an unpleasant dream during a troubling sleep."

Of course they put Beloved aside because "remembering seemed unwise," and there is irony here. But while the novel's brilliance lies in its capacity to summon up guilt and anger no one could assuage in nine lifetimes, the burden of its resolution is simply "Accept yourself." This is not to dismiss the possibilities of healing, only to say that its details are skimped a bit. Nor is it to say that people foully wronged cannot find a way to go on loving their lives—obviously they do. But the psychological groundwork is not given amply enough here to convince us that once the ghost of a great wrong is felled, ordinary life, not madness, can resume.

Morrison has always had an exhaustive and generous understanding of the complexity of community, and the voices of the town are unfailingly heard and accounted for; many of her novels have begun and ended with them. They make a noisy chorus. Her folks drag one another down, hold one another up, betray and soothe and protect with a wholly realistic unpredictability and lack of hypocrisy. And, proof of the necessity of those others, the actions of her characters always have ramifications in the community: everyone is affected. (Remember the flowers that refuse to bloom, the robins that plague the town.)

In Beloved, Morrison is at pains to show us how much strength her people have summoned to get them through, to keep on keeping on in spite of every effort to lay them low. But the energy and audacity of her book is in its pain and in the ambivalence of its characters toward their memories, their forgetting. As in many folk and fairy tales, the witch-spirit is the one that prevails in memory and nightmare. No one who has not been haunted, Sethe thinks, knows "the downright pleasure of enchantment, of not suspecting but knowing the things behind things." In addition to its other surprises, Beloved brings us into the mind of the haunter as well as the haunted. That is an invitation no other American writer has offered, let alone fulfilled with such bravery and grace.

Now go read the book and let's be ready, say in six months, to talk about it.

Aunt Medea

Stanley Crouch

Much of the Afro-American fiction written over the last 25 years derives from a vision set down by James Baldwin, who described the downtrodden as saintly. According to Baldwin, those who had suffered most knew life best; they had more to tell the world. Though Negroes had been taught to hate themselves, though they were emasculated, driven mad, or driven to drink or to drugs, Baldwin insisted that somewhere in the souls of those black folk were truths that might set everyone free:

> I do not mean to be sentimental about suffering—enough is certainly as good as a feast—but people who cannot suffer can never grow up, can never discover who they are. That man who is forced each day to snatch his manhood, his identity out of the fire of human cruelty that rages to destroy it knows, if he survives his effort, and even if he does not survive it, something about himself and human life that no school on earth—and, indeed, no church—can teach. He achieves his own authority, and that is unshakable. This is because, in order to save his life, he is forced to look beneath appearances, to take nothing for granted, to hear the meaning behind the words. If one is continually surviving the worst that life can bring, one eventually ceases to be controlled by a fear of what life can bring; whatever it brings must be borne. And at this level of experience one's bitterness begins to be palatable, and hatred becomes too heavy a sack to carry.

Baldwin's success as the voice of the racially oppressed proved that something had changed in American entertainment. The United States had no sense of tragedy because Americans hate losers, William Carlos Williams observed in his emotionally brambled *In the American Grain;* but with Baldwin the claim to martyrdom, real or merely asserted, began to take on value. One no longer had to fear the charge of self-pity when detailing the suffering of one's group. Catastrophic experience was elevated. Race became an industry. It spawned careers, studies, experts, college departments, films, laws, hairdos, name changes, federal programs, and so many *books.* Blessed are the

Reprinted from *The New Republic* 197, 19 October 1987, 38–43. Reprinted by permission of *The New Republic,* © 1987, The New Republic, Inc.

victims, the new catechism taught, for their suffering has illuminated them, and they shall lead us to the light, even as they provide magnets for our guilt.

Toni Morrison's new novel is another patch in that quilt, the most recent proof of the course of racial letters since Baldwin. It was not long before feminist ideology brought its own list of atrocities to the discussion: the horrors wrought by the priapic demon of sexism. Men and their obsession with manhood, with conquest, with violence, with the subjugation of the opposite sex and even the environment itself, were the problem. They had made things so bad that some feminists felt comfortable saying that "woman is the nigger of the universe," usurping a term of insult, and opening the way for those black women who would rise to contend for the martyr's belt that had been worn so long by the black man.

The influence of feminism on writing by black women led to work that was charged with corroborating the stereotypes of bestial black men. Zip Coon, the dangerous darkie whose pedigree stretched back to the minstrel show, became a stock character in black feminist writing. Old Zip replaced Uncle Tom as the lowest form of black life. In various manifestations he threw his children out the window, abused his wife until she murdered him, raped his daughter and drove her mad, or made intimate life so harsh and insensitive that lesbianism was the only human alternative. A pipsqueak in the world, he was hell on wheels at home. As Diane Johnson, writing on Toni Morrison and Gayle Jones, noted:

> In a demoralized subculture, everyone is a victim, but women, especially girls, are actually the most defenseless. . . . Morrison and Jones present them also as cleverer, more interesting, and eventually more homicidal than men; men are childlike, barely sentient, and predatory. Nearly all the women characters in these works have been sexually abused and exploited, usually as children.

Baldwin, Malcolm X, Eldridge Cleaver, and others had sung the same song, but now the circle of culprits was expanded. White America was still racist, violent, spiritually deficient, and exploiting, but the venom formerly reserved for Caucasians was spewed far enough to drench black men as well. Though black men clearly experienced racism, the worst of them were not above taking advantage of patriarchal conventions and brutally lording over their families—in the same way Southern white trash had used racism as an instrument of release whenever they were frustrated and Negroes were available to absorb the shocks of their passions. What might have begun as rightful indignation quickly decayed to a self-righteous, bullying whine and, went the claim, was turned inward, on one's own.

Black feminist writing was especially resented by those black men who had enjoyed the social, political, and sexual benefits resulting from the smug cartoonish version of "black manhood" promoted by radical organizations. That stylized image supposedly restored the patriarchal privilege denied by bondage and racism. Black feminists challenged the predictability of protest writing by black men, and the idiot cards of "positive black images," criticizing the plots and portraits as incomplete, as failing to tell the entire story and avoiding the problems of personal responsibility. The majority of black male writers had been content to see the difficulties experienced by black women at the hands of black men as no more than the byproducts of racism, but Negro feminists protested something different. As Johnson observed, "Undoubtedly, white society is the ultimate oppressor, and not just of blacks, but, as Morrison and Jones show, the black person must first deal with the oppressor in the next room, or in the same bed, or no farther away than across the street."

So the martyr's belt hadn't been worn very well by the self-declared champ. But exposing the shortcomings in protest writing by black men didn't automatically make writing by black women any better. Writers like Alice Walker revealed little more than their own inclination to melodrama, militant self-pity, guilt-mongering, and pretensions to mystic wisdom. What the Walkers really achieved was a position parallel to the one held by Uncle Remus in *Song of the South:* the ex-slave supplies the white children and the white adults with insights into human nature and the complexity of the world through his tales of Brer Rabbit. Better, these black women writers took over the role played by the black maids in so many old films: when poor little white missy is at a loss, she is given guidance by an Aunt Jemima lookalike.

Toni Morrison gained more from these changes in black literary fashion than anybody else. As an editor at Random House, she was one of the most powerful people in the New York literary world. With *Song of Solomon,* which appeared in 1979, she became a best-selling novelist too, proving that the combination of poorly digested folk materials, feminist rhetoric, and a labored use of magic realism could pay off. Shrewdly Morrison separated herself from the speeches and writing produced in the middle to late '60s by Stokely Carmichael, LeRoi Jones, Eldridge Cleaver, and H. Rap Brown, but avoided any serious criticism of their views. She told an interviewer that "those books and political slogans about power were addressed to white men, trying to explain or prove something to them. The fight was between men, for the king of the hill." Yet none of the black women whom Morrison proceeded to celebrate—Toni Cade Bambara, Gayle Jones, Alice Walker—took any significant positions of their own against the wrongheadedness of a black politics that mixed a romanticized African past with separatist ideas, virulent anti-white racism, and threats to overthrow the government of the United States "by any means necessary." Morrison didn't either.

What Morrison did do was consolidate her position as a literary conjure woman. Consider, for example, Mary Gordon's fantasy about her. It provides a generous taste of the spiritual and intellectual status that Morrison assumed in the dream world of white women:

I once dreamed that she bought a huge old Victorian mansion. It would one day be beautiful, but now it was a wreck, with cobwebs, broken windows, mice, rats, and vermin everywhere. I asked her how she was going to deal with all that mess. She simply said, "No problem," and waved her arms in the air. Immediately the rats and roaches disappeared and the house was beautiful.

Hoo doo to you too.

Beloved, Morrison's fourth novel, explains black behavior in terms of social conditioning, as if listing atrocities solves the mystery of human motive and behavior. It is designed to placate sentimental feminist ideology, and to make sure that the vision of black woman as the most scorned and rebuked of the victims doesn't weaken. Yet perhaps it is best understood by its italicized inscription: *"Sixty Million and more."* Morrison recently told *Newsweek* that the reference was to all the captured Africans who died coming across the Atlantic. But sixty is ten times six, of course. That is very important to remember. For *Beloved,* above all else, is a blackface holocaust novel. It seems to have been written in order to enter American slavery into the big-time martyr ratings contest, a contest usually won by references to, and works about, the experience of Jews at the hands of Nazis. As a holocaust novel, it includes disfranchisement, brutal transport, sadistic guards, failed and successful escapes, murder, liberals among the oppressors, a big war, underground cells, separation of family members, losses of loved ones to the violence of the mad order, and characters who, like the Jew in *The Pawnbroker,* have been made emotionally catatonic by the past.

That Morrison chose to set the Afro-American experience in the framework of collective tragedy is fine, of course. But she lacks a true sense of the tragic. Such a sense is stark, but it is never simpleminded. For all the memory within this book, including recollections of the trip across the Atlantic and the slave trading in the Caribbean, no one ever recalls how the Africans were captured. That would have complicated matters. It would have demanded that the Africans who raided the villages of their enemies to sell them for guns, drink, and trinkets be included in the equation of injustice, something far too many Afro-Americans are loath to do—including Toni Morrison. In *Beloved* Morrison only asks that her readers tally up the sins committed against the darker people and feel sorry for them, not experience the horrors of slavery as they do.

Morrison, unlike Alice Walker, has real talent, an ability to organize her novel in a musical structure, deftly using images as motifs; but she perpetually interrupts her narrative with maudlin ideological commercials. Though there are a number of isolated passages of first-class writing, and though secondary characters such as Stamp Paid and Lady Jones are superbly drawn, Morrison rarely gives the impression that her people exist for any purpose other than to deliver a message. *Beloved* fails to rise to tragedy because it shows no sense of the timeless and unpredictable manifestations of evil that preceded and followed American slavery, of the gruesome ditches in the human spirit that prefigure all injustice. Instead, the novel is done in the pulp style that has dominated so many renditions of Afro-American life since *Native Son*.

As in all protest pulp fiction, everything is locked into its own time, and is ever the result of external social forces. We learn little about the souls of human beings, we are only told what will happen if they are treated very badly. The world exists in a purple haze of overstatement, of false voices, of strained homilies; nothing very subtle is ever really tried. *Beloved* reads largely like a melodrama lashed to the structural conceits of the miniseries. Were *Beloved* adapted for television (which would suit the crass obviousness that wins out over Morrison's literary gift at every significant turn) the trailer might go like this:

"Meet Sethe, an ex-slave woman who harbors a deep and terrible secret that has brought terror into her home. [Adolescent sons are shown fleeing.] Meet Paul D, who had a passion for Sethe when they were both slaves, but lost her to another. [Sethe shown walking with first husband Halle, smiling as Paul D looks on longingly.] During slavery they had been treated as human beings at Sweet Home in Kentucky by the Garners. [Garners waving to their slaves, who read books, carry guns into the woods, seem very happy.] That was before the master died, the mistress took sick, and schoolteacher, the cruel overseer, took over. [Master Garner on deathbed, Mrs. Garner enfeebled, schoolteacher being cruel.] No longer treated like human beings, reduced to the condition of work animals, the slaves of Sweet Home plot to escape. [Slaves planning escape around a fire.] Sethe, swollen with child, bravely makes her way to Ohio, determined to see that the child is born free! [Sethe trudging along with great determination.] And there, in Ohio, the terrible deed takes place. [Slave catchers dismounting and Sethe running into a barn with her children.] Sethe's home is ruled by the angry spirit of an innocent child, until Paul D returns to her life. [House shaking, Paul D holding onto table as he shouts.]

"Now they are together, but the weight of the past will not let them live in the freedom they always dreamed of. Then the mysterious Beloved appears and becomes part of the family, charming Denver, Sethe's only remaining child, and the horrible past begins to come clear. [Scenes of Africans in the holds of ships.] Relive some of America's most painful moments—slavery, the Civil War, the efforts made by ex-slaves to experience freedom in a world that was stacked against them from the moment they were sold as work animals. But, most of all, thrill to a love story about the kinds of Americans who struggled to make this country great. [Sethe, Paul D, and Denver walking hand-in-hand.]"

Beloved means to prove that Afro-Americans are the result of a cruel determinism:

... [that's] what Baby Suggs died of, what Ella knew, what Stamp saw and what made Paul D tremble. That anybody white could take your whole self for anything that came to mind. Not just work, kill, or maim you, but dirty you.... Dirty you so bad you forgot who you were and couldn't think it up.

This determinism is also responsible for the character of Sethe, the earth mother heroine who might be called Aunt Medea. Mistakenly thinking that they will be sent back to slavery, Sethe gathers her four children for slaughter, and kills one daughter before she is stopped. When the novel opens, it is 1873. The ghost of the dead daughter has been haunting Sethe's home for years, frightening off neighbors, shaking, rattling, and rolling the house.

The book's beginning clanks out its themes. Aunt Medea's two sons have been scared off: there is the theme of black women facing the harsh world alone. Later on in the novel, Morrison stages the obligatory moment of transcendent female solidarity, featuring a runaway indentured white girl, Amy Denver, who aids pregnant Sethe in her time of need:

A pateroller passing would have sniggered to see two throwaway people, two lawless outlaws—a slave and a barefoot whitewoman with unpinned hair—wrapping a ten-minute-old baby in the rags they wore. But no pateroller came and no preacher. The water sucked and swallowed itself beneath them. There was nothing to disturb them at their work. So they did it appropriately and well.

Woman to woman, out in nature, freed of patriarchal domination and economic exploitation, they deliver baby Denver. (Amy is also good for homilies. While massaging Sethe's feet, she says, "Anything dead coming back to life hurts." When Sethe quotes the girl as she tells Amy's namesake the story of her birth, Morrison writes, "A truth for all times, thought Denver." As if that weren't gooey enough, there's the fade-out: "Sethe felt herself falling into a sleep she knew would be deep. On the lip of it, just before going under, she thought, 'That's pretty. Denver. Real pretty.' ")

Then there is the sexual exploitation theme, introduced in a flashback in the opening pages: for ten minutes of sex, the impoverished Sethe gets the name "Beloved" put on the gravestone. This theme in particular is given many variations. One of the most clumsy comes in an amateurishly conceived flashback designed to reveal that even Sethe's mother had a touch of Medea:

Nighttime. Nan holding her with her good arm, waving the stump of the other in the air. "Telling you. I am telling you, small girl Sethe," and she did that. She told Sethe that her mother and Nan were together from the sea. Both were taken up many times by the crew. "She threw them all away but you. The one from the crew she threw away on the island. The others from more whites she also threw away. Without names, she threw them. You she gave the name of the black man. She put her arms around him. The others she did not put her arms around. Never. Never. Telling you. I am telling you, small girl Sethe."

It doesn't get much worse, or the diction any more counterfeit.

Baby Suggs, Sethe's mother-in-law, is philosophical about the house ghost, and introduces the stoicism theme when it is suggested that they move away. "Not a house in the country ain't packed to its rafters with some dead Negro's grief. We lucky this ghost is a baby," she tells Sethe. "My husband's spirit was to come back in here? or yours? Don't talk to me. You lucky. You got three left. Three pulling at your skirts and just one raising hell from the other side. Be thankful, why don't you? I had eight. Every one of them gone away from me. Four taken, four chased, and all, I expect, worrying some-body's house into evil." Through Baby Suggs we will eventually learn how right Paul D is to conclude that "for a used-to-be slave woman to love . . . that much was dangerous, especially if it was her children she had settled on to love. The best thing, he knew, was to love just a little bit; everything, just a little bit, so when they broke its back, or shoved it in a croaker sack, well, maybe you'd have a little love left over for the next one."

Morrison is best at clear, simple description, and occasionally she can give an account of the casualties of war and slavery that is free of false lyricism or styl-ized stoicism:

> Sethe took a little spit from the tip of her tongue with her forefinger. Quickly, lightly she touched the stove. Then she trailed her fingers through the flour, parting, separating small hills and ridges of it, looking for mites. Finding none, she poured soda and salt into the crease of her folded hand and tossed both into the flour. Then she reached into a can and scooped half a handful of lard. Deftly she squeezed the flour through it, then with her left hand sprinkling water, she formed the dough.

Or Paul D remembering the people he saw on the road after making his escape from slavery, people

> who, like him, had hidden in caves and fought owls for food; who, like him, stole from pigs; who, like him, slept in trees in the day and walked by night; who, like him, had buried themselves in slop and jumped in wells to avoid reg-ulators, raiders, paterollers, veterans, hill men, posses, and merrymakers. Once he met a Negro fourteen years old who lived by himself in the woods and said he couldn't remember living anywhere else. He saw a witless coloredwoman jailed and hanged for stealing ducks she believed were her own babies.

But Morrison almost always loses control. She can't resist the temptation of the trite or the sentimental. There is the usual scene in which the black woman is assaulted by white men while her man looks on; Halle, Sethe's husband, goes mad at the sight. Sixo, a slave who is captured trying to escape, is burned alive but doesn't scream: he sings "Seven-o" over and over, because his woman has escaped and is pregnant. But nothing is more contrived than the figure of Beloved herself, who is the reincarnated force of the malevolent ghost that was chased from the house. Beloved's revenge—she takes over the house, turns her mother into a servant manipulated by guilt, and becomes more and more vicious—unfolds as portentous melodrama. When Beloved finally threatens to kill Sethe, 30 black women come to the rescue. At the fence of the haunted property, one of them shouts, and we are given this: "Instantly the kneelers and the standers joined her. They stopped praying and took a step back to the beginning. In the beginning there were no words. In the beginning was the sound, and they all knew what that sound sounded like."

Too many such attempts at biblical grandeur, run through by Negro folk rhythms, stymie a book that might have been important. Had Morrison higher intentions when she appropriated the conventions of a holocaust tale, *Beloved* might stand next to, or outdistance, Ernest Gaines's *The Autobiography of Miss Jane Pittman* and Charles Johnson's *Oxherding Tale,* neither of which submits to the contrived, post-Baldwin vision of Afro-American experience. Clearly the subject is far from exhausted, the epic intricacies apparently unlimited. Yet to render slavery with aesthetic authority demands not only talent, but the courage to face the ambiguities of the human soul, which transcend race. Had Toni Morrison that kind of courage, had she the passion necessary to liberate her work from the failure of feeling that is sentimentality, there is much that she could achieve. But why should she try to achieve anything? The position of literary conjure woman has paid off quite well. At last year's PEN Congress she announced that she had never considered herself American, but with *Beloved* she proves that she is as American as P. T. Barnum.

A House Divided

JUDITH THURMAN

If you think about what's most frightening in a horror picture, what "gets" you, it isn't the images but the soundtrack. The reason, perhaps, is that human beings listen in the womb, and hearing is one of the first sensory experiences—one of trust and connection but also, later, of helpless vigilance. The ear listens for the heartbeat, and the footstep, and to the dark—and, in literature, for a certain unwilled cry, to be heard in works as different as the poetry of George Herbert and the stories of Kafka.

That cry resounds from the void in which an infant endures its anguish, rage, yearning, hunger, and worthlessness. A writer can't make a story of that experience, perhaps because language is a relation, and can only describe other relations. But a writer can make a story of the drama of that helplessness as it's played out in and perpetrated upon the world; and it is through that drama that the best fiction engages us in history.

Beloved (Knopf; $18.95), Toni Morrison's fifth novel, is such a piece of fiction. Her protagonist is a former slave woman named Sethe, living near Cincinnati after the Civil War with the last of her four children—a teenage girl named Denver, with whom she was pregnant at the time of her escape from a Kentucky plantation called Sweet Home. Sethe's two sons have run away from her. Her formidable mother-in-law has just died. Her husband has not been heard from since the day that he and the other slaves attempted to board the "train" of the Underground Railroad. And Sethe's house is haunted by the ghost of her third child, a furious infant called Beloved, who died there—her throat cut—eighteen years before.

Despite the richness and authority of its detail, *Beloved* is not primarily a historical novel, and Morrison does not, for the most part, attempt to argue the immorality of slavery on rational grounds, or to make a dramatic case for her heroine's act of violence—the way, for example, Styron does in *The Confessions of Nat Turner.* She treats the past as if it were one of those luminous old scenes painted on dark glass—the scene of a disaster, like the burning of Parliament or the eruption of Krakatoa—and she breaks the glass, and recomposes it in a disjointed and puzzling modern form. As the reader struggles

Reprinted from *The New Yorker,* 2 November 1987, 175–80. Reprinted by permission of the author.

with its fragments and mysteries, he keeps being startled by flashes of his own reflection in them.

I would like to consider, for a moment, the relation of that fractured scene to the intact, glassed-over family portrait that is beamed into millions of living rooms on a weekly television program called *The Cosby Show.* Bill Cosby has become America's ideal parent, and the household he heads is much the same as the one at which he aims his commercials for automobiles, cameras, computers, stocks and bonds, peppy soft drinks, and Jell-O. What he really pitches, though, is reassurance, and what is most distinctive about him, as salesman, is his amalgam of maternal and paternal qualities. Cosby is rich and powerful, unlike most mothers; he is tender and present, unlike most fathers. His main role, at least as an actor, is to instill trust in children while disarming their parents' fears of them, and he does this so well that he fulfills what must be a vast yearning for the kind of perfect nurturing that almost no one gets, and that would permit the kind of self-mastery that almost no one achieves—most rarely, the children of poor, single-parent families in a ghetto.

Cosby has five children of his own, and he has published his thoughts on raising them in a book called *Fatherhood,* which restates a number of homely truths—basic articles in the implicit social contract of the middle-class family. "Even though your kids may not be paying attention," he advises us, "you have to pay attention to them all the way"; "real fatherhood means total acceptance of the child"; "the most important thing to let them know is simply that you're there"; "kids have one guiding philosophy, and it's greed"; and their "baffling behavior . . . is the same today as it was when Joseph's brothers peddled him to the Egyptians." Cosby's book contains no references to his own past, and there is nothing, except for his picture on the jacket, that identifies him as a black man—nor should there have to be. But his blackness, I think, italicizes his message—the way a contrasting typeface indicates that a passage has a double, an unconscious, an exotic, or a revealed meaning.

Cosby's assimilated American family lives in a state of grace that he invites his audience to contemplate and to share, and it is in many ways an ironic counterpart of Morrison's riven and haunted family. For who were the slaves but the selfless "ideal parents" of their white masters?

As *Beloved* opens, one of the former slaves turns up on Sethe's doorstep near Cincinnati. Paul D is "the last of the Sweet Home men," and in the score of years since Sethe last saw him he has been a prisoner on a chain gang, a fugitive living in the wilderness, a laborer for both sides in the Civil War, and a vagabond. Sethe learns from him that his brother, Paul A, was captured and hanged; that their comrade Sixo—"the wild man"—was "crisped" and shot; and that her husband, Halle, was last seen squatting next to a butter churn with expressionless eyes, smearing the clabber on his face:

"Did you speak to him?"
"I couldn't."

"Why!"
"I had a bit in my mouth."

She, in turn, recounts her story. After she put her children safely aboard the "train" and went back to wait for her husband, she was cornered in the barn by the nephews of her master. Inured as he is to the brutality of white men, Paul D is still astounded that the boys would have "pulped" Sethe's back when she was pregnant. Yet it isn't the beating that she wishes to impress upon him:

"They used cowhide on you?"
"And they took my milk!"
"They beat you and you was pregnant?"
"And they took my milk."

The scene in which the nephews force Sethe to suckle them is one of the most shocking in a novel stocked with savagery of every description, physical and verbal, and the point that it doesn't register as such for Paul D is an important one. It is not because he lacks compassion—Morrison has endowed him with an almost mystical (perhaps even sentimental) tenderheartedness. But, as a man, his experience of slavery has been different from Sethe's, as a woman, and if his hardships have been more extreme they have also been less damaging to his pride. That pride has been invested in his own attributes: his strength, his mobility, his manhood, his ability to survive. Hers has been invested in her maternity and confused with her maternity, and until that confusion is resolved, which is the real business of the narrative, she is still, and in every sense, a slave/mother.

Sethe and her two daughters, one flesh and one spirit, are trapped in a void at the core of *Beloved,* trapped by a powerfully cohesive but potentially annihilating force—maternal love—that scatters and repels the male characters of the novel. Paul D puts it one way when he tells Sethe, "Your love is too thick." Baby Suggs, Sethe's mother-in-law, describes it another way when she says, "A man ain't nothing but a man. But a son? Well now, that's *somebody*." What she also means, in the context of her own life, is "A woman ain't nothing but a woman. But a mother? Now, that's somebody."

Morrison goes on to amplify Baby's remark, and it is worth pausing at this passage—less for its own sake than because it suggests the kind of impassioned polemic that *Beloved* does not, ultimately, succumb to:

It made sense for a lot of reasons because in all of Baby's life, as well as Sethe's own, men and women were moved around like checkers. Anybody Baby Suggs knew, let alone loved, who hadn't run off or been hanged, got rented out, loaned out, bought up, brought back, stored up, mortgaged, won, stolen or seized. So Baby's eight children had six fathers. What she called the nastiness of life was the shock that she received upon learning that nobody stopped playing checkers just because the pieces included her children. Halle she was able to keep the longest . . . Given to her, no doubt, to make up for *hearing* that her two girls . . . were sold and gone and she had not been able to wave goodbye.

This language is powerful but manipulative. It is meant to awe us, and it does—like the tiny human figure that a model-builder sets next to a pyramid. The abolitionist novels and tracts of the last century aimed for the same effect. They exposed the plight of the Negro as a slave, a victim, a hero, but not as an individual, not as a familiar. When Morrison sets Baby Suggs and all her griefs on one tray of the scale, she defies us to supply our own moral counterweight—and, of course, we fail.

The occasional excesses of rhetoric (and sentimentality) in *Beloved* may reflect an anxiety in Morrison that she attributes to her heroine: a need to overfeed and overprotect her children. Paul D tries to warn Sethe about it, but she won't listen to him, asserting, grandiosely, that she will "protect [Denver] . . . while I'm live and . . . when I ain't." One of the ironies of the novel is, in fact, that its author hovers possessively around her own symbols and intentions, and so determines too much for the reader—flouting her own central moral principle and challenge. For throughout *Beloved* Morrison asks us to judge all her characters, black and white, according to the risks they take for their own autonomy and in honoring that of others.

Sethe, Paul D, and Denver are a fascinating family "unit" in part because they are so familiar: a middle-aged single mother, sexually out of practice, whose desire takes her by surprise; a middle-aged man ready to compromise with his own need to wander; and a lonely, "secretive" adolescent who strains their relationship. Denver is jealous and resentful of Paul D, particularly when he exorcises the ghost of her baby sister—her only companion. She comforts herself with carbohydrates and by daydreaming about the glorious adventure of her own birth, in a rowboat—she was dragged from her mother's womb, prematurely, by a young white girl. But Sethe has, in fact, never fully "delivered" Denver. Fat, dreamy, submissive, fearful of the world, and fixated on her moment of entry into it, Denver will be forced to complete the labor by herself.

Morrison makes this family romance just novelistically comfortable and promising enough so that one resents the apparition of a supernatural intruder: a thirsty and beautiful young woman who walks out of the pond behind the house and takes it over. She has no past, or refuses to recall one. There are no lines on her hands and feet, although there are faint scars, like fingernail scratches, on her forehead. She calls herself by the name of the dead baby—Beloved—so there isn't much suspense, either about her identity or about her reasons for coming back. But we are meant to feel, I think, that we are actually losing something to Beloved—losing a story, a family, just as they were becoming real. The family's members are seduced away by her, and forced to serve her, which they do in a trance; and the role of memory in the novel is, at least in part, to inflict enough vivid and specific pain to dispel the trance.

What is most physically striking about Beloved is her smoothness: she's the dark glass of the picture. What is most poignant about her is that, like any vindictive child but unlike most ghosts or vampires, she ("it") is "not evil, just sad." And you finally have to decide between your sympathy with her greed for love and your desire to see the others go on living—the same private choice, I suppose, that one has to make between the claims of past grief and potential happiness.

A number of critics, and Morrison herself, have described Beloved as a "ghost story," but that is a somewhat deceptive and sensational tag for it. The characters themselves take the same, almost casual attitude toward ghosts that they do toward violent death, and, as Baby Suggs reminds Sethe when she thinks of moving, "What'd be the point? . . . Not a house in the country ain't packed to its rafters with some dead Negro's grief." As a monster, a helpless but omnipotent "it," Beloved belongs to the family that Caliban and the monster in Mary Shelley's Frankenstein belong to. Freud, in an essay called "The Uncanny," suggests a way to understand them. "The uncanny," he writes, "is that class of the terrifying which leads back to something long known to us, once very familiar." The German word for uncanny is unheimlich (and a haunted house is an unheimliches Haus). But he interprets the prefix un not as a grammatical negation of what is "homelike" but as a "token of repression" for what is most secretly terrifying and desirable about home— what drives one away from it and compels one to resurrect it.

The slaves in Beloved recall their bondage to Sweet Home with the same mixture of homesick love and dread: "Although there was not a leaf on that farm that did not make [Sethe] want to scream, it rolled itself out before her in shameless beauty." They were treated humanely there—insidiously so. Their master, Mr. Garner, was a man who encouraged them to "correct" and "even defy him. To invent ways of doing things . . . to buy [the freedom of] a mother, choose a horse or a wife, handle guns, even learn reading." But the illusion of autonomy, Morrison suggests, is more debilitating, and perhaps, in the long run, crueller, than a full consciousness of servility. The slaves discover when they are turned over to a fiend named schoolteacher, Garner's heir, that they have been their master's creatures all along. "How 'bout that?" Paul D reflects. "Everything rested on Garner being alive. Now ain't that slavery or what is it?"

It's important to the story that one of Paul D's first acts when he moves in with Sethe is to break her house up—smash her furniture and dishes—as a way of ridding her of the ghost. But he can't destroy her perverse attachment to the memory, to the idea of Sweet Home—in part because the roles of master and slave, mother and child, have been fused within her. This fusion is, I think, what we experience as most sinister, claustrophobic, and uncanny in the novel, and it's what drives home the meaning of slavery.

"I am Beloved and she is mine," the ghost daughter repeats, like a vow or a litany. She means that Sethe is hers—Sethe's body, her attention, her time—and she steals Sethe's "milk" more ruthlessly than the nephews did. "Beloved she my daughter. She mine," Sethe says, claiming a privilege that the law did not accord even the slave owner: he could breed or whip or starve or separate his slaves but not murder them. And in surrendering to each other, in claiming to own each other, Sethe and Beloved create a monster like slavery itself: a greedy infant with a parent's "supernatural" power.

Morrison has a dreamer's gift for choosing names and images, and for the ironic doubling of meanings which gives a dream its cohesiveness and makes it an experience of pure retrospect but pure present. Like a dream, however, the novel is vulnerable to the kind of morning-after synopsis that one critic gave it when, quoting coolly from its steamier passages, he labelled it a "soap opera."

It's worth considering the nature of the objections that people who don't like the better kind of Romantic opera make to those who do. The staging is contrived; the plot heaves; the passions are grandiose and the myths obsolete; no one has a sense of humor. "*Espressivo* at any price," Nietzsche says, scowling, "and music in the service, the slavery, of poses—*that is the end.*"

Morrison is essentially an operatic writer, and as a "production" *Beloved* has some of the excesses that Nietzsche objected to in Wagner. She doesn't eschew melodrama in her big, violent scenes, or weeping in her domestic ones. There is a chorus of stock characters—good neighbors, evil prison guards, a messenger of the gods called Stamp Paid, and even a tree named Brother. The prose is rife with motifs and images that the narration sometimes orchestrates too solemnly. Paul D's last speech to Sethe is not the only one that trembles on the edge of pathos: "Me and you, we got more yesterday than anybody. We need some kind of tomorrow."

But if you read *Beloved* with a vigilant eye, you should also listen to it with a vigilant ear. There's something great in it: a play of human voices, consciously exalted, perversely stressed, yet holding true. It gets you.

Ghost Story

Thomas R. Edwards

A novel like Toni Morrison's *Beloved* makes the reviewer's usual strategies of praise and grumbling seem shallow. I find it hard not to dwell on passages like this description of a fugitive slave trying to get out of the Old South, where what is seen and felt so delicately mirrors the condition of the observer:

> And in all those escapes he could not help being astonished by the beauty of this land that was not his. He hid in its breast, fingered its earth for food, clung to its banks to lap water and tried not to love it. On nights when the sky was personal, weak with the weight of its own stars, he made himself not love it. Its graveyards and low-lying rivers. Or just a house—solitary under a chinaberry tree; maybe a mule tethered and the light hitting its hide just so. Anything could stir him and he tried hard not to love it.

But the writing itself is beside the point, even though the book would have little point without it. One can only try to suggest something of what it is like to find one's way through an extraordinary act of imagination while knowing that one has missed much, that later reading will find more, and that no reader will ever see all the way in.

Beloved is unlike anything Morrison has done before. Where her previous novels—*The Bluest Eye, Sula, Song of Solomon,* and *Tar Baby*—dealt with the experience of black people, especially black women, in modern America, this one goes back into history, and behind history into the materials of myth and fantasy that sober history usually thinks it is duty-bound to rationalize or debunk or ignore. Before the Civil War, on a Kentucky farm called Sweet Home, a group—a family, in a sense—of slaves lived more or less contentedly under the fairly enlightened rule of reasonably humane masters, the Garners. Mr. Garner conversed with his field hands, consulted their views about their work, treated them as men, not implements. Mrs. Garner managed the female house servants kindly and helped them with what they didn't know. Still, institutional if not personal inhumanity remained—even Mrs. Garner

Reprinted from *The New York Review of Books* 34, 5 November 1987, 18. Reprinted with permission from *The New York Review of Books.* © 1987, Nyrev, Inc.

was amused by her girl Sethe's hope that her union with Halle Suggs might be dignified by a marriage ceremony, and while Garner readily agreed to free Halle's crippled mother, Baby Suggs, he charged Halle far more in future Sunday labor than her market value justified. As Edens go, Sweet Home had its flaws—"it wasn't sweet and it sure wasn't home," one of its inmates recalls. But Sethe's response to this witticism—"But it's where we were. . . . All together. Comes back whether we want it to or not"—states a need for connection with the past that the book will dwell upon.

Sweet Home fell apart in the 1850s when Garner died and the farm was taken over by a theorizing sadist, called schoolteacher by the slaves—he was a great one for measuring heads and keeping notes—whose brutality to his human livestock drove them to attempt mass escape. Sethe managed to smuggle her three young children across the Ohio to Baby Suggs and, after an epic birthing in the fields, got there finally herself. But the men were killed, tortured, imprisoned, scattered by their bid for freedom.

This is the story's background, told in flashbacks. Now it is 1873, the war is long over, slavery has been abolished. Sethe lives in Baby Suggs's house outside Cincinnati, where she cooks in a restaurant; Baby herself is dead, as is Sethe's older daughter; her sons ran away in early adolescence, not to be heard of again. She lives in seclusion with her daughter Denver, the child she bore during her escape, who is thought "simple" by others and fears to leave the house alone. Sethe and Denver are avoided by their black neighbors, evidently because their house is haunted by the troubled, violent spirit of the daughter who died, known only as Beloved from the pathetically brief inscription on her tombstone.

Beloved thus proposes to be a ghost story about slavery, and Morrison firmly excludes any tricky indeterminacies about the supernatural. This ghost of the elder daughter is no projection of a neurotic observer, no superstitious mass delusion. Various sensible characters witness its manifestations and accept their reality; and unlike most writers of reasonably serious supernatural fiction— Dickens, Wilkie Collins, Sheridan Le Fanu, M. R. and Henry James—Morrison provides us no cozy corner from which to smile skeptically at the thrills we're enjoying. If you believe in Beloved at all you must accept the ghost in the same way you accept the other, solidly realistic figures in the story.

The ghost is violently exorcised by one of the men from Sweet Home, Paul D, who finds his way to Cincinnati after years of imprisonment and wandering to offer Sethe love and release from her history of suffering. But then Morrison, with even more daring indifference to the rules of realistic fiction, brings to Sethe's house a lovely, historyless young woman who calls herself Beloved and is unquestionably the dead daughter's spirit in human form. Beloved moves right in, drives the male recalcitrance of Paul D out of the house, captivates Denver, and begins her conquest of Sethe's own troubled heart.

This new Beloved is no mere apparition. She is solidly physical, indeed she perfects her humiliation of Paul D by seducing him. At one extraordinary moment we see her struggling to keep body and soul together:

> Beloved looked at the tooth and thought, This is it. Next would be her arm, her hand, a toe. Pieces of her would drop maybe one at a time, maybe all at once. Or on one of those mornings before Denver woke and after Sethe left she would fly apart. It is difficult keeping her head on her neck, her legs attached to her hips when she is by herself. Among the things she could not remember was when she first knew that she could wake up any day and find herself in pieces.

This is the grotesque comedy of certain moods of folklore, in which figures of extrahuman potency and menace are partly humanized by assuming some of our own vulnerability; though they try to conceal it, they do speak our language after all. But of course they mostly don't—their sketchy familiarity is in fact what makes them so dangerous, and Beloved is not finally a beneficent intruder.

To speculate about why Morrison should have created such a character and what she means to her, it may be well to stand back a bit. Black experience in America of course originates in slavery, which is to say that it begins with the behavior of white people. The whites in the book—the people without skin, Beloved calls them—are good, bad, or indifferent, but this is almost irrelevant, as if the white world were for blacks something like the third-rate carnival that performs, listlessly, for the colored of Cincinnati: "Two pennies and an insult were well spent if it meant seeing the spectacle of whitefolks making a spectacle of themselves." For many blacks, however sadly, the issue may not be so much what exactly they have suffered from racism as how they can survive it. And survival points to the heart of this book, the question of memory.

Sethe's "serious work," she reflects while kneading bread in the restaurant, is "beating back the past," but of course the past is not simply an enemy but the source of our present selves. She vividly remembers the horrors she fled from at Sweet Home, but she does not often willingly remember a later horror, of which she was not just a victim but also an agent. After her escape, while living with Baby Suggs, she once beat back the past by trying and, except in one case, failing to kill her children when the sadistic schoolteacher appeared with the sheriff to claim his lost property and take Sethe and her children back to Kentucky. (In the event, he judged her to be damaged goods and went home without her.) This tragedy, barely hinted at until the book is half over, puts a new light on things. It explains why Baby Suggs's tough spirit failed late in her life, why Sethe's boys always slept holding hands until they were old enough to flee, why Denver is afraid of going out and so mistrusts visitors like Paul D, why Sethe is avoided by her neighbors. Most important, it explains why the spirit of Beloved, the child Sethe did kill, so yearns for acceptance and love.

Beloved's demand is to be remembered, to regain some form of life in the love of her tormented mother. Men are not very responsive to such an appeal; the boys run away, Paul D drives out the ghost and contends less successfully with the reincarnated Beloved in his hope of convincing Sethe to live in "the world." That world includes his serious love for her, but it also includes schoolteacher, the Klan, the prison Sethe served time in after the murder, and other white horrors. By remembering Beloved, cherishing her in her newfound flesh, Sethe avoids "life" in a way that her life's own nature amply justifies, but hers is also, the book seems to say, a response to experience that may be most tempting, and dangerous, to women and especially to mothers.

Here Morrison's understanding and sympathy come into admirably intricate play. She knows and respects what slavery does to men, how dreadfully it wounds what for better or worse defines the manhood that most men cherish—physical capacity, pride of dominance, freedom of will and action. But she knows that it can do something subtler and perhaps worse to women, something that here centers on the figure of Baby Suggs, dead now but an abiding presence in the minds of her daughter-in-law Sethe and her granddaughter Denver, though significantly not so in the mind of Beloved, who died too young to have known her grandmother's power. Baby knew what life in the world is like, that "Being alive was the hard part," as Sethe says later; she knew that some of the worst horrors of slavery are small and specific, like not seeing your children grow up—as seven of her children, by different fathers, died or were sold away before maturity—or having, like Sethe, to be told by white women how to nurse and care for your own babies. She tried to persuade Sethe that the past is better accepted than fought against: "Lay em down, Sethe. Sword and shield. . . . Both of em down. Down by the riverside. . . . Don't study war no more. Lay all that mess down." Or, more tersely, "Good is knowing when to stop."

Baby Suggs is the matriarch, the goddess of home; after she was freed, her body broken, she made "a living with . . . her heart" as a lay preacher around Cincinnati, conducting Saturday services in the woods at which children laughed, men danced, and women wept, and then all laughed and danced and wept together until they were exhausted and ready for Baby's offer of "her great big heart." Her gospel was love, but not a kind that white religion has much to say about:

Yonder they do not love your flesh. They despise it. They don't love your eyes; they'd just as soon pick em out. No more do they love the skin on your back. Yonder they flay it. . . . Love your hands! Love them. Raise them up and kiss them. Touch others with them, pat them together, stroke them on your face 'cause they don't love that either. *You* got to love it, you! . . . No, they don't love your mouth. *You* got to love it. This is flesh I'm talking about here. Flesh that needs to be loved. . . . And all your inside parts that they'd just as soon slop for hogs, you got to love them. The dark, dark liver—love it, love it, and the beat and beating heart, love that too. More than eyes or feet. More than lungs that have yet to draw free air. More than your life-holding womb and your life-giving private parts, hear me now, love your heart. For this is the prize.

None of Morrison's people have entire access to truth, and Baby's eloquent celebration of the flesh and its affections seems to her a lie when she is dying, shaken (we later understand) by Sethe's violation of her own children's flesh. Once she preached that the only grace her people could have was "the grace they could imagine. That if they could not see it, they would not have it." But she ends by thinking, "There was no grace—imaginary or real—and no sunlit dance in a Clearing could change that." But it's to Baby's remembered comfort that Sethe returns in her later tribulations, and Baby's doctrine of the body as the seat of love and grace that identifies the wrenching ambiguity of Beloved herself. Beloved yearns to exist and be loved in the flesh by the mother who, driven frantic by memory, violated that flesh so grievously. But finally it seems clear to Beloved, so imperfectly lodged in her improvised new body, that "we are all trying to leave our bodies behind"; her desire, as with certain creatures of classical folklore, is not to exist as a separate, integral self but to fuse with her mother in a single "hot thing" that yet preserves her self as object as well as subject: "I want to be there in the place where her face is and to be looking at it too."

This impossible desire leads the novel to its catastrophe and resolution, a kind of reprise of the original tragedy in which Beloved is dismissed, though not exactly defeated, and Sethe uncertainly begins to see that she herself, and not Beloved, may be her own "best thing." And Beloved's thwarted desire points back toward what I take to be the story's center. "To be there . . . and to be looking at it too" is the terrible paradox of memory, of history itself, the hopeless yet necessary wish still to *be* a part of what we can understand only because it and we no longer are what we were, or think we may have been. At the simplest, most personal level, Sethe wants to preserve her memories—in effect, herself—against the distractions of living in the present, in the "world," that Paul D's love, and in a way Baby Suggs's too, offer as compensation. In an important way Sethe is right to want this: her history matters; her own children can know nothing of slavery except through the stories she tells them, and her people (in Morrison's own longer view) will be imaginatively cheated, their dignity cheapened, if stories like hers are lost.

Yet memory, isolated from immediate life, is terribly dangerous. It permits guilt and self-loathing and hatred of others (however well deserved) to batten on themselves. Beloved is *all* memory—hers seems to be a collective racial memory whose "personal" contents mingle with recollections of the Middle Passage from Africa. She loves both sweets and her mother's stories too well, and as she grows obese and insatiable in her domination of the household, Sethe herself becomes increasingly demoralized, loses her job, begins to starve. Stories are important—they are in fact all we have of the past—yet at the end the voice that tells Beloved's story insists that hers is "not a story to pass on," even though that voice has been passing it on for 275 pages. It should not be told, it *will* be told—the paradox is unresolvable. The memory—personal, political, poetical—of a social horror of such magnitude may distort or cancel living possibilities; but living possibilities, pursued without regard for such memories, are pretty sure to be trivial, empty possibilities in the end.

Though it is hard for a white, male reader to be sure about this, I would suppose that in *Beloved* Morrison means to help thoughtful black people, especially women, to create or re-create an imagination of self that "white history" or "male history" has effectively denied them, even while showing them how easily such an imagination can become self-defeating. What I am sure about is that this book will convince any thoughtful reader, of any sex or color, that Toni Morrison is not just an important contemporary novelist but a major figure of our national literature. She has written a work that brings to the darkest corners of American experience the wisdom, and the courage, to know them as they are.

Ties That Bind

Marsha Jean Darling

In recent decades gifted Black American women writers like Toni Morrison have come to figure prominently as the conveyors of their own valuing and imagining. In *Beloved,* we watch as the lines of cause and effect extend all the way from the world of incarnate human life-force into the world of discarnate spirit life-force. *Beloved* is at once the title of this extraordinary novel, the name of a baby girl spirit, and the name given a young woman who appears to be the "living dead." In *Beloved* the "dead dead" and the "living dead" come to 124 Bluestone Road, Cincinnati, Ohio, to reckon and be reckoned with.

Beloved challenges, seduces, cajoles and enjoins us to visualize, contemplate, to know, feel and comprehend the realities of the material world of nineteenth-century Black women and men. We enter the inner psychological and psychic world of a sensitive human being, a woman called Sethe, who is mother, worker and wife. We sense and are touched by the etheric world of her murdered baby, whose manifestation as a spirit or "haint" hints at some unfinished business around personal injustice. And we are confronted with, see, hear and feel the emotional and physical world of a traumatized young woman who has survived the Middle Passage and taken on an identity as "Beloved" in search of the kindness and love denied throughout years of suffering.

Beloved, unlike Morrison's earlier work, is a historical novel. But the distant years it encompasses are as important for us all as if they had just occurred. Although this is the story of a small group of Black people who must construct lives out of the turbulent years of American slavery, the Civil War and what is commonly referred to as the Reconstruction Era, it is also a story about the world in which we now live. It is a story about kinship, family, survival, the reasons death is welcomed, and the terms on which the "dead" actually leave the living.

The story is fashioned from the particulars of a factual account first published in the mid-1850s. Margaret Garner, a Black woman who had escaped enslavement in Kentucky, succeeded in slashing the throat of one of her chil-

Reprinted from *The Women's Review of Books* 5, March 1988, 4–5. Reprinted by permission of the author.

dren while attempting to kill them all as she was about to be captured and re-enslaved. American history is replete with accounts of Black mothers slaying their unborn and infant young rather than see the institution of slavery consume still another generation.

Morrison's novel opens some eighteen years after Sethe has killed one of her daughters. A free woman in 1873, she remembers her past under slavery. The impulse to "re-memory" is linked to her many attempts to reconcile her personal actions with her values, her intentions and her concrete material situation.

Sethe lived on a plantation in Kentucky with her husband Halle, their children and four other Black men. But when Sweet Home's owner dies, his widow's brother, "schoolteacher," and two nephews bring with them a very different regime. They brutalize and humiliate their new "possessions": Sethe, about to give birth to another baby, is savagely beaten and physically molested with schoolteacher's approval. She and the men resolve to escape through the network that links the Underground Railroad with free territory.

Sethe does escape, giving birth to her fourth child, Denver, on the way to freedom. But her flight across the Ohio River to Cincinnati, where Halle's mother Baby Suggs lives, does not protect her from the slave-catcher's legally sanctioned pursuit. Sethe is reunited with her other three children, who had been sent ahead earlier and arrived safely. But freedom is short-lived: schoolteacher, his nephew, a slave-catcher and the local sheriff descend on the house. At the prospect of being recaptured and returned to Sweet Home and slavery, something happens inside Sethe: she tries to kill all of her children, and succeeds in cutting the throat of the infant girl whom she calls "dearly Beloved."

For the next eighteen years the baby's spirit is present at 124 Bluestone Road, and in all those years Sethe—who does escape the recapture attempt—has to account to herself and others for her desperate actions. One day in 1873 Paul D, one of the Sweet Home men, makes his way to 124 Bluestone Road. In the course of building a relationship with him, Sethe is asked outright for her version of what Paul D has heard from others. As she reveals her motivations to her friend, now her lover, we hear a passionate woman who is intensely loyal to her own sense of right action:

> "I couldn't let all that go back to where it was, and I couldn't let her nor any of em live under schoolteacher. That was out." . . . Simple: she was squatting in the garden and when she saw them coming and recognized schoolteacher's hat, she heard wings. Little hummingbirds stuck their needle beaks right through her headcloth into her hair and beat their wings. And if she thought anything, it was No. No. Nono. Nonono. Simple. She just flew. Collected every bit of life she had made, all the parts of her that were precious and fine and beautiful, and carried, pushed, dragged them through the veil, out, away, over there where no one could hurt them. Over there. Outside this place, where they would be safe . . .

> "I stopped him . . . I took and put my babies where they'd be safe . . . It's my job to know what is and to keep them away from what I know is terrible. I did that." (pp. 163–165)

We hear more of Sethe's mind later in the narrative, after the otherwise thoughtful and accepting Paul D has judged her actions as morally and ethically untenable, and her love for her children as "too thick." When Sethe knows she must account to her "dearly Beloved," the child whose physical presence is increasingly insistent, she thinks telepathically to the spirit and to the nineteen-year-old woman whom she perceives as the physical incarnation of Beloved's spirit:

> I have felt what [slavery] felt like and nobody walking or stretched out is going to make you feel it too. Not you, not none of mine, and when I tell you you mine, I also mean I'm yours. I wouldn't draw breath without my children. (p. 203)

In *Beloved,* rights, responsibilities and individual accountability are central themes, as are motherhood, strong healing men and the African doctrine of last things. Although the novel begs us to travel back to the nineteenth century, it frames questions which are not bound by specific time and place. What are the entitlements and boundaries of "mother's love"? Why is the "precious interior, the loved self, whatever it is, suppressed or displaced and put someplace in the children, in the lover, in the man"? And why do the same women who surrender so much of themselves possess so strongly, even to the point of acting in ways that compromise their in-earnest attempt to love? In a society of mixed messages about personal accountability and responsibility, how did the choices people made affect their lives and the lives of those immediately about them—those in the body, as well as those who had passed on over? What were the consequences of action on one's will, when social custom and the letter of the law conspired to deny or usurp the perception that one had a will?

Sethe is inseparable from her children; there is no sense of self separate from the way in which mother's love consumes her, and those "precious and fine and beautiful" parts of her which have displaced her self. In a profound way, mother's love, which is shared, committed and loyal, is a killer: it empowers itself to set the terms under which the life it has brought forth and nurtured will prevail. Even as we read of an action that on some level is comprehensible, we also feel the baby spirit's rage urging us to ask: Do good intentions and destructive acts amount to injustice? Who is responsible, where is the tragedy? Sethe's mother love does and undoes itself; it is nurturing and destructive, empowered and tragically unjust.

The social order set in place during the early years of European settlement evolved into the social relations that reinforced the desperation Sethe would feel about the vulnerability of her children. Legislation like the Virginia statute of 1662 validated white male sexual abuse of Black women and ensured the continuing existence of the slave force by using Black women as breeders, whether the fathers were Black or white men. Law and practice worked together to dismantle the nuclear core of Black families.

Sethe, acting as the mother she thought she should be, lived in a society that legally and socially attempted to reduce her to the behavior and status of a human baby machine. Trying to empower herself as a conscious human being, she chose to run away from the degradation of enslavement. But after the escape to Ohio she poignantly sums up the new challenge she confronts: "Freeing yourself was one thing; claiming ownership of that freed self was another."

Freeing oneself to act and claiming ownership and responsibility for one's freed self are major issues in Sethe's life. Hers is a world defined by injustice, a pervasive, consuming, destructive injustice that struck at body and soul. What is tragic about her is that she is driven to act against herself (and her children who are also "herself"), and must later answer to her own desperate actions.

White society constantly abrogates its responsibility. Its accountability extends only to contracts and laws, not to any moral accountability on the part of the individual; in fact, that accountability is constantly being denied behind a facade of "blaming the victim." Neither schoolteacher, with his obsessive, pseudoscientific counting up of the animal characteristics Sethe inherently possesses, nor his nephews, who are learning how to debase still another generation of their fellow human beings, nor the white sheriff, who would no doubt claim to be just doing his job with the force of law at his disposal as he judges those the law has dispossessed, have to assume any moral responsibility of their own. Authority without responsibility brought the tyranny that was slavery.

Black people in *Beloved* constantly negotiate a physical and spirit world: people think to each other, and know what is in another person's mind. Reading it makes one wonder how much of this understanding should be attributed to telepathic communication, either with the ancestor spirits or through mediums able to connect spirit and human energies. In the African tradition, religion and life were inextricably linked in practical as well as esoteric ways. Sethe's world was deeply inscribed with a concrete understanding of traditional African religion and its beliefs about mother's right, communality and the continuum that linked ancestors and unborn spirits with the incarnate; her consciousness reflects this deeply rooted cultural pattern.

In our own time, many people do not accept that the events of material reality account for only one level of existence. The possibility of having and using this knowledge consciously is often dismissed as imaginary, "otherworldly." Toni Morrison asks us to recognize that death is an event along an individual and communal continuum. Death matters; death is an integral part of living consciousness in African religious understanding. And in *Beloved* we are ever close to Death.

ESSAYS

◆

The Opening Sentences of *Beloved*

Toni Morrison

124 was spiteful. Full of a baby's venom.

Beginning *Beloved* with numerals rather than spelled out numbers, it was my intention to give the house an identity separate from the street or even the city; to name it the way "Sweet Home" was named; the way plantations were named, but not with nouns or "proper" names—with numbers instead because numbers have no adjectives, no posture of coziness or grandeur or the haughty yearning of arrivistes and estate builders for the parallel beautifications of the nation they left behind, laying claim to instant history and legend. Numbers here constitute an address, a thrilling enough prospect for slaves who had owned nothing, least of all an address. And although the numbers, unlike words, can have no modifiers, I give these an adjective— spiteful (There are three others). The address is therefore personalized, but personalized by its own activity, not the pasted on desire for personality.

Also there is something about numerals that makes them spoken, heard, in this context, because one expects words to read in a book, not numbers to say, or hear. And the sound of the novel, sometimes cacaphonous, sometimes harmonious, must be an inner ear sound or a sound just beyond hearing, infusing the text with a musical emphasis that words can do sometimes even better than music can. Thus the second sentence is not one: it is a phrase that properly, grammatically, belongs as a dependent clause with the first. Had I done that, however, (124 was spiteful, comma, full of a baby's venom, or 124 was full of a baby's venom) I could not have had the accent on *full* [/ u u / u / u pause / u u u u / u].

Whatever the risks of confronting the reader with what must be immediately incomprehensible in that simple, declarative authoritative sentence, the risk of unsettling him or her, I determined to take. Because the *in medias res* opening that I am so committed to is here excessively demanding. It is abrupt, and should appear so. No native informant here. The reader is snatched, yanked, thrown into an environment completely foreign, and I

Reprinted from "Unspeakable Things Unspoken: The Afro-American Presence in American Literature," *Michigan Quarterly Review* 28, no. 1 (Winter 1989): 1–34. © 1989 Toni Morrison. Reprinted by permission of International Creative Management.

want it as the first stroke of the shared experience that might be possible between the reader and the novel's population. Snatched just as the slaves were from one place to another, from any place to another, without preparation and without defense. No lobby, no door, no entrance—a gangplank, perhaps (but a very short one). And the house into which this snatching—this kidnapping—propels one, changes from spiteful to loud to quiet, as the sounds in the body of the ship itself may have changed. A few words have to be read before it is clear that 124 refers to a house (in most of the early drafts "The women *in the house* knew it" was simply "The women knew it." "House" was not mentioned for seventeen lines), and a few more have to be read to discover why it is spiteful, or rather the source of the spite. By then it is clear, if not at once, that something is beyond control, but is not beyond understanding since it is not beyond accommodation by both the "women" and the "children." The fully realized presence of the haunting is both a major incumbent of the narrative and sleight of hand. One of its purposes is to keep the reader preoccupied with the nature of the incredible spirit world while being supplied a controlled diet of the incredible political world.

The subliminal, the underground life of a novel is the area most likely to link arms with the reader and facilitate making it one's own. Because one must, to get from the first sentence to the next, and the next and the next. The friendly observation post I was content to build and man in *Sula* (with the stranger in the midst), or the down-home journalism of *Song of Solomon* or the calculated mistrust of the point of view in *Tar Baby* would not serve here. Here I wanted the compelling confusion of being there as they (the characters) are; suddenly, without comfort or succor from the "author," with only imagination, intelligence, and necessity available for the journey. The painterly language of *Song of Solomon* was not useful to me in *Beloved*. There is practically no color whatsoever in its pages, and when there is, it is so stark and remarked upon, it is virtually raw. Color seen for the first time, without its history. No built architecture as in *Tar Baby,* no play with Western chronology as in *Sula;* no exchange between book life and "real" life discourse—with printed text units rubbing up against seasonal black childtime units as in *The Bluest Eye.* No compound of houses, no neighborhood, no sculpture, no paint, no time, especially no time because memory, pre-historic memory, has no time. There is just a little music, each other and the urgency of what is at stake. Which is all they had. For that work, the work of language is to get out of the way.

Nameless Ghosts:
Possession and Dispossession in *Beloved*

Deborah Horvitz

Toni Morrison's fifth novel, *Beloved* (1987), explores the insidious degradation imposed upon all slaves, even when they were owned by, in Harriet Beecher Stowe's term, "a man of humanity."[1] The novel is also about matrilineal ancestry and the relationships among enslaved, freed, alive, and dead mothers and daughters. Equally it is about the meaning of time and memory and how remembering either destroys or saves a future. Written in an antiminimalist, lyrical style in which biblical myths, folklore, and literary realism overlap, the text is so grounded in historical reality that it could be used to teach American history classes. Indeed, as a simultaneously accessible and yet extremely difficult book, *Beloved* operates so complexly that as soon as one layer of understanding is reached, another, equally as richly textured, emerges to be unravelled. Morrison has referred to her novel as a "ghost story"[2] and begins and ends with Beloved, whose name envelopes the text.

The powerful corporeal ghost who creates matrilineal connection between Africa and America, Beloved stands for every African woman whose story will never be told. She is the haunting symbol of the many Beloveds— generations of mothers and daughters—hunted down and stolen from Africa; as such, she is, unlike mortals, invulnerable to barriers of time, space, and place. She moves with the freedom of an omnipresent and omnipotent spirit who weaves in and out of different generations within the matrilineal chain. Yet, Morrison is cautious not to use Beloved as a symbol in a way that either traps the reader in polemics or detaches one from the character who is at different times a caring mother and a lonely girl. Nor is Beloved so universalized that her many meanings lose specificity. She is rooted in a particular story and is the embodiment of specific members of Sethe's family. At the same time she represents the spirit of all the women dragged onto slave ships in Africa and also all Black women in America trying to trace their ancestry back to the mother on the ship attached to them. Beloved is the haunting presence

First published in *Studies in American Fiction* 17, no. 2 (Autumn 1989): 157–67. Reprinted by permission of *Studies in American Fiction* and Northeastern University.

who becomes the spirit of the women from "the other side."[3] As Sethe's mother she comes from the geographic other side of the world, Africa; as Sethe's daughter, she comes from the physical other side of life, death. There is a relationship, too, between Beloved's arrival and the blossoming of Sethe's memory. Only after Beloved comes to Sethe's house as a young woman does Sethe's repression of countless painful memories begin to lift. Beloved generates a metamorphosis in Sethe that allows her to speak what she had thought to be the unspeakable.

In *Beloved* the ghost-child who comes back to life is not only Sethe's two-year-old daughter, whom she murdered eighteen years ago; she is also Sethe's African mother. This inter-generational, inter-continental, female ghost-child teaches Sethe that memories and stories about her matrilineal ancestry are life-giving. Moreover, Beloved stimulates Sethe to remember her own mother because, in fact, the murdered daughter and the slave mother are a conflated or combined identity represented by the ghost-child Beloved.

Mother-daughter bonding and bondage suffuses Morrison's text. Sethe's nameless mother is among the African slaves who experienced the Middle Passage and, late in the text, she relates that ordeal through a coded message from the ship revealing that she too is a Beloved who, like Sethe, has been cruelly separated from her own mother. This cycle of mother-daughter loss, perceived abandonment, betrayal, and recovery is inherent in and characterizes each mother-daughter relationship in the novel. But in the present tense of the novel—Ohio in 1873—Sethe barely remembers, from so long ago,

> her own mother, who was pointed out to her by the eight-year-old child who watched over the young ones—pointed out as the one among many backs turned away from her, stooping in a watery field. Patiently Sethe waited for this particular back to gain the row's end and stand. What she saw was a cloth hat as opposed to a straw one, singularity enough in that world of cooing women each of whom was called Ma'am. (p. 30)

This is mainly how she remembers her mother, simply as an image, a woman in a field with a stooped back in a cloth hat.

Sethe does, however, have one other quite specific memory of this obscure mother, of what may have been their only interaction following the two weeks the nameless Ma'am was allowed to nurse her. She remembers that Ma'am

> picked me up and carried me behind the smokehouse. Back there she opened up her dress front and lifted her breast and pointed under it. Right on her rib was a circle and a cross burnt right in the skin. She said, "This is your ma'am. This," and she pointed. "I am the only one got this mark now. The rest dead. If something happens to me and you can't tell me by my face, you can know me by this mark." Scared me so. All I could think of was how important this was and how I needed to have something important to say back, but I couldn't

think of anything so I just said what I thought. "Yes, Ma'am," I said. "But how will you know me? How will you know me? Mark me, too," I said. "Mark the mark on me too." (p. 61)

Because Sethe is not marked,[4] she thinks she has no link with her mother. In fact, before Beloved helps Sethe's memory unfold, Sethe firmly believes that because Ma'am is physically dead, they are not emotionally tied. When her mother was hanged, Sethe did not know why. Probably Ma'am was caught trying to escape from the plantation, but the daughter born in bondage refuses to believe her mother could have run. It would mean that she left Sethe behind, emphasizing in this generation the continuous pattern of severed mother-daughter relationships. In other words, her memories of Ma'am are buried not only because their relationship was vague and their contact prohibited but also because those recollections are inextricably woven with feelings of painful abandonment. If Sethe remembers her mother, she must also remember that she believes her mother deserted her.

As Sethe tells this story to Denver and Beloved,[5] she becomes frightened: "She was remembering something [Ma'am's language] she had forgotten she knew" (p. 61). Murky pictures and vague words begin to creep into her mind and she knows that they come from that place inside her—the place Paul D refers to as the locked and rusted tobacco tin—that stores but can never lose, forgotten memories. Ma'am's language erupts into her conscious mind signaling the beginning of Sethe's slow metamorphosis. "Something privately shameful . . . had seeped into a slit in her mind right behind the . . . circled cross" (p. 61), and she remembers that she does or did have a link with her mother that transcends the cross in the circle. She is afraid to remember but ashamed not to. Recollections of "the language her ma'am spoke . . . which would never come back" creep into her consciousness (p. 62). She remembers one-armed Nan, the slave who was in charge of Sethe and the other children on the plantation where Sethe grew up. Nan "used different words" (p. 62), words that expressed her mother's native African, and these words link Sethe back both to her mother and to her mother's land, the place where women gathered flowers in freedom and played in the long grass before the white men came:

> Words Sethe understood then but could neither recall nor repeat now. She believed that must be why she remembered so little before Sweet Home except singing and dancing and how crowded it was. What Nan told her she had forgotten, along with the language she told it in. But the message—that was and had been there all along. Holding the damp white sheets against her chest, she was picking meaning out of a code she no longer understood. Nighttime. (p. 62)

Although Sethe has forgotten the words of her mother's language, they continue to exist inside her as feelings and images that repeatedly emerge as a code that she relies on without realizing it. This code holds animated, vital memories, such as the one of her mother dancing juba, as well as the most painful fact of Sethe's life: her mother's absence.

Sethe is shocked as she continues to find meaning in a code she thought she no longer understood. She remembers that she felt the dancing feet of her dead mother as she was about to give birth to Denver. Pregnant and thinking she is going to die because her swollen feet cannot take another step, she wants to stop walking; every time she does so, the movement of her unborn child causes her such pain that she feels she is being rammed by an antelope. Although Sethe wonders why an antelope, since she cannot remember having ever seen one, it is because the image of the antelope is really an image of Ma'am dancing. Sethe's antelope kicking baby and her antelope dancing mother are one and the same:

> Oh but when they sang. And oh but when they danced and sometimes they danced the antelope. The men as well as the ma'ams, one of whom was certainly her own. They shifted shapes and became something other. Some unchained demanding other whose feet knew her pulse better than she did. Just like this one in her stomach. (p. 31)

Stored in childhood but only now unlocked, the link between the unborn Denver's kicks and the dead ma'am's kicks as she danced the antelope erupts in Sethe's memory. As she bears the next generation in her matrilineal line, Sethe keeps her mother's African antelope dancing alive: she links the pulses of her unchained, vigorously moving mother and her energetic, womb-kicking daughter forever.

A second and perhaps the most crucial part of this story from her past is that Sethe, as Nan tells her, is the only child her mother did not kill:

> She told Sethe that her mother and Nan were together from the sea. Both were taken up many times by the crew. "She threw them all away but you. The one from the crew she threw away on the island. The others from more whites she also threw away. Without name she threw them. You she gave the name of the black man. She put her arms around him. The others she did not put her arms around. Never. Never. Telling you. I am telling you, small girl Sethe . . ." (p. 62)

Conceived with a Black man in love, rather than with a white master through rape, Sethe, named after her father, is the only child her mother allowed to survive.

Significantly, she is flooded with these memories in response to questions from her own daughter, Beloved, who wants to know everything in Sethe's memory and actually feeds and fattens on these stories. What Beloved demands is that Sethe reveal memory and story about her life before Sweet Home, memory about her African speaking, branded mother and her life right after Sweet Home when she cut Beloved's throat. In other words, because they share identities, the ghost-child's fascination lies in the "joined" union between Sethe's mother and herself. Sethe's memory is being pried wide open by Beloved's presence. She forces Sethe to listen to her own voice and to remember her own mother, her ma'am with the special mark on her body, along with her mother's native language, songs, and dances.

This cycle of mother-daughter fusion, loss, betrayal, and recovery between Sethe and her mother plays itself out again in the present relationship between Sethe and Beloved. Beloved transforms from a lonely, affectionate girl into a possessive, demanding tyrant, and her ruthlessness almost kills Sethe. There is even a connection between this ruling Beloved and the slave-driver. Because any attempt to possess another human being is reminiscent of the slave-master relationship, Denver links Sethe and the slave-drivers when she warns Beloved that Sethe, like "the men without skin" from the ship, "chews and swallows" (p. 216). Beloved is furious and ferocious. When she first comes to the farmhouse where Sethe and Denver live, she appears because the other side is lonely—devoid of love and memory. She yearns for Sethe and cannot take her eyes off her. "Sethe was licked, tasted, eaten by Beloved's eyes" (p. 55). But what starts out as a child's love and hunger for a mother from whom she has long been separated turns into a wish to own Sethe, to possess her, to merge with her and be her. Beloved gets rid of Paul D and eventually excludes Denver from their play. Just as the disembodied baby ghost Beloved hauntingly possessed Sethe, so the flesh-and-blood adolescent Beloved tries to own and dominate her. Sethe is as haunted by the girl's presence as she was by her absence because possession of any kind involving human beings is destructive.

These "possessive" attachments raise the important moral dilemma underlying Sethe's act; either Sethe must be held accountable for Beloved's death or the institution of slavery alone killed the child. If Morrison wants to humanize and individualize the "great lump called slaves,"[6] then perhaps she is suggesting that Sethe, like any individual, is answerable and responsible for her own actions. The namesake for Beloved's Sethe is the biblical Seth, born to replace his brother, the murdered Abel. Perhaps Morrison's Sethe, too, is a "replacement" for her brothers and sisters murdered by the system of slavery and lost to her nameless ma'am. If so, then the inevitable confrontation between Sethe, the replacement child saved by her ma'am, and Beloved, the protected child murdered by hers, represents the impossible choice available to the enslaved mother.

Certainly one reason Beloved comes back is to pass judgment on Sethe. When Sethe first realizes that Beloved is the ghost of her third child, she wants desperately for the girl to understand that she tried to kill her babies so that they would be protected from captivity forever. Sethe assumes Beloved will forgive her. She does not. For Beloved, her mother's protection became the act of possession that led to her own death, which was murder. Beloved becomes mean-spirited and exploits her mother's pain. Sethe gives Beloved story after story of her love and devotion to her. She tells her how nothing was more important than getting her milk to her, how she waved flies away from her in the grape arbor, how it pained her to see her baby bitten by a mosquito, and how she would trade her own life for Beloved's. Sethe tries to impress upon her how slavery made it impossible for her to be the mother she wanted to be.

For Sethe her children are her "best thing" (p. 272), yet they have all been ruined. The murdered Beloved torments Sethe, Howard and Buglar have left home, and Denver is so afraid of the world that it is only starvation that forces her off the front porch. Sethe begs the ruling Beloved not only for forgiveness for the obvious but also for the return of her "self." But Beloved does not care:

> She said when she cried there was no one. That dead men lay on top of her. That she had nothing to eat. Ghosts without skin stuck their fingers in her and said beloved in the dark and bitch in the light. Sethe never came to her, never said a word to her, never smiled and worst of all never waved goodbye or even looked her way before running away from her. (p. 242)

What is most striking here is that Beloved responds to Sethe's entreaties not only in the language of the murdered daughter but also in the tortured language of the "woman from the sea" (p. 62). Death and the Middle Passage evoke the same language. They are the same existence; both were experienced by the multiple-identified Beloved.

To appreciate fully Beloved's attack on her mother, it is important to look back to Morrison's previous pages, written without punctuation, composed of some lines written in complete sentences with spaces after them, while others are not (pp. 210–14). The writing is fluid, open, created in the first person with no names and no reference to time or place. This rhetoric communicates what may at first appear to be an unintelligible experience, a story of images which the reader must grope and finally fail to figure out. In fact, breaking the barriers of form, this key passage, much like Morrison's ghost moving beyond human barriers, communicates the death-like Middle Passage suffered by Sethe's mother. She, Sethe's mother, is the woman "from the sea."

In the remembered ghost story, a woman is crouching on a ship where there is not enough room; there is bread that she is too hungry to eat and so little water that she cannot even make tears. Prisoner on a rat-infested ship where she is urinated on by the "men without skin" (p. 210), which is how the clothed white men look to her, she uses words almost identical to the ones Beloved shouts at Sethe: Beloved says "dead men lay on top of [me]" (p. 241); the speaker "from the sea" says "the man on my face is dead" (p. 210). Beloved tells Sethe that "ghosts without skin stuck their fingers in [me]" (p. 241); the woman from the ship says that "he puts his finger there" (p. 212). Beloved blames Sethe for not coming to her, not smiling and not waving goodbye before she left her; the woman on the ship says "she was going to

smile at me she was going to   a hot thing" (p. 212). The point is that
"Beloved" exists in several places and has more than one voice. While in the
pages of unpunctuated writing she is the voice of the woman on the ship,
thirty pages later she uses almost the same words as Sethe's daughter, and
each voice shouts to a Sethe.[7] At the end of this section, the collective voice
screams: "I am not dead   Sethe's is the face that left me   Sethe sees
me see her now we can join   a hot thing" (p. 213). The "hot thing,"
referred to repeatedly by both voices, expresses the passion that permeates
the text, the fantasy that it is possible to join with and possess the lost
Beloved. It expresses the desperately writhing and thwarted wish to be both
"self" and "other" so as to regain the lost Beloved by becoming her. This is
what each means when she says "her face is my own," or "the woman is there
with the face I want   the face that is mine" (p. 211). The "hot thing"
expresses the wish to join, merge, and fuse with the lost mother.

Referring to the dead slaves being dumped overboard, the voice of the
woman from the sea says "the men without skin push them through with
poles" (p. 211), and then the speaker, Sethe's mother, enraged and mournful,
protests: "The woman is there with the face I want   they fall into the sea
if I had the teeth of the man who died on my face I would bite the circle
around her neck   bite it away" (p. 211). Terrified and outraged by the
iron collar placed on the slaves, she wants to "bite the circle around her neck
bite it away" because she knows the woman hates its being there. The "woman
with the face I want" is never definitively identified, but at the very end of the
novel, Morrison, referring to the African women whose stories are lost, writes,
"they never knew . . . whose was the underwater face she needed like that" (p.
275). Perhaps she, "the woman with the face I want," the lost underwater,
drowned face, is someone on the ship with Sethe's mother. Most likely, given
that she sees her own face reflected in the "underwater face," she is her own
mother, Sethe's grandmother. If so, there is another generation in the line of
tortured, invisible women, all of them Beloveds, who have been cruelly severed
from their mothers and daughters. The loss of "the underwater face" represents
not only the death of a woman, but the death of a mother and therefore the
rupture of the mother-daughter bond, probably the strongest, most important
relationship women can have. In this novel grief is not only for one deceased
woman but for the empty space that she leaves inside all her daughters.

The two voices, Sethe's ma'am's and her daughter's, both of them
Beloveds, merge. Yet within the fused voice, each describes her own, individual experience of horrific loss:

> I am Beloved and she is mine. [Sethe] was about to smile at me when the men
> without skin came and took us up into the sunlight with the dead and shoved
> them into the sea. Sethe went into the sea. . . . They did not push her. . . . She was
> getting ready to smile at me. . . . All I want to know is why did she go in the water
> in the place where we crouched? Why did she do that when she was just about
> to smile at me? I wanted to join her in the sea but I could not move. (p. 214)

From the "place where we crouched," the slave ship, Sethe's mother has lost someone who jumped in the water—the woman Morrison says will never be known, but surely it is Sethe's grandmother. The author creates a fluidity of identity among Sethe's mother, Sethe's grandmother, and the murdered two-year-old, so that Beloved is both an individual and a collective being. They are the primary losses to Sethe, more so, even, than her husband, Halle. Beloved is the crucial link that connects Africa and America for the enslaved women. She is Sethe's mother; she is Sethe herself; she is her daughter.

Although at different times Sethe, her mother, and her daughter all live with the agonizing feeling that they have been betrayed by their mothers, perhaps most heart-breaking is the image of mother-daughter separation evoked when Beloved insists that a "Sethe," voluntarily and without being pushed, went into the sea. The agony stems from the child's assumption that she is being deliberately abandoned by her ma'am. A little girl stands on an enormous ship not understanding why her mother jumps overboard. Beloved lost her mother when she "went into the sea instead of smiling at [her]" (p. 214). And Sethe's mother wants an unidentified, lost woman on the ship, probably her ma'am, to know how urgently she tries "to help her but the clouds are in the way" (p. 210). This Beloved, Sethe's mother, wants desperately either to save her own mother or die with her, but she loses her again "because of the noisy clouds of smoke" (p. 214). (Beloved also says she lost "Sethe" again "because of the noisy clouds of smoke.") There was a riot on the ship and the noisy clouds of smoke were caused by guards' gunfire, which prevented the daughter from reaching her mother. Perhaps the sick slaves were forced overboard; maybe it was a mass suicide or an attempt to escape through the water. Or the gunfire could have occurred in Africa, before the ships were boarded, when the white traders were hunting down and capturing native Blacks.[8] What is clear is that a woman on the ship went into the sea leaving a girl-child alone, bereft; and each was to the other a Beloved. What is also clear is that the novel is structured by a series of flashbacks, which succeed in bridging the shattered generations by repeating meaningful and multi-layered images. That is, contained in the narrative strategy of the novel itself are both the wrenching, inter-generational separations and the healing process.

The American and African Beloveds join forever in the last two pages of the novel as symbols of the past—exploding, swallowing, and chewing—and fuse with these same images in the present. The sickening fear of her body exploding, dissolving, or being chewed up and spit out links each enslaved Beloved with her sister in captivity. Africa is "the place where long grass opens" (p. 274), the slave ship is the crouching place, and the ghost-child is the girl seen "that day on the porch" (p. 274). The Beloved from each place is another's matrilineal heritage and future; and each Beloved merges with her other "selves" in the shared and horrific fear of losing her body. The gap is bridged between America and Africa, the past and the present, the dead and the living, the flesh and the spirit. But they are joined in a specific shared, secret horror, perhaps the most devastating effect of the violence heaped upon them by "the men without skin." Each lives in terror that her body will disintegrate or, quite literally, explode. Earlier in the text the ghost-child loses a tooth and

> Beloved looked at the tooth and thought, This is it. Next would be her arm, her hand, a toe. Pieces of her would drop maybe one at a time, maybe all at once. Or on one of those mornings before Denver woke and after Sethe left she would fly apart. It is difficult keeping her head on her neck, her legs attached to her hips when she is by herself. Among the things she could not remember was when she first knew that she could wake up any day and find herself in pieces. She had two dreams: exploding and being swallowed. When her tooth came out—an odd fragment, last in the row—she thought it was starting. (p. 133)

She cannot remember when she first knew "she could wake up any day and find herself in pieces," not simply because she was only two when her mother cut her throat, but because the fear predates her birth; it comes from the Beloveds in Africa and the ship: "In the place where long grass opens, the girl who waited to be loved and cry shame erupts into her separate parts, to make it easy for the chewing laughter to swallow her all away" (p. 274). The voice on the ship repeatedly hears "chewing and swallowing and laughter" (p. 212). The point is that enslaved women, not in possession of their own bodies, survived barbaric beatings, rapes, and being "swallowed" without total decompensation by emotionally dissociating themselves from their bodies. The price they paid was, of course, an enormous one; those that survived often did so with no shred of basic integrity or dignity regarding their bodies. The imagery emphasizes, too, those African women who did not survive the Middle Passage—those who were chewed up, spit out, and swallowed by the sea—those whose bodies and stories were never recovered. Morrison, speaking of the women whose stories are lost, says they are "disremembered" (p. 275), meaning not only that they are forgotten, but also that they are dismembered, cut up and off, and not re-membered.

The very end of the novel paradoxically appears to belie the crucial theme of the book, that it is imperative to preserve continuity through story, language, and culture between generations of Black women. The authorial voice says repeatedly "this is not a story to pass on" (p. 275), although it seems in this text that not to repeat is to lose stories crucial to Black heritage and American history and to the personal lives of Black women.

The paradox is the one posed by memory and history themselves when past memories hurt so much they feel as though they must be forgotten. Sethe could not pass on her mother's story for the same reason that, before Beloved came, she could not talk about the murder: "Every mention of her past life hurt. The hurt was always there—like a tender place in the corner of her mouth that the bit left" (p. 58). Remembering horrors of such enormous magnitude can cause a despair so profound that the memories cancel out the possibility of resolution or pleasure in the present and future. For example, the happiness that seemed possible between Sethe and Paul D at the carnival was obliterated by the past, in the form of Beloved's arrival that very day. However, Morrison implies, even though memory of the past can prevent living in the present, to pursue a future without remembering the past has its own and even deeper despair for it denies the reality and sacrifice of those who died. Assuming individual and collective responsibility is a crucial concern of *Beloved,* and it is a responsibility to remember.[9]

Like Sethe, Beloved herself is trapped by painful memories of the past at the end of her narrative. When white Mr. Bodwin comes to pick up Denver, Sethe becomes terrified because she associates Bodwin's hat with schoolteacher's. She temporarily forgets where she is and who he is, and she tries to kill him. Sethe runs from Beloved into the crowd of women outside her house. The ghost-child, left "Alone Again" (p. 262), watches Sethe run "away from her to the pile of people out there. They make a hill. A hill of black people, falling" (p. 262). What Beloved sees is the "little hill of dead people" from the slave ship; she sees "those able to die . . . in a pile" (p. 211). She sees "rising from his place with a whip in his hand, the man without skin, looking. He is looking at her" (p. 262). While Sethe sees Bodwin as schoolteacher, Beloved sees him as a slave-driver from the slave ship looking at her, suggesting again that Beloved, the daughter, is also the woman "from the sea," Sethe's mother. She runs away, naked and pregnant with stories from the past, back to the water from which she emerged, where the narrator says she will be forgotten.

The paradox of how to live in the present without cancelling out an excruciatingly painful past remains unresolved at the end of the novel. At the same time, something healing has happened. Sethe's narrative ends with her considering the possibility that she could be her own "best thing." Denver has left the front porch feeling less afraid and more sure of herself. Now that Beloved is gone there is the feeling that perhaps Sethe can find some happiness with Paul D, who "wants to put his story next to hers" (p. 273). As the embodiment of Sethe's memories, the ghost Beloved enabled her to remember and tell the story of her past, and in so doing shows that between women words used to make and share a story have the power to heal. Although Toni Morrison states that "it was not a story to pass on" (p. 274), she herself has put words to Beloved's tale. Though the ghost-child-mother-sister returns, unnamed, to the water, her story is passed on.

Notes

1. Harriet Beecher Stowe, *Uncle Tom's Cabin* (New York: The New American Library, 1966), p. 11.
2. Toni Morrison quoted by Judith Thurman, "A House Divided," *The New Yorker* (November 2, 1987), p. 175.

3.   Toni Morrison, *Beloved* (New York: Alfred A. Knopf, Inc., 1987), p. 215. Because the novel is so newly published, there is no body of criticism on it. For substantial reviews, however, see Judith Thurman; Thomas R. Edwards, "Ghost Story," *The New York Review of Books* (November 5, 1987), p. 18; Margaret Atwood, "Haunted by Their Nightmares," *The New York Times Book Review* (September 13, 1987), p. 1; and Marsha Jean Darling, "In the Realm of Responsibility: A Conversation with Toni Morrison," *The Women's Review of Books* (March, 1988), p. 7. For discussion of Morrison's work in general up to *Beloved,* see Mari Evans, *Black Women Writers* (1950–1980) (New York: Doubleday, 1983), pp. 339–70; Barbara Christian, *Black Women Novelists* (Westport: Greenwood Press, 1980), pp. 137–79; Barbara Christian, *Black Feminist Criticism* (New York: Pergamon Press, 1985), pp. 47–63. For an analysis from a Marxist perspective of Morrison's first four books, see Susan Willis, *Specifying* (Madison: Univ. of Wisconsin Press, 1987), pp. 83–109. Among the essays available on Morrison's first four novels, a particularly interesting one is on the character of Sula in *Sula:* Naana Banyiwa-Horne, "The Scary Face of the Self: An Analysis of the Character of Sula in Toni Morrison's *Sula,*" *Sage,* 2, No. 1 (1985), pp. 28–31. Elizabeth Ammons offered insightful comments regarding Toni Morrison and *Beloved,* and her scrupulous readings of this paper were enormously helpful to me.

4.   Morrison often marks the bodies of her female characters. In *Song of Solomon,* Pilate has no navel; in *Sula,* Sula has a birthmark over her eye; in *Beloved,* Sethe's mother is branded with the cross in the circle and Sethe is permanently marked from the whipping on her back. Their bodies as well as their minds and souls are indelibly marked as different, "other," strange and witchy. As alienated women, they share being motherless. Each lost her mother to a violent death, and the marked bodies are associated with loss. Sethe's markings symbolize her separation from her mother because, in a sense, they are the "wrong" marks. She begged her mother to brand her with a cross in a circle, so she could be permanently marked as her mother's daughter. And Pilate's lack of a navel questions whether she ever had a matrilineal connection. Also, Morrison reminds us that it is the mind, soul, spirit, *and* body that unforgettably mark the identities of these women.

5.   Sethe tells this story about her mother to Denver and Beloved in response to Beloved's questions. The child asks Sethe if her ma'am ever fixed up her hair, a question reminiscent of the one Hannah asks Eva in *Sula* when she wants to know if, twenty-eight years ago, when they were almost starving to death, Eva played games with her children. See Toni Morrison, *Sula* (New York: The New American Library, 1973), p. 68.

6.   Toni Morrison quoted by Darling, p. 7.

7.   Although Sethe is the daughter of "Ma'am," born in bondage on a Southern plantation, Morrison also uses the name "Sethe," on at least one occasion, to open the possibility that there are other, perhaps many, "Sethes." The text reveals a Sethe in Africa and also one on the ship: "Sethe . . . picked yellow flowers in [Africa] the place before the crouching" (p. 214), and a Beloved lost a Sethe when she [Sethe] "went into the sea" (p. 214). Perhaps "Sethe," like "Beloved," traveled across continents and through generations.

8.   For information on the Middle Passage, see W. O. Blake, *History of Slavery and Slave Trade* (Columbus: J and H Miller, 1859). This book consists of actual testimony given before the House of Commons by a slave ship captain. The report discusses the horrors on the ship that we also hear from Morrison's voice "from the sea": crowding, crouching, suicide by drowning. Also important for the primary documents it contains is *Documents Illustrative of the History of the Slave Trade to America,* Vol. 2, ed. Elizabeth Donnan (Washington: Carnegie Institution of Washington, Division of Historical Research, 1931). For more recent discussion of the Middle Passage, see John B. Boles, *Black Southerners 1619–1869* (Lexington: Univ. of Kentucky Press, 1983).

9.   Morrison herself very clearly expresses these ideas about memory in her interview with Darling, p. 5.

Temporal Defamiliarization
in Toni Morrison's *Beloved*

Brian Finney

Beloved, Toni Morrison's fifth published novel, has been received with a mixture of adulation (it topped the best-seller lists and was awarded the 1988
Pulitzer Prize) and reserve (she was passed over for both the National Book
Award and the National Book Critics Circle Award, leading to a protest in
the *New York Times Book Review* by forty-eight Black writers). Such controversy generally signals the arrival of a major new work. It is the contention of
this article that *Beloved* is indeed an important addition to the tradition of
American fiction. The novel is highly innovative, not in the postmodernist
sense of drawing attention to its textuality, but in more subtle linguistic ways
that originate in the Black tradition of oral narrative. For her the most distinctive feature of that tradition is its language, what she describes as "its
unpoliced, seditious, confrontational, manipulative, inventive, disruptive,
masked and unmasked language" ("Unspeakable Things Unspoken" 11).
Indeed it is the incorporation of this tradition into the mainstream of the
novel which helps make this book such an important landmark in the history
of fiction.

In an interview she gave after the publication of her fourth novel, *Tar
Baby,* Toni Morrison explained what she understood by the oral tradition:
"Black people have a story, and that story has to be heard. There was an articulate literature before there was print." An important part of that story was
the experience of slavery. The vital question is how to tell that story: "The
fact is that the stories look as though they come from people who are not
even authors ... They are just told—meanderingly—as though they are
going in several directions at the same time" (McKay 427). In *Beloved* Toni
Morrison offers an artful simulacrum of this most natural of narrative methods. In particular she appears to drift between past and present in a way
which both baffles and intrigues her readers. The more one examines the
actual time shifts in the novels the more one appreciates the skill with which
she manipulates the reader for very special purposes. Further, the Black oral

First published in *Obsidian II* 5, no. 1 (Spring 1990): 20–36. Reprinted by permission of *Obsidian II.*

tradition encourages the listener/reader to contribute to the story as well. As she says in the same interview, those "who are listening comment on it and make it up too," much in the way the preacher of a sermon "expects his congregation to listen, participate, approve, disapprove, and interject almost as much as he does." Part of her narrative strategy, then, is to position the reader within the text in such a way as to invite participation in the (re)construction of the story, one which is usually complicated by an achronological ordering of events.

In effect, the distance between what the Russian Formalist called the *fabula* (the chronological ordering of events) and the *syuzhet* (the order in which events are actually presented in the narrative) in *Beloved* is almost as great as can be tolerated by most modern readers. And just as listeners are induced by the teller's "meandering" technique to intervene in order to make sense of the story, so the reader of *Beloved* is virtually forced by Toni Morrison's narrative strategy to make sense of the jumps in time, place and causality by attending to the connections and associations that the jumps create. This is why, she has explained, the novel opens *in media res*. "I wanted the compelling confusion of being there as they (the characters) are; suddenly, without comfort or succor from the 'author,' with only imagination, intelligence, and necessity available for the journey" ("Unspeakable Things" 33).

Partly for my own satisfaction and partly for the purposes of pursuing the argument that will be advanced in this article, I found myself taking this process of extrapolating the *fabula* from the *syuzhet* further than is necessary for a first appreciation of the novel. There is enough internal evidence in the novel to date virtually all the important events in the *fabula*. If one is to understand fully the way in which the *syuzhet* creates meaning for the reader, it is necessary to summarize the major time periods with which the novel is concerned.

The two principal periods between which the novel moves backwards and forwards are 1850–1855 and 1873–1874. One can also characterize these two moments culturally as that of slavery in the antebellum South and that period dubbed (somewhat ironically) by historians as Reconstruction. Or one can identify them spatially as Sweet Home, the Kentucky farm run by Mr. and Mrs. Garner with the help of five male slaves (the three Pauls, Halle, and Sixo) and one female slave (Sethe, who replaced Baby Suggs), and 124 Bluestone Road, the house on the outskirts of Cincinnati which the Bodwins made available to Baby Suggs in 1850 when her son Halle had bought her freedom from slavery by doing extra work on Sundays. The past is the Confederate South, the present is the Union North, and the meeting point between the two is the Ohio River that symbolizes a geographical, historical, cultural and ethical divide which the major protagonists of the novel have to cross—not once but many times in the unfolding of the *syuzhet*.

The novel's present time extends from the summer of 1873, when Paul D arrives at 124 (haunted by the not-quite-two-year-old murdered daughter of Sethe) in the first chapter, to the spring of 1874, when he returns there in the penultimate chapter after the twenty-year-old Beloved has disappeared. During this brief period Paul D arrives in the summer of 1873, drives out the baby ghost, becomes Sethe's lover, wins over Denver's loyalty, is seduced by the reincarnated Beloved that fall, and leaves 124 in the winter after hearing the story of Sethe's infanticide from Stamp Paid. After this, Sethe becomes so involved with Beloved that Sethe abandons any attempt to earn a living for the three of them. Early in 1874 Denver is forced to venture out from 124 for the first time since she abandoned her lessons with Lady Jones (after hearing about her mother's murder of her sister from Nelson Lord) and find food and money for the family. That spring, Denver is hired nights to look after the aging Bodwins. When Mr. Bodwin arrives to collect Denver for her first night's employment, Sethe mistakes him for schoolteacher and is just prevented by Denver and the neighborhood women from murdering the old man with an ice-pick. Beloved disappears and Paul D returns.

Although the book's past concentrates on the period 1850–1855, Baby Suggs's experience extends back to before 1840, the year after Mr. Garner bought her and her last son, Halle—back to her years as a slave in Carolina when she gave birth to seven previous children by six different fathers. 1850 is the year in which Mr. Garner buys the thirteen-year-old Sethe to replace Baby Suggs in the kitchen. The following year she chooses Halle as her mate and the couple have four children in successive years—Howard, Buglar, "Beloved" and Denver. In 1855 Mr. Garner dies and a sick Mrs. Garner invites schoolteacher and his two nephews to run the farm. Schoolteacher's harsh treatment of the slaves leads to their plan to escape that August. Sethe and her children manage to escape, but only after she has been sexually abused by the nephews and then flogged for informing Mrs. Garner about it. Sixo is killed by schoolteacher. Halle is so traumatized by witnessing the nephews' abuse of Sethe that he probably gives up trying to escape (the novel makes a point by remaining ambiguous about what happened to him). Paul D is captured and sold to Brandywine. With the assistance of Amy, a poor young white woman, Sethe manages to cross the Ohio (giving birth to Denver on the journey) and rejoin her children at 124. Two months after the escape, schoolteacher and company arrive to reclaim Sethe and her children under the terms of the notorious Fugitive Slave Law of 1851. Rather than allow them to return to a life of slavery, Sethe tries to kill all four of her children and succeeds in murdering Beloved.

We learn about events during the intervening period between this crucial year, 1855, and the present, 1873–74, in a highly fragmented manner. In almost every case the event is introduced to throw light on some aspect of the present. However, to complete the reconstruction of the *fabula,* the major events affecting Sethe and her family are in chronological order: 1855: Sethe and Denver spend three months in prison, while Baby Suggs gives up her preaching in the clearing and takes to her bed in despair; 1862–63: Denver attends Lady Jones's "school"; 1863–65: Denver becomes mute after learning of her mother's act of infanticide; 1864–65: Howard and Buglar leave home to escape the haunting; 1865: Baby Suggs dies. Simultaneously we learn about Paul D's history since being sold to Brandywine in 1855. His experiences include 86 days in a convict chain gang, 18 months living with a woman in Wilmington, Delaware, being bought by the Northpoint Company, working for both armies during the Civil War, and drifting around the North for seven years before turning up at Sethe's door.

However, this is far from how the *syuzhet* works. As readers, we piece together the *fabula* from a *syuzhet* that coils about itself and unwinds in just that meandering manner that Toni Morrison associates with the Black tradition of oral narrative. The book relies heavily on what narratologists call redundancy, the repetition of *fabula* events. Indeed, it appears to foreground such redundancy for its own thematic purposes. Almost every significant incident from the past is recounted or remembered on more than one occasion. In part, this is because the past is placed at the disposal of the present; in part it is the result of telling the story through the eyes of a number of characters into each of whose minds we are given privileged access by the omniscient narrator. Above all it reflects the difficulty all the major characters have in thinking and talking about the almost unthinkable and unspeakable experience of slavery. Morrison's repeated use of redundancy allows for the return of the repressed. All the major characters who have survived life as slaves have repressed that life to the detriment of their freed existence after the Civil War. And they bear the burden of that repressed past into the visible form of the cherrychoke tree that has been cut into Sethe's back by her owner's whip, in the marks of the iron collar that still circle Paul D's neck, and in Baby Suggs's broken hip.

The mental block which accounts for the complexity of the *syuzhet* is shared by the characters and their creator alike. Toni Morrison has confessed that at first she didn't think the horrific story of slavery could be written at all. But the more she thought about it (and she thought about it for ten years before starting to write it) the more she became convinced that this particular story could only be told in the form of fiction. "Historians can't do it—they can't speculate. They've got to decide that they're going to talk about 'ages' and 'issues' and 'great men' and 'forces.' These people didn't know they were living 'in the age of . . . ' They just thought, 'what about tomorrow?' " (Kastor B12). Seen in this light, *Beloved* constitutes a major contribution to what Claudia Tate has termed "reclamations of slavery," recent attempts by Black writers to come to terms with the pain of reliving the experience of slavery in their art. Although *Beloved* is set in the mid-nineteenth century, it is about a haunting that won't go away. Only by returning to the past can the present lead on to the future. That is why the *syuzhet* takes its highly involuted form. The behavior and reactions of the major characters make sense only when contextualized by their past.

Above all, the entire novel is an attempt to understand what forces—both historical and personal—could cause Sethe to murder her two-year-old daughter; could induce a mother to feel that it is preferable to kill her own children rather than allow them to return to a past form of living. Her action implicitly judges the life of a slave to be a worse fate than death, a prolonged death-in-life. The horror of what the past represents and the lengths to which it was capable of making its victims go is given haunting living embodiment in the shape of Beloved. Her nightmarish existence in the purgatorial world from which she has escaped confirms the reality of the condition of slavery; Sethe and the other escapees, including Baby Suggs, have escaped only its actual physical bondage, for it continues to haunt their unconsciousness and to bedevil their present lives. Beloved's ghostly presence acts as a controlling metaphor for the book as a whole and is at the center of the operation of the *syuzhet*.

Nevertheless, the convoluted nature of the *syuzhet* is the result of more than the searing effects of slavery on the book's ex-slaves. At least Toni Morrison complicates matters by portraying the majority of the white characters in the book as generally sympathetic. Mr. and Mrs. Garner, the owners of Sweet Home, are atypical of the average slave-owner, treating their slaves with respect and imposing fewer restrictions than were normal. Further, Sethe manages to escape only with the help of Amy Denver, a poor young white woman who dresses her bleeding back with spiders' webs and helps to deliver her baby. The one white family representing the North in the book is that of the Bodwins, who belong to the abolitionist movement and help all three generations—Baby Suggs, Sethe and Denver—to make a new life in Cincinnati. Only schoolteacher is truly tyrannical, the ruthless and frightening wielder of absolute power over the slaves he owns.

And yet—the Garners are still slaves owners, however liberal. This is what is so confusing to Sethe—that Sweet Home can combine such powerful images of beauty and happiness with the nightmare images of schoolteacher's brief reign. Baby Suggs is shown to suffer from the same contradictory feelings about the Garners. When Mr. Garner delivers her to the Bodwins, Toni Morrison has Mr. Garner, the Bodwins and Baby Suggs define their different positions on the issue of slavery. Miss Bodwin speaks first:

"We don't hold with slavery, even Garner's kind."
"Tell em, Jenny. You live better on any place before mine?"
"No, sir," she said. "No place."
"How long was you at Sweet Home?"
"Ten year, I believe."
"Ever go hungry?"
"No, sir."
"Cold?"
"No, sir."
"Anybody lay a hand on you?"
"No, sir."

"Did I let Halle buy you or not?"

"Yes, sir, you did," she said, thinking, But you got my boy and I'm all broke down. You be renting him to pay for me way after I'm gone to Glory. (145–46)

Amy is also a mixture of compassion and prejudice, telling Sethe, "You don't know a thing. End up dead, that's what. Not me" (80). Even the abolitionist Bodwins keep by their back door a container for small change in the form of a Black boy on his knees into whose open mouth money was placed. "Painted across the pedestal he knelt on were the words 'At Yo Service' " (255). Slavery might epitomize the worst aspects of racism, but racism persists in the North in less conscious forms. So it is no surprise that Baby Suggs is torn apart by conflicting emotions of gratitude and deep resentment, as are Sethe, Paul D and others of her generation. Sethe's first memory of Sweet Home in the opening section of the book typifies the ambiguous hold that the past exercises over her: "although there was not a leaf on that farm that did not make her want to scream, it rolled itself out before her in shameless beauty" (6). Beauty is so entangled with horror in her memory that she cannot trust her own senses and dares not at first hope that life might have better in store for her with the arrival of Paul D than the past has led her to expect. Toni Morrison has always been interested in "the complexity of how people behave under duress . . . the combinations of virtue and flaw, of good intentions gone awry, of wickedness cleansed and people made whole again" (McKay 420, 423).

A further complicating factor is the way in which their white slave owners have all but appropriated the very language the ex-slaves use. A poignant example of this occurs when schoolteacher accuses Sixo of stealing a shoat. Sixo redefines his taking the shoat as "Improving your property, sir." He explains: "Sixo take and feed and Sixo give you more work." The double grammatical use to which Sixo puts his own name in this sentence indicates the contortions to which the slave is put to make the whiteman's language serve his purposes. "Clever," Toni Morrison comments, "but schoolteacher beat him anyway to show that definitions belonged to the definers—not the defined" (190). The active tense is reserved for the white slave owner who places his slaves in the grammatical role of past passive. The *syuzhet* places this incident from 1855 within an episode belonging to the winter of 1874–75 in which Sethe resorts shamefacedly to stealing insignificant items from her employer, Mr. Sawyer. Her reason for doing so is revealing: "she just didn't want the embarrassment of waiting out back of Phelps store with the others till every white in Ohio was served before the keeper turned to the cluster of negro faces looking through a hole in his back door" (189). The reader is left to deduce the connection between the two events brought into juxtaposition by the *syuzhet*—racism (the linguistic or spatial designation of Blacks as the Other) persists beyond the demise of its legal institutionalization.

Toni Morrison uses naming in this book as the epitome of the continuing and haunting presence of the past. The benevolent Mr. Garner insists on calling Baby Suggs "Jenny Whitlow" because her previous owner, Whitlow, called her Jenny on the bill-of-sale. But she insists on retaining the name of her "husband," Suggs, who used affectionately to call her Baby, "because how could he find or hear tell of her if she was calling herself some bill-of-sale name?" (142). Her name then is a constant reminder of her forcible separation from Suggs in the past as well as of her continuing hope that she might find him again in the North. Names reinforce the *syuzhet* by complicating the present with the confusions of the past. To be named by others is to be deprived of identity. So Stamp Paid, for instance, decides to change the name his white master gave him (Joshua) after he has been forced to hand over his wife to his master's son for sexual gratification. "With that gift, he decided that he didn't owe anybody anything. Whatever his obligations were, that act paid them off" (185). Not only does he choose to pay and stamp his own bill-of-sale, but he tries to extend his freedom to others: "Beaten runaways? He ferried them and rendered them paid for; he gave them their own bill-of-sale, so to speak. 'You paid it; now life owes you'" (185).

The importance of naming in the novel extends to the farm whose name, Sweet Home, becomes even more of a linguistic anomaly for the slaves whose home it also is after the arrival of schoolteacher. A major movement in the novel is towards an understanding on the part of Paul D (the anonymity of whose name is indicative in itself) that Garner's liberal attitude managed to conceal from them all the essential similarity between his values and those of schoolteacher. As Paul D tells himself, "Garner called and announced them men—but only on Sweet Home, and by his leave. Was he naming what he saw or creating what he did not?" (220). Paul D has no trouble that Halle and Sixo "were men whether Garner said so or no." But he is less sure about his own manhood. "Oh, he did manly things, but was that Garner's gift of his own will?" (220). The institution of slavery has the effect of separating a man from his own understanding of what constitutes manhood. No wonder all the Black characters in the book are haunted by such a past, one in which white men owned both them and the language by which they defined themselves. No wonder that almost half the book is occupied with memories of a past which invalidates the present freedom of its ex-slaves. Besides, that freedom supposedly offered by the period of Reconstruction (the novel's present) is made a mockery of by the lynchings and killings that Paul D has witnessed: "Eighteen seventy-four and white folks were still on the loose. Whole towns wiped clean of Negroes; eighty-seven lynchings in one year alone in Kentucky; four colored schools burned to the ground; grown men whipped like children; children whipped like adults; black women raped by the crew; property taken, necks broken" (180).

The relationship between *fabula* and *syuzhet* in this book is more than a matter of temporal distortion. It entails a manipulation of time, place and causality. Yet if time is predominant, as Gerard Genette has shown, it is itself divisible into at least three aspects—order, duration, and frequency (chapters 1–3). The matter of frequency is particularly pertinent to this novel, since, as has already been noted, so many of the most important events in the past are recounted more than once. Toni Morrison skillfully combines the technique of redundancy with that of delayed and distributed exposition in order to embrace the painful, enduring subject of slavery. Take, for instance, the brief period of time in 1855 when schoolteacher arrives at Sweet Home, changes the retinue, foils most of the escape bid and turns up at 124 to reclaim Sethe and her children. This relatively brief segment of the *fabula* is told in no fewer than twelve separate sections of the *syuzhet*.[1] Only in the twelfth of these sections (218–229) do we learn the full details of what happened on the day of the slaves' planned escape through the drunken musings of Paul D as he sits on the porch steps of the church where he has taken refuge from a world which would seemingly not allow him to make a new life for himself and Sethe. Throughout, the *syuzhet* subordinates (by delaying) revelation of prior events to the needs of the narrative present.

The first references to schoolteacher in the opening section of the book are brief and enigmatic. On page nine a short paragraph appears to adopt the stance of an omniscient narrator in order to explain how after Mrs. Garner was widowed "schoolteacher arrived to put things in order." "But," we learn, "what he did broke three more Sweet Home men and punched the glittering iron out of Sethe's eyes." Eight pages later Sethe, in explaining to Paul D how her back came to be scarred, recounts how she had been abused by "those boys." When they found out that she had told Mrs. Garner about their treatment of her, schoolteacher "made one open up my back, and when it closed it made a tree" (17). Paul D helps the reader understand that the tree was caused by whipping her with cowhide, but the reader's comprehension of the part schoolteacher played in Sethe's and Paul's past is extremely sketchy at this stage of the novel and seems to have more to do with the characters' present feelings than what happened in the past. Gradually the reader is made to realize that the past lives on in the present, despite Sethe's conviction that "the future was a matter of keeping the past at bay" (42), and despite Paul D's attempt to lock up the past in the tobacco tin lodged in his chest. The novel follows the tortuous way in which the past forces itself on the attention of them all, even Denver for whom "the past was still waiting" (42). The most painful and therefore necessarily the most repressed memories are the last to surface in the consciousness of the main characters.

The novel's three-part structure throws further light on the changing way in which the past lives on in the present. Part One covers the half a year (from summer to winter) during which Paul D comes to live with Sethe until he leaves her. Much of this, the longest part of the book, consists of flashbacks to the pre-Civil War past, which are cut short or censored by both Sethe and Paul D because they cannot handle the full "rememory" as Sethe calls it.

What Sethe does allow herself to recall are the details of her escape, pregnant, and bleeding all over her back, during which she gave birth to Denver, the only child still to be a part of her life. We also get glimpses of her life with Baby Suggs and of Baby Suggs's life prior to the appearance of schoolteacher at 124. And there is a brief account of the most horrific period of Paul D's past with the chain gang. But that section ends informing us that it was some time before he could lock away the memory of 1855 in his tobacco tin. "By the time he got to 124 nothing in this world could pry it open" (113). Finally the penultimate section gives an objective and highly selective account of schoolteacher's arrival and Sethe's arrest. In the last section she circles around the central incident of her murdering her two-year-old daughter without being able to tell Paul D about it. Paul D's departure symbolizes the split that has occurred between them due to their inability to deal with the past, a past which literally haunts them and parts them.

Part Two covers the period from Paul D's departure (during which Sethe and Beloved grow closer together) to Stamp Paid's discovery of Paul D at the church when he explains Sethe's action in murdering her daughter. To complement this movement towards understanding and eventual forgiveness, most of the flashbacks in this part concern the period from schoolteacher's takeover to the abortive escape. This is the bleakest part of the book, symbolized by the winter they all endure. The past is taking its revenge on them as Beloved begins to turn malevolent and Paul D allows his tobacco tin to spill out its contents that "made him their play and prey" (218).

Part Three moves from winter to spring, from the deterioration at 124, climaxing in Sethe's mistaken attack on Mr. Bodwin, to Beloved's disappearance and Paul D's return and reconciliation with Sethe. The only significant flashback in this section is the account of Paul D's past during and after the Civil War, one in which he enters into a new life of freedom. In Part Three the present dominates the narrative. The past has been finally laid to rest—not forgotten but defused, deprived of its ability to dominate and diminish the present. At the end of the penultimate section of the book, Paul D echoes Baby Suggs's earlier sentiments when he says to Sethe, "me and you, we got more yesterday than anybody. We need some kind of tomorrow" (273). Yet the fact that Toni Morrison chooses to finish the book with a section of prose-poetry evoking the elusive ghost of Beloved, acts as a reminder that the memory of her and the sixty million or more slaves who are estimated to have died in the course of the two hundred years during which slavery flourished (see the dedication) continues to haunt civilization, an injustice that can never be undone.

From the opening sentence of the book onward, the novel's most prominent means of bringing the past into the lives of Sethe, Denver, and Paul D is the use of the supernatural—first in the form of the ghost of the baby she killed and then in the appearance of the twenty-year-old Beloved (the age the baby would have been had it survived). Beloved acts as the personification of the action of the *syuzhet*. She is the past brought to life in the present. Toni

Morrison's use of the supernatural is another important way in which she incorporates the Black oral tradition into the mainstream of the novel. As she told Nellie McKay, "her parents told thrilling and terrifying ghost stories, and her mother sang and played the numbers by decoding dream symbols as they were manifest in a dream book that she kept. She tells of a childhood world filled with signs, visitations, and ways of knowing that encompassed more than concrete reality" (McKay 414). This is not the first novel in which she has drawn on her family's and her race's belief in a supernatural world. In previous works, avocado trees and butterflies are endowed with strong opinions and a woman is born without a navel. She confessed to Gloria Naylor that while writing this book she felt haunted by its characters: "I have to call them by their names and ask them to reappear and tell me something or leave me alone even" ("A Conversation" 586).

Haunting, the irruption of the past into the present, is central to an understanding of how the novel works. It is itself a major theme of the book. It constitutes an important structuring device for the handling of the *syuzhet*. And it acts as a key metaphor throughout the novel. According to Toni Morrison, one of the purposes of the "fully realized presence of the haunting . . . is to keep the reader preoccupied with the nature of the incredible spirit world while being supplied a controlled diet of the incredible political world" ("Unspeakable Things" 32). Ghosts from the past haunt everyone in the book, even the young Denver. They make their presence felt within as well as independent of the major characters. From the opening pages of *Beloved* the presence of ghosts is taken for granted by the Black characters. As Baby Suggs says, "Not a house in the country ain't packed to its rafters with some dead Negro's grief" (5). Ella echoes her sentiments: "You know as well as I do that people who die bad don't stay in the ground" (188).

But Toni Morrison boldly gives flesh to a past that won't go away by making the ghost of Sethe's murdered daughter one of the major characters in the book. She has said that she decided to have Beloved perform two roles. "For the characters in the book, she would indeed be the character returned." However, "for the reader she would be a real person, a real character with a life elsewhere. But their desires meet. Her needs blend with theirs" (Kastor B12). This double perspective illustrates not only her attitude towards the supernatural but the role she allocates to the reader whom she expects to participate in and yet act as interpreter of the narrative. Maybe Beloved did have a past in which she was locked up to serve her white captor's sexual appetite (*Beloved* 119). Is this where her nightmare image of one of the men without skin comes from? Yet the major role she performs is to act as the external embodiment of Sethe's past. She is the living presence of both Sethe's love for her children that she could never wholly allow herself to feel as a slave, and the guilt she feels for the act of murder (which is both a form of self-murder and an act of selfless love) that the institution of slavery forced on her. As Margaret Atwood pointed out in her review of the book, in her creation of

Beloved Toni Morrison draws on her knowledge of folklore (something she shares with Zora Neale Hurston) which has it that "the dead cannot return from the grave unless called, and it's the passions of the living that keep them alive" (55). Both Sethe and Denver give life to Beloved by their different desires, desires which are, however, contaminated by distrust of the world beyond 124, and by Sethe's guilt.

Beloved's ghostly presence in the book points to one of the major themes that Toni Morrison has said informs not just this book, but the trilogy she plans on writing, of which this novel is the opening volume. She came across the central facts of the novel (Sethe's infanticide to prevent her children's return to slavery) in a clipping from *The Black People's Almanac*. The original slave woman's name was Margaret Garner. But whereas in reality Margaret Garner was sent back after the trial to her "owner," Toni Morrison is more interested in staging a continuing confrontation between mother and dead daughter. Toni Morrison has explained: "She was not permitted to be a mother, and that is such an elemental desire." The only person naturally qualified to question Sethe's action is the dead child, "because you knew a woman like that *would* be haunted by what she had done" (Kastor B12). "And I thought, it's interesting because the best thing that is in us is also the thing that makes us sabotage . . . our perception of the best part of ourselves" ("A Conversation" 585). Looked at in Lacanian terms, Sethe is a subject split between desire and being.[2] Her desire for unity with the object of that desire, Beloved, is interdicted by the male intervention of schoolteacher and the white patriarchal order for which he stands.

What most animates Beloved, then, is Sethe's own strangled maternal passions, strangled not just by her decision to save Beloved by killing her, but by the conditions that slavery enforced on her, which meant that she hardly had time for her children while serving the Garners. Beloved's presence, then, reinforces the strategy employed by the *syuzhet*. Both narrative elements contribute to one of the less obvious, but extremely contemporary themes of the novel, "the ways in which we displace the individual self into the beloved," as Toni Morrison has put it. "And we let the best part of us flourish in something other than ourselves and get completely erased. But no one would want to take that away, so that you're negotiating the tension" (Kastor B12). Seen from this point of view, the novel traces Sethe's displacement of self back to its roots, examines its destructive potential in the present, and attempts to find some way of laying to rest the anger from her ghostly past while reintegrating the love that she has wholly displaced into her own life. Quite early in the book Baby Suggs indicates to her, using a speech rhythm close to a form of oral poetry, the path to such reintegration when she preaches in the clearing: " 'Here,' she said, 'in this place here, we flesh; flesh that weeps, laughs; flesh that dances on bare feet in grass. Love it. Love it hard' " (88). Sethe evolves from someone completely owned by her white possessors, through someone who gives all of herself to the personification of her dead daughter (still a part of her past), to someone who begins to realize at the end that, as Paul D tells her, " 'You your best thing, Sethe. You are' " (273). Her uncertain reply, " 'Me? Me?' " leaves the way open for a continuation of this problematic theme of displacement in the next volume of the trilogy where Toni Morrison plans to resurrect Beloved in a 1920s Harlem milieu (Kastor B12).

In *Beloved* Toni Morrison has personalized the legacy of slavery that the *syuzhet* has so skillfully interwoven with the post-Civil War narrative. In one sense all her books are about what she has described as "the evolution of self in Black women" (Randolph 106). Ultimately the novel is as much concerned with the effects of that legacy on the Black community at large as the interaction between Sethe and Beloved. According to Toni Morrison, in this book she was "trying to explore how a people . . . absorbs and rejects information on a very personal level about something [slavery] that is indigestible and unabsorbable, completely. Something that has no precedent in the history of the world, in terms of length of time and the nature and specificity of its devastation." Accordingly, "nobody in the novel, no adult black person, survives by self-regard, narcissism, selfishness. They took the sense of community for granted" (Washington 58). The community can be supportive (in the mass escapes, the meetings at the clearing and the gathering of Ella and the neighboring women to exorcise the ghost of Beloved) or malevolent (after the party Baby Suggs throws)—when they all suffer the consequences. What finally brings about the disappearance of the ghost whose voice has come to represent "the mumbling of the black and angry dead" (198) is in part the collective will of the entire Black community. Their singing "broke over Sethe and she trembled like the baptized in its wash" (261). Sethe is washed clean of her sin and guilt by the Black community. It is equally significant that Beloved disappears immediately after Sethe has directed her anger at the man whom she mistakenly takes to be schoolteacher. This time round she does not try to sacrifice those nearest to her heart. Instead, she directs her fury at the white source of her agonized condition. The past is not repeated but left behind. So that it is fitting that Beloved, the embodiment of a past that has haunted Sethe in particular, should also be left behind at this critical juncture in the novel.

Ultimately the novel is about the haunting of the entire Black race by the inhuman experience of slavery, about the damage it did to their collective psyche and the need to summon all the skills of their community (including that of oral narrative) to exorcise this ghost that will otherwise turn destructive. This is done not by banishing it to the haunting purgatory that Beloved describes, but by accepting it and turning to each other for the strength to go forward in life. The title of the book derives in part from Romans 9:25 which Toni Morrison quotes as the epigraph of the novel: "I will call them my people, which were not my people; and her beloved, which was not beloved." It comes from a passage in which St. Paul is justifying the incomprehensible ways of God to doubters. The verse immediately following the one quoted by

Toni Morrison reads: "And it shall come to pass, that in the place where it was said to them, Ye are not my people; there shall they be called the children of the living God." *Beloved* gives fictional expression to a belief that the Black community through the suffering and injustice that it has suffered has earned for itself that title. "I want my work to capture the vast imagination of the people," Toni Morrison told Nellie McKay. "That is, I want my books to reflect the imaginative combination of the real world . . . while at the same time they encompass some great supernatural element" (428). The success with which she has accomplished this ambitious project leaves this reader waiting eagerly for the next volume in the trilogy.

Notes

1. Pages 9 and 16–17; 36–37; 42; 67–72; 125–26; 148–51; 157–58; 163; 190–91; 193–98; 220; 262; and 282–89.
2. Cf Jacques Lacan, *Écrits. A Selection*. London: Tavistock Publications, 1977, especially sections 3 and 9.

Works Cited

Atwood, Margaret. "Haunted by Their Nightmares." *New York Times Book Review,* 13 Sept. 1987: 1+.

Genette, Gerard. *Narrative Discourse. An Essay in Method.* trans. Jane E. Lewin. Cornell UP, 1980.

Kastor, Elizabeth. "Toni Morrison's 'Beloved' Country." *The Washington Post,* 5 Oct, 1987: B1+.

Lacan, Jacques. *Écrits. A Selection*. London: Tavistock Publications, 1977.

McKay, Nellie. "An Interview with Toni Morrison." *Contemporary Literature* 24.4 (Winter 1983): 413–429

Morrison, Toni. *Beloved*. New American Library, 1987.

———. "Unspeakable Things Unspoken: The Afro-American Presence in American Literature." *Michigan Quarterly Review* 28:1 (Winter 1989): 1–34.

Naylor, Gloria and Toni Morrison. "A Conversation." *The Southern Review* 21.3 (July 1985): 567–593.

Randolph, Laura B. "The Magic of Toni Morrison." *Ebony* 43.9 (July 1988): 102–104+.

Washington, Elsie. "Toni Morrison Now." *Essence* 18.6 (October 1987): 108+.

Toni Morrison's Ghost:
The Beloved Who Is Not Beloved

Elizabeth B. House

Most reviewers of Toni Morrison's novel *Beloved* have assumed that the mysterious title character is the ghostly reincarnation of Sethe's murdered baby, a flesh and blood version of the spirit Paul D drives from the house. Judith Thurman, for example, writes in *The New Yorker* that the young stranger "calls herself by the name of the dead baby—Beloved—so there isn't much suspense, either about her identity or about her reasons for coming back."[1] In *The New York Review of Books,* Thomas R. Edwards agrees that the "lovely, historyless young woman who calls herself Beloved . . . is unquestionably the dead daughter's spirit in human form,"[2] and, concurring with these ideas, the *Ms.* reviewer, Marcia Ann Gillespie, adds that "Beloved, blindly seeking retribution, is a succubus leeching Sethe's . . . spirit."[3] Similarly, Stanley Crouch, in his *New Republic* review, chides Morrison for creating unreal characters and then laments that "nothing is more contrived than the figure of Beloved herself, who is the reincarnated force of the malevolent ghost that was chased from the house."[4] And, in the same vein, Carol Rumens says in the *Times Literary Supplement* that the baby ghost, after being driven from the house, "loses little time in effecting a more solid manifestation, as a young woman runaway." Then Rumens faults Morrison for using a spirit as a main character, for, as she says, "the travails of a ghost cannot be made to resonate in quite the same way as those of a living woman or child."[5]

Clearly, these writers evaluate Morrison's novel believing that Beloved is unquestionably a ghost.[6] Such uniform acceptance of this notion is surprising, for evidence throughout the book suggests that the girl is not a supernatural being of any kind but simply a young woman who has herself suffered the horrors of slavery.

In large part, Morrison's Pulitzer Prize-winning fifth novel is about the atrocities slavery wrought both upon a mother's need to love and care for her children as well as a child's deep need for a family: Sethe murders her baby

First published in *Studies in American Fiction* 18, no. 1 (Spring 1990): 17–26. Reprinted by permission of *Studies in American Fiction* and Northeastern University.

girl rather than have her taken back into slavery;[7] Baby Suggs grieves incon-
solably when her children are sold; Sethe sees her own mother, a woman who
was brought from Africa on a slave ship, only a few times before the woman is
killed;[8] Denver loves her mother, Sethe, but also fears the woman because she
is a murderer. These and other incidents illustrate the destruction of family
ties brought by slavery, and Beloved, seen as a human being, emphasizes and
illuminates these themes.

Unraveling the mystery of the young woman's identity depends to a
great extent upon first deciphering chapters four and five of Part II, a section
that reveals the points of view of individual characters. Both of these chapters
begin with the line "I AM BELOVED and she is mine," and in these narratives Morrison enters Beloved's consciousness. From Beloved's disjointed
thoughts, her stream-of-conscious rememberings set down in these chapters,
a story can be pieced together that describes how white slave traders, "men
without skin," captured the girl and her mother as the older woman picked
flowers in Africa. In her narrative, Beloved explains that she and her mother,
along with many other Africans, were then put aboard an abysmally crowded
slave ship, given little food and water, and in these inhuman conditions, many
blacks died. To escape this living hell, Beloved's mother leaped into the
ocean, and, thus, in the girl's eyes, her mother willingly deserted her.

In order to grasp the details of this story, chapters four and five of Part II
must be read as a poem: thus, examining the text line by line is often necessary. As Beloved begins her narrative, she is recalling a time when she was a
young girl, for she says "I am not big" (p. 210) and later remarks again "I am
small" (p. 211). However, the memory of these experiences is so vivid that, to
her, "all of it is now" (p. 210). One of the first traumas Beloved describes is
being in the lower hold of a slave ship. The captured Africans have been
crouching, crammed in the overcrowded space for so long that the girl thinks
"there will never be a time when I am not crouching and watching others who
are crouching" and then she notes that "someone is thrashing but there is no
room to do it in" (p. 210). At first the men and women on the ship are separated, but then Beloved says that "storms rock us and mix the men into the
women and the women into the men   that is when I begin to be on the
back of the man" (p. 211). This person seems to be her father or at least a
father figure, for he carries the young girl on his back. Beloved says "I love him
because he has a song" and, until he dies on the ship, this man sings of his
African home, of the "place where a woman takes flowers away from their
leaves and puts them in a round basket   before the clouds" (p. 211).

These lyrics bring to mind the first scene in Part II, chapter four.
Beloved's tale begins with the girl watching her mother as the woman takes
"flowers away from leaves   she put them in a round basket. . . . She fills
the basket   she opens the grass" (p. 210). This opening of the grass is
probably caused by the mother's falling down, for Beloved next says, "I
would help her but the clouds are in the way." In the following chapter, the

girl clarifies this thought when she explains, "I wanted to help her when she was picking the flowers, but the clouds of gunsmoke blinded me and I lost her" (p. 214). Thus, what the girl is remembering is the capture of her mother by the men without skin, the armed white slave traders. Later, Beloved sums up her story by explaining that the three crucial points in her life have been times when her mother left her: "Three times I lost her: once with the flowers because of the noisy clouds of smoke; once when she went into the sea instead of smiling at me; once under the bridge when I went in to join her and she came toward me but did not smile" (p. 214). Thus, the slave traders' capture of her mother is the first of three incidents that frame the rest of Beloved's memories.

Once incarcerated on the ship, Beloved notices changes in her mother. She remembers seeing the diamond earrings, "the shining in her ears" (p. 211), as they were picking flowers. Now on the ship, her mother "has nothing in her ears," but she does have an iron collar around her neck. The child knows that she "does not like the circle around her neck" and says "if I had the teeth of the man who died on my face I would bite the circle around her neck   bite it away   I know she does not like it." Sensing her mother's unhappiness, her longing for Africa, Beloved symbolizes the woman's emotions by ascribing to her a wish for physical items: "She wants her earrings   she wants her round basket" (p. 211).

As Beloved continues her tale, she explains that in the inhuman conditions of the ship, many blacks die. She says "those able to die are in a pile" and the "men without skin push them through with poles," evidently "through" the ship's portholes, for the hills of dead people "fall into the sea which is the color of the bread" (p. 211). The man who has carried her on his back is one of those who succumbs, and as he takes his last breath, he turns his head and then Beloved can "see the teeth he sang through" (p. 211). She knows that "his song is gone," so now she loves "his pretty little teeth instead" (p. 212). Only after the man's head drops in death is the girl able to see her mother; Beloved remembers, "when he dies on my face I can see hers   she is going to smile at me." However, the girl never receives this gesture of affection, for her mother escapes her own pain by jumping into the ocean, thus committing suicide. The scene is etched in Beloved's memory: "They push my own man through   they do not push the woman with my face through   she goes in   they do not push her   she goes in   the little hill is gone   she was going to smile at me" (p. 212). Beloved is haunted by this second loss of her mother for, unlike the separation caused by the slave traders' attack, this time the mother chooses to leave her. The girl agonizes as she tries to understand her mother's action and later thinks that "all I want to know is why did she go in the water in the place where we crouched? Why did she do that when she was just about to smile at me? I wanted to join her in the sea but I could not move" (p. 214).[9]

Time passes and Beloved notes that "the others are taken   I am not taken" (p. 212). These lines suggest that when the other slaves are removed from the ship, Beloved, whose beauty is noted by several characters, is perhaps kept by one of the ship's officers.[10] At any rate, she is now controlled by a man who uses her sexually, for "he hurts where I sleep" (p. 212), thus in bed, and "he puts his finger there." In this situation, Beloved longs for her mother and explains, "I wait on the bridge because she is under it" (p. 212). Although at this point she may be on an inland bridge, Beloved is most likely waiting for her mother on the ship's bridge; if she is being kept by one of the vessel's officers, the girl would logically be there. But, wherever she is at this time, Beloved last saw her mother as the woman went into the sea; thus, the girl associates water with her parent and believes she can be found in this element.

Beloved's stream-of-consciousness narrative then jumps to the time, apparently several years later, when she arrives at the creek behind Sethe's house. Morrison does not specify exactly how Beloved comes to be there, but various characters give possible explanations. The most plausible theory is that offered by Stamp Paid who says, "Was a girl locked up in the house with a whiteman over by Deer Creek. Found him dead last summer and the girl gone. Maybe that's her. Folks say he had her in there since she was a pup" (p. 235). This possibility would explain Beloved's "new" skin, her unlined feet and hands, for if the girl were constantly kept indoors, her skin would not be weathered or worn. Also, the scar under Beloved's chin could be explained by such an owner's ill-treatment of her. Morrison gives credence to Stamp Paid's guess by having Sethe voice a similar hypothesis and then note that her neighbor, Ella, had suffered the same fate. When Beloved first comes to live with the family, Sethe tells Denver "that she believed Beloved had been locked up by some whiteman for his own purposes, and never let out the door. That she must have escaped to a bridge or someplace and rinsed the rest out of her mind. Something like that had happened to Ella . . ." (p. 119). In addition, Beloved's own words suggest that she has been confined and used sexually. The girl explains to Denver that she "knew one whiteman" (p. 119), and she tells Sethe that a white man "was in the house I was in. He hurt me" (p. 215). In a statement that reveals the source of her name, Beloved says that men call her "beloved in the dark and bitch in the light" (p. 241), and in response to another question about her name, she says, "in the dark my name is Beloved" (p. 75).

Whatever situation Beloved has come from, when she reaches the creek behind Sethe's house, she is still haunted by her mother's absence. The lonely girl sees the creek, remembers the water under the ship's bridge where she last glimpsed her mother, and concludes that her lost loved ones are beneath the creek's surface. In her soliloquy, Beloved links the scene to her mother and father figure by evoking images of the African mother's diamond earrings and the father's teeth. She says that she knows the man who carried her on his back is not floating on this water, but his "teeth are down there where the blue is . . . so is the face I want the face that is going to smile at me" (p. 212). And, in describing the creek she says, "in the day diamonds are in the water where she is and turtles[11] in the night I hear chewing and swallowing and laughter   it belongs to me" (p. 212). The diamonds Beloved thinks she sees in the water are most likely reflected bits of sunlight that make the water sparkle. Similarly, the noises the girl interprets as "chewing and swallowing and laughing" are probably made by the turtles. Alone in the world, Beloved's intense need to be with those she loves undoubtedly affects her interpretation of what her senses perceive.[12]

If Stamp Paid is right and the girl has been locked up for years, then she has not had normal experiences with people or places. She lacks both formal learning and the practical education she would have gained from a family life. These deficiencies also undoubtedly affect her perceptions, and, thus, it is not especially surprising that she does not distinguish between the water under the ship's bridge and that in the creek behind Sethe's house. To the untutored girl, all bodies of water are connected as one.

Apparently, Beloved looks into the creek water, sees her own reflection, and concludes that the image is her mother's face. She then dives into the water, believing that in this element her mother will at last give her the smile that was cut short on the slave ship. Beloved says,

> "I see her face which is mine   it is the face that was going to smile at me
> in the place where we crouched   now she is going to   her face comes
> through the water . . . her face is mine   she is not smiling. . . . I have to
> have my face   I go in. . . . I am in the water and she is coming   there
> is no round basket   no iron circle around her neck." (pp. 212, 213)

In the water, Beloved cannot "join" with the reflection, and thus she thinks her mother leaves her for a third time; distraught, she says, "my own face has left me   I see me swim away. . . . I see the bottoms of my feet   I am alone" (p. 213).

Beloved surfaces, sees Sethe's house, and by the next day she has made her way to the structure. Exhausted by her ordeal, the girl is sleeping near the house when Sethe returns from the carnival.[13] Beloved says,

> "I come out of blue water. . . . I need to find a place to be. . . . There is a
> house. . . . I sit   the sun closes my eyes   when I open them I see the
> face I lost   Sethe's is the face that left me. . . . I see the smile. . . . It is the
> face I lost   she is my face smiling at me   doing it at last." (p. 213)

Thus, when Beloved awakens and sees Sethe smiling at her, the girl mistakenly thinks that the woman is her long lost mother. In the second half of her narrative, Beloved even more clearly states her erroneous conclusions when she asserts, "Sethe is the one that picked flowers . . . in the place before the crouching. . . . She was about to smile at me when the men without skin came and took us up into the sunlight with the dead and shoved them into the sea. Sethe went into the sea. . . . They did not push her . . ." (p. 214).

What finally emerges from combining Beloved's thoughts and the rest of the novel is a story of two probable instances of mistaken identity. Beloved is haunted by the loss of her African parents and thus comes to believe that Sethe is her mother. Sethe longs for her dead daughter and is rather easily convinced that Beloved is the child she has lost.

Morrison hints at this interpretation in her preface to the novel, a quotation from Romans 9:25: "I will call them my people, which were not my people; and her beloved, which was not beloved." As Margaret Atwood notes, the biblical context of these lines emphasizes Paul's message that people once "despised and outcast, have now been redefined as acceptable."[14] However, Morrison's language, especially in the preface, is rich in meaning on many levels. In view of the ambiguity about Beloved's identity found in the rest of the novel, it seems probable that in this initial line Morrison is suggesting an answer to the riddle of who Beloved really is or, to be more exact, who she is not. The words "I will call . . . her beloved, which was not beloved" suggest that the mysterious girl is not really Sethe's murdered daughter returned from the grave; she is "called" Beloved, but she is not Sethe's child. Also, the line "I will call them my people, which were not my people" hints that Beloved mistakenly thinks Sethe and her family are her blood kin.

Seen in this light, Beloved's story illuminates several other puzzling parts of the novel. For example, after Sethe goes to the Clearing and feels that her neck is being choked, Denver accuses Beloved of causing the distress. Beloved replies, " 'I didn't choke it. The circle of iron choked it' " (p. 101). Since she believes Sethe and her African mother are the same person, Beloved reasons that the iron collar her African mother was forced to wear is bothering Sethe.

Beloved's questions about Sethe's earrings are one reason the woman comes to believe that the mysterious girl is her murdered child. Before her death, Sethe's baby girl had loved to play with her mother's crystal earrings. Sethe had "jingled the earrings for the pleasure of the crawling-already? girl, who reached for them over and over again" (p. 94). Thus, when Beloved asks "where your diamonds? . . . Tell me your earrings," the family wonders, "How did she know?" (p. 63). Of course, Beloved asks this question remembering the "shining" in her African mother's earrings, the diamonds that were probably confiscated by the slave traders. However, Sethe thinks Beloved is remembering the crystal earrings with which the dead baby played.

This instance of misunderstanding is typical, for throughout the novel Sethe, Denver, and Beloved often fail to communicate clearly with each other. In fact, the narrator describes Beloved's and Denver's verbal exchanges as "sweet, crazy conversations full of half sentences, daydreams and misunderstandings more thrilling than understanding could ever be" (p. 67). This evaluation is correct, for as the three women talk to each other, each person's understandings of what she hears is slanted by what she expects to hear. For example, Denver, believing Beloved to be a ghost, asks the girl what the "other world" was like: " 'What's it like over there, where you were before? . . . Were you cold?' " Beloved, of course, thinks Denver is asking her about Africa and the slave ship, and so she replies, " 'Hot. Nothing to breathe down there and no room to move in' " (p. 75). Denver then inquires whether Beloved saw her dead grandmother, Baby Suggs, or Jesus on the other side: " 'You see Jesus? Baby Suggs?' " and Beloved, remembering the death-laden ship, replies that there were many people there, some dead, but she did not know their names. Sethe has a similar conversation with Beloved and begins "Tell me the truth. Didn't you come from the other side?" and Beloved replies "Yes. I was on the other side" (p. 215). Of course, like Denver, Sethe is referring to a life after death world, while Beloved again means the other side of the ocean, Africa.

Encased in a deep and destructive need for what each thinks the other to be, Sethe and Beloved seclude themselves in Sethe's house, Number 124, and the home becomes like a prison cell for the two disturbed women. They separate themselves completely from the rest of humanity, even Denver, and they begin to consume each other's lives: Beloved continually berates Sethe for having deserted her. Sethe devotes every breath to justifying her past actions to Beloved. Their home life deteriorates to the point that the narrator says "if the whitepeople . . . had allowed Negroes into their lunatic asylum they could have found candidates in 124" (p. 250).

Sethe's and Beloved's obsession with the past clearly affects their perception of what happens when the singing women and Edward Bodwin approach Sethe's house. Ella and the other women are there, singing and praying, hoping to rid Sethe of the ghost they think is plaguing her. Edward Bodwin is the white man who helped Sethe when she was jailed for murdering her baby; now he has come to give Denver a ride to her new job. However, when Sethe comes out of her house and views the scene, her mind reverts to the time when another white man, her slave owner, had come into the yard.

On that fateful day Sethe had killed her child, and she had first sensed danger when she glimpsed her slave master's head gear. When she saw the hated "hat, she heard wings. Little hummingbirds stuck their needle beaks right through her headcloth into her hair and beat their wings. And if she thought anything, it was No. No. Nono. Nonono. Simple. She just flew" (p. 163). Years later, as Sethe stands holding Beloved's hand, she sees Bodwin approach, and her unsettled mind replays her thoughts from long ago. She recognizes "his . . . hat wide-brimmed enough to hide his face but not his purpose. . . . She hears wings. Little hummingbirds stick needle beaks right through her headcloth into her hair and beat their wings. And if she thinks anything, it is no. No no. Nonono. She flies" (p. 262). Apparently deciding that this time she will attack the white intruder and not her own child, Sethe rushes toward Bodwin with an ice pick. Ella strikes Sethe, and then the other women apparently fall on the distraught mother, pinning her to the ground.

As this commotion occurs, Beloved also has a sense of *déjà vu*. First, the girl stands on the porch holding Sethe's hand. Then Sethe drops the hand, runs toward the white man and group of black women, and Beloved thinks her mother has deserted her again. Remembering that her African mother's suicide came after the hill of dead black people were pushed from the slave ship, Beloved sees the horrible scene being recreated:

> But now her hand is empty. . . . Now she is running into the faces of the people out there, joining them and leaving Beloved behind. Alone. Again . . . [she is running away]. Away from her to the pile of people out there. They make a hill. A hill of black people, falling. And above them all, . . . the man without skin, looking. (p. 262)

Beloved connects this "hill" of falling people with the pile of dead blacks who were pushed from the ship, and, terrified, the girl apparently runs away.

In his introduction to *The House of the Seven Gables*, Nathaniel Hawthorne notes that romances, one of the literary traditions to which *Beloved* is heir, are obliged to reveal the "truth of the human heart."[15] And, in *Beloved*, Morrison does just that. An important facet of this truth is that emotional ghosts of hurt, love, guilt, and remembrance haunt those whose links to family members have been shattered; throughout the novel, Morrison shows that family ties can be severed only at the cost of distorting people's lives. In *Beloved*, Morrison also shows that past griefs, hurts ranging from the atrocities of slavery to less hideous pains, must be remembered, but they should not control life. At the end of the novel, Paul D tells Sethe " 'me and you, we got more yesterday than anybody. We need some kind of tomorrow' " (p. 273). And, throughout *Beloved*, Morrison's theme is that remembering yesterdays, while not being consumed by them, gives people the tomorrows with which to make real lives.

Notes

1. Judith Thurman, "A House Divided," *The New Yorker* (November 2, 1987), p. 178.

2. Thomas R. Edwards, "Ghost Story," *The New York Review of Books* (November 5, 1987), p. 18.

3. Marcia Ann Gillespie, "Out of Slavery's Inferno," *Ms.,* 16, No. 5 (1987), 68.

4. Stanley Crouch, "Aunt Medea," *The New Republic* (October 19, 1987), p. 42.

5. Carol Rumens, "Shades of the Prison-House," *The Times Literary Supplement* (October 16–22, 1987), p. 1135.

6. A few other reviewers take the more moderate position of expressing puzzlement about Beloved rather than claiming that she is either ghost or human. For example, in her *New York Times* review of the novel, Margaret Atwood concludes, "The reader is kept guessing; there's a lot more to Beloved than any one character can see, and she manages to be many things to several people." See "Haunted by Their Nightmares," *The New York Times Book Review* (September 13, 1987), p. 50. Similarly, in a *Newsweek* piece, Walter Clemons writes that "Beloved . . . has an anterior life deeper than the ghostly role she fulfills in the . . . household she visits." See "A Gravestone of Memories," *Newsweek* (September 28, 1987), p. 75. And, Paul

Gray in a *Time* review says that "the flesh-and-blood presence of Beloved roils the novel's intense, realistic surface. This young woman may not actually be Sethe's reincarnated daughter, but no other explanation of her identity is provided." See "Something Terrible Happened," *Time* (September 21, 1987), p. 75.

7.   Walter Clemons notes that Morrison took the germ of Sethe's story from a newspaper account of an 1855 event: "In 1855 a runaway slave from Kentucky named Margaret Garner was tracked by her owner to Cincinnati, where she had taken refuge with her freed mother-in-law. Cornered, she tried to kill her four children. Afterward, she was quite serene about what she had done." See "A Gravestone of Memories," *Newsweek* (September 28, 1987), p. 74.

8.   Sethe's own need for a parent is expressed in a pained suspicion that her mother had been hanged for attempting to run away, an action that would have separated the woman not only from the horrors of slavery but also from her own daughter. Speaking to Beloved in a stream-of-conscious remembering, Sethe explains, "My plan was to take us all to the other side where my own ma'am is. They stopped me from getting us there, but they didn't stop you from getting here. . . . You came right on back like a good girl, like a daughter which is what I wanted to be and would have been if my ma'am had been able to get out of the rice long enough before they hanged her and let me be one. . . . I wonder what they was doing when she was caught. Running, you think? No. Not that. Because she was my ma'am and nobody's ma'am would run off and leave her daughter, would she? Would she, now?" (p. 203). Toni Morrison, *Beloved* (New York: Knopf, 1987), p. 203. All further references to *Beloved* appear in the text.

9.   In an interview with Walter Clemons, Morrison brought to his attention *Beloved*'s dedication, "Sixty Million and more," and explained that "the figure is the best educated guess at the number of black Africans who never even made it into slavery—those who died either as captives in Africa or on slave ships." Morrison notes, too, that "one account describes the Congo as so clogged with bodies that the boat couldn't pass. . . . They packed 800 into a ship if they'd promised to deliver 400. They assumed that half would die. And half did." And, the author wryly adds, "A few people in my novel remember it. . . . Baby Suggs came here out of one of those ships. But mostly it's not remembered at all." See "A Gravestone of Memories," *Newsweek* (September 28, 1987), p. 75. Of course, Beloved is the most important person in the novel who remembers the slave ships' horrors. However, Morrison does not reveal that fact here; she merely hints at it.

10.   Although in 1807 Congress banned importations of slaves into the United States after January 1, 1808, the decree did not stop captured Africans from entering the country. In his classic work *The Suppression of the African Slave-Trade to the United States of America: 1638–1870* (New York: Russell and Russell, 1965), W. E. B. Du Bois notes that violations of the slave trade ban were especially prevalent in the deep South and during the middle of the nineteenth century. In fact, Du Bois says, "the slave trade laws, in spite of the efforts of the government, . . . were grossly violated, if not nearly nullified, in the latter part of the decade 1850–1860" (p. 183). Du Bois notes, too, that during this period, American ships illegally but routinely carried African slaves not only to the United States but also to South American countries, especially Brazil (p. 186). The first page of *Beloved* is set in 1873. Thus, the mysterious young woman, Beloved, could have entered the United States on one of the many American slave ships which sailed illegally in the late 1850s. Another possibility is that the girl was brought to the United States after the rest of the ship's cargo was delivered to another country, such as Brazil. The lines "the others are taken I am not taken" (p. 212) could suggest that after the other slaves were unloaded in South America, Beloved was forced to accompany one of the ship's officers to the United States.

11.   In *The Golden Bough,* James G. Frazier notes that several American Indian groups believed that the dead souls of their relatives returned to earth in the form of water turtles. See *The Golden Bough: A Study in Magic and Religion* (New York: Macmillan, 1940), pp. 502–05. This concept fits with Morrison's use of the turtles in the scene in which Beloved decides that her lost loved ones are beneath the creek's surface.

12.   I am indebted to William J. House for discussing psychological theories of human perception and memory with me.

13.   The narrator says that all of Sethe's neighbors are eager to see the carnival, a show that advertises performances by people who have two heads, are twenty feet tall, or weigh a ton, and "the fact that none of it was true did not extinguish their appetite a bit" (p. 48). That Sethe and Denver attend this carnival immediately before meeting Beloved foreshadows their willingness, in fact their need, to believe that the mysterious girl is something other than an ordinary human. Neither the carnival world nor Beloved's status as a child returned from the dead is based on truth, but both provide much desired escapes from the pain of everyday reality.

14.   Margaret Atwood, "Haunted by Their Nightmares," *The New York Times Book Review* (September 13, 1987), p. 50.

15.   Nathaniel Hawthorne, "Preface," *The House of the Seven Gables* (Boston: Houghton Mifflin, 1964), p. 3. Also, Hawthorne's "Custom House" introduction to the *The Scarlet Letter* contains an intriguing use of the word "Beloved." Explaining the atmosphere necessary for the writing of his romances, Hawthorne describes a moonlit night and notes that "where the Actual and the Imaginary . . . meet . . . Ghosts might enter . . . without affrighting us. It would be too much in keeping with the scene to excite surprise, were we to look about us and discover a form, beloved, but gone hence, now sitting quietly in . . . this magic moonshine. . . ." See "The Custom-House," *The Scarlet Letter* (New York: W. W. Norton, 1962), p. 31.

Beloved: "Woman, Thy Name Is Demon"

Trudier Harris

If we think of Toni Morrison's work on a continuum from *Sula* (1974), where she begins the transformation of woman from human being to something other than human and where she experiments with sentience beyond death, through *Tar Baby* (1981), with its talking trees and butterflies, then *Beloved* (New York: Knopf, 1987), with its emphasis on the temporal transcendence of the grave, is a natural extension of those ideas. The ancient tree mothers who would claim Jadine as their sister by drowning her in tar if necessary are not so far removed from the single-mindedness of Beloved, who would kill Sethe as quickly as she would claim her as mother. In exploring the novel's basis in folk traditions, some prevailing ideas about the female body, especially those grounded in myth and fear, are especially illuminating.

Stereotypical conceptions of the female body as "Other" have pervaded oral and written literature. In contemporary times, athletes are warned against intimacy with women before important competitions, some husbands believe their wives poison food if they are allowed to cook while menstruating, and yet others believe their penises could literally be engulfed by women's vaginas. We could document a host of additional persistent and often destructive images of women; underlying these notions is a basic clash between the masculine (those who have power and voice) and the feminine (those who are acquiescent and silent but potentially destructive), which is also worked out in Morrison's novel. These folk and popular stereotypes about the female body have often been bolstered by "scientific" research.

For example, in 1968 psychiatrist Wolfgang Lederer published a volume called *The Fear of Women.*[1] It is a storehouse of information on the control of female images throughout the ages, on how the female body was used to account for a plethora of problems in the world. As early as medieval times, woman stood as Frau Welt ("Mrs. World"), a deceptively beautiful damsel from the frontal view, who, upon being viewed from the rear, showed a disgusting, maggot-filled eruption crawling with snakes, frogs, and other vile

Reprinted from *Fiction and Folklore: The Novels of Toni Morrison* by Trudier Harris (Knoxville: University of Tennessee Press, 1991), 151–64. © 1991 by Trudier Harris. Reprinted by permission of the author.

creatures with whom she shared inclinations to make man's righteous path in the world difficult if not impossible. The ability to engulf and destroy, as well as to poison the air, were commonplace notions about women. Lederer documents those practices in certain cultures where menstruating women were encouraged to walk over newly plowed and planted fields in order to poison the insects and ensure the growth of the crops.

The blood that flowed every month concentrated the distinguishing differences between men and women that Lederer documents so carefully. And not only was woman the bleeder, but she was also insatiable in her desire for blood. Kali, the Indian goddess, is the epitome of the bloodthirsty female on the rampage against human, especially *man*-kind. Tales about her illustrate the recurring ambivalence of the traditions. On the one hand, woman is the mother/nurturer; on the other, she is the goddess/destroyer.

As recently as 1986, a song played repeatedly on black radio stations was the Isley Brothers' "Insatiable Woman." Its upbeat tempo, coupled with the soothing voice of the male singing the lyrics, quickly lulled one into forgetfulness against its evil intent. The female body, the singer complained, could never be satisfied; no matter what he gave—probably sperm donations—she wanted more. Obviously he could not keep delivering the donations at the rate at which she could receive them, so he could only verbally affirm: "Baby, I'm yours," and perhaps hope that she would let him be. The song and the verbal tradition it perpetuates of the engulfing, never-satisfied woman recalls the tale of the preacher and the pretty young woman. Preacher tales, a special subcategory of African-American folk narrative, frequently debunk the authority and prestige of ministers. Preachers are invariably painted as greedy; they especially love fried chicken, alcohol, and money. They are also impious and sexually unrestrained. As the story goes, a preacher who thought he would take advantage of her parents' absence and seduce a young woman gets the tables slightly turned on him. He sends her upstairs to the bedroom and maintains that he will be up shortly to "scare" her, his euphemism for sexual intercourse. He discovers, however, that her receptivity is longer than his stamina. After three trips upstairs and increasingly weaker, near crawling returns, when she requests that he come upstairs and "scare" her yet another time, he responds: "Well, BOO, goddamn it!"[2]

The female body, as it has been written in the oral tradition and in sexist literature, is in part a source of fear, both an attraction and a repulsion, something that can please, but something that can destroy. The tricksters of tradition find one of their chores the task of bravely entering the vagina to break those teeth that tradition has long identified with it. Such actions are considered heroic—and at times helpful even to the woman herself, for the poor dear never realizes what difficulty she is in until some man tells her and proceeds to rescue her. And in *his* ending to the tale, she usually appreciates the rescue and indeed becomes more decorous in her sexual habits. Witchlike, Other, Strange, Fearful—that is how the female body has been characterized.

In many instances the attributes center upon the demonic, as indeed many of those traditions I've described would encompass. Women could be witches or healers—depending upon point of view—only because they were in some way in league with the devil. Or indeed, just the nature of being female was considered evil—without the specific connotations of satanic contact.

The nature of evil—the demonic, the satanic—those are the features of the female body as written by Toni Morrison in *Beloved*. We can describe the title character as a witch, a ghost, a devil, or a succubus; in her manipulation of those around her, she exerts a power not of this world. In her absence of the tempering emotions that we usually identify with humankind, such as mercy, she is inhumanly vengeful in setting out to repay the one upon whom she places the blame for her too-early demise. We should note that this is not the first time that Morrison has called woman Demon.

In *Sula*, she begins the transformation of woman from human being to something other than human. The people in the Bottom make Sula into a witch whom they believe to be in league with the forces of evil if not with the devil himself. They believe that she makes Teapot fall off her steps, that she causes Mr. Finley's death when he chokes on a chicken bone, and that she is a witch who can make herself appear much younger than she is. Her suprahuman qualities lead them to ostracize her to the point of circumventing the rituals that usually apply to death and funerals in black communities. Sula's demise, however, points to another source for comparison with Beloved. Sula's sentience beyond death, presented briefly in the book, is enough to signal that Morrison has drawn no final lines between the planes of life and death. Indeed, Morrison has asserted that the call of one of the stories that inspired *Beloved* worked on her so strongly that it may have surfaced unwittingly in her earlier novels: ". . . I had been rescuing [the dead girl] from the grave of time and inattention. Her fingernails maybe in the first book; face and legs, perhaps, the second time. Little by little bringing her back into living life."[3]

Following the African belief that the demise of the body is not the end of being, which David Bradley develops so vividly in *The Chaneysville Incident* (1981), Morrison hints with Sula what becomes her major preoccupation in *Beloved*. During her life, Sula has given some insight into the actions of those who are set apart or deemed demonic. They owe allegiance only to themselves; Sula is interested only in making herself, Beloved is interested only in claiming and punishing her mother. Their desires are foremost; the wishes of others are inconsiderable. Sula sleeps with her best friend's husband without compunction; Beloved sleeps with her mother's lover. Though one is alive and the other returned from the dead, at several points the actions of the two characters are strikingly similar in motivation and execution.

The world view in *Sula* prepares us for the seeming topsy-turviness of *Tar Baby*, with its racing blind horsemen and mythic life forms, for the other-worldliness represented by Pilate's lack of a navel in *Song of Solomon*, and for the emphasis on the temporal transcendence of the grave in *Beloved*. Remember, too, that Eva talks to Plum after his death (he comes back to tell her things) and that Valerian sees Michael's ghost in the dining room on the night that Son intrudes into the island world. Morrison has well prepared her readers, therefore, for complete suspension of disbelief in the human and natural worlds. The female body reduced to desire makes Sula kindred in spirit and objective to Beloved. Consider, too, that Ajax, Sula's lover, leaves her when he begins to fear her body as woman, when he judges that she wants to trap him into marriage, or at least domesticity.

Woman's body is a threat to men in *Beloved* as well; that is the vantage point from which we see what happens in the novel. Paul D's arrival at Sethe's house brings with it the ancient fear of women. When he enters the house haunted by Beloved's ghost, it becomes the enveloping enclosure of the vagina; the vagina dentata myth operates as Paul D *feels* the physical threat of the house. The red light of the baby's spirit drains him, makes him feel overwhelming grief, feminizes him. Sethe and Denver live in the presence of the spirit; they may be annoyed by the spirit of the "crawling-already?" baby, but they have little to fear from it as females. Indeed, there is evidence that Beloved may be nurturing them into acceptance of her later physical, human manifestation. They comment at one point that "the baby got plans" (37).

For Paul D, however, the house is immediately his enemy, a veritable threat. He perceives that it bodes no good for him, and he senses—more than he knows—that the contest is between male and female spirits. Walking through the "pulsing red light," "a wave of grief soaked him so thoroughly he wanted to cry. It seemed a long way to the normal light surrounding the table, but he made it—dry-eyed and lucky" (9). To cry is to be broken, diminished as a man. Holding himself together against such a feminine breakdown, Paul D already views the house as a threat to his masculinity. He therefore enters it like the teeth-destroying tricksters of tradition entered the vagina, in the heroic vein of conquering masculine will over female desire. The competition, as it develops, then, seems initially unfair—a grown man against a baby. The supernatural element of the baby's spirit neutralizes the inequality somewhat, but the spirit of maleness in this initial battle seems stronger even than Beloved's supernaturalism. In his confrontation with the house, Paul D *wills* Beloved's spirit away. His vocal masculine will is stronger than her silent, though sometimes noisy, desire. The power of his voice to command behavior, even that of spirits, is ultimately stronger than the spirit's desire to resist.

Or at least that is one possible reading of the confrontation. Another would be to explore it from the perspective of Beloved's demonic nature. In this seeming rite of exorcism, it is not Beloved who is removed, but Paul D who is lulled into a false sense of victory. The demonic Beloved voluntarily leaves the scene in order to prepare for a greater onslaught of female energy. In seemingly forcing Beloved to leave, Paul D, like the heroes of tradition, gives to Sethe and Denver the peace that they have been unable or unwilling to give to themselves. Presumably he has made the society better. The house is quiet, he and Sethe can pretend to be lovers, and the women can contemplate such leisure activities as going to a circus.

By blending the temporal and the eternal planes of existence, however, Morrison gives Beloved the upper hand for most of the novel. As the shapeshifter who takes on flesh-and-blood human characteristics, Beloved introduces a logic and a world view into the novel that defy usual responses to such phenomena. Certainly in the black folk tradition, a ghost might occasionally appear among the living—to indicate that all is well, to teach a lesson, or to guide the living to some good fortune, including buried treasure. There are few tales, however, of revenants that actually take up residence with living relatives. One such tale, "Daid Aaron," which is from the Gullah people, centers upon the theme of revenge. Aaron refuses to go to the dwelling of the dead because his wife is already showing signs of her intention to have other suitors. But then, that's a male/female conflict as well. The widow finally gets rid of Aaron when he requests that her fiddler suitor provide dance music. Aaron dances gleefully and madly, faster and faster, until he comes apart, literally bone by bone.[4] Whether she knew of such tales or not, Morrison has asserted that she and her family members "were intimate with the supernatural" and that her parents "told thrillingly terrifying ghost stories."[5]

Beloved has a brief experience that brings to mind the possibility of disintegration comparable to Aaron's. She pulls a tooth, then speculates:

> Next would be her arm, her hand, a toe. Pieces of her would drop maybe one at a time, maybe all at once. Or on one of those mornings before Denver woke and after Sethe left she would fly apart. It is difficult keeping her head on her neck, her legs attached to her hips when she is by herself. Among the things she could not remember was when she first knew that she could wake up any day and find herself in pieces. She had two dreams: exploding, and being swallowed. When her tooth came out—an odd fragment, last in the row—she thought it was starting. (133)

But Beloved does not decay. Like a vampire feeding vicariously, she becomes plump in direct proportion to Sethe's increasing gauntness. Vengeance is not the Lord's; it is Beloved's. Her very body becomes a manifestation of her desire for vengeance and of Sethe's guilt. She repays Sethe for her death, but the punishment is not quick or neat. The attempt to choke Sethe to death in Baby Suggs's clearing and the lingering pain of that encounter is but the beginning of Beloved's taking over the women's lives. Before she can accomplish that, however, she must extricate the most formidable opposition, Paul D. In another demonic parallel in the male/female clash, she becomes the traditional succubus, the female spirit who drains the male's life force even as she drains him of his sperm. Beloved makes herself irresistible to Paul D, gradually forcing him, through each sexual encounter, to retreat farther and farther from the territory she has claimed as her own. Her "shining" or sexual latching on to him causes him initially to sleep in a rocking chair in the kitchen, then in Baby Suggs's keeping room behind the kitchen, then in the store-room, and finally in the "cold house" outside the main house. *"She moved him,"* and Paul D "didn't know how to stop it because it looked like he was moving himself" (114—emphasis added). Their three weeks of sexual encounters in the cold house result in a guilty Paul D trying to confront Sethe with the news only to find that he cannot; Beloved's control over him, together with his discovery of Sethe's killing of her baby, force him off the premises alto-gether. After all, what option does he have? To stay is to contemplate the vio-lations he has committed—sleeping with a woman who has been much abused and abusing her further by sleeping with her daughter/ghost. To go or to stay is to contemplate a possible further evil—having slept with the devil—either in the form of the mother or the daughter.

Paul D's departure makes clear that Beloved has not only used her body to drain him physically, but spiritually as well. He becomes a tramp of sorts, sleeping where he can, drinking excessively, literally a shadow of his former self. From the man who was strong enough to exorcise a spirit, Paul D reverts to his wandering, unsure of his residence from day to day and unclear about what kind of future, if any, he has. The picture of him sitting on the church steps, liquor bottle in hand, stripped of the very maleness that enables him to caress and love the wounded Sethe, is one that shows Beloved's power. There is no need for her to kill Paul D; she simply drains him sufficiently to make him one of the living dead, in a limbo-like state from which he cannot extri-cate himself as long as Beloved reigns at 124 Bluestone Road. For this male warrior, therefore, the demonic female has won over him in the very realm he has used to define himself; his sexual fear of woman is justified.

But the parasitic Beloved is not content to destroy maleness; she also attacks femaleness. Or, I should say it is perhaps less femaleness that she attacks in Sethe than motherhood, another symbol of authority almost mascu-line in its absoluteness. We could say, then, that as far as Beloved is concerned, Paul D and Sethe are in some ways shaped from the same mold—those who have the power to command, those who have power over life and death. In her resolve to escape from slavery, Sethe, like Jean Toomer's Carma, is "strong as any man."[6] In the resolve that keeps her going during the ordeal of Denver's birth she is again, stereotypically, strong as any man. In her determination to kill her children to keep them from being remanded to slavery, she is again as strong as any man. Beloved's anger with Sethe for having killed her may be centered in mother love, but it is also centered in the patriarchal authority that Sethe assumed unto herself in killing Beloved, in becoming the destructive, authoritative mother/goddess. Beloved's war against Sethe, then, can be read from one perspective as a further attack against masculine privilege, against the power over life and death that is stereotypically identified with males or with those masculine mother/goddesses.

Think, too, about how Sethe is viewed in the community. Comparable to Sula, she is too proud, too self-sufficient, too independent, generally too much on her own for the neighbors. Her rugged individualism is more characteristic of males than females of the time. The more feminine thing would be for her to need help from the community. She neither seeks nor accepts any before Beloved arrives; later, she is too transformed to care.

Perhaps we are sufficiently encouraged, then, to see Sethe as a masculine presence that the female demon seeks to exorcise. Beloved symbolically begins feeding upon Sethe as the succubus feeds upon males; she takes food from her mouth, eats whatever there is to eat, and inspires Sethe to leave her job, thereby relinquishing her ability to feed herself, and causing her to shrink, to become diminished in stature as well as in self-possession. By denying to Sethe the power to support herself, Beloved initially attacks Sethe's spirit of independence. She sends her into a stupor comparable to that of Paul D. But Beloved is not content to stupefy Sethe; she is after her life force. She drains her by slowly starving her and, as the neighbors believe, beating her (255). The apparently pregnant Beloved blossoms, glows, and continues to get plump as the shrinking Sethe literally becomes a skeleton of her former self. Like Paul D, Sethe loses willpower, thereby losing the ability to control her own body or her own destiny. She and Paul D are assuredly slaves to Beloved's desire as Sethe and the Pauls were literally slaves earlier. Beloved becomes the arbiter of life and death, so playfully so that Sethe acquiesces in her own decline.

It is in part the playfulness of the situation that tones down its potentially destructive side. With Beloved, Sethe has the opportunity to live out two fantasies. First of all, she can be mother to the daughter she has never known. Giving all her time and attention to Beloved makes it easy for the demon to execute her desire. On the other hand, by giving all to Beloved, Sethe becomes childlike, pleading for acceptance by a harsh "parent" who is more intent upon cruel punishment than understanding forgiveness. By relinquishing her will to survive, Sethe again becomes Beloved's willing victim.

Their relationship raises questions about Morrison's intentions in the novel. Is guilt the central theme, thereby making it understandable how Sethe acquiesces in her own slow destruction? Does the guilt deserve the punishment of the demonic? Is infanticide so huge a crime that only otherworldly punishment is appropriate for it? If, on the other hand, we understand, accept, and perhaps even approve of the dynamic that allowed a slave mother to kill rather than have her children remanded to slavery, would not the dominant theme be love? After all, Sethe has precedence in her action; her own mother killed some of her children rather than allow them to be slaves, or to recognize her own forced depravity in having given birth to them (62). If the theme is love, what warrants allowing Sethe to be so violated for her love of Beloved?

As the novel develops, it would seem that Beloved's *desires,* irrational as they are, are the acceptable force driving the story. I emphasize desire as opposed to will simply because Beloved is not to be denied in what she wants. Her desire is for a mother, and she will have that mother even if it means killing her in the process of claiming her. She desires Paul D and takes him in spite of her mother's involvement with him. As it manifests itself in the novel, desire is unbridled id, self-centered and not to be easily denied.[7] Will, on the other hand, can be altruistic; Paul D wills Beloved out of 124, it can be argued, in part to bring a measure of peace to Sethe and Denver. The destructive, irrational force is pure desire, which in turn is perhaps the most otherworldly. It is out of desire for something that spirits are able to make the journey between the two worlds. Beloved, the personification of desire, thus epitomizes the demonic.[8] Her lack of caring is spiteful retaliation for not being allowed to live; she is the unleashed force of the childish mentality at which her life ended. Twenty years in body, but eighteen months in mind, she is the objective, physical distillation of desire.

Beloved's characterization ultimately makes her "Thing," unhuman, unfeeling, uncaring except in the perpetuation of what she wants. Like Frau Welt, she cannot live up to the promise of herself; to become involved with her is to be destroyed. As Thing, Beloved has no consistently seen reflective trait; the point of view of the narrative encourages us to see her as the traditional vampire. We see her inner thoughts for only brief moments, which do not evoke undue sympathy for her. We are left to judge her objectively, to infer motive from a distance, and thereby to solidify our evaluation of her as demonic. Her actions suggest that she has ultimate power of judgment, that vengeance is indeed hers, that her brand of justice has no guiding morality to temper it with mercy.[9]

In her amorality, Beloved shares kinship with some of the tricksters of tradition—ever guided by personal desires and frequently identified as masculine. Such figures are recognizable by the power they wield, without consideration for those being affected by that power. Brer Rabbit kills the elephant simply to escape detection for a crime he has committed, or he avenges himself on the entire alligator family because of an insult by Brer Alligator. Unleashed and unrestrained, Brer Rabbit is limited only by the power of imagination that conceived the cycle of tales in which he stars. With her supernatural dimension, Beloved has no obvious limits. Nonetheless, she ultimately seems subject to a force greater than herself.

A potentially troublesome part of the novel is how Beloved is exorcised from 124. Paul D's initial driving of her spirit from the premises is merely temporary. She is finally exorcised not by individuals working in isolation but by a community of effort directed against her presence. And that community of effort comes from a group of women, women who call upon ancient and contemporary messages, murmuring incantations and singing songs, to control Beloved. Is Morrison suggesting finally that women, who may themselves be demonic—or *because* they are demonic—are the only force with sufficient power to control that evil? Is it a question of good versus evil? Are the women who send Beloved away in any way identified with the forces of good? Most of them are certainly not the image of stereotypically traditional churchgoing black women. Nor do they pursue the exorcism from altruistic motivations. Rather, like Richard Wright's District Attorney Ely Houston pursuing the murderous Cross Damon in *The Outsider* (1953), they are simultaneously attracted to and repulsed by the evil in their midst. They see in it tiny mirrors of the selves they have suppressed, and they want it extracted before it touches them too greatly or even has the potential to reclaim them. And they are offended. They "didn't mind a little communication between the two worlds, but this was an invasion" (257).

In other words, Beloved is a threat to them in the psychological sphere as effectively as Sula is a threat to the women in the Bottom in the sexual sphere. Extending the philosophy from that novel, where the community is content to recognize evil and let it run its course, the women in *Beloved* cannot afford that detachment. Letting Beloved run her course may mean the destruction of them all. They must exorcise that part of themselves, therefore, that is a threat to them. If thy right eye offend thee, pluck it out. This is not a farfetched philosophy when we consider that throughout history it is frequently women who cast sanctions most vehemently upon other women.

Exorcising the demonic part of the self so that all women are not judged to be demons—that is what the women are about in getting Beloved to leave 124. And how do they accomplish this? With a combination of pagan and religious rituals. They initially find power in numbers as they gather in a group of thirty to move toward 124. They raise their voices in singing and in religious murmurs as they march along the road. The comparative images that come to mind are straight out of *The Golden Bough.* The voices raised serve the same function as the sticks and pans villagers of pretechnological cultures might have used to drive evil spirits from their midsts. The act of singing itself serves as a chant, perhaps as the proverbial "witch doctor" of ancient times might have used to implore or command that some living/hearing evil take its leave from the environs of the innocent and the helpless.

What the pregnant Beloved sees then, as she comes to the front door of 124, is that those with whom she identifies as well as despises are organized against her. The mothers are multiplied many times over, as are the breasts of the women in Eloe, Florida, whom Jadine confronts in *Tar Baby;* against the demands of that immutable force of potential mother/goddesses, who seem to represent justice without mercy, Beloved can only retreat. The vengeance of parents punishing recalcitrant children is ultimately stronger than will or desire.

But Beloved's retreat may in reality be a departure from a battlefield where she has won, accomplished what she set out to do. Consider what happens as the white Mr. Bodwin drives up. In the near-reenactment of what happened at Beloved's death, it becomes clear that Sethe is nearly deranged. She is decidedly no longer the figure of authority and independence that she had been before Beloved's arrival. When she takes the ice pick in hand to save Beloved once again, the same set of imperatives does not apply. Slavery has ended; the man approaching is a rescuer rather than an enslaver; Sethe needs rescue *from* Beloved rather than rescuing her from someone else. Reduced to irrationality engendered by the wiping out of eighteen years of her life, Sethe is now the recalcitrant child, in need of correcting and nurturing (252). In this reading of the scene, Beloved can leave instead of being sent away because she has accomplished two things. First, she has caused Sethe to become temporarily deranged. Second, the result of that derangement is that Sethe acts without thought, instinctively, to save Beloved. What Beloved could not see as a "crawling-already?" baby, she is now able to see as an adult: that her mother's action, many years before and in its current duplicate, was indeed one of love. This reading does not mean that the demon changes her nature, but that she achieves her desire: tangible evidence that her mother loved her best of all. Ironically, to achieve that goal is simultaneously to risk eventual destruction of the individual of whom the evidence was required.[10]

Again, Beloved either leaves voluntarily or is driven out. Whatever interpretation we accept, one thing is clear: Sethe and Beloved cannot exist on the same plane. If Sethe is to live, Beloved must depart. If Beloved stays, Sethe can only die. The trip from beyond, though, is apparently a one-time thing. Once removed from 124, the undelivered, restless Beloved roams the neighboring territory, her footprints a reminder that she is there but her desire fulfilled sufficiently so that she cannot return all the way to 124. Her inability to return is attested to in the return of Here Boy, the dog, to 124 and in the return of Paul D, the masculine presence. Of the animals traditionally believed to sense ghosts and evil spirits, dogs are perhaps first on the list.[11] When Here Boy takes up residence again, that is the folkloristic signal that Beloved will not be returning. When Paul D finds the energy to pursue Sethe again, to experience the returning of sexual desire as well as general concern for another human being, that is also a signal that Beloved will not be returning. Paul D's presence means health for Sethe, the opposite of what Beloved's presence meant. With the novel ending on a sign of health, there will at least be calm at 124.

And what of Beloved? The demon comes and goes. Humans interact with it, but it ultimately transcends them, returns to another realm of existence controlled only by human imagination. Morrison lifts Beloved from a void and returns her there. Her footprints relegate her to kinship with Big Foot and other legendary if not mythical creatures. Beloved goes from imagination to humanoid to legend, basically unchanged in her category as demon, the designation of Other that makes it impossible for her to be anything but eternally alone.

Notes

1.   The volume depends upon stereotypical conceptions of women, but it is nonetheless an interesting historical recapitulation of traditional perceptions of femaleness; Lederer, *The Fear of Women*.

2. Daryl Cumber Dance, *Shuckin' and Jivin': Folklore from Contemporary Black Americans* (Bloomington: Indiana University Press, 1978), 56–57.

3. Gloria Naylor and Toni Morrison, "A Conversation," *Southern Review* 21 (July 1985): 593. While this comment could apply to the writing practice Morrison gained in her previous novels in preparation for writing the difficult tale of a mother killing her child, it could also apply to touching briefly on the unorthodox ideas that would inform the substance of *Beloved.* See pp. 583–84 of the above interview for Morrison's discussion of the two incidents that shaped the idea for *Beloved:* that of Margaret Garner, the slave woman who preferred death rather than slavery for her children, and that of an eighteen-year-old dead girl photographed in Harlem by James Van der Zee; the girl had sacrificed her own life in order to allow the jealous lover who had shot her sufficient time to escape the scene of the crime.

4. See "Daid Aaron," in *The Book of Negro Folklore*, ed. Langston Hughes and Arna Bontemps (New York: Dodd, Mead & Co. 1958), 175–78.

5. Jean Strouse, "Toni Morrison's Black Magic," *Newsweek*, 30 Mar 1981, 52–57.

6. Jean Toomer, *Cane* (New York: Boni and Liveright, 1923), 16.

7. Indeed, some of the comments that Charles Scruggs makes about desire in *Song of Solomon* could also apply to *Beloved*. See "The Nature of Desire in Toni Morrison's *Song of Solomon*," *Arizona Quarterly* 38 (Winter 1982): 311–35.

8. While Terry Otten also recognizes Beloved's demonic nature and the fact that she is "an evil thing," he asserts that she may be "a Christ figure come to save," "the 'beloved' one come to reclaim Sethe and from whom Sethe seeks forgiveness." See Otten, *The Crime of Innocence in the Fiction of Toni Morrison* (Columbia: Univ. of Missouri Press, 1989), 84, 85. In *Toni Morrison*, Wilfred D. Samuels and Clenora Hudson-Weems assert that Paul D is a Christ figure (Boston: Twayne Publishers, 1990, 134). Instead of this designation, with its attendant connotation of absolute goodness, perhaps it would be more productive to view Paul D in the ambivalent mode of some of Morrison's earlier heroes, such as Milkman and Son.

9. For a discussion of the multiple voices and characters Beloved represents in the novel, see Deborah Horvitz, "Nameless Ghosts: Possession and Dispossession in *Beloved*," *Studies in American Fiction* 17 (Autumn 1989): 157–67. On the other hand, Elizabeth B. House, in "Toni Morrison's Ghost: The Beloved Who Is Not Beloved," *Studies in American Fiction* 18 (Spring 1990): 17–26, argues that Beloved is not a ghost but merely a runaway who has suffered the blights of slavery. These in turn intersect coincidentally with Sethe's relationship to her deceased daughter.

10. Otten comments that "in attacking [Bodwin], Sethe achieves an exorcism; in saving Beloved by offering herself, she at last frees herself from the demonic presence that will not release her from the past. Once Sethe acts to save Beloved, retestifying to her love, the ghost disappears"; *The Crime of Innocence*, 94.

11. See *The Frank C. Brown Collection of North Carolina Folklore*, vol. 7, ed. Wayland D. Hand (Durham, N.C.: Duke University Press, 1961, 1964), 144, 145, 147. Dog ghosts are also painted in the lore as being some of the most benign spirits humans can encounter. See J. Mason Brewer, *Dog Ghosts and Other Texas Negro Folk Tales* (Austin: Univ. of Texas Press, 1958).

"Breaking the Back of Words": Language, Silence, and the Politics of Identity in *Beloved*

BARBARA HILL RIGNEY

The most valuable point of entry into the question of cultural (or racial) distinction, the one most fraught, is its language—its unpoliced, seditious, confrontational, manipulative, inventive, disruptive, masked and unmasking language.

—(Morrison, 1990, 210)

A consideration of language is primary in the development of theoretical paradigms as these relate to all literatures, but particularly to the African American feminine/feminist text. This is especially true in a critical approach to Toni Morrison's works, for it is only through an analysis of her language that we can reconstruct an idea of the political and artistic revolution she represents. "Confrontational," "unpoliced," hers is the language of black and feminine discourse—semiotic, maternal, informed as much by silence as by dialogue, as much by absence as by presence. Morrison seems to *conjure* her language, to invent a form of discourse that is always at once both metaphysical and metafictional.

One of the freedoms Morrison claims in her novels is to move beyond language, even while working *through* it, to incorporate significance beyond the denotation of words, to render experience and emotion, for example, as musicians do. Morrison says that she wishes to accomplish "something that has probably only been fully expressed in music. . . . Writing novels is a way to encompass this—this something" (McKay, 1). If *Beloved* is not, as Morrison writes, "a story to pass on" (274), then it is certainly one to be sung. Morrison describes "the sound of the novel, sometimes cacophonous, sometimes harmonious, [which] must be an inner ear sound or a sound just beyond hearing,

Material from *The Voices of Toni Morrison,* Barbara Hill Rigney (Columbus: Ohio State University Press, 1991). © 1991 by Ohio State University Press. Reprinted by permission.

infusing the text with a musical emphasis that words can do sometimes even better than music can" (Morrison, 1990, 228). Sethe often recounts her "rememories" in the form of songs, made-up ballads for her children, which constitute a transmission of history and of culture, but it is also her conversation, even her thoughts, which are musical. Beloved's own voice is "gravelly" with "a song that seemed to lie in it. Just outside music it lay, with a cadence not like theirs" (60). All women's songs, Morrison indicates, are "just outside music"; often also they are codes, ways to break an enforced silence; they constitute a protest. Cixous writes in "The Laugh of the Medusa," "In women's speech, and in their writing, that element which never stops resonating, which, once we've been permeated by it, profoundly and imperceptibly touched by it, retains the power of moving us—that element is the song: first music from the first voice of love which is alive in every woman" (312). And also in Morrison's terms, music and the singing of women have a power beyond words, a transcendent meaning that can provide "the right combination, the key, the code, the sound that broke the back of words . . . a wave of sound wide enough to sound deep water and knock the pods off chestnut trees" (261). All songs in Morrison's texts represent subversion, and they speak the lost language of Africa, the language of Sethe's mother "which would never come back" (62), and a heritage of freedom.

The mother-tongue is, in fact, a recurrent evocation in all of Morrison's works, whether spoken or sung, whether by women or men; it is like music, but less intelligible, far more mystical, a sound that transcends language, a primal cry that echoes from pre-history. The Word of the father and even of the biblical God is re-written by the singing women at the end of *Beloved* who know that "In the beginning there were no words. In the beginning was the sound, and they all knew what that sounded like" (259).

Karla Holloway and Stephanie Demetrakopoulos write in *New Dimensions of Spirituality* that "Black women carry the voice of the mother—they are the progenitors. . . . Women, as carriers of the *voice*, carry wisdom—mother wit" (123). Throughout Morrison's novels, women are the primary tale-tellers and the transmitters of history as well as the singing teachers; only they know the language of the occult and the occult of language and thus comprise what Morrison has called a "feminine subtext" (1990, 220). Mary Helen Washington also maintains that there is a "generational continuity" among black women in which "one's mother serves as the female precursor who passes on the authority of authorship to her daughter and provides a model for the black woman's literary presence in this society" (147).

In all her novels, Morrison implies the primacy of the maternal and the semiotic over the symbolic language of the father. Beyond the male "I" and outside of the metaphysics of binary opposition of western humanism lies what Julia Kristeva has called the "she-truth" of the semiotic; here is Morrison's mother-wit of the conjure woman, the expression of which is so central in her novels and particularly in *Beloved*. Kristeva writes in *Desire in Language:*

No language can sing unless it confronts the Phallic Mother. For all that it must not leave her untouched, outside, opposite, against the law, the absolute esoteric code. Rather it must swallow her, eat her, dissolve her, set her up like a boundary of the process where "I" with "she"—"the other," "the mother"— becomes lost. Who is capable of this? "I alone am nourished by the great mother," writes Lao Tzu. (19)

As Cixous also says of the writer of feminine discourse, "There is always within her at least a little of that good mother's milk. She writes in white ink" (1986, 312).

All of Morrison's female characters exist primarily in maternal space, living in the houses of their mothers and their grandmothers, comfortable with the female worlds and the matriarchal social structures these houses represent. Inevitably, the houses themselves exude exoticism just as do the women who live in them. The "house of many rooms" (*Sula,* 26) in which Sula lives with Eva and Hannah is as whimsically constructed, with gratuitous stairways and doorways, as the lives of its inhabitants, and it is a testament to female power and autonomy in its refutation of male logic and practicality. Similarly, Pilate's house in *Song of Solomon,* which she shares with Reba and Hagar, is defined as female space; empty of furniture, on the edge of the black community and therefore of both the black and the dominant cultures, it is characterized by the pervasive presence of sunshine and the smell of pine trees. Baby Suggs's house in *Beloved,* where Sethe comes to live with her daughters, is inhospitable to males in general; Sethe's sons flee its confines on the first page of the novel and it is not the baby ghost alone which at first prevents Paul D from entering and, finally, from being able to sleep or live at 124 Bluestone Road, for, as the first sentence of the novel makes clear, "124 was spiteful." This pattern of women living communally which Morrison depicts with such frequency is an arrangement that is not unusual given the historical and sociological realities of African American economic exigency. However, the persistence of the female triad as image in Morrison's fiction has also to do with an inquiry into the dangerous secrets of women's lives, their ways of knowing, and especially into their language and the wisdom and truth which it expresses.

But ambiguities are inherent in the image, and in Morrison's novels the maternal space, even for women, is fraught with danger as well as with desire. For the child, Denver, in *Beloved,* the womb space is at first sweet and full of secrets. Just outside of her mother's house, a ring of trees forms a narrow room, a cave of "emerald light": "In that bower, closed off from the hurt of the hurt world, Denver's imagination produced its own hunger and its own food, which she badly needed because loneliness wore her out. *Wore her out.* Veiled and protected by the live green walls, she felt ripe and clear, and salvation was as easy as a wish" (28–29). Eventually Denver leaves the female space of Sethe's house; her "salvation" lies after all in a confrontation with a larger world, but not, however, until she has learned the mother tongue, drunk the mother's milk, mixed though it literally is with blood. Such relationships are also potentially damaging for the mother as well as the daughter; Beloved's desire to re-enter the womb almost kills her mother. Although Sethe is a willing host, the community women are correct that "Sethe's dead daughter, the one whose throat she cut, had come back to fix her. Sethe was worn down, speckled, dying, spinning, changing shapes and generally bedeviled" (255). That which Beloved has sought in Sethe is the maternal space, the "loneliness that can be rocked. Arms creased, knees drawn up; holding, holding on, the motion, unlike a ship's, smooths and contains the rocker. It's an inside kind—wrapped tight like skin" (274).

In *Beloved* it is the daughter, Beloved, who is the primary aggressor, but Denver is haunted also by a memory of maternal violence: "Her eye was on her mother, for a signal that the thing that was in her was out, and she would kill again" (240). Fear of maternal aggression, for both men and women, is as justifiable in Morrison's novels as it is in the work of a number of psychoanalysts, including Nancy J. Chodorow in *Feminism and Psychoanalytic Theory:* "cemented by maternal and infantile rage, motherhood becomes linked to destruction and death" (85). However, for both Morrison and Chodorow, female children are more likely than their brothers to survive, even benefit, from the encounter. While all children, Chodorow argues in *The Reproduction of Mothering,* are originally and essentially "matrisexual" (95), girls experience the pre-Oedipal phase as less threatening than do boys: "Because of their mothering by women, girls come to experience themselves as less separate than boys, as having more permeable ego boundaries" (93). Chodorow quotes Freud's statement in "Female Sexuality": "One insight into this early pre-Oedipal phase in girls comes to us as a surprise, like the discovery in another field of the Minoan-Mycenaean civilization behind the civilization of Greece" (92).

Morrison, too, renders this phase poetically, and in her novels it is not merely a phase but a condition of living, there being no interruption by the father in most instances, no violation of the feminine world of mothers and daughters by the Oedipal law. And, always in Morrison, this pre-Oedipal state encompasses space that is forbidden by the fathers; it is erotic, beyond masculine "law" and order, a wild zone. Sethe's house becomes a veritable witch's nest, a semiotic jungle in which language itself defies convention and the laws of logic; voices merge and identities are indistinguishable:

> I am Beloved and she is mine. . . . I am not separate from her   there is no place
> where I stop   her face is my own and I want to be there in the place where her
> face is and to be looking at it too   a hot thing. . . . she is the laugh   I am the
> laughter   I see her face which is mine. . . . she knows I want to join   she chews
> and swallows me   I am gone   now I am her face   my own face has left me
> I see me swim away   a hot thing   I see the bottoms of my feet   I am alone
> I want to be the two of us   I want the join. . . . a hot thing   now we can join
> a hot thing . . . (210–13)

It is not surprising that Stamp Paid cannot enter the house, for what he hears from outside is "a conflagration of hasty voices—loud, urgent, all speaking at once so he could not make out what they were talking about or to whom. The speech wasn't nonsensical, exactly, nor was it tongues. But something was wrong with the order of the words and he couldn't describe or cipher it to save his life" (172). What Stamp Paid hears and what excludes him is the mother tongue, the feminine language, which defies and almost precludes male understanding. Later Stamp Paid decides that what he has heard is the "mumbling of the black and angry dead," a natural response to white people, who, he says, believe that

> under every dark skin was a jungle. Swift unnavigable waters, swinging screaming baboons, sleeping snakes, red gums ready for their sweet white blood. In a way, he thought, they were right. . . . But it wasn't the jungle blacks brought with them to this place from the other (livable) place. It was the jungle whitefolks planted in them. And it grew. It spread. (198)

Stamp Paid is only partly right; it is not merely a black jungle he intuits, but a black *woman's* jungle, a linguistic wilderness, the mumbo-jumbo of the conjure world, "the thoughts of the women of 124, unspeakable thoughts, unspoken" (199). When, finally, Denver understands that she must extricate herself from this pre-Oedipal stew or starve to death, it is like stepping "off the edge of the world" (239).

All of Morrison's works are about silence as well as about language, whether that silence is metaphysical or physically enforced by circumstance. All African Americans, like a great many immigrants to America, write and speak in a language they do not own as theirs. Historically, the dominant culture has enforced black silence through illiteracy, through the metaphoric and the actual insertion of the bit in the mouth which inevitably results in "the wildness that shot up into the eye the moment the lips were yanked back" (71). The point of Morrison's novels, in fact, is to give a voice to the voiceless, to speak the unspeakable on the part of the speechless, to tell just "how offended the tongue is, held down by iron" (71).

Like silence, absence is metaphysical in Morrison's texts. Morrison explains in "Unspeakable Things Unspoken" that "invisible things are not necessarily 'not-there'; that a void may be empty, but is not a vacuum. In addition, certain absences are so stressed, so ornate, so planned, they call attention to themselves; arrest us with intentionality and purpose . . ." (210). Clearly, the significant silences and the stunning absences throughout Morrison's texts become profoundly political as well as stylistically crucial. Morrison describes her own work as containing "holes and spaces so the reader can come into it" (Tate, 125); such intent is testament to her rejection of theories which privilege the author over the reader. Morrison disdains such hierarchies in which the reader as participant in the text is ignored:

"My writing expects, demands participatory reading, and I think that is what literature is supposed to do. It's not just about telling the story; it's about involving the reader. . . . we (you, the reader, and I, the author) come together to make this book, to feel this experience" (Tate, 125).

Morrison indicates in each of her novels that images of the zero, the absence, the silence that is both chosen and enforced, are ideologically and politically revelatory. The history of slavery itself, Morrison writes in *Beloved,* is "not a story to pass on," but rather is something that is "unspeakable," unconscionable, unbearable. Among the heinous crimes of slavery was its silencing of its victims; how perversely ironic it is that "schoolteacher" does not come to Sweet Home to teach literacy, but to take notes, to do scholarship on the measurement of black craniums. Ironic, too, is the fact that schoolteacher's notes are taken in ink which Sethe, quite possibly functionally illiterate, has manufactured. Paul D cannot read the newspaper account of Sethe's crime, and, even in freedom, Denver must lurk outside and beneath the window of the reading teacher's house.

Morrison's characters are inevitably politically muted in spite of the lyrical language of the mother which Morrison always provides for them. They themselves do not articulate or perhaps realize the political ramifications of certain of their actions, but Morrison repeatedly translates the body itself into political "speech." Sethe trades ten minutes of sex for a single inscription, "the one word that mattered," on her daughter's tombstone, thus almost literally translating her body into the written word. Sethe's motivation for the murder of her child is, obviously, a desperate attempt to protect that child from what she considers a fate far worse than death, but Morrison also renders this act as the ultimate statement, the most significant transcendence of the word, an act of the body that is, like slavery itself, truly "unspeakable."

Silence exists also in the text of *Beloved* itself, as, according to Wilfred D. Samuels and Clenora Hudson-Weems, was the case in the original slave narratives, characterized by "not what history has recorded . . . but what it has omitted" (96). Samuels and Hudson-Weems quote Morrison as saying of slave narratives: "somebody forgot to tell somebody something. . . . My job becomes how to rip that veil" (97). But Morrison's own "veils," indicative of the kind of pain the writing of *Beloved* entailed, remain implicit in the text which itself is a revision, an inversion, and, finally, a subversion of traditional value systems which privilege presence over absence and speech over silence. The central paradox, however, is that the silence of women echoes with reverberation, speaks louder than words: "What a roaring," writes Morrison (181).

In all of Morrison's fictions what is left unsaid is equally as important as what is stated and specified, what is felt is as significant as what is experienced, what is dreamed is as valid as what transpires in the world of "fact." And none of these conditions of being is rendered as opposites; there are no polarities between logic and mysticism, between real and fantastic. Rather, experience for Morrison's characters is the acceptance of a continuum, a recognition that the mind is not separate from the body nor the real separate from that which the imagination can conceive. She writes from the maternal space, which is consciousness but also the unconscious, the dream world; but those dreams have substance, teeth, and they are part of a world conception in which terms like "fact" seem superfluous. "Magic realism" is not, for Morrison, an oxymoron. In an interview with Grace Epstein, Morrison talks about the significance of dreams, their practical value for winning at the numbers game when she was a child in Lorain, Ohio, and about how their validity was unquestioned, particularly by her mother, who "thought" rather than "dreamed" her sleeping experiences:

> It was like the second life she was living, so that dreamscape, then, becomes accessible, a separate part, and it's functional in some respects. As a child the problem is trying to establish what is real and what is not real. Since my dreams were real in the sense they were about *reality* some dream life could spill over into the regular life; that's where the enchantment came from. (5)

Narrative itself is dream-like in Morrison's fiction: diffused, fluid, always erotic.

Beloved also represents a denial of literary conventions about plot development and traditional boundaries. The personal history of Sethe and her daughters is revealed ever so gradually, fragmented into symbols, and, finally, becomes one with the history of all African Americans. Everyone tells or sings the story of slavery and the escape into a freedom that is also, paradoxically, still a form of slavery. And, each tale, each aspect of the monomyth, is re-told, elaborated upon, rendered in circles and silences by every character in the novel. Sethe's recounting of her story to Paul D is accompanied by a physical act of making circles and is emblematic of all tale-telling in the novel: "At first he thought it was her spinning. Circling him the way she was circling the subject. Round and round, never changing direction, which might have helped his head. . . . listening to her was like having a child whisper into your ear so close you could feel its lips form the words you couldn't make out because they were too close" (161). But the largest circle and the deepest secrets are those told us by that same enigmatic, pervasive omniscience which is Morrison herself.

Just as she challenges the dominant cultural view of language and signification, so Morrison also subverts traditional western notions of identity and wholeness. Patricia Waugh, in *Feminine Fictions: Revising the Postmodern*, is not alone in her observation that the death of the self is characteristic of all postmodern fictions, which thus act to undermine traditional philosophies by contradicting "the dualistic, objective posturing of western rationality" (22). More central to the present concern is Waugh's argument that "for those marginalized by the dominant culture, a sense of identity as constructed through impersonal and social relations of power (rather than a sense of identity as the reflection of an inner 'essence') has been a major aspect of their self-concept long before post-structuralists and postmodernists began to assemble their cultural manifestos" (3). If this is true particularly for women, as Waugh maintains, how much more radical might be the deconstruction of the self as a concept in fiction by those doubly marginalized by race as well as gender?

Morrison's own "self" does not appear in her fiction; she does not write autobiography, as she has emphasized in a number of interviews, nor do her characters speak so much as individuals as members of a group, a race. Even the physical marks carried by so many of Morrison's characters, like the crossed circle mandala branded beneath the breast of Sethe's mother, or even the choke-cherry tree scars on Sethe's own back, represent membership rather than separation or individuality. If these marks distinguish at all, they distinguish a racial identity, for most are either chosen or inflicted by the condition of blackness itself, by the institution of slavery which "marked" its victims literally and figuratively, physically and psychologically. "If something happens to me and you can't tell me by my face, you can know me by this mark," Sethe's African mother tells her. And the child Sethe answers, "Mark me, too . . . Mark the mark on me too" (61). Whether this is the mark of Cain or the blood stain of a Passover, a curse or an anointment, it denotes a sisterhood (and sometimes a brotherhood as well) of Africa, which in itself is a political statement that is both subversive and confrontational.

The verbal equivalent of such marks is the name, which, also like marks, does not necessarily designate an individual self so much as a segment of community, an identity larger than self. As Morrison has said in an interview with Thomas Le Clair:

> If you come from Africa, your name is gone. It is particularly problematic because it is not just *your* name but your family, your tribe. When you die, how can you connect with your ancestors if you have lost your name? That's a huge psychological scar. (28)

Of least importance in Morrison's novels are those names which are a part of the dominant signifying order, those denoting ownership, appropriation, those originating in slavery, those which deny group identity and African origins. In *Beloved,* Baby Suggs recalls her slave name as Jenny Whitlow; only as Mr. Garner delivers her into freedom can she turn and ask him, "why you all call me Jenny?" Her lack of a name—"Nothing. . . . I don't call myself nothing" (141)—is testament to the "desolated center where the self that was no self made its home" (140). Baby Suggs has no "self" because she has no frame of reference by which to establish one, no family, no children, no context: "Sad as it was that she did not know where her children were buried or what they looked like if alive, fact was she knew more about them than she knew about herself, having never had the map to discover what she was like" (140).

Similarly, Paul D is one of a series of Pauls, identified alphabetically by some anonymous slaveholder, while Sixo is presumably the sixth of an analogous group. Stamp Paid, born Joshua under slavery, has, however, chosen and devised his own symbolic name which represents a rejection of a tradition of white naming as well as a celebration of freedom. His name is also and more specifically a symbol of freedom from debt; because he suffered under slavery and because he "handed over his wife to his master's son" (184), he has paid in misery any obligation to humanity, he believes, although his continued activity as a conductor on the Underground Railroad would indicate otherwise. All African Americans are, in essence, "Stamp Paid," Morrison implies.

Sethe's name is one of the few chosen by a mother, and that name is a mark of blackness and of acceptance into tribe and culture. As Nan tells the "small girl Sethe," "She threw them all away but you. The one from the crew she threw away on the island. The others from more whites she also threw away. Without names, she threw them. You she gave the name of the black man" (62). Whether this name is derived from that of the Egyptian god, Seth, or from the Biblical Seth, it represents, like most of the names which Morrison designates as chosen, a sense of heritage and a context of relational identity.

And Beloved, whose birth name we never learn, takes her identity from the single word on her tombstone and from the love her mother bears her, the paradox of which is reflected in the novel's epigraph from *Romans:* "I will call them my people, which were not my people; and her beloved, which was not beloved." Finally, Beloved has no identity other than that merged with the "Sixty Million and more" of the dedication, all those who suffered the outrage of enslavement.

For Morrison, when history and the concept of reality become so brutal, so horrific and unnatural, the only "natural" element becomes the supernatural. The validity of myth and the acceptance of manifestations beyond nature inform *Beloved* from the first page to the last: "Not a house in the country ain't packed to its rafters with some dead Negro's grief" (5), says Baby Suggs, who knows that the spirit world is everywhere—in the houses, in the trees, in the rivers, manifested in hellish light or in hands that reach out to caress or to strangle. That Beloved returns "out of blue water" (213) to plague her family and fill the house at 124 Bluestone Road with "baby's venom" (3) is no surprise, for the women in that house "understood the source of the outrage as well as they knew the source of light" (4). Thus does Morrison reimagine the "real" and redefine history, language, and the purpose of art itself.

Works Cited

Chodorow, Nancy J. *Feminism and Psychoanalytic Theory.* New Haven: Yale University Press, 1989.
———. *The Reproduction of Mothering: Psychoanalysis and the Sociology of Gender.* Berkeley: University of California Press, 1978.

Cixous, Helene. "Castration or Decapitation?" trans. Annette Kuhn. *Signs* 7, no. 11 (Autumn 1981): 41–55.

———. "The Laugh of the Medusa." In *Critical Theory Since 1965,* ed, Adams and Searle, 309–20. Tallahassee: Florida State University Press, 1986.

Epstein, Grace. "An Interview with Toni Morrison." *Ohio Journal* 9, no. 3 (Spring 1986): 3–8.

Holloway, Karla F. C., and Stephanie Demetrakopoulos. *New Dimensions of Spirituality: A Biracial and Bicultural Reading of the Novels of Toni Morrison.* New York: Greenwood Press, 1987.

Kristeva, Julia. *Desire in Language: A Semiotic Approach to Literature and Art,* ed. Leon S. Roudiez, trans. Thomas Goza, Alice Jardine, and Leon Roudiez. New York: Columbia University Press, 1980.

Le Clair, Thomas. " 'The Language Must Not Sweat': A Conversation with Toni Morrison." *New Republic* (March 1981): 21–29.

McKay, Nellie Y., ed. *Critical Essays on Toni Morrison.* Boston: G. K. Hall, 1988.

Morrison, Toni. *Beloved.* New York: Knopf, 1987.

———. *Song of Solomon.* New York: Signet, 1978.

———. *Sula.* New York: Bantam, 1975.

———. "Unspeakable Things Unspoken: The Afro-American Presence in American Literature." In *Modern Critical Views: Toni Morrison,* ed. Harold Bloom, 201–30. New York: Chelsea House, 1990.

Samuels, Wilfred D., and Clenora Hudson-Weems. *Toni Morrison.* Boston: Twayne Publishers, 1990.

Tate, Claudia. *Black Women Writers at Work.* New York: Continuum, 1989.

Washington, Mary Helen. *Invented Lives: Narratives of Black Women, 1860–1960.* New York: Doubleday, 1987.

Waugh, Patricia. *Feminine Fictions: Revising the Postmodern.* New York: Routledge, 1989.

The Telling of *Beloved*

EUSEBIO L. RODRIGUES

Beloved is a triumph of storytelling. Toni Morrison fuses arts that belong to black oral folk tradition with strategies that are sophisticatedly modern in order to create the blues mode in fiction, and tell a tale thick in texture and richly complex in meaning. The reader has to be a hearer too. For the printed words leap into sound to enter a consciousness that has to suspend disbelief willingly and become that of a child again, open to magic and wonder.

"124 was spiteful": thus the narrative shock tactics begin.[1] Here is no fairy tale opening but an entrance (124 is not a number but a house as the last sentence of the first paragraph will confirm) into a real unreal world. Toni Morrison's narrator—it is a woman's voice, deep, daring, folkwise—has full faith in her listeners (curious males have gathered around her) and in their ability to absorb multiple meanings. She plunges *in medias res* and begins her tale with the arrival of Paul D.

Paul's arrival sets the story in motion. Outraged by the spiteful persecution of a "haunt" that resents his sudden irruption into a house it has taken possession of, Paul attacks it and drives it out. The incident has a tremendous impact—on Paul, on Sethe, who has resigned herself to a certain way of life, on Denver, who feels deprived of the only companion she ever had, and especially on the listener, who is bewildered, utterly disoriented. For he is flung into a dark fictional world without any bearings or explanations. He has to be patient and wait for light to filter in through cracks in the thick darkness. Exhalations from the dim past arise—a baby is furious at having its throat cut, a grandmother's name is Baby Suggs, a baby is born in 1855, Sethe's milk is taken—but they lack meaning and cannot, yet, be chronologically aligned or connected with the events of the present, the year 1873.

Toni Morrison begins the slow process of conjuring up a world that has receded into the past. Here is no extended Proustian act of remembering a lost world with the help of a madeleine dipped in tea. For the past, racial and personal, seared into the being of her characters, has to be exorcized by "rememory." Unspeakable, it emerges reluctantly. The major characters,

This essay first appeared in *The Journal of Narrative Technique* 21, no. 2 (Spring 1991): 153–69. Reprinted by permission of *The Journal of Narrative Technique*.

Sethe and Paul, have to tear the terrible past, bit by painful bit, out of their being so that they, and Denver, can confront it and be healed. Toni Morrison's narrator will stage an extended blues performance, controlling the release of these memories, syncopating the accompanying stories of Sixo, Stamp Paid and Grandmother Suggs, making rhythms clash, turning beats into offbeats and crossbeats, introducing blue notes of loneliness and injustice and despair, generating, at the end, meanings that hit her listeners in the heart, that region below the intellect where knowledge deepens into understanding.

The structural ordering of this "aural" novel is not spatial but musical.[2] It consists of a title, a dedication to Sixty Million and more, an epigraph from an obscure Biblical passage, and three unequal parts. Part I, of eighteen sections, appears to be lopsidedly long, a stretch of 163 pages; Part II, with its seven sections, goes on for 70 pages; Part III, of 3 sections and only 38 pages, ends with a word that is an isolate, at once a re-dedication and a whispered prayer, Beloved.

Part I takes its time in order to establish the many modes Toni Morrison uses to create a world. Her narrator begins the tale, and immediately allows an interplay of voices to begin. Torn fragments of the past float out of Sethe and Paul, who have met again after eighteen long years. Their voices join those of Baby Suggs, dead for eight years, and of Denver, for whom only the present matters. The voices set a world spinning, the world of slaves and slavery whose horrors can no longer be visualized today but whose sounds of pain and suffering still linger on. They issue out of the shared stories of Sethe and Paul D set in two focal regions: in Sweet Home, a farm in Kentucky, where events take place that project and compress rural slave life before 1865; and in 124 Bluestone Road on the outskirts of Cincinnati, Ohio, an urban setting that highlights the painful consequences of post Civil War freedom. The narrator transforms the interlinked stories of Sethe and Paul into a paradigm of what it meant to be a slave, especially a woman slave in America.

History, however, is not treated as mere documentary. For that readers could turn to slave narratives. Toni Morrison makes history integral to her novel. In musical terms her narrative melodies are sung against the ground-beat of historical detail. The details are thrown in casually, understated, as in the true blues idiom, to intensify the horror. Baby Suggs's eight children had six fathers. Men were put out to stud, slave women were sold suddenly, children vanished into the unknown. After the war there was chaos, black human blood cooked in a lynch fire stank (180), there was madness, segregation, the South was "infected by the Klan" (66). Before the war hangings were common (Sethe saw her mother's unrecognizable corpse cut down), slaves were branded (Sethe's mother's identification mark was a cross and circle burnt into the skin under her breast), and an iron bit was thrust into the mouth for days as punishment (Paul complained not about sucking iron but about his intense need to spit). What happened before the slaves got to America was, for them, only a dim memory. At times Sethe remembers her mother dancing the antelope (there is no such animal in America) and remembers, at times, faintly, the ghostly voice of Nan, her mother's friend, speaking about a sea voyage in a language Sethe knew but has now forgotten (62). The memories of the other characters do not extend to the African past. The narrator will devise a way to resurrect this past.

But before this past can spring to life for the community of listeners (women, their work done, have joined the semi-circle now), the present has to be made alive and exciting. The telling therefore does not begin from a point fixed in time. Nor will the narrator use symbolism (an overused mode), or channel her stories through points of view (too thin, too limited), or through a consciousness that flows like a stream. The words will not have a Hemingway translucence but a Faulknerian density, for the language, slow moving, will be thick with history. Tenses will shift when needed to quicken pace. The oral-aural mode will use repetition to intensify the experience. Words will be repeated; phrases and images will be used over and over again to generate rhythmic meanings; fragments of a story will recur, embedded in other fragments of other stories. A born bard, the narrator, a blueswoman, will cast a spell on her audience so that fragments, phrases, words accelerate and work together to create a mythic tale.

The words repeated are simple but vibrant. Plans, repeated to warn slaves not to make any, for they have no future, anything could happen any time. Interlinked words, pieces, parts, sections, warn a slave about the lack of a unitary self. The slave is a bundle of pieces, of names, food, shelter provided by changing masters; a collection of fractured parts, outer and inner, that have been defiled. Sethe knows she could easily break into pieces. That is why Baby Suggs bathed the rescued Sethe in sections; that is why Paul D will have to wash off Sethe's defilement part by piece by section at the end, before his love (like that of Sixo's woman) can make the pieces come together. Beloved, it becomes clear, is afraid of breaking up into pieces, an indication that she is a composite of slave pieces of the past.

Smile/smiling: these word-forms, tossed out casually at first (7, 50), begin to resound when associated with Beloved, who emerges from the water smiling mysteriously, fascinating Denver. They gather more resonance when Sethe connects the smile with her mother's smile, and realizes that her mother "had smiled when she did not smile" (203), realizes further that it was the iron bit clamped on the tongue that had produced that perpetual smile. It was the same smile worn by the Saturday prostitutes who worked the slaughterhouse yard on pay day. Sethe's own smile, as she makes these connections, is one of knowledge. Paul D, during the telling of his story to Sethe, can understand why, when he was led away, iron bit in the mouth, his hatred had focused on Mister, "the smiling boss of roosters" (106). What Paul saw on the rooster was a white smile of supreme contempt and arrogance, a looking down on one less than a chicken. In Part III the full force of the word-forms rings loud and clear. Beloved smiles dazzlingly before she explodes out of existence. What remains at the end is the scar on her handsawed throat, the "smile under the chin" (275), the memory for Sethe of "the little shadow of a smile" (239). Smiling, the listener realizes, is a silent statement of endurance. To smile is to know the horror of what it means to be a slave.

The narrator makes words function as musical notes. She also makes use of musical phrases together with chordal accompaniments to produce assonance, consonance, dissonance. "Wear her out" (13): associated at first with the young Denver, who is always tired, this phrase is applied to Sethe and then modulated and amplified when linked with Baby Suggs and Stamp Paid. Stamp Paid himself feels bone tired (176) towards the end; only then does he understand the marrow weariness that made Baby Suggs give up the struggle, and get into bed to die. "Lay it all down" (174), she advises Sethe and Denver, echoing a line out of a spiritual. Sword and shield, lay it all down; she urges resignation, it's useless to fight, one cannot ever defend oneself. The phrase becomes a refrain, a burden (in both senses), that insists on the unbearable weight of racial suffering and injustice.

Images and metaphors of food intensify this suffering. "The stone had eaten the sun's rays" (40): a mere trick of style, did the verb not compel listener and reader to pause, for "eaten" springs out of the consciousness of the famished Sethe. Sethe is constantly chewing and swallowing; she keeps "gnawing" (162) at the past. The narrator uses the language of hunger lest her listeners forget essential truths, that all food was decided and provided by the masters, and that hunger was yet another burden of slave life. Sugar was never provided; that's why Denver and Beloved crave sweet things. The only food the slave mother could provide her babies was her own milk. "All I ever had," Sethe tells Paul (159). That's why she felt outraged when the two white boys stole her nursing milk. That is why she was ready to bite out the eyes, to gnaw the cheek of anyone who would stop her from getting to her starving baby. That's what drove her on from Kentucky to Ohio.

Milk, more than just food, was the flow of love Sethe wanted to release into her babies. Denver, sucking on a bloody nipple, took in Sethe's milk with her sister's blood. The baby sister never did get enough of Sethe's milk. That is why, when she returns as Beloved, she has a "hungry" face. Sethe, says the narrator, "was licked, tasted, eaten by Beloved's eyes" (57). Beloved was "greedy" to hear Sethe talk, and Sethe "feeds" her with stories of the past it always hurt her to tell others, even Denver. The narrator's language becomes thick with insistent references to and images and metaphors of food and hunger, so that listener and reader become aware of many slave hungers—for food, for things sweet, for an understanding of the past, for communion, for community, and, above all, for a form of sustenance slaves were deprived of, love. It was dangerous to love, for the beloved could be torn away at any time. Beloved, as name, title and emanation, now gathers significance but the meanings do not come together yet. Nor can the hearers grasp the connections between food and religion—"the berries that tasted like church" (136), the Biblical references to "loaves and fishes" (137), the setting-up of the food after Baby Suggs's funeral. All connections and meanings, all notes and musical phrases, will be made to converge and resonate in Parts II and III.

Before such a convergence can occur there has to be an awareness of the magical sounds of the language through which meanings flow. Toni Morrison undermines the heaviness of print by turning word-shapes into word-sounds in order to allow her narrator to chant, to sing, to exploit sound effects. ". . . No. No. Nono. Nonono" (163): these staccato drumbeats—single, double, triple—translate Sethe's fears of the threatening white world into ominous sounds. Word-sounds enact the rhythmic steps of a dance: "A little two-step, two-step, make-a-new-step, slide, slide and strut on down" (74). A page presents consecutive paragraphs that have a one-word beginning, "but" with a period (223). The reader can see the pattern the "buts" make; the listener hears the repeated thuds that drive in the utter futility of slaves making plans to escape. At one point the narrator refers to Sethe's "bedding" dress made up of pieces Sethe put together—two pillow cases, a dresser scarf with a hole in it, an old sash, mosquito netting (59). The strange adjective is used to trigger an ironic rhyme-echo, for a slave woman could never have a "wedding" with a ceremony and a preacher, but only a coupling. Sad, but full of admiration and affection for Sethe, the narrator herself turns celebrant, the music of her language transforming the mating into a unique fertility rite in a tiny cornfield, witnessed by their friends who partake of the young corn. Fourteen-year-old Sethe's virgin surrender to Halle, her moments of pain and joy, have as accompaniments the dance of the cornstalks, the husk, the cornsilk hair, the pulling down of the tight sheath, the ripping sound, the juice, the loose silk, the jailed-up flavor running free, the joy (27). Light monosyllabic sounds bring this epithalamium to a close: "How loose the silk. How fine and loose and free."

Beloved makes many aural demands for its musical patterns are many. Toni Morrison turns her narrator into a Bakhtinian ventriloquist who throws her voice into Baby Suggs. Oh my people, cries Baby Suggs, that preacher without a church, calling out to her congregation in the Clearing, repeating the words "here" and "yonder," and "flesh" and "heart" and "love," exhorting her people to love their unloved flesh, their beating hearts, so moving them that they make music for her dance (89). By using repetition for emphasis, participles for movement, internal rhyme and alliteration, the narrator heightens the voice and the word-patterns of Paul D (who cannot read) to translate into thudbeats the unspeakable fears and cravings of forty-six chain-linked chain-dancing men pounding away at rocks with their sledge hammers:

> They sang it out and beat it up, garbling the words so they could not be understood; tricking the words so their syllables yielded up other meanings. They sang the women they knew; the children they had been; the animals they had

tamed themselves or seen others tame. They sang of bosses and masters and misses; of mules and dogs and the shamelessness of life. They sang lovingly of graveyards and sisters long gone. Of pork in the woods; meal in the pan; fish on the line; cane, rain, and rocking chairs. (108)

Toni Morrison endows her narrator with a voice that has both range and energy, without being artificial or literary. It is a human voice, warm and friendly, not detached or distant, a voice that reaches out to touch the whole village community now gathered around her. She is, after all, their bard; she knows their language and can speak the vernacular. There is no need, therefore, for any comments, or for the language of explanations; only the need for a heightening of the black idiom in order to summon up a world buried in their racial memory.

Hence the language intensification. "Knees wide open as the grave" (5): this startling simile erupts as Sethe remembers rutting among the headstones to get the seven letters of "Beloved" chiseled for free. A flirtation "so subtle you had to scratch for it" (7): Sethe's verb springs out of her world; the implied image is that of hens in a farmyard. A memory of something shameful seeps "into a slit" in Sethe's mind (61); she is poised on "the lip" of sleep (85); Beloved has "rinsed" certain memories out of her mind, explains Sethe to Denver (119). The language becomes intensely vibrant at times, as when Paul D suddenly realizes he was completely wrong about Sethe:

> This here Sethe was new. The ghost in her house didn't bother her for the very same reason a room-and-board witch with new shoes was welcome. This here Sethe talked about love like any other woman; talked about baby clothes like any other woman, but what she meant could cleave the bone. This here Sethe talked about safety with a handsaw. This here new Sethe didn't know where she stopped and the world began. (164)

The verbal phrase, "cleave the bone," the repetition of "talked," of "like any other woman," the repetition of thematic words used earlier in the story, "love," "safety," "world," the insertion of "here" between "this" and "Sethe" to colloquialize the phrase, its repetition three times, and then the modulation into a four beat phrase "this here new Sethe"—all work together to produce the thick flow of Paul's realization.

Toni Morrison's ability to charge the vernacular with power and sound enables her to give a mythic form to the story of her people, the Afro-Americans. Oh my people, cries Toni Morrison, hear the voice of the bard. This bard is a Blakean *griot* in whom the ancestral experience is stored and who can see and sing the past, present, and future. She sings an ongoing story of the savage uprooting of sixty million and more, of a sea passage from Africa to America, of selves fractured and reduced to things lower than animals, of freedom imposed by others from the outside, and then the painful process of healing, of the achieving of inner freedom, and of slowly discovering themselves as human beings in a new world. It is a story of generations, of two hundred years and more compressed in time and channeled through a few individuals. The telling is a teaching, too, directed to the generations yet to come, lest they forget. History had to be transformed into myth.

Toni Morrison has her narrator employ the technique of circling round and round the subject that Sethe, her central character, uses for telling the essentials of her story to Paul D: "Circling, circling, now she was gnawing something else instead of getting to the point" (162). All the stories—that of Sethe and Paul D, of Baby Suggs and Stamp Paid, of Beloved and Denver, and of Sixo—have their chronologies fractured and the "pieces" made to spin together to form one story, monstrous and heroic. The fragments keep sliding into and out of each other for they cannot be separated. Their love for each other makes Sethe's story Paul's too. The stories of Baby Suggs and Stamp Paid tell of an earlier generation. The stories of Sixo and the Cherokee Indians present yet another account of suffering and injustice. Denver's story leads into the future, while Beloved's reaches to the past. Sure her people will slowly understand the story of their own past, the narrator begins with Sethe.

Sethe, in 1873, has resigned herself to her situation. Isolated from the Bluestone community, terrified of the exhalations of the past she kept buried within her damaged being, Sethe needs healing. The re-entry of Paul D and of Beloved into her life begins the slow process that leads her to understanding, love and community. Sethe is compelled to re-live two ordeals, the birth of Denver and the killing of her third child.

The story of Sethe's harrowing escape and of Denver's miraculous birth takes eight sections of Part I (up to p. 85) to be told, but the narrator does not release all its meanings. Certain clues are offered; the listener gets accustomed to a mode of telling that involves delay, repetition, and a slow but controlled release of information. Sethe casually mentions "that girl looking for velvet" (8) to Paul D. Only later (32) is her name, Amy, revealed (the first clue, the name, from Old French, means *beloved*). The story is relayed through dialogue, recall and narration. Sethe begins the narrative; Denver remembers parts that Sethe told her, and, as if under a spell, she "steps into the told story" (29) to recreate it for Beloved. The narrator takes over and finishes the telling which is exciting, full of horror and pathos and beauty. She smuggles in significant truths through the words of Amy—that anything dead coming back to life hurts (35), that nothing can heal without pain (78)—that she hopes some of her listeners will ponder. The unexpected aria that bursts out of the narrator towards the end, just after the birth of Denver, is a musical celebration the audience can respond to but cannot understand, yet:

> Spores of bluefern growing in the hollows along the riverbank float toward the water in silver-blue lines hard to see unless you are in or near them, lying right at the river's edge when the sunshots are low and drained. Often they are mistook for insects—but they are seeds in which the whole generation sleeps con-

fident of a future. And for a moment it is easy to believe each one has one—will become all of what is contained in the spore: will live out its days as planned. This moment of certainty lasts no longer than that; longer, perhaps, than the spore itself. (84)

The story of Sethe's other ordeal is told in "pieces" that are scattered through all 18 sections of Part I, and that have to be put together. The focus is on two consecutive days, four weeks after Sethe's arrival at 124. On the first day the whole community is invited to a feast, a communion, a ritual "celebration of blackberries that put Christmas to shame" (147). The second day is one of foreboding for Baby Suggs, who smells two odors, one of disapproval, the other of a "dark and coming thing." What happens in the shed appears to be both a killing and a ritual sacrifice, the red blood spurting out of the cut throat of the baby held against the mother's chest.

The horror is not immediate, nor are the details graphic. The scene has a stabbing intensity, for it is a chill horror that takes time to penetrate and implode. The narrative tactics shift; the temperature of the language drops. The scene (section 16 of Part I, 148–153) is relayed through four voices that slide one into the other to form a "white" composite. That of the slave catcher presents a hunter calculating his profit: "Unlike a snake or a bear, a dead nigger could not be skinned for profit and was not worth his own dead weight in coin" (148). The nephew simply cannot understand why and how a mere beating could cause such a reaction. The schoolteacher presents a doleful view of "creatures God has given you the responsibility of" (150). The sheriff sees before him a proof that freedom should not have been imposed so soon on these poor savages. The language of all four voices is cold, aloof, detached, clinical. After all these are creatures and cannibals, aren't they, what else can one expect. Drenched in savage irony the scene becomes almost unbearable. Mercifully the narrator takes over; the ironic mode loses its edge but still continues with the sudden entry (as in a Hitchcock movie) of two white children, one bearing shoes for Baby Suggs to repair. The unmentioned color emits a tiny scream as the narrator's voice drops into silence at the end: "The hot sun dried Sethe's dress, stiff as rigor mortis" (153).

The story of Sethe and her ordeals forms the spinning center around which the other stories of collapse spin. The outer circle is made up of the stories of the Cherokee (yet another people decimated, and uprooted from the lands they owned) and of Sixo the Indian, Paul's "brother," who laughs when his feet are roasted and sings "Seven-O!, Seven-O!" before he is shot. Then the story of Baby Suggs, seventy years old, who had proclaimed the gospel of love after she got her freedom. She realizes that she had preached a lie, and that it was all useless. White folks came into my yard, she says, using the language of understatement. She "lays down" in bed to die there. Two sentences sum up the slave life of Paul, whose heart has become a rusty tobacco tin into which he has stuffed his experiences: "It was some time before he could put

Alfred, Georgia, Sixo, Halle, his brothers, Sethe, Mister, the taste of iron, the sight of butter, the smell of hickory, notebook paper, one by one, into the tobacco tin lodged in his chest. By the time he got to 124 nothing in this world could pry it open" (113). How much is a nigger supposed to take, he asks. All he can, Stamp Paid replies, and Paul can only repeat why why why why why. The Stamp Paid story is of one who had dedicated his entire life to the rescue and service of his people. He finds himself in a state of despair in 1874, nine years after his people were set free. He had found in his boat a tiny red ribbon that smelt of skin and embodied for him all the lynchings and the burnings that his people still had to endure. "What *are* these people? You tell me, Jesus. What *are* they?" (180) he asks.

The narrator is confident that this question to Jesus will direct her audience (some white people have drifted into the group now) to the Christian dimensions of her tale. After all, they also have been sustained and comforted by their Christian faith and by the Bible. They would pick up the Biblical references to "loaves and fishes" during the celebratory feast, to Stamp Paid's real name, Joshua (the successor to Moses), and to the origins in Genesis of Sethe's name. They would realize that Baby Suggs had lost faith in the God she once believed in; that Stamp Paid, who had relied on the Word and who had believed that "these things too will pass" (179), abandoned his efforts to rescue the inhabitants of 124 menacingly "ringed with voices like a noose" (183). And they would sense that additional help was needed from other sources to deal with things "older, but not stronger, than He Himself was" (172).

Listeners (aware of African religious beliefs) and readers (familiar with books by Janheinz Jahn and Geoffrey Parrinder, and with the Indic tradition) slowly begin to realize that Beloved has sprung out of pre-Christian sources. A complex creation, Beloved is made up of "pieces" that Toni Morrison has spun into being so skillfully that it is difficult to isolate their sources. Some elements derive from the Afro-American belief, shared by the Bluestone community, that the unfulfilled dead can return to the scene of their former existence. According to Baby Suggs almost every house is "packed to its rafters with some dead Negro's grief" (5). Other elements spring from the belief, purely African, that "the departed are spiritual forces which can influence their living descendants. In this their only purpose is to increase the life force of their descendants."[3] Toni Morrison fuses these elements with others of her own invention in order to intensify her tale and raise it to the level of myth. She makes her narrator control the pace of the telling, releasing the story slowly so that listener and reader are persuaded to accept Beloved as a "presence," allowing a number of meanings to accumulate so that, at the end, it becomes a story of haunting significance.

In the beginning the baby ghost is merely a disturbance, mysterious not to Sethe and Denver but to the listeners, exciting their interest in a good story. Only after the Thursday carnival,[4] after Beloved returns from the other side of the grave, does the tale become more than a ghost story. Toni Morrison set herself two fictional problems. She had to delay Sethe's recognition of Beloved as her baby daughter, while allowing Denver to be aware that Beloved is her sister almost from the beginning. The second problem was to provide Beloved with a voice and a language. Toni Morrison carefully controls the release of details about Beloved. That Beloved is a nineteen-year-old (the age she would have been had she lived) who acts like a baby in the beginning is clear (though not to Sethe who is distracted by her love of Paul D): Beloved has sleepy eyes, her hands and feet are soft, her skin is flawless, she cannot hold her head up, she is incontinent. She "grows" up in the course of a few days because Sethe "feeds" her with stories of her own past. This "feeding," a form of narrative strategy, allows the novelist to evoke Sethe's past for her readers, and it allows Sethe to exorcize what she had kept buried within herself. Sethe's rememory pours out of her in response to the many questions Beloved keeps asking, using a strange, raspy voice. It takes over four weeks for Beloved's "gravelly" voice, with its African cadence, to shift unobtrusively into the rhythms of Afro-American speech.

The talks with Sethe establish the reality of Beloved as a human being. The scenes with Denver and with Paul suggest that Beloved is also a catalytic life force. The shed behind 124 becomes the locale where the racial past is reenacted. Beloved "moves" Paul D (the way slaves were moved from place to place; there was nothing they or Paul could do about it), "like a rag doll" (126, 221), out of Sethe's bed and into the dark shed where she forces him, much against his will, to have sex with her, and to call her by her true name, Beloved, not the one the "ghosts without skin" called her in the daylight, bitch (241). Paul turns into a version of Seth, the black man on the slave ship whom Sethe's mother loved and after whom Sethe was named. The dark shed becomes the ship's hold as Beloved forces Denver to re-live the experience of panic, suffocation and thick darkness (with cracks of daylight) where the self is reduced to nothing. These painful experiences will be healing (as Amy had said). Denver, who belongs to the future, lives through a racial past without whose knowledge she would not be complete. Paul's rusty tobacco tin, which "nothing *in this world* could pry open" (my italics), opens up into a red, warm heart.

Before presenting Sethe's sorrows and sufferings the narrator halts the recitative and turns into a blueswoman, making a trio of voices sing "unspeakable thoughts, unspoken" (199). The timing of this musical interlude sung by a mother and her two daughters is exactly right: Paul D has been made to leave 124; Sethe knows that her baby has come back from the other side; and the past has been disinterred. The interlude of four sections (200–217) provides a time of rest and slowdown before the final narrative outburst.

The first two sections (200–209) open with the voiced thoughts of Sethe and of Denver, recapitulating, in fragments, the significant moments of their past. The third section (210–213) begins in the present with "I am Beloved and she is mine." Then the I swells into a collective choric I that comes as if from a distant time and place, as though sixty million and more voices had been compressed into one. Toni Morrison could use only a few typographical devices to activate print into tempo.[5] All punctuation is banished (except for the period that ends the opening sentence). There is quadruple spacing between sentences and there are double gaps between paragraphs. These pauses slow down the voice and make it resonate, so that a lamentation fills the air as the African beginnings of the horror are reenacted. Visual details blur and dissolve: women crouch in the jungle picking flowers in baskets, there is gunsmoke during the hunt for slaves, the men are crammed into the ship's hold,[6] children and women, naked, crouch on the deck and on the bridge, storms at sea force men and women to be packed together, there is the sweet rotten smell of death, corpses are stacked in piles on the deck and then pushed out into the sea with poles, suicide by jumping into the sea and rapes are common.

Out of such visual horror arise cries of anguish as beloved is torn from beloved, women from their children, mothers from their daughters. The anguish is never ending, for "all of it is now it is all now" (210). The past is still present, as those who have listened to the tale so far know. Beloved becomes the embodiment of all slave daughters; Sethe stands for generations of slave mothers. Denver experiences something worse than death, the utter lack of self in the shed (123); Paul trembles uncontrollably in Georgia (106) like the man in the hold packed so tight he had no room even to tremble in order to die (211); Sethe experiences choking (96) to make her know what it felt like to wear an iron circle around her neck (213); Beloved gazes in tears at the turtles in the stream behind 124 (105), as if her earlier self were looking for her Seth who had leapt from the bridge of the slave ship. All experiences repeat or parallel each other. The fourth section returns the listeners to the present where the trio of voices chant a dirge in liturgical fashion as the interlude ends.

The narrator then takes up again the story of Sethe, who lavishes all her love on her baby daughter, excluding Denver and feeding the uncomprehending Beloved with explanations, telling her that she had to kill her in order to save her. Beloved grows monstrously fat devouring Sethe's love while Sethe wastes away. Denver, through whom most of Part III is channeled, does not understand what is happening but is afraid there could be another killing.

Both reader and listener have to understand why Beloved and Sethe behave in this unnatural manner. Sethe does not realize that Beloved's demands are not those of a human being, but of an impersonal life force that has got what it wanted, but cannot stop its blind, unreasonable demands for more. The narrator calls her "wild game" (242). The Bluestone community refers to her as an "it" that will destroy Sethe, who has committed a crime. Sethe, on the other hand, believes that "what she had done was right because it came from true love" (251).

Toni Morrison does not judge Sethe. Neither does her narrator allow her listeners to pass judgment on Sethe. The Bluestone community cannot forgive what they regard as an act of senseless murder. Even Baby Suggs was horrified on that day, and fell on her knees begging God's pardon for Sethe (152, 153, 203). Denver, who is afraid of her mother even though she loves her (102), has an inkling of what it was that drove Sethe on: it was a "something" in her mother that made it all right to "kill her own" (205). The thing was "coiled" up in her, too, for Denver felt it leap within her at certain moments (102, 104).

What the "thing" is is never made clear. But Sethe's story provides some clues. The process begins at edenic Sweet Home, that "cradle" (219) of innocence, at the moment when Sethe's knowledge of evil begins, the knowledge that the white world, in the person of schoolteacher, considered her part animal. He had told his nephews to categorize Sethe by setting down her animal characteristics on the right, her human ones on the left (193). Overhearing these words, Sethe feels her head itch as if somebody were sticking fine needles in her scalp (193).[7] During the escape, before the meeting with Amy, Sethe senses a *"something"* that came out of the earth into her and impelled her to attack: "like a snake. All jaws and hungry" (31).

It was this "something," a blind animal force perhaps, that leapt within Sethe just before the killing. At the sight of schoolteacher's hat she heard wings: "Little hummingbirds stuck their needle beaks right through her headcloth into her hair and beat their wings" (163). Stamp Paid, who was present, saw a dramatic change in Sethe, whose face "beaked"[8] and whose hands worked like claws before she snatched up her children "like a hawk on the wing," and dragged them into the shed (157).

Stamp Paid tries to tell Paul D that love drove Sethe to "outhurt the hurter" (234). Paul cannot understand such love. Too thick (164), he tells Sethe, adding that Sethe had two legs not four, implying that she was not an animal but a human being (165). A "forest" sprang up between them, adds the narrator who, reluctant to explain anything to listener or reader, compels them to ponder the image of the forest.

Yet another clue had been provided earlier when, asked by Paul to have his baby, Sethe thought: "Unless carefree, motherlove was a killer" (132). Paul D had observed that, for a slave, any form of love was fraught with danger, and that human love needed freedom. One can only speculate that mother love, when not allowed free expression and growth in human society, remains a primal instinct. Fiercely possessive and predatory, it kills to protect the young from the enemy. That explains perhaps why there are so many animal references. Slaves were regarded as property, as possessions, as animals.

In this light Sethe's act of murder transforms itself from a mere killing into a ritual sacrifice of the beloved, an expression of the helpless rage and outrage of many slave mothers who either wanted to or did kill their young to deliver them from slavery.[9] But one sin cannot cancel out another. 124

with its shed is more than a gray and white house: it becomes the arena where the resurrected past demands vengeance and threatens to overwhelm the present. A ritual atonement is needed. Denver, the future, has to step out of this dark world to seek help. She goes to the community.

With a few deft touches all through Parts I and II, the narrator has established the reality of the Bluestone community, a loosely knit group of colored folks living at the city's edge. They are a good bunch, Stamp Paid tells Paul D, a little proud and mean at times, but ready to help anyone in need. They had two meeting centers: the Church of the Holy Redeemer with Reverend Pike as preacher, and the Clearing in the woods where that unchurched preacher, Baby Suggs, holy, restored their faith in themselves and in their bodies. 124, at that time, had been a "cheerful, buzzing house" (86), a way station and a place of refuge for runaways, where Baby Suggs provided food, comfort and help. What led to the estrangement between 124 and the community is not quite clear, but the narrator is confident that her listeners (their circle has now expanded into a vast human congregation) will understand and forgive human failings.

A few listeners might be aware of the term *hubris,* but all would know that pride and arrogance were sins that could lead to misunderstanding. Baby Suggs knew that she had been guilty of pride on the day of the celebration, knew that she had "offended them by excess" (138). That is why, on the next day, she could smell the disapproval of the community. The ninety friends and neighbors were guilty too, of enjoying the feast of "loaves and fishes" and then displaying anger, envy and resentment towards the provider. Sethe, too, is guilty, of arrogantly isolating herself and not going to the community for help, even after the death of Baby Suggs. The setting-up after the funeral did not lead to communion. Sethe did not eat of their food, and they would not eat what she provided. It is Stamp Paid, that Soldier of Christ (171), who tries to help. Driven by a sense of guilt and by the memory of his friend, Baby Suggs, he tries to pass through two barriers: the circle of nightmarish voices, and the door that remains locked despite his knocking. He abandons his efforts to reach the inhabitants of 124.

Having made her listeners fully aware of the many meanings of 124, the narrator now quickens the pace of the telling. The tempo increases, the sound effects grow intense. "124 was loud," the opening of Part II (169), echoes the opening of Part I, "124 was spiteful," and there is a re-echo in the opening of Part III, "124 was quiet" (239). Quiet because its inhabitants, locked in a meaningless love, were starving and would die of hunger. Denver is afraid of stepping off the porch of this prison:

> *Out there where* small things scratched and sometimes touched. *Where* words could be spoken that would close your ears shut. *Where,* if you *were* alone, feeling could overtake you and stick to you like a shadow. *Out there where there were* places in which things so bad had happened that when you *were* near them it

would happen again. Like Sweet Home *where* time didn't pass and *where,* like her mother said, the bad was waiting for her as well. How would she know these places? What was more—much more—*out there were* whitepeople and how could you tell about them? (italics mine) (244–45)

The listener can easily respond to the reference to Sweet Home as a place where time had stopped, to the rhyme-echoes and repetition (with variation) of "out there," "where," and "were" that enact Denver's fears and hesitations, and trigger Denver's rememory of the rats in prison and her sudden deafness.

Neither Sethe nor Denver can hear the loud voices that menace 124. Only Stamp Paid, that witness of his people's sufferings, listens and can recognize the two sets of voices: the roaring of all the slaves who were lynched and burned; and the terrified mutterings, near the porch, of whites (like the schoolteacher who had created a "jungle" in Sethe) in whom the jungle of hate and terror had entered. The pack of haunts is ready to pounce.

The listeners can tell the end is near. The narrator summons up techniques that tellers of tales use to create suspense—tantalizing pauses, breaks in the narrative, switches and cross-telling (like cross-cutting in film). It is an ominous Friday, three in the afternoon, a steaming tropical day reeking with foul odors. Three narrative movements converge: Bluestone women, thirty of them, led by Ella, make their way to 124 to rescue Sethe from the devil child; Mr. Bodwin, who had helped in the defense of Sethe, is on his way to 124 (where he had been born), to fetch Denver, who is waiting for him on the porch; Sethe, inside 124, uses an ice pick to break some ice for the sweating Beloved.

To amplify her story the narrator now summons her co-tellers, the blueswoman and the bard. The blueswoman vocalizes the rhythms of the approaching mumbling chorus of thirty women (significantly, no man, not even Stamp Paid, is present). Some of them kneel outside the yard, as though in church, and begin a series of responses to a prayer call: "Yes, yes, yes, oh yes. Hear me. Hear me. Do it, Maker, do it. Yes" (258). Then Ella begins to holler,[10] an elemental cry that sweeps all the women to the very beginning, of time perhaps, even before the Christian Word. "In the beginning was the sound," the blueswoman announces (259).

The narrative pauses, then the narrator switches to Edward Bodwin, driving a cart to 124, haunted by time and by the recent wars and the fight over abolition that made him lose faith in what his father had told him, that human life is holy. The narrative breaks again to Sethe and Beloved standing on the porch of 124. The three movements converge and combine.

The blueswoman becomes one with the community of women out of whose being sounds explode, and rise to a crescendo of pure sound. More than a speech act, it is a *mantra*like utterance that rises from the creative female depths of their self, an act of exorcism:[11] "Building voice upon voice until they found it, and when they did it was a wave of sound wide enough to sound deep water and knock the pods off chestnut trees. It broke over Sethe and she trembled like the baptized in its wash" (261). The reference to water, the word "sound" used as a verb and noun, the allusion to Baby Suggs and to her powers associated with nature, "tremble," the word linked with Paul D, the double implication of "wash," all insist that this unpremeditated rite combines a pre-Christian archetypal cleansing with Christian baptism. Beloved's dazzling smile suggests that she does "understand" what has happened. But the listeners are puzzled.

It is the bard who knows what has been exorcized and begins to chant, switching from the past to the present tense because "all is now." The events of the past are once again made present. The words used earlier for what happened in 1855 (the definite green of the leaves, the staccato drumbeats of Sethe's fears) are repeated and relayed through Sethe's rememory. But this time, ice pick in hand, Sethe (after she sees Edward Bodwin's hat) attacks not her beloved but the "schoolteacher" attacker, a normal human reaction for the "thing" has been exorcized out of her. Denver and the women move in to stop her. The words used in the interlude (pile, faces, people, the man without skin) are also repeated to summon back from the remote past Beloved's ordeals on the slave ship. Then Beloved, her belly swollen with the past, vanishes. But this monstrous African past cannot be completely exorcized. It will linger on, wanting to be at least remembered.

The listeners, held spellbound by these events, experience catharsis. The tale has reached into their hearts and touched basic human emotions. It moves them, but not to action. For Toni Morrison is an artist, not a sociologist or a politician. Like Conrad, who wanted, before all, to make his readers *see,* Toni Morrison wants to make her people *listen* and, like the spirit of Baby Suggs urging Denver (244), know the truth about themselves and their "roots." Like Conrad, too, Toni Morrison feels compelled to "render the highest kind of justice to the visible universe."[12] The institution of slavery is condemned, but all white people are not. The listeners remember Amy (a "slave" herself who, significantly, is on her pilgrim way to Boston), the Garners (Sethe looked upon Mrs. Garner as if she was her mother), the Bodwins, even the sheriff (who had looked away when Sethe nursed Denver). But Toni Morrison insists that true freedom is essential and that equality between peoples is of absolute necessity. That is why the goodness of the Garners and the Bodwins is somehow flawed: on a shelf in the Bodwin house Denver sees a black boy figurine kneeling on a pedestal that reads: "At Yo Service" (255).

Toni Morrison's sense of justice and compassion leads her to introduce notes of hope. The many Christian references suggest such a possibility, especially the name of the community church, and the redemptive tree of suffering that Sethe carries on her back and will carry for a lifetime. Paul's love will heal Sethe, rescue her from the fate that befell Baby Suggs, and put her pieces together. In the tableau at the end Paul touches Sethe's face as he whispers his tribute to her: "You your best thing, Sethe. You are" (273). The story of Sethe and Paul will gradually recede into the past. Denver *is* the future. She is the child of the race, "my heart," Stamp Paid tells Paul D (265). Lady Jones can see "everybody's child" in her face (246). Clever and intelligent, she will go to Oberlin. Denver is like Seven-O, which is not just a cry of warning to his woman, but a continuation of Sixo, the name of his "seed" which she bears away with her. Denver needs no tribute, for the narrator has already sung an aria to celebrate her birth; she is the seed "in which the whole generation sleeps confident of the future" (84).

With the stories of Sethe, Paul, and Denver told, the narrator and the bard know that the telling has to come to a stop. Their listeners have been rapt into a mythic world. But humankind cannot live there for long. The account of what happened to Paul D, which balances the story of Sethe, allows the listeners to return to ordinary human reality. When Paul D and Stamp Paid talk about what happened at 124, a strange laughter, like Sixo's, erupts out of them. "To keep from cryin' I opens my mouth an' laughs," as Langston Hughes puts it.[13] Narrator and bard have finished their tasks, but something remains to be done. The blueswoman takes over.

She begins to keen, as though at a wake, a ceremony held in order to remember, to celebrate, and then to forget. But the lament soon changes into the sound of a Biblical voice from on high (sounded in the epigraph), that summons an alien people unto itself and calls them beloved.[14] The community remembers what Sethe rememoried, the voice of the preacher at the baby's funeral telling them who they are, addressing them all as Dearly Beloved. The voice of the blueswoman now develops a powerful hum, for she expresses, as in basic blues, not her own feelings but those of all her people. It uses not the minor (though it sounds plaintive) but the major mode of the classical blues. The words are unimportant for they all have been heard before, except the twice repeated, two-word word, "disremembered," which associates memory with pieces.[15] The blueswoman and the community know that the past can linger on but has to be laid to rest. As in a blues ending they announce, then repeat, then repeat again, mixing the past and present tenses, that it was/is "not a story to pass on." Till, finally, the blueswoman allows her voice to sink into silence after a whispered prayer, Beloved.

Notes

1.   Toni Morrison, *Beloved* (New York: New American Library, 1987), 3. Hereafter page references will be cited in the text. Other page references will help the reader to locate specific moments in this complex novel. Toni Morrison calls attention to the significance of the opening sentence of *Beloved* in "Unspeakable Things Unspoken: The Afro-American Presence in American Literature," *Michigan Quarterly Review,* Winter 1989: 31–32.

2.   Toni Morrison comments on the oral-aural qualities of her fiction in an interview: "Ah well, that may mean that my efforts to make aural literature—A-U-R-A-L—work because

I do hear it. It has to be read in silence and that's just one phase of the work but it also has to *sound* and if it doesn't *sound* right . . . Even though I don't speak it when I'm writing it, I have this interior piece, I guess, in my head that reads, so that the way I hear it is the way I write it and I guess that's the way I would read it aloud. The point is not to need the adverbs to say how it sounds but to have the sound of it in the sentence, and if it needs a lot of footnotes or editorial remarks or description in order to say how it sounded, then there's something wrong with it." (Christina Davis, "Interview with Toni Morrison," *Présence Africaine* 145, 1st Quarterly 1988: 148).

3. Janheinz Jahn, *Muntu* (New York: Grove Press, Inc., 1961) 110. A. K. Forbes (*Ras Mala: Hindu Annals of Western India* [New Delhi, India: Heritage Publications, 1973] 674) refers to spirits called bhoots: "Bhoots are . . . daimons—spirits of men or women deceased . . . still unhappily entangled in human passions, desires, or anxieties . . . seeking to inflict pain, to practise delusion, or to enjoy pleasure through the instrumentality of a living human body, of which they take temporary possession."

4. That was a bad sign according to Stamp Paid (235). Geoffrey Parrinder (*African Traditional Religion* [London: Sheldon Press, 1974]) has a chapter on Nature Gods (pp. 43–54). He refers to a grave-digging ceremony that uses a prayer that begins: "Earth, whose day is Thursday. . . ." The references to water gods and to the snake cult could help in explaining some elements in the novel. Toni Morrison also makes references to directional signs, left and right, which are significant in Indic culture.

5. Faulkner experimented with italics and other devices to project mind-voice in some of his novels, especially in *Light in August*. He wanted his publishers to use different colored inks for the Benjy section of *The Sound and the Fury*.

6. In the *Time* interview (May 22, 1989, p. 120) Toni Morrison refers to "travel accounts of people who were in the Congo—that's a wide river—saying, 'We could not get the boat through the river, it was choked with bodies.' That's like a logjam. A lot of people died. Half of them died in those ships." In his introduction to *Adventures of an African Slaver* by Captain Theodore Canot (New York: Dover Publications Inc., 1969) Malcolm Cowley mentions a strange phenomenon: that "in Bonny River . . . the bodies of slaves washed backwards and forwards with the tide, the women floating, it is said, face downwards; the men on their backs, staring into perpetual clouds which were almost the color of their eyes" (IX). In the slaveship's hold "the slaves were packed as tightly as cases of whisky. . . . The slaves were laid on their sides, spoon-fashion, the bent knees of one fitting into the hamstrings of his neighbour. On some vessels they could not even lie down; they spent the voyage sitting on each other's laps" (XII). Beloved demonstrates this position to Denver in the shed when she "bends over, curls up and rocks" (124).

7. There are two other references to birds in Sethe's hair (188). Mrs. Garner thinks Sethe has lice in her hair (195).

8. That is why Paul D keeps repeating to Stamp Paid (154–158) that the mouth shown on the newspaper clipping wasn't Sethe's.

9. No statistics on slave infanticide are available. Deborah Gray White (*Ar'n't I a Woman?* [New York: W. W. Norton and Co., 1985] 88) writes: "In 1830 a North Carolina slave woman was convicted of murdering her own child. A year later a Missouri slave was accused of poisoning and smothering her infant, and in 1834, Elizabeth, one of James Polk's slaves, was said to have smothered her newborn. No one will ever know what drove these women to kill their infants, if they did. Some whites thought slave women lacked maternal feelings, yet a few women who killed their children claimed to have done so because of their intense concern for their offspring."

10. The holler was a call or a cry used in the fields in the south. According to Tilford Brooks (*America's Black Heritage* [New Jersey: Prentice-Hall Inc., 1984] 52), "the holler is perhaps the most important single element in the blues, partly by virtue of the intensity of its personal expression."

11.   *Mantra* is a Sanskrit term difficult to translate and impossible to define. The most recent book on the subject is a collection of essays edited by Harvey P. Alper, *MANTRA* (State University of New York Press, 1989). According to Fritz Staal, mantras "are used in ritual or meditation to bring about effects that are stated to be 'ineffable' and 'beyond language.' " They represent rudiments of something that existed before language. André Padoux quotes from Abhinavagupta who describes the hissing sounds/vibrations that appear in the throat of a woman at the moment of orgasm: "In this context, such a sound, since it issues spontaneously from the depths of the self, goes beyond the bounds of ordinary human existence. It is felt as going back to the source of life . . ." (304). These quotations may help in the understanding of *Beloved*. Those interested in knowing about the Indic tradition should read a recent book of essays edited by Alf Hiltebeitel, *Criminal Gods and Demon Devotees* (State University of New York Press, 1989), especially the essay by David M. Knipe, "Night of the Growing Dead: A Cult of Virabhadra in Coastal Andhra," 123–156.

12.   Joseph Conrad, *The Nigger of the Narcissus,* ed. R. Kimborough (W. W. Norton & Co., 1979), 145.

13.   Used by Janheinz Jahn as an epigraph to his chapter on the blues, p. 217.

14.   The passage from Romans 9:25 is a modified quotation from Hosea 2.23, which implies that God looks forward to the day when his people will once more be his people. According to F. F. Bruce (*The Letter of Paul to the Romans* [Michigan: W. B. Eerdman's Publishing Co., 1985] 185), "what Paul does here is to take this promise, which referred to a situation within the frontiers of the chosen people, and extract from it a principle of divine action which in his day was reproducing itself on a world-wide scale."

15.   Deborah Horvitz, in her insightful pioneering essay on *Beloved* ("Nameless Ghosts: Possession and Dispossession in *Beloved,*" *Studies in American Fiction* 17, no. 2, Autumn 1989: 157–167) offers an analysis of this word.

Beloved: A Womanist Neo-Slave Narrative; or Multivocal Remembrances of Things Past

BERNARD W. BELL

"What is curious to me," Toni Morrison occasionally says in her lectures, "is that bestial treatment of human beings never produces a race of beasts." Since her childhood in Lorain, Ohio, she has been fascinated by the uncommon efforts of common black people to deal creatively with their double consciousness and socialized ambivalence.

As first defined in 1897 by W. E. B. Du Bois in "Strivings of the Negro People," double consciousness was not the sociopsychological and sociocultural experience of all ethnic immigrants and hyphenated white Americans. Rather, it was the complex double vision of Americans of African descent whose humanity and culture had been historically devalued and marginalized by people of European descent. For Du Bois, it was a mythic blessing and a social burden: an ancestral gift for making sense of life, a product of institutionalized racism, and a dialectical process in American society involving the bearers of residual sub-Saharan African cultures, on the one hand, and bearers of residual Western cultures, on the other hand. For many contemporary Afro-Americans, it is the striving to reconcile one's ancestral African past—however remote, mythic, or spiritual—with one's American present, one's ascribed identity with one's achieved identity; to reconcile the politics of race with the politics of sex; to reconcile being a subject with being an object, and being an outsider with being an insider.

In an apparent rewriting of Du Bois's metaphor of double consciousness and sociologist Robert E. Park's 1928 theory of the marginal man (a racial and cultural hybrid or creole), the term *socialized ambivalence* was coined in 1937 by anthropologist Melville J. Herskovits in *Life in a Haitian Valley* to signify the anthropological adjustment of Haitians to the sociopsychological conflict that resulted from the contradictory cultural imperatives of European colonialism and African traditions. In applying this model to the United States, one notes the ambivalence expressed in the mixed emotions of most

First published in *African American Review* 26, no. 1 (1992): 7–15. © Bernard W. Bell; reprinted with the permission of the author.

Americans of African descent about ideologies of integration and separation and in our shifting identification between white hegemonic and black non-hegemonic cultural systems as a result of institutionalized racism. *Double Vision,* Ralph Ellison's 1964 rewriting of Du Bois's metaphor (in *Shadow and Act*), is a fluid, ambivalent, laughing-to-keep-from-crying perspective toward life as expressed in the innovative use of irony and parody in Afro-American folklore and formal art.

How, then, do ordinary black people cope with the sexist customs, racist absurdities, and class exploitation of American life? Drawing on remembrances of her family's tradition of telling ghost stories and her longstanding fascination with literature, Morrison began attempting to answer this question creatively and expanded her commitment by joining a writers' workshop at Howard University in 1962. The short story which she began in that workshop became the nucleus of *The Bluest Eye* (1970) and the apprenticeship for her major achievements in poetic realism and Gothicism: *Sula* (1973), *Song of Solomon* (1977), *Tar Baby* (1981), and the Pulitzer-Prize-winning *Beloved* (1987).

Beloved contains Toni Morrison's most extraordinary and spellbinding womanist remembrances of things past. As Alice Walker's epigraphs to *In Search of Our Mothers' Gardens* suggest, *womanist* connotes "a black feminist or feminist of color"; a woman who, among other things, is audaciously "committed to [the] survival and wholeness of entire people, male *and* female" (xi). As Wilfred D. Samuels and Clenora Hudson-Weems remind us in their bio-critical study *Toni Morrison,* because of the silences in the slave narratives due to authorial compromises to white audiences and to self-masking from a painful past, Morrison sees her role as a writer as bearing witness to "the interior life of people who didn't write [their history] (which doesn't mean that they didn't have it)" and to "fill[ing] in the blanks that the slave narrative left" (97).

Unlike James Baldwin, who also defined his role as bearing witness, Morrison privileges the authority and epistemology of black and Third World women in America. "I use the phrase 'bear witness' to explain what my work is for," she told Steve Cannon and Ntozake Shange in 1977.

> I have this creepy sensation . . . of loss. Like something is either lost, never to be retrieved, or something is about to be lost and will never be retrieved. Because if we don't know . . . what our past is, . . . if we Third-World women in America don't know it, then, it is not known by anybody at all. . . . And somebody has to tell somebody something. (qtd. in Samuels and Hudson-Weems 139)

As narrative strategy, remembrance, in Morrison's words, is "a journey to a site to see what remains have been left behind and to reconstruct the world that these remains imply" (qtd. in Samuels and Hudson-Weems 97). As in Marcel Proust's *The Remembrance of Things Past,* the recovery of lost experience is triggered by some external, ostensibly insignificant event. For example, in *Beloved* Sethe

> worked hard to remember as close to nothing as was safe. Unfortunately her brain was devious. She might be hurrying across a field, running practically, to get to the pump quickly and rinse the chamomile sap from her legs. Nothing else would be in her mind. . . . Then something. The plash of water, the sight of her shoes and stockings awry on the path where she had flung them; or Here Boy lapping in the puddle near her feet, and suddenly there was Sweet Home rolling, rolling, rolling out before her eyes, and although there was not a leaf on that farm that did not make her want to scream, it rolled itself out before her in shameless beauty. It never looked as terrible as it was and it made her wonder if hell was a pretty place too. Fire and brimstone all right, but hidden in lacy groves. Boys hanging from the most beautiful sycamores in the world. It shamed her—remembering the wonderful soughing trees rather than the boys. Try as she might to make it otherwise, the sycamores beat out the children every time and she could not forgive her memory for that. (6)

On a sociopsychological level, *Beloved* is the story of Sethe Suggs's quest for social freedom and psychological wholeness. Sethe struggles with the haunting memory of her slave past and the retribution of Beloved, the ghost of the infant daughter that she killed in order to save her from the living death of slavery. On a legendary and mythic level, *Beloved* is a ghost story that frames embedded narratives of the impact of slavery, racism, and sexism on the capacity for love, faith, and community of black families, especially of black women, during the Reconstruction period. Set in post-Civil-War Cincinnati, *Beloved* is a womanist neo-slave narrative of double consciousness, a postmodern romance that speaks in many compelling voices and on several time levels of the historical rape of black American women and of the resilient spirit of blacks in surviving as a people.

As the author has explained in interviews and as a sympathetic white minister's report in the February 12, 1856, issue of the *American Baptist* reveals (see Bassett), at the center of *Beloved* is Morrison's retelling of the chilling historical account of a compassionate yet resolute self-emancipated mother's tough love. Margaret Garner, with the tacit sympathy of her sexagenarian mother-in-law, cut the throat of one of her four children and tried to kill the others to save them from the outrages of slavery that she had suffered. Guided by the spirits of the many thousands gone, as inscribed in her dedication, Morrison employs a multivocal text and a highly figurative language to probe her characters' double consciousness of their terribly paradoxical circumstances as people and non-people in a social arena of white male hegemony. She also foregrounds infanticide as a desperate act of " 'thick' " love (164) by a fugitive-slave mother "with iron eyes and backbone to match" (9). " 'Love is or it ain't,' " Sethe, the dramatized narrator/protagonist, says in reproach to a shocked friend, Paul D. " 'Thin love ain't love at all' " (164).

Indignantly reflecting on Paul D's metonymic reprimand that she " 'got two feet . . . not four' " (165), she later expands on their oppositional metaphors in reverie: "Too thick, he said. My love was too thick. What he know about it? Who in the world is he willing to die for? Would he give his privates to a stranger in return for a carving?" (203).

The implied author, the version of herself that Morrison creates as she creates the narrative (see Booth 70–75, 138, 151), brilliantly dramatizes the moral, sexual, and epistemological distances between Sethe and Paul D. After their first dialogue, a trackless, quiet forest abruptly appears between them. This metaphorical silence is an ingenious, ironic use of the technique of call and response that invites the implied reader—in Wolfgang Iser's words, that "network of response-inviting structures, which impel the reader to grasp the text" (34)—to pause and take stock of his or her own ambivalent moral and visceral responses to this slave mother's voicing of her thick love.

Thematically, the implied author interweaves racial and sexual consciousness in *Beloved*. Sethe's black awareness and rejection of white perceptions and inscriptions of herself, her children, and other slaves as nonhuman—marking them by letter, law, and lash as both animals and property—are synthesized with her black feminist sense of self-sufficiency. Sethe reconciles gender differences with first her husband Halle Suggs, and later Paul D, in heterosexual, endogamous relationships that affirm the natural and Biblical principles of the racial and ethnic survival of peoplehood through procreation and parenting in extended families. Although the implied author blends racial and sexual consciousness, the structure and style of the text foreground the ambivalence of slave women about motherhood that violates their personal integrity and that of their family.

Foregrounding the theme of motherhood, Morrison divides the text into twenty-eight unnumbered mini-sections, the usual number of days in a woman's monthly menstrual cycle, within three larger, disproportionate sections. Within these sections, Sethe experiences twenty-eight happy days of "having women friends, a mother-in-law, and all of her children together; of being part of a neighborhood; of, in fact, having neighbors at all to call her own" (173). Also within these sections, the passion and power of memory ebb and flow in a discontinuous, multivocal discourse of the present with the past. Unlike the univocal, nineteenth-century slave narratives, in which plot rides character in the protagonist's journey of transformation from object to subject, *Beloved* is a haunting story of a mother's love that frames a series of interrelated love stories (maternal, parental, filial, sororal, conjugal, heterosexual, familial, and communal) by multiple narrators. These stories begin in 1873 and end in 1874, but flash back intermittently to 1855. In the flashbacks and reveries, the omniscient narrator invokes ancestral black women's remembrances of the terror and horror of the Middle Passage. She also probes the deep physical and psychic wounds of Southern slavery, especially the paradoxes and perversities of life on Sweet Home plantation in Kentucky, and recalls Sethe's bold flight to freedom in Ohio in 1855. Freedom, as Paul D's and Sethe's stories most dramatically illustrate, is "to get to a place where you could love anything you chose—not to need permission for desire" (162).

The metaphors of personal and communal wholeness in the text heighten the psychological realism of its womanist themes of black kinship, motherhood, sisterhood, and love. Besides the structural analogue to a woman's natural reproductive cycle, the text frequently and dramatically highlights metaphors and metonyms for the agony and ecstasy, despair and hope, of loving, birthing, nurturing, and bonding. Heart, breasts, milk, butter, water, and trees—these recurring tropes first appear in the opening eight mini-sections as the vehicles for controlling the psychological, emotional, and moral distances among the narrators, characters, and implied reader, who participate, on various levels, in Sethe's historical and mythic quest.

After the omniscient narrator introduces us to the restless, spiteful spirit of Sethe's two-year-old daughter Beloved, we are quickly and irrevocably drawn into the vortex of conflicting values and feelings of the text. On one hand, we are drawn emotionally and psychologically closer to Sethe through her unrelenting memory of the terrible price she has paid for loving her daughter so dearly; but on the other, like Paul D and Ella, we are at first morally repelled by her gory act of infanticide. When slave catchers and schoolteacher suddenly appear in the family's Ohio yard to return Sethe and her children to slavery, she not only cuts Beloved's throat with a handsaw and attempts to kill her other three, but she subsequently trades ten minutes of sex on her daughter's grave with an engraver, as his son watches, to pay him for carving the word *Beloved* on her daughter's headstone.

Our sympathies for Sethe are strengthened, however, through her grim reverie and dialogue with Paul D. Through them we discover that, earlier in 1855, while pregnant with Denver and before she could escape with her husband Halle to join their children in Ohio with the milk to nurse her baby girl, she was outrageously violated. "I am full God damn it of two boys with mossy teeth," she remembers, "one sucking on my breast the other holding me down, their book-reading teacher watching and writing it up." Weaving into her story the additional gruesome details provided eighteen years later by Paul D, who knew her from their shared years of slavery on the ironically named Sweet Home plantation, the horror continues:

Add my husband to it, watching, above me in the loft—hiding close by—the one place he thought no one would look for him, looking down on what I couldn't look at at all. And not stopping them—looking and letting it happen. . . . There is also my husband squatting by the churn smearing the butter as well as its clabber all over his face because the milk they took is on his mind. And as far as he is concerned, the world may as well know it. (70)

Again we note the implied author's privileging of metaphor and metonym over black dialect to achieve just the right aesthetic balance between the poetics and polemics of the long black song of the many thousands gone that she skillfully orchestrates to engage our hearts and mind.

The collusion of many antebellum white women with the brutalization of black women is suggested by the ineffectual tears of the plantation mistress, Mrs. Garner, whom Sethe tells about the attack. In retaliation, Mrs. Garner's wryly named brother-in-law, who studies and treats slaves as animals, orders one of his nephews to whip Sethe. " 'Schoolteacher made one open up my back,' " Sethe tells Paul D, " 'and when it closed it made a tree. It grows there still' " (17). The ugly scar on her back is described as having the trunk, branches, leaves, and blossoms of a chokecherry tree by Amy Denver, the runaway, ragged, and hungry indentured white girl who, in sharp contrast to Mrs. Garner, not only massages Sethe's swollen feet but also helps to deliver her baby on the Ohio River bank. Unlike most of the black female narrators, Amy, whose quest for velvet rather than love is the principal sign of her racial, sexual, and class difference, is not raped, and she stands as the implied author's brightest ray of hope for black and white sisterhood. When Paul D hears about Sethe's stolen milk and bitter-fruit tree, he bends down behind her in the kitchen, "his body an arc of kindness," and holds her breasts in his hands as he "rub[s] his cheek on her back and learn[s] that way her sorrow, the roots of it; its wide trunk and intricate branches" (17). Symbolically, the chokecherry tree signifies the physical and psychic suffering of slavery that Paul D shares with Sethe.

As the text unfolds with the ebb and flow of characters, events, and memories, these figures of speech are developed in free association and free indirect discourse—the linguistic fusion of two narrative voices. Occasionally, the implied author's consciousness merges with the narrator's, the narrator/protagonist's with the characters', the past with the present, and the black female's with the male's. These techniques compel the reader viscerally and cerebrally to fill in the gaps in the text of the fragmented, yet complementary, embedded stories and memories of Baby Suggs, Nan, Sethe's mother, Ella, Stamp Paid, and Paul D. The implied reader is moved by these illustrative comparisons and contrasts to reconstruct and reconsider the unspeakable human cost of American slavery, racism, and sexism, then and now—to whites as well as blacks, to men as well as women—and to sympathize with Sethe, black mothers, and black families in their struggle against white male hegemony to affirm their self-worth as a racial group.

The Gothic story of Sethe's loving and losing Beloved is thematically and emotionally emblematic of the historical struggle for survival with self-respect and love of black families that has been passed on orally and spiritually from generation to generation. " 'Not a house in the country ain't packed to its rafters with some dead Negro's grief,' " Sethe's sixty-year-old mother-in-law tells her. " 'You lucky. You got three left. . . . I had eight. Every one of them gone away from me. Four taken, four chased, and all, I expect, worrying somebody's house into evil' " (5). Sethe tells her daughters the horror story of her mother as passed on to her by Nan, the one-armed slave wet nurse and cook who became her surrogate mother. For Sethe was nursed only two or three weeks by her mother, a field slave branded with a circle and cross under her breast, before she was turned over to Nan, who, along with Sethe's mother, had been raped many times by crew members during the Middle Passage. The children fathered by these and other whites, Sethe's mother threw away. " 'Without names, she threw them,' " Nan tells young Sethe in a pidgin tongue that implicitly valorizes the ancestral life-bestowing power of naming rituals, a tongue and ritual bonding that are only a dim memory for Sethe. " 'You she gave the name of the black man. She put her arms around him. The others she did not put her arms around. Never. Never' " (62).

Ella, an agent on the Underground Railroad who twice rescues Sethe, believes in root medicine but not love. As a result of Ella's having been regularly abused sexually while in puberty by her master and his son, " 'the lowest yet,' " she considers sex disgusting and love a "serious disability." She remembers having delivered, "but would not nurse, a hairy white thing, fathered by 'the lowest yet' " (258–59). While she understands Sethe's rage in the shed, she regards Sethe's reaction as prideful and misdirected. Even so, ". . . Ella didn't like the idea of past errors taking possession of the present . . . of sin moving on in the house, unleashed and sassy" (256). Morally and emotionally, the relationship of the past to the present is relative, not absolute.

Similarly, Baby Suggs, an "unchurched preacher" who is driven to bed to think about the colors of things by the un-Christian ways of white Christians, passes on the bittersweet wisdom of her years in stories she tells to her granddaughter Denver and her daughter-in-law Sethe. Baby Suggs's heart, her faith and love, began to collapse twenty-eight days after Sethe's arrival, when white slave catchers violated her home and terrorized Sethe into killing Beloved, the daughter of the only son Baby Suggs was allowed to mother, Halle. "What she called the nastiness of life," the sympathetic implied author tells us in free indirect discourse,

> was the shock she received upon learning that nobody stopped playing checkers just because the pieces included her children. Halle she was able to keep the longest. Twenty years. A lifetime. Given to her, no doubt, to make up for *hearing* that her two girls, neither of whom had their adult teeth, were sold and gone and she had not been able to wave goodbye. To make up for coupling with a straw boss for four months in exchange for keeping her third child, a boy, with her—only to have him traded for lumber in spring of the next year and to find herself pregnant by the man who promised not to and did. That child she could not love and the rest she would not. "God take what He would," she said. And He did, and He did, and He did and then gave her Halle who gave her freedom when it didn't mean a thing. (23)

The double consciousness and double vision here (which some readers will recognize as analogous to Mikhail M. Bakhtin's theory of double-voiced or dialogic texts) are apparent in the interplay and interweaving of the represented discourse, time frames, and perspectives of the implied author and Baby Suggs.

In addition to the three basic types of represented discourse (direct, simple indirect, and free indirect), five different yet related linguistic codes and their concomitant ideologies (i.e., their implicit, related systems of beliefs and values) are present in *Beloved:* standard American English, rural black vernacular English, black feminist discourse, black patriarchal discourse, and white male hegemonic discourse. The two dominant voices, however, are in standard American English and black feminist discourse. For example, the implied author and the dramatized narrator/protagonist, Sethe, want Beloved and the implied reader to understand that, far worse than Beloved's grisly death, is

> that anybody white could take your whole self for anything that came to mind. Not just work, kill, or maim you, but dirty you. Dirty you so bad you couldn't like yourself anymore. Dirty you so bad you forgot who you were and couldn't think it up. And though she and others lived through and got over it, she could never let it happen to her own. The best thing she was, was her children. Whites might dirty *her* all right, but not her best thing, her beautiful, magical best thing—the part of her that was clean. (251)

In contrast, Denver tells her sister Beloved the legend of her birth and of the white girl with "no meanness around her mouth" whose name she bears (77).

In an apparent rewriting of Faulkner's narrative strategy in dramatizing Shreve and Quentin's reconstruction and reliving of Charles Bon and Henry Sutpen's fatal kinship in *Absalom, Absalom!,* Morrison employs Denver to voice the manner and degree to which storyteller, story, and primary audience of *Beloved* share a concord of sensibilities in a residually oral culture which sanctions the dynamic coexistence of the spoken and written word, the metaphysical and physical, the mythic and historic:

> Denver was seeing it now and feeling it—through Beloved. Feeling how it must have felt to her mother. Seeing how it must have looked. And the more fine points she made, the more detail she provided, the more Beloved liked it. So she anticipated the questions by giving blood to the scraps her mother and grandmother had told her—and a heartbeat. The monologue became, in fact, a duet as they lay down together, Denver nursing Beloved's interest like a lover whose pleasure was to overfeed the loved. (78)

Near the end of the novel, in sections 22 and 23, the consciousness of Sethe, Denver, and Beloved merge in free indirect discourse and surrealism.

Unlike Morrison's *The Bluest Eye* and the womanist texts of Alice Walker, in *Beloved* black men are not stereotyped as "low-down dirty dog[s]," like the nameless Assistant and the Wild Child's anonymous impregnator in

Meridian (59–61, 24) and Mr. _____ and even God in *The Color Purple* (170, 164). Although circumstances may reduce some to debasing themselves with cows, clabber, or the daughters of their lovers, Baby Suggs, Sethe, and the implied author agree: " 'A man ain't nothing but a man . . .' " (23). Even Garner, the benevolent master of Sweet Home, stands out among his white neighbors for treating his slaves (Paul D, Paul A, Paul F, Halle, and Sixo) like men. " 'Bought em thataway, raised em thataway,' " he boasts with dramatic irony. Garner allows Halle to hire himself out on weekends for five years to buy his mother's freedom, allows his slaves to have guns, and even allows them to marry rather than breed them like animals. Thus, although Sethe was a desirable young girl of thirteen when she arrived at the plantation, the Sweet Home men, who were all in their twenties and "so sick with the absence of women they had taken to calves," did not rape her. They "let the iron-eyed girl be, so she could choose" (10). Clearly, the theme, protagonist, structure, and style privilege a black woman's perspective, but sexual politics complements rather than dominates racial politics in the implied author's celebration of black people as more than the dehumanized victims of brutal social oppression.

In her multivocal celebration of the spiritual resiliency of black people, black men and women are physically and psychologically violated by slavery, racism, and sexism in the text. (These violations were exacerbated by the infamous Fugitive Slave Act of 1850, which legalized the kidnapping and enslavement of any black person anywhere in the United States.) With Garner's death, "schoolteacher broke into children what Garner had raised into men" (220). So after Paul F is sold, the other slaves attempt unsuccessfully to escape. Sixo is burned alive and shot; Paul A is hanged and mutilated; Sethe is raped and beaten; and Halle loses his mind after witnessing his wife's violation. Paul D is forced to wear a three-spoked collar and mouth bit while waiting to be sold down river where he and other black prisoners are terrorized with fellatio and death. Paul D's reverie explains his subsequent seduction by Beloved while he is Sethe's lover as "more like a brainless urge to stay alive" than a desire to have fun (264). Also "dirtied" by whites, Stamp Paid, the conductor on the Underground Railroad who ferries Sethe to Ohio and snatches Denver from death in a woodshed, was born Joshua. But

> . . . he renamed himself when he handed over his wife to his master's son. Handed her over in the sense that he did not kill anybody, thereby himself, because his wife demanded he stay alive. . . . With that gift, he decided that he didn't owe anybody anything. Whatever his obligations were, that act paid them off. (184–85)

For the characters, narrator, and the implied author, the scars of sexual, racial, and class oppression on the soul—the price of the ticket for the journey from slavery to freedom and from object to subject—are more horrible than those on the body.

Even so, the struggle to survive with justifiable self-respect rather than inordinate self-esteem or self-debasement prevails for those who affirm ties to their ethnic community. When the community perceives excessive pride in Sethe and Baby Suggs, as illustrated by the former's "stand offishness" and the latter's extravagant blackberry party, it feels insulted and rejected—which is why no one from the community warns them about the slave catchers' approach. After sixty years of a life with less sunshine than rain, Stamp Paid reflects, ". . . to belong to a community of other free Negroes—to love and be loved by them, to counsel and be counseled, protect and be protected, feed and be fed—and then to have that community step back and hold itself at a distance—well, it could wear out even a Baby Suggs, holy" (177). But Ella and the community of thirty black women come praying and singing to Sethe's rescue after Denver reaches out to the community and after Beloved "t[a]k[es] flesh" in the world as a "devil-child" and nearly hounds Sethe to death (257–61).

The arrival, departure, and return of Paul D, however, provide the frame-story for Sethe's realization of personal wholeness in the community and Morrison's synthesis of sexual and racial politics. With Paul D's arrival at Sethe's haunted house, she can suddenly "trust things and remember things because the last of the Sweet Home men was there to catch her if she sank" (18). In her mind's eye, "there was something blessed in his manner. Women saw him and wanted to weep. . . . Strong women and wise saw him and told him things they only told each other . . ." (17). Paul D leaves Sethe after being shocked by her confession of infanticide and after responding insensitively about the number of feet Sethe has. This remark is associated in the minds of the protagonist and, with mixed emotions, the implied reader with schoolteacher's belief and value systems as dramatized in his listing of Sethe's "characteristics on the animal side" (251).

Paul D returns to 124 Bluestone Road after Denver and the choral community of black women break Beloved's evil spell because he wants to take care of Sethe, who has withdrawn in despair to die in Baby Suggs's bed. As he proceeds to rekindle the will to live of the woman who, as Sixo said of his woman, is " 'a friend of [his] mind' " by bathing her, he remembers how she "left him his manhood" by not mentioning his being collared like a beast. Putting "his story next to hers" as the framestory closes in a romantic vignette, he holds her hand and tells her that she is her best thing and that " '. . . we got more yesterday than anybody. We need some kind of tomorrow' " (273).

In her multivocal remembrances of things past, Morrison probes the awesome will to live of her characters in order to celebrate the truth and resiliency of the complex double consciousness of their humanity. What she has wrought in *Beloved* is an extraordinarily effective Gothic blend of postmodern realism and romance as well as of racial and sexual politics.

Works Cited

Bakhtin, Mikhail M. *The Dialogic Imagination: Four Essays.* Trans. Caryl Emerson and Michael Holquist. Ed. Holquist. Austin: U of Texas P, 1981.

Bassett, P. S. "A Visit to the Slave Mother Who Killed Her Child." *American Baptist* 12 Feb. 1856: n.p. Rpt. *The Black Book.* Comp. Middleton Harris, et al. New York: Random, 1974. 10.

Booth, Wayne C. *The Rhetoric of Fiction.* Chicago: U of Chicago P, 1961.

Du Bois, W. E. B. "Strivings of the Negro People." *Atlantic* Aug. 1897: 194–96.

Ellison, Ralph. *Shadow and Act.* New York: Random, 1964.

Herskovits, Melville J. *Life in a Haitian Valley.* New York: Knopf, 1937.

Iser, Wolfgang. *The Act of Reading.* Baltimore: Johns Hopkins UP, 1978.

Morrison, Toni. *Beloved.* New York: Knopf, 1987.

Park, Robert E. *Introduction to the Science of Sociology.* 2nd ed. Chicago: U of Chicago P, 1928.

Proust, Marcel. *Remembrance of Things Past.* Trans. C. K. Scott Moncrieff and Terence Kilmartin. Vol. 1. New York: Vintage, 1982.

Samuels, Wilfred D., and Clenora Hudson-Weems. *Toni Morrison.* Boston: Twayne, 1990.

Walker, Alice. *The Color Purple.* New York: Harcourt, 1982.

———. *In Search of Our Mothers' Gardens.* New York: Harcourt, 1983.

———. *Meridian.* New York: Harcourt, 1976.

Call and Response as Critical Method: African-American Oral Traditions and *Beloved*

MAGGIE SALE

Presenting herself as a proponent of "Black art," Toni Morrison distinguishes her position from that of early advocates of the Black Aesthetic, some of whom believed in a single, "politically correct" way to write African-American literature, stating, "Nothing would be more hateful to me than a monolithic prescription for what Black literature is or ought to be" ("Memory" 389). She is aware that not all U.S. authors of African descent focus on African-American culture or characters, either stylistically or thematically, and that white authors sometimes write about black characters. Morrison willingly recognizes "that there are eminent and powerful, intelligent and gifted Black writers who not only recognize Western literature as part of their own heritage but who have employed it to such an advantage that it illuminates both cultures" (389). Yet she wants to distinguish her approach from those that actively utilize Western or European literary forms and traditions.

In her own writing, Morrison works within a specific aesthetic, if not literary, tradition, and describes her project this way: "I simply wanted to write literature that was irrevocably, indisputably Black, not because its characters were, or because I was, but because it took as its creative task and sought as its credentials those recognized and verifiable principles of Black art" (389). Thus Morrison rejects the prescriptiveness associated with the Black Aesthetic, while choosing to use a number of the theoretical concepts developed within it. In attempting "to write literature that [is] irrevocably, indisputably Black," Morrison privileges "those recognized and verifiable principles of Black art"[1] which she details in the following passage:

> If my work is faithfully to reflect the aesthetic tradition of Afro-American culture, it must make conscious use of the characteristics of its art forms and translate them into print: antiphony, the group nature of art, its functionality, its improvisational nature, its relationship to audience performance. . . . (388–89)

First published in *African American Review* 26, no. 1 (1992): 41–50. © Maggie Sale; reprinted with the permission of the author.

The characteristics listed here are aspects of African-American oral traditions, and are interrelated rather than discrete. Antiphony or call and response, function, improvisation, and audience performance can all be thought of as part of the group or communal nature of art. This theory of art is interactive, process-oriented, and concerned with innovation, rather than mimetic, product-oriented, or static. Call-and-response patterns provide a basic model that depends and thrives upon audience performance and improvisation, which work together to ensure that the art will be meaningful or functional to the community.

My argument is that Morrison's latest novel, *Beloved,* is an oral text shaped by the principles outlined above, with a special emphasis on improvisation and call-and-response patterns. Such a reading goes beyond the vexed question of authorial intent—i.e., reading *Beloved* the way that Morrison says that we should—by showing the importance of incorporating the above-stated principles of African-American oral traditions into ways of thinking about history and systems of critical inquiry. *Beloved* not only presents "new" perspectives, but foregrounds the power and problematics of perspective itself; this text suggests a complex method of reading and interpreting that values multiplicity rather than codification and polemic, while simultaneously refusing the problematic notion that all positions are equally valid.

Call-and-response patterns, developed in spirituals and play and work songs, are related to the group or communal nature of art; these patterns both value improvisation and demand that new meanings be created for each particular moment. The valuing of these characteristics suggests that importance lies not only in what is said, but also in how it is said. The assumption is that a story will be repeated and will change with every telling, and that the success of the telling, and so of the particular story, resides not so much in its similarity to the original as in its individual nuances and its ability to involve others. Improvisation gives authority to the improviser based on how well he or she recreates the story to fit individual and group needs as they present themselves at the specific moment of the telling. Such a theory of art demands and values change over continuity, within a given, agreed upon structure.

Structured on these principles, *Beloved* presents a new way of conceiving of history, one that refuses and refutes master versions of history. Such master versions value certainty and exactitude and claim authority through a covert and convenient erasure of the teller's (writer's) perspective. They collapse the multiplicity of voices available at any given historical moment into an artificial and repressive synthesis of diverse material, which presents itself as definitive. Most histories of slavery, traditional and revisionist, follow this model by presenting themselves as authoritative versions of this vexed past superseding all other representations. In contrast, *Beloved* does not assert a "definitive" version of the Margaret Garner case, the historical event upon which the novel is based,[2] but rather offers several contradictory versions of Garner's (hi)story, which exist simultaneously, yet complementarily. In this schema, each version gains authority from the performance and persona of the teller, from her or his ability to involve and persuade others. The teller is implicated in her or his particular version of the (hi)story and each version, or (hi)story, is as "true" as the teller (writer) can make it, where that "truth" depends upon an alliance and agreement between teller and listener.[3] Within the novel, individual (hi)stories are told, listened to, and believed depending upon the relation between teller and listener. Similarly, these individual (hi)stories combine to create the text of *Beloved,* whose (hi)story as a whole is told (written), listened to (read), and believed depending upon the relation between teller (writer) and listener (reader).

Thus in this conception of history, derived from call-and-response patterns and the communal nature of art, the always operative, but sometimes masked, factor of perspective is foregrounded. In contrast to master versions of history, which erroneously present themselves as independent of their makers and so of any particular perspective, the history created in *Beloved* both emphasizes the importance of perspective and requires the articulation of multiple perspectives. Because it is performative in nature and communally based, this kind of (hi)story depends upon the repeated interaction of the one and the many; recognition, authority, and responsibility for this (hi)story not only require but relish audience participation, the contributions of many tellers (writers) and listeners (readers).

These principles from African-American oral traditions have a powerful effect when used to evoke the sense of an enslaved past. *Beloved*'s black characters are by and large "illiterate": The Sweet Home men are not interested in learning how to read because "nothing important to them could be put down on paper" (*Beloved* 125); others can write only their names; Sethe can recognize seventy-five written words; only Stamp Paid, Lady Jones, and eventually Denver can actually read. The picture of Sethe accompanying the newspaper article detailing her "crime" is emblematic of how the majority of African Americans in the nineteenth century were objects of writing, rather than its producers and consumers. *Beloved* thus represents a different population of enslaved and formerly enslaved people from that represented by the antebellum slave narrators and the authors of postbellum autobiographies.[4] While *Beloved* cannot be said to recreate the "actual" oral traditions of enslaved African Americans, Morrison's use of the principles outlined above inserts a contemporary sense of African-American oral traditions into her representation of an enslaved and formerly enslaved past. These principles are, in some form, descendants of African and enslaved cultures. Thus Morrison uses the descendant to form the ancestor, creating a text and a sense of the past that are, in her words, "irrevocably, indisputably Black."

A number of elements from these oral traditions influence the narrative strategies and thematics of *Beloved,* and significant among them are the ways in which call-and-response patterns are "translated into print." A familiar antiphonal form appears thematically at the end of the novel: "Denver saw only lowered heads, but could not hear the lead prayer—only the earnest syllables of agreement that backed it: Yes, yes, yes, oh yes. Hear me. Hear me. Do it, Maker, do it" (258). Earlier on, inanimate objects act the part of an underscoring chorus; when Sethe makes it clear she doesn't want Paul D sleeping outside in the cold any longer, "she smile[s] at him, and like a friend in need, the chimney cough[s] against the rush of cold shooting into it from the sky" (130). Baby Suggs, holy, as woods preacher, sends out a healing call to different sections of the community, and they respond with laughing, dancing, crying, and finally with an answering song so that she might dance (87–89). Call-and-response patterns both structure and are the theme of Sethe and Beloved's relationship. Sethe's guilt, which she acknowledges only to her murdered child, keeps that child alive and eventually calls her back into the physical world. Beloved calls Sethe to account once Sethe realizes who she is, and Sethe responds endlessly but uselessly, since the healing response is not reciprocal. When Sethe and Beloved become locked in a narrowing spiral that threatens to destroy the mother even as it feeds the child, Denver leaves her self-imposed exile, calling the women of the community, who respond with food and later with spiritual assistance.

When considered in a larger frame, call-and-response patterns are related to audience (reader) participation in that the text suggests, or calls, implicitly asking for a response. One example is how stories are left unfinished or unclarified: We never learn exactly what happened to Halle, either before Sethe was attacked or afterward; or what happened to Howard and Buglar—or even, finally, to Beloved. In some cases, as with Sethe's sons, there is no participation on the part of the reader because the boys leave the narrative unambiguously, and speculation is not called for. But Morrison's representation of Beloved invites readers to respond, to think over her appearance, her disappearance, her symbolic being, to be active in creating the meaning of this text. A different kind of example, one external to the text, is how Morrison's representation of Sethe and her act of infanticide challenges readers to examine their own responses to this event and the circumstances surrounding it. *Beloved* presents and clarifies social problems without resolving them, and so raises, or calls out, issues to be discussed, or to be responded to, by readers or the community.[5] This call for communal response is part of the contemporary healing process that this text is involved in.

124 Bluestone Road, when it was a way station on the Underground Railroad, is described as a place "where bits of news soaked like dried beans in spring water—until they were soft enough to digest" (65). The text of *Beloved* functions in a similar way for contemporary readers: as a textual space in which the horrors of slavery and the sometimes equally horrific responses to it by the (formerly) enslaved are not simply denied, or justified, or explained away, but are presented through an empowering use of oral traditions and language so that they become *digestible*.[6] This approach encourages multiple

ways of seeing and interpreting, and so gives readers access to difficult material that encourages responses that are not exclusively defensive or justifying, but complex and often contradictory. The novel itself does not judge Sethe's act of infanticide, although certain characters do; the point is not simply to judge, but to move, as readers, through the many positions that make up this complex situation.

Beloved's approach to slavery is markedly different from previous representations either of this particular event or of a (formerly) enslaved past, which most often posit a singular or one-dimensional response pattern. The abolitionist press, for example, represented Margaret Garner's act of infanticide as in the heroic tradition of the American fight for Liberty, calling upon readers to sympathize unequivocally with Garner, as they would with Patrick Henry.[7] As Rachel Myers points out, this polemical interpretation erases the emotional cost of Garner's decision: Her choice to kill her baby is appropriated into an abolitionist discourse that denies the complexity of her emotional life, as well as her subjectivity. Conversely, because pro-slavery writers figured slavery as an uplifting institution for heathen Africans, where a divinely sanctioned aristocracy gently rested on the labor of contented slaves, in their discourse an act such as Garner's is marked as barbaric, bloodthirsty, and deviant, and calls for a shocked, condescending, even angry response. These are just two examples that illustrate a locking into position, characteristic of polemics, that obstructs or denies the validity of any other view, and which prevents this difficult past from becoming "digestible." *Beloved* presents a new way of conceiving this past, simultaneously allowing for conflict, inequality, multiplicity, and healing—a point I will return to shortly.

In addition to call-and-response patterns, improvisation and repetition are incorporated thematically and structurally in the text of *Beloved*. Repetition is one way storytellers remember their narratives and cue their listeners regarding important elements.[8] An example of repetition that involves improvisation comes when Sethe and Halle make love for the first time in the corn field: "How loose the silk. How jailed down the juice. . . . How loose the silk. How quick the jailed-up flavor ran free. . . . How loose the silk. How fine and loose and free" (27). This kind of progression is characteristic of the blues and is a simple form of improvisation. A more complicated progression is evident in the way "one thousand feet of the best hand-forged chain in Georgia" becomes "dance two-step to the music of hand-forged iron" becomes "they chain-danced over the fields" (107–08). These progressions are not the same as the common literary motif of repeating images or themes. The patterns I've quoted here occur close to one another in the text, within a few sentences or paragraphs, rather than as threads running through and organizing the entire narrative, and as such they form brief moments in the text that are analogous to a single song.

The latter example comes from the chapter in which Paul D's experience on a chain gang in Alfred, Georgia, is related; it is told as a scene of instruction, an experience that has to be remembered and passed on, though no one wants to, in a novel that "is not a story to pass on" (275). This difficult remembering is also part of the contemporary healing process, where the stories in *Beloved* come back in pieces small and "soft enough to digest" (65); these stories de-authorize the original figures in power—in the case of Paul D's story, the "whitemen" whose power lay in the guns they held—because they are retold by methods that authorize the teller and the thematically disenfranchised through the foregrounding of their perspectives. In this particular story, repetitions with variations emphasize the oral aspect of the story so that the tale takes on the quality of a fable. This brief chapter is thematically similar to the antebellum slave narratives in its representation of almost unbelievable escape from the depths of degradation, yet it rewrites these earlier narratives with an oral rather than a literary style. Thus, *Beloved* presents a heroic story that is analogous to the antebellum narratives, but which articulates the experience of a population not otherwise represented in nineteenth-century texts, in a style perhaps more appropriate to that experience.

Improvisation or, in this case, repetition with variations also structures the first section of the novel and the way Sethe's escape from slavery and the events leading up to her baby's death are told over and over from a number of different perspectives. This process of retelling describes the outermost circling paths of a deepening and narrowing spiral that is the form of the novel. Each of these circling paths is demarcated by the peeling away of emotional defenses to reveal an individual character's remembered story about the infanticide or events leading up to it. The remembered stories come in digestible bits and pieces, emphasizing slightly different or new material depending on the particular perspective, which, when considered together, move chronologically toward the act. The center of the spiral, the place to which the circling stories lead, is the relationship of Sethe and Beloved, the second half of the novel spinning on the unresolvable emotional fact of a mother's killing her daughter in an attempt to keep her safe. During the first section readers are asked simply to piece the stories together, a job much like Ella's "listen[ing] for the holes—the things the fugitives did not say" (92). Because most of these partial stories involve Sethe's rather miraculous escape from slavery, readers are given views of Sethe that ingratiate her to them before they are exposed to the harshness of her act. It is not until Sethe and Beloved claim one another, and lock all others outside, an event marked by the disappearance of their perspectives from the narrative, that readers are forced, whatever their earlier impressions, to see this relationship as entirely exclusive and, therefore, in the terms set by the novel, as deeply destructive.

In order to make connections among the emotional stakes, the concepts of history, and the principles of oral traditions at issue here, I want next to consider two points on this deepening spiral: Denver's telling of her birth to Beloved, and Sethe's attempt to tell Paul D why she reacted as she did when schoolteacher stepped into her yard. In the opening chapter of the novel,

Sethe alludes to the "whitegirl" who had called her beaten back a chokecherry tree, and a little later Denver "step[s] into the told story" (29) of this "whitegirl's good hands" and how they had healed Sethe's grotesquely swollen feet. Yet because Sethe has seldom spoken to Denver of the past, when asked to tell the story of her mother's escape and her own birth, Denver has to "swallow twice to prepare for the telling, to construct out of the strings she had heard all her life a net to hold Beloved" (76). In each of these progressive scenes a story with similar elements is reworked with different emphases, so that readers (the external audience) learn more of the story but, just as importantly, they learn about the respective tellers through the elements they emphasize. For Sethe, the stolen milk is more important than the whipping she receives, because the milk's being taken is an outrage not only upon her physical body, but also upon her "motherlove"; Denver attaches particular importance to the "whitegirl" who named her, Amy, and the story of her own birth, the only story of her mother's about slavery that includes her.

In the following scene between Beloved and Denver, Beloved's obsession to hear about Sethe and Denver's need to hold Beloved's attention affect the story's (re)construction, determine how the tale is told:

> The monologue became . . . a duet as they lay down together, Denver nursing Beloved's interest like a lover whose pleasure was to overfeed the loved. . . . Denver spoke, Beloved listened, and the two did the best they could to create what really happened, how it really was, something only Sethe knew because she alone had the mind for it and the time afterward to shape it: the quality of Amy's voice, her breath like burning wood. (78)

The story of "what really happened" is a fiction created from mutual need, in this case the needs of the two characters, but this idea is also applicable to the intentions of a text and the needs of its readers. Denver develops the story from bits and pieces, "strings she had heard all her life" (76), creating with Beloved a particular narrative that would not otherwise exist. Even for Sethe, who "had the mind for it" (78), the story has to be shaped from the loose recollections of memory, where the quality of a character's voice and the feel of her fingers are as important as what she says.

The passage reveals the process of creating oral history out of memories and how this process depends upon the interaction between the perspectives and needs of teller(s) and listener(s). The implications of this passage move beyond the boundaries of the text to challenge notions of objectivity in the creation of history: Who is saying (or writing) what to whom, and how they're saying (or writing) it, is of the utmost importance to the meaning of what gets said (written). Not only does Beloved foreground its own construction as history and fiction, but it asserts that all historical narratives participate in a similar fictionalizing that reveals as much about the writer (teller) as it recovers of the past.

Three other versions of "what really happened" immediately precede Sethe's own: those of Baby Suggs, schoolteacher, and Stamp Paid. Both Baby Suggs's and Stamp Paid's stories recall the party the day before, and the resulting resentment of the community with its tragic consequences. Schoolteacher's chapter is the only one in the novel entirely given over to a white perspective; he judges Sethe's act with the distorting assumption of racial superiority characteristic of a pro-slavery stance. To schoolteacher, the infanticide and Sethe's attempt to kill her other children is simply "testimony to the results of a little so-called freedom imposed on people who needed every care and guidance in the world to keep them from the cannibal life they preferred" (151). By the time Sethe tells her own version at the end of the first section of the novel, the spiraling stories have narrowed toward a spin, "round and round the room" (159). Her story is different from each of the earlier versions, not a recounting of the event at all, but a painting of Sethe's relationship with Beloved as it was under slavery in an attempt to give Paul D enough pieces so that he might draw her same conclusion. But

> Sethe knew that the circle she was making around the room, him, the subject, would remain one. That she could never close in, pin it down for anybody who had to ask. If they didn't get it right off—she could never explain. (163)

This passage suggests that only someone who already shares Sethe's particular perspective, her position, could understand why she killed her child. Yet one of the novel's projects is to get readers to do exactly that: move to a position from which they can understand why Sethe did what she did and claims what she does. The novel's structure also insists that readers move among positions and inhabit multiple perspectives.[9]

This structural insistence is thematically paralleled in the way the tellings of Sethe's act of infanticide move along a circling path demarcated by elements that cannot be resolved: Sethe's desperate situation as a runaway woman with children being remanded to slavery; her deep offense at schoolteacher's suggestion of her inhumanity; the marvel of her escape with all her children; the frightening intensity of her claim to her children, bred from slavery's very denial of this claim; her child's extreme helplessness coupled with her crude, unflinching violence. These elements are presented in such a way that any one of them constitutes only a part of the whole, each needing to be balanced by a consideration of all of the others. Thus Sethe's circling and the spiraling stories are a metaphor for what is asked of readers: the refusal to rest on any single element.

In the first section, readers move through the various versions of Sethe's story, all of which are told from more or less empathetic perspectives. But when Paul D forces Sethe to look at her memories, to try to explain them to him, she locks herself into a single position, that of justification. This locking into position enables Sethe to recognize Beloved as her daughter, but it also sets her into a spinning pattern with that murdered and resurrected child from which she cannot, and perhaps does not want to, escape. When Sethe locks the door of 124 (198), just as she has locked herself into justification, the women become stuck in a web of possession that excludes readers—"You are mine / You are mine / You are mine" (217)—and that eventually excludes Denver. This exclusion proves too much for Denver; excluded once from the world outside 124 by a boy recalling the time she spent in jail with her mother, Denver is forced back into that world when Beloved and Sethe exclude her from their lives. Denver's journey out into Cincinnati breaks her off from the deadly spiral of her mother and sister, and she begins a new cycle, her own spiral, but now one that widens rather than narrows. As Denver develops the ability to participate in the community, to move between positions, her character becomes the narrative focus of the last section of the novel. Denver, born on her mother's road to freedom, emerges as the agent of this battered family's recuperation and regeneration.

This representation of Sethe's complex emotional life and the difficulty of her situation challenges schoolteacher's figuring of her as an animalistic cannibal, and the equally one-dimensional representations of Margaret Garner in the abolitionist and mainstream presses as either a heroine or a monster. Such one-dimensional representations of Garner/Sethe indicate a locking into position that denies the validity of other positions and that is characteristic of linear, definitive history. But *Beloved* insists on a flexibility among perspectives that rhetorically challenges both traditional and revisionist conceptions of history that are presented through linear arguments.

Despite this plurality, *Beloved*'s method of revisioning the past does not authorize all perspectives equally; schoolteacher's perspective is articulated, but it is not sanctioned, and the positions of both the "good" slave-holding Garners and the abolitionist Bodwins are deeply problematized. Amy Denver is the only white character who has a positive relation with Sethe, made possible, the text implies, by her similar status as an abused, but now escaped, indentured servant. One might conclude from this that only the perspectives of "whitepeople" are not given equal weight and validity, and this is true within the context of the novel: Whereas Sethe once believed ". . . she could discriminate among [whitepeople]. . . . she had come to believe every one of Baby Suggs' last words . . ." (188) that all evil in the world came from white folks. Yet I would argue that the perspectives of the "whitepeople" are problematic not because of an essential, immutable difference between white and black people, which is after all the premise upon which the justification for slavery rests, but because of the way "whitepeople" operated within the context of slavery and continue to operate, to a greater or lesser extent, within the racist society that is its legacy. An ideology of Anglo-Saxon supremacy fundamentally organized the cultural logic of the United States before the Civil War, affecting all peoples living within that context. The perspectives of those who benefited from these notions of racial superiority included a fundamental inability to appreciate racial and cultural difference—a tendency which characterized the thinking of even the most progressive abolitionists. It is this inability that links the diverse perspectives of the Bodwins, the Garners, and schoolteacher in Morrison's novel; it is this inability that *Beloved* articulates but absolutely refuses to authorize.

For those who were specifically oppressed by the nineteenth-century ideology of white supremacy, traditional and "mainstream" representations of slavery have continued the legacy of oppression by distorting and ignoring their experience. *Beloved* grows out of and joins with a contemporary movement begun by scholars such as John Blassingame, Eugene Genovese, and Herbert Gutman to shift the terms of the representation of slavery by re-envisioning this vexed past from the perspective of the enslaved.[10] Yet *Beloved* should also be seen as entering this contemporary dialogue, this complex call and response, on terms similar to Angela Davis's *Woman, Race and Class,* Deborah Gray White's *Ar'n't I A Woman,* and Sherley Anne Williams's *Dessa Rose,* all of which respond not only to the negative stereotyping of African Americans in traditional histories of slavery, but also to the lack of attention paid specifically to the importance of gender and the experience of enslaved women in the first wave of revisionist histories. Like other revisionist projects of the past two decades, *Beloved* shifts the terms of representation by moving those marginalized by traditional and "mainstream" histories to the center, and forcing those traditionally at the center to the margins. Yet unlike many other revisionist projects, the center presented in *Beloved* is multiple, contradictory, and unresolvable. Authority for this center rests not in the false rigor of a singular argument or polemic, but in its persuasiveness and the alliances built between the text (teller) and its audience/readers/listeners.

This essay began with a discussion of Morrison's formulation of her work's relation to Black art and the Black Aesthetic; I would like to end by rethinking this formulation in the context of my discussion of *Beloved.* Morrison's refusal of the prescriptiveness of the Black Aesthetic is embodied in the form of *Beloved,* in which a politically informed, multivocal discourse values innovation and difference rather than continuity and similarity. I join with Hazel Carby in thinking that contemporary movements to create an African-American literary tradition, as with all traditions, tend "to create unity out of disunity and to resolve the social contradiction, or differences, between texts" (127). I would like to suggest a different stance, one that refuses to reproduce the marginalizing project of tradition and canon building, and adopts instead the interactive, dialogic model of interpretation presented in *Beloved,* both within critical systems at large and within our own individual practices as critics. An adoption of this model would foreground the ideological, without resorting to prescriptions; it would transform the tone and methods of critical discourse by allowing for complexity, contradiction, and differences, without accepting all positions as equally valid.

Notes

1.   It is uncertain whether Morrison thinks that a white writer utilizing the principles she sets forth here would produce African-American literature, or whether all three characteristics are needed—i.e., principles of "Black art," an African-American author, and African-American characters.

2.   Rachel Myers has shown that the historical record of this event is at best unstable, differing versions of it appearing in both contemporary accounts and later historiography. Here are a few basic "facts" provided by the *National Anti-Slavery Standard*. On the night of January 27, 1856, two families, totaling seventeen people, escaped from Kentucky over the ice into Ohio, staying there overnight before being recaptured. Margaret Garner apparently killed one of her children with a handsaw when she realized they would be retaken. The court case that ensued centered on states vs. federal rights, and a testing of the Fugitive Slave Law. Garner was remanded to slavery, sold down river, and disappeared from the historical record. (See, for example, *NASS* 29 Jan. 1856: 2; 7 Feb. 1856: 3; and Myers.)

3.   Sherley Anne Williams problematizes scholarly notions of truth and appeals to something similar to what I am arguing for in *Beloved* when she comments in the Author's Note to *Dessa Rose:* "This novel then is fiction; all the characters, even the country they travel through, while based on fact, are inventions. And what is here is as true as if I myself had lived it" (x).

4.   Antebellum slave narratives and postbellum autobiographies form a major portion of the writing done by African Americans in the nineteenth century. Both genres were written for particular purposes: the antebellum narratives to assert the basic humanity and worth of the enslaved and thus force the abolition of slavery, and the postbellum autobiographies to construct slavery as a training ground for a new, eminently capable labor force. On one basic level literacy marks the difference between the authors of these texts and the characters in *Beloved,* but the requirements of these nineteenth-century genres also called for specific kinds of self-representation that are substantially different from the representations of the (formerly) enslaved in Morrison's text. (See Foster, *Witnessing;* Andrews.)

5.   Morrison remarks, "To make the story appear oral, meandering, effortless, spoken—to have the reader feel the narrator without identifying that narrator, of hearing him or her knocking about, and to have the reader work with the author in the construction of the book—is what's important" ("Rootedness" 341).

6.   In *Beloved,* the term *digestible* has a very different meaning from that associated with the contemporary criticism of consumer culture. In a TV interview, Morrison described slavery as the "great undigestible," a past that most refuse to contemplate, but which continues to affect the present by virtue of its solidity and tenacity. Contemporary criticism of consumer culture uses the term *digestible* to describe the least oppositional art, such as television situation comedies and soap operas, especially formulated to "go down easy."

7.   "And what deed of noble heroism ringing through the world, what proud action, showing that the brave man tramples on life as on a dishonoured burden when the oppressor would clutch at his liberties, is like this stern deed of the poor ignorant black woman, done among her enemies in a dark corner of the land? . . . What does she do? . . . The slavehunters are at the door! She must choose for the innocent girl. On one side, Slavery—its nameless wrongs eating into the soul—its heart-agonies—its degradation—its unrewarded toil—its prostitution and shame; on the other Liberty! She chose as the noble of all ages have chosen—as you, reader, would choose for your babe! . . . It is not frenzy, though done in inspiration; it is the noblest instinct" ("Slave Mother of Cincinnati").

Frances Ellen Watkins Harper presents a more complex vision of Garner's situation in her poem "The Slave Mother." When describing Garner's successful escape, Harper calls her "heroic mother," but at the moment when Garner realizes that "the hunter {is at her} door," Harper shifts her characterization of Garner to "the mournful mother" (Harper qtd. in Foster, *Brighter* 85).

8. Simple examples include the repetition of *it rained* (109–10) when Paul D escapes the chain gang, and *nobody saw them falling* (174–75) when Sethe, Denver, and Beloved go ice skating.

9. This idea has parallels in postulations of contemporary feminist theory. Teresa de Lauretis, for example, discusses this notion in terms of differences among women, differences within feminism, differences within individual women, and the importance of flexibility among these varying positions.

10. It should be noted that a number of black and/or leftist writers have articulated perspectives of the enslaved for many years, among them Benjamin Quarles, Herbert Aptheker, and Arna Bontemps. However, despite the efforts of these scholars, the opposing, but equally disempowering theories of plantation life represented in U. B. Phillips's *Life and Labor in the Old South* (1929), and its fictional counterpart Margaret Mitchell's *Gone With the Wind* (1937), and Stanley Elkins's *Slavery,* and its fictional counterpart William Styron's *The Confessions of Nat Turner* (1967), retained cultural dominance until the 1970s.

Works Cited

Andrews, William L. "The Representation of Slavery and the Rise of Afro-American Literary Realism, 1865–1920." McDowell and Rampersad 62–80.

Carby, Hazel. "Ideologies of Black Folk: The Historical Novel of Slavery." McDowell and Rampersad 125–43.

de Lauretis, Teresa. "Feminist Studies/Critical Studies: Issues, Terms and Contexts." *Feminist Studies/Critical Studies.* Bloomington: Indiana UP, 1986. 1–19.

Foster, Frances Smith, ed. *A Brighter, Coming Day: A Frances Ellen Watkins Harper Reader.* New York: Feminist, 1990.

———. *Witnessing Slavery: The Development of Ante-Bellum Slave Narratives.* Westport: Greenwood, 1979.

McDowell, Deborah, and Arnold Rampersad, eds. *Slavery and the Literary Imagination.* Baltimore: Johns Hopkins UP, 1989.

Morrison, Toni. *Beloved.* New York: Knopf, 1987.

———. "Memory, Creation and Writing." *Thought* 59 (1984): 385–90.

———. "Rootedness: The Ancestor as Foundation." *Black Women Writers (1950–1980): A Critical Evaluation.* Ed. Mari Evans. Garden City: Anchor, 1984. 339–45.

Myers, Rachel. "Competing Representations—From Abolitionist Polemic to Twentieth-Century Revision: The Case of Margaret Garner and *Beloved.*" Unpublished essay.

"The Slave Mother of Cincinnati." *National Anti-Slavery Standard* 1 Mar. 1856: 1.

Williams, Sherley Anne. *Dessa Rose.* 1986. New York: Berkley, 1987.

The Making of a Man:
Dialogic Meaning in *Beloved*

Deborah Ayer (Sitter)

Reviewer Stanley Crouch has referred disparagingly to Toni Morrison as a "literary conjure woman" (40), an intended barb that may serve instead as a suggestive compliment. Through the medium of words Morrison summons those unseen presences populating the nether regions of language and closely questions them. What goes on in the ghostly subtext of *Beloved* is an intense debate over the meaning of manhood and the possibility for enduring heterosexual love. The central figure in this debate is Paul D, whose reflections on manhood are muffled by a stronger female voice. Sethe's story seems to dominate, but as Morrison suggests at the end of *Beloved,* the meaning of Sethe's story cannot be fully understood except in relation to his. Paul D's determination to "put his story next to hers" is not just a clever way of bringing closure to this novel (*Beloved* 273). The dialogue between their two stories constructs the context in which Morrison conducts a deeper dialogue with the social meanings of words which have the power to liberate or enslave.

Discussions of manhood and heterosexual love are notably absent from the critical commentary on *Beloved,* which has been read largely as Sethe's story, a tale of fierce maternal love.[1] Critics thus far have minimized Paul D's role, tending to describe him as an interesting minor character. Most would accept Margaret Atwood's assertion that the "central voice belongs to Sethe" (1), an escaped slave woman who, when the novel opens in 1873, is living outside of Cincinnati with her daughter Denver in a house haunted by the spirit of the child Sethe murdered to shield her from the soul-death of slavery. The plot that revolves around Sethe's confrontation with and exorcism of the incarnated ghost (Beloved) and her subsequent reintegration into her community naturally tends to dominate first readings of the novel. The "story" of Paul D, who drives out the spirit from 124 Bluestone Road and is in turn "moved out" by Beloved, is often briefly acknowledged; but, to date, most critics have been "deaf to the dialogue" between these two stories and to the deeper dialogue as well.[2]

First published in *African American Review* 26 no. 1 (1992): 17–29. © Deborah Ayer (Sitter); reprinted with the permission of the author.

A more fully dialogic reading may better accommodate Morrison's repeated assertions that *Beloved* is the story of a *people* rather than a person. She says, "The book was not about the institution—Slavery with a capital S. It was about these anonymous *people* called slaves. What they do to keep on, how they make a life, what they're willing to risk, however long it lasts, in order to relate to one another—that was incredible to me" (Angelo 120, emphasis added). Although the novel began as Sethe's story—Morrison learned about Margaret Garner while editing *The Black Book* in 1975—it evolved into a story about "these *people* who don't know they're in an era of historical interest. They just know they have to get through the day . . . and they are trying desperately to be parents, husbands and a mother with children" (Horn 75, emphasis added). Morrison's conscious focus on collective rather than personal history is further clarified when she says that the novel "has to be the interior life of some people, a small group of people, and everything they do is impacted on by the horror of slavery, but they are also people" ("Toni" B3). As a dialogic reading of *Beloved* demonstrates, the meaning of slavery's impact on a people encompasses more than maternal love; it involves the way internalization of oppressors' values can distort all intimate human relationships and even subvert the self.

Beloved depicts slavery's insidious power to distort the two most basic human emotions and instincts: love and self-preservation. In this novel Morrison explores her most persistent theme, "love or its absence," from every imaginable angle[3]: Sethe's brand of mother love, which is a "killer"; Baby Suggs's loving embrace of her community; Denver's adoration of her father and sister; Beloved's obsessive love for her mother; Stamp Paid's loving allegiance to Paul D; and—the focus of this essay—Paul D's possessive love for Sethe. In the shadow of slavery, love inevitably results in destruction or betrayal of another or oneself. Morrison has said that, when writing *Beloved,* she was especially concerned with the theme of "self-sabotage," with the "ways in which the best things we do so often carry seeds of one's own destruction" ("Toni" B3). This theme is played out in Paul D's love for Sethe, which leads to his self-imposed exile in the basement of a church, just as Sethe's absolute love for her children leads her to take a handsaw to her daughter's throat, resulting in imprisonment and virtual banishment by her community. Morrison shows how every natural instinct and emotion is in some way twisted or stunted by the experience of living in a culture that measures individual worth by resale value and the ability to reproduce oneself without cost.

Morrison does more than simply document distortions of emotion and instinct as the effects of physical enslavement, however; she shows why they persist long after the chains have been severed, tracing their roots in language, in the words with which people name themselves and their relations with others. Language is a primary means for internalizing cultural values, implanting ideals of manhood and womanhood which can be as enslaving as any set of chains, especially for those on the margins of the dominant culture.

In *Beloved* Morrison dramatizes Paul D's enslavement to an ideal of manhood that distorts his images of self and others. Since this ideal is unspoken, embedded in the very words Paul D uses to make sense of his world, it can be interrogated only if it is made to "speak." And since speech implies language, itself invested with cultural values, Morrison's method must be indirect, revealing alternative meanings for "manhood" by expanding the contexts in which the concept appears. The stylistic devices Morrison uses to amplify meanings and create new contexts for understanding slavery's inhuman legacy are inherently dialogic and are best approached through the kind of stylistic analysis advocated by Mikhail Bakhtin.[4] Paul D's story, which is a meditation on manhood played out in the novel's shadowy subtext, must be heard if Sethe's story of fierce maternal love is to be understood. Through the dialogic interaction between these stories, Morrison suggests new possibilities for love which endures.

The probable reason that Paul D's story has gone unheard lies in the indirect way in which Morrison explores the themes of manhood and enduring love. Embedded in her language and metaphors, like half-formed thoughts, they influence the reader's judgment of people and actions in the novel without ever necessarily reaching the level of conscious awareness. Bakhtin's theory of language is useful here in understanding the dialectical play of these themes in *Beloved*. As Bakhtin asserts, language is "ideologically saturated." Words are never neutral but always "taste" of the thoughts, points of view, and value judgments of the people using and receiving them. In any utterance a struggle goes on between two opposing tendencies of language: centripetal forces seeking to stabilize language into a unitary and "officially recognized" system and centrifugal forces seeking to disunify and decentralize language, accentuating its diversity and multivocality (271–72). A detailed analysis of any utterance—spoken or written—must take into account the tension between these two opposing forces. Paul D's meditation on manhood becomes an arena in which the values of the dominant white culture are challenged by values rooted in African culture.

The critique of Western values is not new to Morrison's work. Her novels, essays, and conversations reflect the intensity of her struggle to give life to the experience and consciousness of African-American people, to articulate and validate a world view other than that of the dominant culture.[5] In *The Bluest Eye,* Western values are ironically introduced through a grade-school primer's idealized portrait of family life (among white folks), and in *Sula* such values underlie a cruel "Nigger joke" and an inverted world which locates the "Bottom," home of the Black community, on an infertile hillside. *Song of Solomon* represents the spiritual death of white middle-class values in the materially rich but emotionally impoverished household of Macon Dead, while in *Tar Baby* the values of the—ironically—imperial Valerian Street lure his servants' niece, Jadine, into a life of inauthenticity.

In each of these novels Morrison contrasts white Western values with those of a Black person, household, or community which, however maimed or broken, is portrayed as the source of the communal love, warmth, and sustenance necessary for spiritual wholeness. Frequently in her later works, positive values are associated with specific practices of West African culture: naming traditions, ancestor worship, acceptance of the supernatural, harmony with nature, and the linking of individual wholeness to rootedness in a community.[6] Whether Morrison's implicit distinctions between "Western" and "African" values are generalizations in need of closer examination is not at issue here; rather my focus is on *how* the dialogue between opposed values is heard through Morrison's manipulation of language and metaphor in *Beloved*. Since the interrogation of dominant cultural values is carried on in the spaces Morrison creates—through the juxtaposition of words and points of view, and in the play of nuance and allusion—it is accessible only through close textual analysis, the approach which "has been most repressed," Henry Louis Gates argues, "in the received tradition of Afro-American criticism" (*Figures* ix).[7]

Morrison proceeds by indirection because to state a position directly— were it possible to articulate that position—would not be persuasive. If meaning depends on the context in which a word occurs—who speaks, where, when, and to whom—and if language, is, as Bakhtin says, already "overpopulated with the intentions of others" (294), then Morrison must weave her "message" through the already existing social atmosphere of words in such a way that the reader can "hear" it. In other words, the novelist persuades not by pronouncing this or that as so but by creating a context which opens the reader's mind, making it possible to think what is normally unthinkable because such thoughts are foreign to the reader's orientation to the world. An enlarged perspective prevents judging Sethe and Paul D by absolute standards of morality or justice; it recognizes the complexity of their motives and enlists our sympathy.[8]

To sensitize her readers to alternative world views, Morrison uses a variety of structural and stylistic devices which expand the context so that characters' motives and actions acquire new meanings. The fragmentary structure of the narrative is deliberately disorienting; and narrative circumlocution, in which the same story is retold many times, makes the reader strain to hear— and construct—the meaning behind the words. For example, in referring to the opening of the novel she says: "The reader is snatched, yanked, thrown into an environment completely foreign, and I want it as the first stroke of the shared experience that might be possible between the reader and the novel's population. Snatched just as the slaves were from one place to another . . . without preparation and without defense" ("Unspeakable" 32). Morrison also manipulates narrative point of view to convey multiple perspectives simultaneously, both at the level of the sentence and of the scene, forcing her readers to think before they judge.[9] And she amplifies meanings through "saturated language." Not only are stories repeated in ever newer contexts, but words and images are made to swell with nuances and associations derived from both within and without the text.[10]

Morrison's most characteristic stylistic device, however, is the construction of metaphors which, as they are elaborated in the work, accumulate an almost inexhaustible range of meanings. For her, a metaphor is "a way of seeing something, familiar or unfamiliar, in a way you can grasp it" (Bakerman 58). If she can imagine the right metaphor, then the work flows, for it is in the metaphor that "the information lodges" ("Toni" B3). Metaphors enable Morrison to speak indirectly, to amplify meanings through intratextual allusions and by "signifying" on other literary texts and cultural associations.[11]

One of the central metaphors in *Beloved* is, of course, the scar on Sethe's back. As Morrison has said, "Once I know what the shape of the scar is . . . then I can move" ("Toni" B3). The scar's shape is first mentioned when Sethe tells Paul D, " 'I got a tree on my back and a haint in my house' " (15). That the two attach different meanings to this "tree" becomes apparent in a bedroom scene occurring early on. How radically their versions of the tree differ gradually emerges, however, and the metaphor's full significance can be understood only by tracing its pathway through the novel. Beginning as a simple visual comparison between a scar and tree, this metaphor swells with increasingly complex meanings until it becomes the locus of a debate between Western and African ideals of manhood. The most concentrated example of Morrison's multivocal style, the "tree" begins to resonate in the bedroom scene which enacts in miniature the major action of *Beloved*. A close analysis of this scene reveals how Morrison builds the multilayered context through which she orchestrates her meanings. As the tree is "dialogized," we become aware of competing definitions of manhood, womanhood, and love.[12]

After a tender episode in the kitchen where both relax their guard, Paul D and Sethe rush to bed, only to experience failure and disappointment. Embedded in the context in which Morrison situates their lovemaking are the values of fairy tale and romance implicit in Paul D's image of himself as a demon-slaying hero returned to claim his prize. By juxtaposing this image against a harsher reality, Morrison questions the values on which the image is based. An instance of what Bakhtin would call an "inserted genre" (355), the embedded romance motif is one way in which Morrison creates semantic depth in the novel. These values comment most forcefully on Paul D's purported love for Sethe and the obstacles to this love: Romantic illusion is followed by romantic disillusion, and both are subjected to reality testing.

When Paul D and Sethe fail to satisfy each other in the cramped upstairs bedroom at 124 Bluestone Road, the nubile maiden Paul D has dreamed of for twenty-five years turns into a hag before his eyes. The hero who has slain the dragon and spirited the maiden away on the wings of his pent-up desire turns away from her sagging breasts "that he could definitely live without" and the "revolting clump of scars" on her back (21). Sethe feels his withdrawal and bitterly reflects, "But maybe a man was nothing but a man. . . . They encouraged you to put some of your weight in their hands and as soon as you felt how light and lovely that was, they studied your scars and tribulations, after which they did what he had done: ran your children out and tore up the house" (22). The mature matron dismisses the returned hero with a contemptuous sneer.

Typically, Morrison would have ended the scene here—the frustrated lovers held apart by mutual distrust and blame—as she had done many times before: Sula and Ajax/A. Jacks (she didn't even learn his name until after he had abandoned her), Milkman and Hagar, Son and Jadine—even Cholly Breedlove and Pauline. In earlier novels, love between men and women could not endure, and Morrison frequently dismissed romantic values summarily.[13] But she chose a different fate for these lovers, permitting them indirect fulfillment, implicit in the language which concludes the scene. Paul D and Sethe restlessly toss and turn, moving in and out of each others' thoughts until, seduced by memories of their shared past, their minds merge orgasmically:

> No matter what all your teeth and wet fingers anticipated, there was no accounting for the way that simple joy could shake you.
> How loose the silk. How fine and loose and free. (27)

How Morrison makes credible this transformation of sexual frustration into fulfillment is understandable only through careful reading of this scene.

At the beginning of the scene, Paul D and Sethe are separated by differences more profound than either realizes, and until these differences can be articulated, reconciliation is impossible. Morrison makes them "speak" in two ways. First, introducing the values of romance—associated with Paul D's dream of Sethe—provides an ironic context for their abortive lovemaking. And second, through the metaphor of the tree, Morrison examines unconscious assumptions preventing their love. For Sethe a "tree" is an emblem of female suffering, whereas for Paul D it is associated with a manly ideal. In the bedroom scene, Morrison explores these disparate associations and their connections with particular cultural values.

When Paul D and Sethe lie side by side in resentful rejection of each other, what is rejected is much more than the shape of the scar on a woman's back. Morrison places their present experience in the context of their past, introduced through their memories of Sweet Home. Romance encounters reality when Paul D's dream of a twenty-five-year-old love is set against a more realistic version of the way things were. Paul D's dream "had been too long and too long ago," the narrator says (20). What was this dream, deferred for twenty-five years only to result in a loss of appetite? When Sethe arrived at Sweet Home she was thirteen years old, the desired object of all the men but Sixo, who was already attached to the Thirty-Mile Woman. The men wanted Sethe for a very basic reason: She was not a cow, and "fucking cows" had been their only experience of sex. The men left it up to her to choose, and Halle won out, so Paul D went back to cows but continued to dream of Sethe. Juxtaposing Paul D's romantic dream with the reality of life at Sweet Home serves to invalidate the dream: Cows and courtly lovers do not mix.

Sethe's failure to be the object Paul D imagined leads him to reject her. His rejection initially takes the form of denying that the scars on her back are a tree, insisting they are, in fact, a "revolting clump of scars" (21). Like a petulant child, Paul D lashes out against Sethe, suggesting the superficiality of his twenty-five-year-old love. The vehemence of Paul D's denial stems from the special significance he attaches to trees, which are connected with an idealized concept of manhood.

Placing Paul D's image in the context of Sethe's image of the tree undercuts the values on which his ideal is based. For Sethe, the tree is the shape of the scar tissue on her back, scars incurred when schoolteacher and his nephews pinned her, six months pregnant, to the earth, first digging a hole so as not to damage their prospective property—the baby she carried within her—and then delivering a whipping so merciless as to strike even Amy Denver dumb. It is Amy, the escaped indentured servant on her way to Boston to purchase some velvet, who gives shape to Sethe's scar:

> "It's a tree. . . . A chokecherry tree. See, here's the trunk—it's red and split wide open, full of sap, and this here's the parting for the branches. You got a mighty lot of branches. Leaves, too, look like, and dern if these ain't blossoms. Tiny little cherry blossoms, just as white. Your back got a whole tree on it. In bloom." (79)

The stark contrast between Amy's fanciful image, described in her calm "dreamwalker's voice," and the reality of suppurating sores on Sethe's back creates an effect of cognitive dissonance. The two images refuse to come together but remain distinct and alternating. Amy's transformation of Sethe's oozing back into an image of gruesome beauty contrasts with the way men in the novel deal with pain: They eschew it through denial (Paul D) or flight (Howard and Buglar) or insanity (Halle).[14] Together, Amy and Sethe create a feminine context against which Paul D's image of the tree must be understood.[15]

Paul D's denial that Sethe has a tree on her back is a case of phallic assertiveness masking his insecurity about his own manhood. He imposes his own (male) conception of a tree, measures her "tree" by it, and finds it lacking. Sethe's scars are not a tree because, in Paul D's view, "trees were inviting," and by implication—especially in the wake of frustrated sex—her "tree" is not (21). Paul's image hearkens back to Sweet Home, where he sat under the comforting branches of a giant sycamore tree, called Brother. The name is not accidental, for Paul D's tree is associated with his experience of male bonding—with the other Sweet Home men, especially Sixo.

The progression of Paul D's thought is intriguing because the connections among a tree, Brotherhood, and Sixo are hardly inevitable, and they range both within and without the text. Through these associations Morrison subtly introduces the values of another culture. That this other culture is African is implied both by the primacy of trees in African culture and by their association with Sixo, whose very name (60) recalls the "Sixty Million and More" to whom Morrison dedicates her novel. In the center of many West African villages stands a large tree (like the baobab in the epic *Sundiata*) around which men gather to make decisions about tribal governance.[16] More telling, however, are the details with which Morrison describes Sixo's difference from the other Sweet Home men. His color, language, and ways suggest his undiluted African ancestry and set him apart from the rest. His color is darker: "indigo with a flame-red tongue" (21). His language and ways are singular: At one point "he stopped speaking English because there was no future in it"; he danced among the trees at night "to keep his bloodlines open" (25); and he walked for thirty-four hours in two days just to spend an hour with his chosen woman. Sixo is drawn on an heroic scale and seems to function as Paul D's spiritual (ancestral?) guide. That Paul D is meditating not on trees but on manhood in Sethe's bedroom is revealed in the concluding words of his reverie: "Now *there* was a man, and *that* was a tree. Himself lying in the bed and the 'tree' lying next to him didn't compare" (22). By accentuating Sixo's "Africanness" and by establishing him as a primary example of manliness, Morrison suggests he represents an African ideal of manhood.

Paul D's preoccupation with trees and manhood operates as a subtext in which the conflict between the values of the West and of Africa is played out. What Paul D perceives as innate manliness may be attributable to Sixo's African upbringing. Rather than in extraordinary deeds and risks—the actions conventionally associated with the heroes of the West—Sixo's true manliness may lie in his unfailing respect for the living and the dead, the natural and the supernatural which in his view—an African view—are one. For example, when he invites the Thirty-Mile Woman to a rendezvous in a deserted stone shelter "that Redmen used way back when they thought the land was theirs," Sixo asks the Redmen's Presence for permission to enter (24). When she fails to meet him there, he asks the wind for help (and gets it). Sixo's ability to live in harmony with the world of spirit and of nature sets him apart. Not until long after the scene in the bedroom does Paul D come to conscious awareness of the qualitative difference between the manliness of Sixo and that of Mr. Garner, the master of Sweet Home.

Although only a brief episode in *Beloved*, the bedroom scene beautifully exemplifies the devices Morrison uses to question cultural values and disrupt cultural complacencies so that new meanings can be heard. By constantly shifting the contexts in which words and actions occur and by strategically juxtaposing Sethe's and Paul D's points of view, she exposes the assumptions underlying his ideal of manliness. It is in this scene that the metaphor of the tree and its different meanings for Paul D and Sethe are first explored: Paul D's symbol of manhood is "put next" to Sethe's emblem of woman's pain. His denial of Sethe's "tree" foreshadows his later desertion. Paul D's refusal to acknowledge that her scars cohere into an awful but beautiful image reveals his inability to accept Sethe's integrity, her wholeness. As the metaphor of the tree develops, it becomes clear that the chief barrier to Paul D's committing himself to Sethe is an ideal of manhood which is threatened by the woman she is.

The metaphor of the tree and the theme of manhood compressed into two paragraphs of Paul D's meditation surface in new contexts as the novel progresses in a relationship more suggestive than defined. Paul D's image of the tree seems at all moments to be an index of his sense of his own manliness. At Sweet Home Paul D is confident that he is a man: Garner has raised him to be one, given him the use of a gun, asked his advice, even allowed him to make decisions—within certain limits. So Paul D envisions a tree huge and comforting. On the chain gang in Alfred, Georgia, however, Paul D can no longer imagine a tree, "old, wide and beckoning," like Brother; his "little love" is an aspen, "too young to call a sapling" (221). This aspen reflects a diminished self. After watching Sixo burn, after the neck collar, after the humiliation of Rooster's gaze, Paul D is changed into something else, and that "something was less than a chicken sitting in the sun on a tub" (72). Manhood becomes radically problematic.

It is unlikely that, even in similar circumstances, Sixo's confidence in his manhood would ever have been shaken. As Paul D's meditation continues, the source of his confusion is revealed. Although Sixo is his model of a manly man, the qualities Paul D associates with manliness originate in the dominant culture of the white slaveholder Mr. Garner. These qualities include strength, courage, and endurance—all of which Sixo possesses—but they are directed toward maximizing the power of the individual to dominate weaker beings. Unlike Sixo, who respects all forms of life, Mr. Garner feels most manly when he is playing lord to someone else's vassal. According to Mr. Garner, the Sweet Home slaves are men—because he has made them so. Schoolteacher challenges this view. Believing that "slave *men*" is oxymoronic, he teaches the Sweet Home men a lesson they do not soon forget: "One step off that ground and they were trespassers among the human race. Watchdogs without teeth; steer bulls without horns; gelded workhorses . . ." (125).

It is only after Beloved takes him in hand that Paul D realizes that Mr. Garner's and schoolteacher's views are fundamentally the same. Paul D had done many conventionally manly things: He "had eaten raw meat barely dead" and "under plum trees bursting with blossoms had crunched a dove's breast before its heart stopped beating. Because he was a man and a man could do what he would" (126). But these heroic feats are no protection against Beloved, who can pick him up and put him down like a rag doll.[17]

Paul D is not convinced he is a man because he locates manhood in an objectified image of another. He responds to Beloved's manipulations by asserting his manhood in a different but standard way: He wants to prove himself a man by virtue of being a father. Making Sethe pregnant will both "document his manhood" (128) and break Beloved's spell. Before he can carry out this plan, however, Stamp Paid hands him some "news" that sends him running for cover.

This news challenges an ideal of womanhood that mirrors the individualistic ideal of manhood. Both must be relinquished if men and women are to have a life, as Morrison suggests through language and imagery. The individualistic hero who feeds on raw meat and dove's bones expects to be complemented by a submissive maiden needing to be rescued from mortal danger. In fairy tales and romances the hero's courage is measured by his ability to battle and slay the dragon, thereby winning possession of the maiden. When the maiden steps out of her assigned role, however, the hero's manhood is threatened, as Morrison demonstrates in the scene in which Paul D confronts Sethe with Stamp Paid's news clipping of the murder and trial.

Paul D had thought he understood the roles he and Sethe were to play: She was the maiden, living "in helpless, apologetic resignation because she had no choice," and he was the hero who "had gotten rid of the danger; beat the shit out of it; run it off the place and showed it and everybody else the difference between a mule and a plow." He learns his error and it terrifies him. "This here Sethe talked about safety with a handsaw"; far more important than what she "had done was what she claimed" (164). Sethe refused to believe it wasn't the only thing to have done. When her back was up against the wall, she didn't faint or weep or cower; she fought back with all the ferocity of a man. Paul D's response is to judge her—not as a man (she couldn't be) but as an animal: " 'You got two feet, Sethe, not four.' " Morrison's metaphor for the impact of these words is a master stroke: "a forest sprang up between them; trackless and quiet" (165). Paul D's tree—sapling or Brother—and Sethe's tree—emblem of suffering—stand at either end of an ever-widening forest.

The forest remains impenetrable until Paul D is able to imagine a new role for himself. His conventional masculine heroism is put into perspective by Sethe's bitter reflection on Paul D's cowardice: ". . . look how he ran when he found out about you and me in the shed. Too rough for him to listen to. Too thick, he said. My love was too thick. What he know about it? Who in the world is he willing to die for? Would he give his privates to a stranger in return for a carving?" (203). Ultimately, Sethe is rescued not by a male hero but by her daughter Denver, who performs an act at least as brave as dragon slaying. She forces herself to venture out into a terrifying world to find work and food for her mother. Denver's behavior conforms to a line of action Morrison regards as distinctively African-American. In talking about *Sula* she has asserted that "black people" regard evil as a natural part of the universe; they are "not terrified by evil, by difference. Evil is not an alien force; it's just a different force" (Tate, "Toni" 129). Thus, Denver does not try to kill whatever evil exists (as Paul D attempted to do); rather she seeks the protection of the community to keep evil at bay, suggesting a healthier alternative to conventional heroic action. Perhaps Denver succeeds where Paul D fails because she acts in accord with communal values.

While Denver is coming to terms with her private demons, Paul D is living in the damp cellar of a storefront church, still trying to find a definition of manhood he can live with. He obsessively returns to the ideal of manhood espoused by Garner and schoolteacher and wonders "how much difference there really was between before schoolteacher and after" (220). A combination of incidents enables Paul D to rejoin the community. Stamp Paid seeks him out to gossip about Sethe's latest escapade (her attempt to stab Mr. Bodwin with an ice pick), and they erupt in a laughter which is cleansing because communal. Then a newly confident Denver welcomes Paul D and calls him by his name, Mr. D—not Paul D Garner, a white man's name—only a letter, a sound, but his. He stops projecting fear and desire outward and takes a good look at himself, worrying about "how *he* left and why" (267, emphasis added). Through Garner's eyes, his walking out on Sethe looks righteous, but measured against Sixo's manliness, it "makes him feel ashamed" (267). Unlocking the tobacco tin, symbol of his repressed feelings of compassion and tenderness, Paul D affirms his commitment to Sethe and heads for 124 Bluestone Road.

Paul D's journey back to Sethe parallels his journey north, to freedom; after escaping from the chain gang, he took the Cherokee's advice to " 'follow the tree flowers. . . . You will be where you want to be when they are gone' " (112). So Paul D followed the dogwood, peach, and cherry blossoms until he got to the apple trees budding with fruit—in Delaware which he mistakenly thought would mean freedom. In retracing his steps eighteen years later, Paul D follows the blossoms not north but to Sethe—who bears a once-blossoming tree on her back. Like the apple trees in Delaware, 124 Bluestone Road contains "blossoms shriveled like sores" (270). Paul D completes his metaphoric journey by returning to the only tree beside which he can be a man, to Sethe whose hair is "like the dark delicate roots of good plants" (271).

Withered blossoms suggest that fruitfulness may follow; Paul D has wandered aimlessly searching for his roots only to find them in a metaphor. Unsure of his welcome, he now treats Sethe gingerly, trying out his new role as man. Fluctuating between command and plea, he struggles to know her wants. He has not come, he says, to count her feet but to rub them. Manhood and womanhood come together in his memory of Sixo's feelings about the Thirty-Mile Woman: " 'She is a friend of my mind. She gather me, man. The pieces I am, she gather them and give them back to me in all the right order' " (272–73). In this context, framed by Sixo's words, Paul D's meditations, Stamp Paid's laughter, and Denver's welcome, by all the pain and humiliation and suffering of their shared and unshared pasts, Paul D arrives at an ideal of manhood for the real world—not of heroes and maidens but of men and women, acting out of blind impulse or with great deliberation in a world in which any gesture of tenderness is precious. Paul D now understands what Sethe's response to his "neck jewelry" means: Her simple refusal to acknowledge it in any way saved him from the "shame of being collared like a beast. Only this woman Sethe could have left him his manhood like that. He wants to put his story next to hers" (273).

Paul D at last satisfies his doubts about his own manhood. It isn't something someone else can confer or take away. No one—even Mr. Garner—can make a man, or break—as schoolteacher tried to do—a man. Witness Sixo. Manhood isn't an organ that can be excised; it is the heart of the man, manifested in the sacredness with which he lives: his respect for the otherness of others, tenderness for their sorrow, and sense of responsibility for helping them to be their " 'best thing[s]' " (273). Paul D's recognition that Sethe *left* him his manhood indirectly acknowledges its existence: One cannot leave people something they do not already have. It is also an indirect affirmation of the kind of woman she is: strong, independent, fierce. The language of his desire is suggestive: He wants "to put his story next to hers." "Next to" speaks of equality—Sethe's story is as important as his. Unlike the hero's story—all ego, possession, and dominance—Paul D's story, like Halle's care for Sethe, comes to suggest "a family relationship rather than a man's laying claim" (25). As Sethe realizes, "her story was bearable because it was his as well—to tell, to refine and tell again" (99). Paul D eventually reaches the same conclusion.

This conclusion is prefigured in the passage enacting their frustrated sex. Morrison places their stories next to one another in alternating passages suggestive of a *pas de deux*.[18] Paul D and Sethe embrace and separate, each executing his or her individual dance; but gradually they work their way back together. What enables their coming together is the ability to smile at themselves. Paul D gives up resenting Sethe for failing to live up to his objectified desire and recognizes his foolishness. This perception makes him smile, think fondly of himself, and consequently open up to Sethe. For her part, Sethe ceases to criticize Paul D for being "nothing but a man" when memories of Sweet Home intrude, along with recollections of Halle's "gesture of tenderness" in taking her in the privacy of the cornfield rather than in her more public quarters. Sethe smiles "at her and Halle's stupidity" (26). These smiles signify recognition of more than one perspective, marking a distance between the individualistic self, ruled by ego, and the contextual self, rooted in community. Together, through indirect speech in the form of private meditation, they reveal the story of what happened in the corn. In the "telling," they become participants and realize their love:

No matter what all your teeth and wet fingers anticipated, there was no accounting for the way that simple joy could shake you.
How loose the silk. How fine and loose and free. (27)

The sexual frustration Sethe and Paul D experience at the outset of the bed-room scene is eventually transformed into sexual fulfillment. What prevents them at first and enables them at last is conveyed indirectly through the mul-tivocal, multilayered, dense verbal texture of Morrison's style.

Paul D's early inability to accept the beauty and coherence of Sethe's scar is connected to an ideal of manhood based on individualism. This absolute—monologic—ideal prescribes a certain kind of "manly" behavior and excludes alternative actions. The counterpart of this manly ideal is an ideal of womanhood, also monologic. Love relationships governed by these values usually fail. As Morrison says, "Always the ego interferes: some pride, some sort of arrogance . . . and it just slips through our fingers" (Bakerman 60).

Paul D's initial ideal of womanhood has no place for the kind of woman Sethe turns out to be, partly because he never really knew her at Sweet Home. She remained an object of his desire: first as an alternative to cows and later as Halle's wife—a man's possession. Later, when forced to confront the results of Sethe's "too-thick" love—the way in which she chose to "rescue" herself and her children—Paul D cannot accept this version of woman and labels her an animal, ironically, just as schoolteacher does. He judges Sethe's action in a vacuum, by an absolute standard. Sethe, on the other hand, judges the situation in terms of its predictable consequences: What would have hap-pened to her and her children if she had *not* acted? Morrison compels her readers to recognize Sethe's dilemma and in so doing precludes judgment and promotes sympathy. Once Paul D enters into dialogue with his assumptions about manhood, assumptions based on white slaveholders' values, and com-pares them with his intimate knowledge of Sixo, the embodiment of African values of community and harmony with natural and supernatural worlds, he gains a new perspective on manhood, on womanhood, and on the possibility for lasting love between man and woman. He returns to Sethe to put his story next to hers.

In *Beloved*, Morrison orchestrates meanings in a dialogue about funda-mental human problems: the meaning of manhood, of womanhood, and of love. By manipulating metaphors and amplifying the meanings of words, she unsettles assumptions and heightens understanding not only of Sethe's act of love/murder but also of the actions of a people and what they had to do to survive. In *Beloved*, Morrison creates a new context for understanding the meaning of slavery, and of freedom.

Notes

1. Reviews and critical commentaries on *Beloved* which focus almost exclusively on female relationships in the novel include Atwood; Christian, " 'Somebody' "; Dudar; Horvitz; Mobley; Sale; Tate, Review; Thurman; and Warner. For an exception, see Cummings.

2. The quoted phrase refers to Mikhail Bakhtin's accusation that "traditional stylistics has been deaf to dialogue"(273). He argues that scholars have practiced linguistics rather than stylistics and have isolated one set of elements in the novel and studied it independently of the dialogic context in which it occurs, thus failing to take into account the "internally dialogic quality of discourse which proper rhetorical analysis may reveal" (269). According to Bakhtin, the "word forms itself in the atmosphere of the already spoken" (280), and its meaning depends not on direct speech but on the context in which it occurs—who speaks it, when, where, and to whom.

3. In an interview with Jane Bakerman, Morrison says, "Actually, I think, all the time that I write, I'm writing about love or its absence. Although I don't start out that way." She later elaborates on this, saying she writes "about love and how to survive . . . *whole* in a world where we are all of us, in some measure, *victims of something*" (60).

4. My analysis of Morrison's style is based on Bakhtin's approach described in "Discourse in the Novel," in which he asserts that the "real task of stylistic analysis is uncovering all the available orchestrating languages in the composition of the novel" (*The Dialogic Imagination* 416). According to Bakhtin, the "meaning of an utterance depends on the context in which it occurs and on the accent which the author gives it" (340). Since language is never neutral, or in Barthes' words, "never innocent," meaning is always a function of at least two consciousnesses. For a different application of Bakhtin's method to *Beloved,* see Mobley's article describing the dialogic interaction between *Beloved* and the genre of the slave narrative, which Morrison seeks to revise in order to make it accessible to modern readers. Mobley argues that *Beloved* represents a "reaccentuation of the past to discover newer aspects of meaning embedded in the slave narrative" (197) and focuses her analysis on Sethe, who represents the "psychological consequences of slavery for women" (192). Mobley does not discuss Paul D's story.

5. For Morrison's statements about her artistic "project," see her interviews with Bakerman and Tate and especially her essays "Rootedness: The Ancestor as Foundation" and "Unspeakable Things Unspoken." See also Davis, and Christian "Contemporary Fables."

6. For discussion of African elements in Morrison's fiction, see Bruck, Campbell, and Lewis.

7. See also *The Signifying Monkey:* "Critics of African-American, Caribbean and African literature have far more often than not directed their attention to the signified, often at the expense of the signifier, as if the latter were transparent" (79). Morrison's concurrence with this critique is suggested in her assertion that "Black literature is taught as sociology, as tolerance, not as a serious rigorous art form" (Angelo 121).

8. Roger Sale describes the effect of Morrison's style in deferring judgment: "For long stretches of *Beloved* we simply don't know how [to respond], because we don't know yet what we're seeing. . . . [Moreover,] Morrison's art makes us gasp at these moments [of horror], then insists we not organize our feelings as if for protest or other action, but instead move back into the heavy verbal texture of her fiction" (82).

9. For example, in the sentence "The sideboard took a step forward but nothing else did" (4), the initial clause represents Sethe and Denver's point of view, their matter-of-fact acceptance of the troublesome ghost. The coordinate clause, however, contains just enough exaggeration to suggest the presence of another point of view—perhaps that of an amused observer who does not believe in ghosts. Furthermore, two of the most freighted scenes in the novel are introduced from the perspectives of white men. The narration of Sethe's murder of her daughter begins inside the consciousness of the slave catcher, while Mr. Bodwin's nostalgic memories of his abolitionist days set the scene for Sethe's attempt to murder him.

10. For example, in the passage describing Sethe's recurrent memory of selling sex to an engraver in return for his carving "Beloved" on a headstone, the marble is described as "pink as a fingernail" (5). This image resonates throughout the novel in associations with the children Baby Suggs "loses," with her obsession with color during her final days, with Stamp Paid's discovery of a red ribbon in the river, and with Sethe's sensual deprivation.

11. According to Henry Louis Gates, *signifyin(g)* is the master trope of African-American discourse, on which he grounds his theory of the Black Aesthetic. Deriving from the Signifying Monkey tales and the Yoruba sacred trickster figure Esu-Elegbara, *signifyin(g)* refers to a technique of indirection, involving repetition and reversal, often resulting in revision of earlier texts. See *Figures in Black* (235–76) for a discussion of Ishmael Reed's use of signifying in *Mumbo Jumbo*, and see *The Signifying Monkey* (170–216) for a discussion of Zora Neale Hurston's use of free indirect discourse in *Their Eyes Were Watching God*. Although an analysis of signifying in *Beloved* is beyond the scope of this essay, I do want to mention several ways in which Morrison seems to be signifying: on Hurston's Janie Starks, who envisions her life as a tree ("and dawn and doom were in the branches"); on the conventional structures of romance and fairy tales, with all their implicit assumptions about relationships between men and women; and on the genre of the slave narrative (discussed by Mobley).

12. For a definition of *dialogize*, see Bakhtin 427.

13. Warner traces the idea of romantic love—one of the "most destructive ideas in the history of human thought"—through Morrison's first four novels, showing how each "examines the entanglement and destruction predicated by romantic love" (8). And she argues that Morrison's fifth novel, *Beloved*, offers the greatest promise for "passionate love without possession" (8). See also Morrison's statement that "love, in the Western notion, is full of possession, distortion, and corruption. It's a slaughter without the blood" (Tate, "Toni" 123).

14. Paul D denies Sethe's tree, symbolizing her suffering; when the ghost becomes too intrusive, Howard and Buglar desert their grandmother, mother, and sister and run off to join the army; and Halle escapes into insanity (smearing clabber all over his face) after witnessing Sethe's "milking" by schoolteacher's nephews. The contrast between the responses of these representative males and the responses of Sethe, Amy, and Baby Suggs are epitomized in Sethe's reflections on her inability to control her "rebellious brain." She thinks it *would* have been a relief to have lost her mind along with Halle, but, she continues, "her three children were chewing sugar teat under a blanket on their way to Ohio and no butter play would change that" (71–72). Women in this novel seem compelled to consider the consequences of any action they might take and to be incapable of acting in their own interest when it conflicts with the interest of beloved others.

15. That Morrison's own associations with trees are closer to Sethe's and Amy's than to Paul D's is evident in her assertion in "Unspeakable Things Unspoken" that, "with all due respect to the dream landscape of Freud, trees have always seemed *feminine* to me" (25–26, emphasis added).

16. For the importance of trees in African culture, see Niane 90 n35.

17. Beloved serves in at least three capacities in this novel: as the incarnated spirit of Sethe's murdered daughter; as an escaped slave who murdered her abusive master; and as the collective racial memory of the Middle Passage, in particular, and of the experience of slavery, in general. If we regard Beloved as a function rather than a person, she represents the memory of slavery which prevents Paul D and Sethe from having a whole life together. Beloved *moves* Paul D out of 124; she promises that, if he will call her by her name, she will leave him alone. But when he says, "Beloved," she does not go. The implication is that Paul D must name (confront) the collective suffering of his race directly before he can be free.

18. I am indebted to Professor Lucy Fultz of Rice University for this idea, which she confirmed in an interview with Toni Morrison at Princeton University in September 1989.

Works Cited

Angelo, Bonnie. "The Pain of Being Black." *Time* 22 May 1989: 120–21.

Atwood, Margaret. "Haunted by Their Nightmares." *New York Times Book Review* 13 Sept. 1987: 1.

Bakerman, Jane. "The Seams Can't Show: An Interview with Toni Morrison." *Black American Literature Forum* 12 (1978): 56–60.

Bakhtin, Mikhail M. *The Dialogic Imagination: Four Essays.* Trans. Caryl Emerson and Michael Holquist. Ed. Holquist. Austin: U of Texas P, 1981.

Bruck, Peter. "Returning to One's Roots: The Motif of Searching and Flying in Toni Morrison's *Song of Solomon.*" *The Afro-American Novel since 1960.* Amsterdam: Grüner, 1982. 289–305.

Campbell, Jane. *Mythic Black Fiction: The Transformation of History.* Knoxville: U of Tennessee P, 1986.

Christian, Barbara. "The Contemporary Fables of Toni Morrison." *Black Women Novelists: The Development of a Tradition, 1892–1972.* Westport: Greenwood, 1980. 136–79.

———. " 'Somebody Forgot to Tell Somebody Something': African-American Women's Historical Novels." *Wild Women in the Whirlwind: Afra-American Culture and the Contemporary Literary Renaissance.* Ed. Joanne M. Braxton and Andrée Nicola McLaughlin. New Brunswick: Rutgers UP, 1990. 326–441.

Crouch, Stanley. "Aunt Medea." *New Republic* 19 Oct. 1987: 40.

Cummings, Katherine. "Reclaiming the Mother('s) Tongue: *Beloved, Ceremony, Mothers and Shadows.*" *College English* 52 (Sept. 1990): 552–69.

Davis, Cynthia. "Self, Society, and Myth in Toni Morrison's Fiction." *Contemporary Literature* 23.3 (1982): 323–42.

Dudar, Helen. "Toni Morrison: Finally Just a Writer." *Wall Street Journal* 30 Sept. 1987: 34.

Gates, Henry Louis, Jr. *Figures in Black: Words, Signs and the "Racial" Self.* New York: Oxford UP, 1987.

———. *The Signifying Monkey: A Theory of African-American Literary Criticism.* New York: Oxford UP, 1988.

Horn, Miriam. "Five Years of Terror." *U.S. News and World Report* 19 Oct. 1987: 75.

Horvitz, Deborah. "Nameless Ghosts: Possession and Dispossession in *Beloved.*" *Studies in American Fiction* 17 (1989): 157–67.

Lewis, Vashti Crutcher. "African Tradition in Toni Morrison's *Sula.*" *Phylon* 48.1 (1987): 91–97.

Mobley, Marilyn Sanders. "A Different Remembering: Memory, History and Meaning in Toni Morrison's *Beloved.*" *Modern Critical Views: Toni Morrison.* Ed. Harold Bloom. New York: Chelsea, 1990. 189–99.

Morrison, Toni. *Beloved.* New York: NAL, 1987.

———. "Rootedness: The Ancestor as Foundation." *Black Women Writers (1950–1980).* Ed. Mari Evans. New York: Anchor, 1984. 339–45.

———. "Unspeakable Things Unspoken: The Afro-American Presence in American Literature." *Michigan Quarterly Review* 28 (Winter 1989): 1–34.

Niane, D. T. *Sundiata: An Epic of Old Mali.* Trans. G. D. Pickett. Harlow: Longman, 1965.

Sale, Roger. "Toni Morrison's *Beloved.*" *Massachusetts Review* 29 (Spring 1988): 81–86.

Tate, Claudia, ed. "Toni Morrison." *Black Women Writers at Work.* New York: Continuum, 1983. 117–31.

———. Rev. of *Beloved. Sisters* (Summer 1988): 40, 46.

Thurman, Judith. "A House Divided." *New Yorker* 2 Nov. 1987: 175–80.

"Toni Morrison's *Beloved* Inspired by a Slave Who Chose to Kill Her Child." *Atlanta Journal and Constitution* 29 Aug. 1987: B3.

Warner, Anne Bradford. "New Myths and Ancient Properties: The Fiction of Toni Morrison." *Hollins Critic* 25 (June 1988): 2–11.

Willis, Susan. "Eruptions of Funk: Historicizing Toni Morrison." *Black American Literature Forum* 16 (1982): 34–42.

Beloved and the Tyranny of the Double

DENISE HEINZE

Beloved is Morrison's most unambiguous endorsement of the supernatural; so rife is the novel with the physical and spiritual presence of ghostly energy that a better term than supernatural would be uncanny, defined by Schelling as "the name for everything that ought to have remained . . . secret and hidden but has come to light."[1] In this case, that which ought to have remained secret is slavery, what Morrison suggests most Americans would like to bury since it is the historical reminder of a national disgrace. Morrison herself delayed the writing of this novel because she could anticipate the pain of recovery and confrontation. She says, "I had forgotten that when I started the book, I was very frightened. . . . It was an unwillingness and a terror of going into an area for which you have no preparation. It's a commitment of three or four years to living inside—because you do try to enter that life."[2] Despite "this terrible reluctance about dwelling on that era," Morrison says she went ahead with the writing of the book because "I was trying to make it a personal experience."[3]

The metaphor for Morrison's reluctance to recall this episode is the configuration of Beloved, part ghost, zombie, devil, and memory. Morrison reveals Beloved in tantalizing degrees until she is manifested as a full-blooded person. Like a childhood trauma, Beloved comes back in snatches until finally her history is retold, a discovery process shared by Morrison, her characters, and the readers as the primary step to collective spiritual recovery. Lloyd-Smith states that "as texts reveal and conceal the repressed" they "renegotiate the relation between the self and the world through the manipulation of image."[4] What began as purgation for the author becomes cathartic for all engaged in the reading process.

The likely medium for this experience is the genre of the fantastic or the uncanny because, as an unchartered reality, it allows the writer more freedom to manipulate Morrison's fictional world: "Roland Barthes has discussed the withholding of revelation (enigma) and the process of elicitation and suppression (the hermeneutic code) by which it is vouchsafed and disclosed. . . . The

Reprinted from *The Dilemma of "Double-Consciousness": Toni Morrison's Novels* by Denise Heinze (Athens: University of Georgia Press, 1993). © 1993 by the University of Georgia Press. Reprinted by permission of the University of Georgia Press and the author.

writer's cul-de-sac is the reader's labyrinth; a thin line of words is the way in and the only way out, and revelation may come or be denied, to either."[5]

Morrison violates, to a certain extent, this revelation process. The reader is aware early on—whether from advanced publicity of the book or Morrison's pointed clues—that the girl Beloved is the murdered two-year-old daughter of Sethe. Thus, the mystery or enigma in the novel does not reside in the origin of the ghostly presence but in the purpose of its manifestation. Morrison withholds from the reader Beloved's raison d'être—why she finally makes an appearance, why she changes physically and emotionally, and why she ultimately disappears. The answer to this particular mystery lies in the ability of her characters and readers to reintegrate and reconcile past and present. For Sethe, she must confront the guilt of her act and in that self-absolution find a future. For Morrison's readers, reconciliation is intimately linked to their ability to recover the past, to dissolve the lineality of time, and overcome the fragmented and distorted notion of past, present, and future. Supernatural to a world with limited notions of reality, Beloved is nothing more or less than a memory come to life that has too conveniently been forgotten.

For Sethe, Beloved represents more of a psychological than a supernatural phenomenon. In this respect, Beloved can be explained in terms of the double, a theme Lloyd-Smith identifies in the literature of the uncanny:

> Within this category come reflections in mirrors, shadows, beliefs in the soul and fear of death, for the double can be a sort of insurance against the death of the ego, stemming from what Freud calls primary narcissism. When this stage has been surmounted, the double reverses its function, and instead of an assurance of immortality it becomes "the uncanny harbinger of death." All of these interpretations, however, have to do with the doubling of the self: what we have often occasion to remark in fiction is the doubling of the *Other*, and especially the other as woman.[6]

The theme of the double is useful in understanding the unusual relationship that develops between Sethe and Beloved. On one level Sethe and Beloved are reunited as mother and daughter, but as the relationship evolves, then disintegrates, more is at work than the reunion of the two. Beloved becomes a monster of sorts, bent on sucking dry the life of Sethe. Though Beloved has every reason to hate her mother, and to desire retribution for a nearly incomprehensible act, she—her spitefulness in particular—seems more a projection of Sethe's imagination than a reincarnation of her daughter.

Beloved's appearance coincides with the surprising and welcome return of Paul D, the very person who can make Sethe happy for the first time. But Sethe knows that life with Paul D cannot be a reality unless she deals with the guilt of the infanticide. Serving a confrontational function, then, Beloved acts as Sethe's double, reliving in stages the moments of her mother's life from infancy to sexual awakening to attempted murder. Beloved becomes Sethe's hair shirt, a painful attempt to heal herself by rediscovering the steps leading to an unspeakable act. Instead of reconciliation, however, Sethe finds those events so repugnant that her life becomes negligible and her double, Beloved, nearly destroys her.

Days after Paul D's arrival, Beloved appears, developmentally and emotionally a two-year-old; she can barely walk, cannot talk clearly or intelligibly, and lies in bed for days after her arrival staring adoringly at Sethe and sucking on candy. Beloved soon grows up, not as Beloved since her life was snuffed out, but as Sethe's alter ego. In this way Sethe, having conjured guilt in the image of her dead child, can attempt to exorcise it.

In the initial or narcissistic stage, Beloved emerges from the water as an infant who can do little more than ogle her mother in wonderment: "Beloved could not take her eyes off Sethe. Stooping to shake the damper, or snapping sticks for kindlin, Sethe was licked, tasted, eaten by Beloved's eyes" (p. 57). But the relationship is not exclusively child-daughter since Sethe does not relish the same attention from her other daughter, Denver: "Sethe was flattered by Beloved's open, quiet devotion. The same adoration from her daughter . . . would have annoyed her; make her chill at the thought of having raised a ridiculously dependent child. But the company of this sweet, if peculiar, guest pleased her the way a zealot pleases his teacher" (p. 57).

The stage of self-love continues as the double regains memory of the past. Beloved feeds off of Sethe's old stories much to the delight of Sethe, who had avoided any mention of it even with Baby Suggs and Paul D, "who had shared some of it and to whom she could talk with at least a measure of calm, the hurt was always there—like a tender place in the corner of her mouth that the bit left" (p. 58). With Beloved there is no such pain: "Perhaps it was Beloved's distance from the events itself, or her thirst for hearing it—in any case it was an unexpected pleasure" (p. 58). Although Beloved's interest is a typically childish proclivity for a parent's distant past, her knowledge of past events that Sethe did not mention—in particular the diamond earrings— suggests a shared memory. Denver wonders about Beloved's recollections: "How did she know?" (p. 63).

Self-love wanes as the double Beloved gets closer to the events of her own death. Gaining strength and conviction from her own martyrdom, Beloved takes it upon herself to be Sethe's judge and jury. But in order to reach this point she must first distance Sethe from Denver and Paul D. She does this systematically, befriending the lonely Denver, seducing Paul D—a transgression less reprehensible if Beloved can be conceptualized as Sethe's double—and finally by demanding exclusive attention and caring from Sethe. Paul D soon walks out and Sethe wonders, not why her life is marked with so much misery, but why "every eighteen or twenty years her unlivable life would be interrupted by a short-lived glory?" (p. 173).

Once the double Beloved has stripped Sethe of any significant other who could provide Sethe with emotional balance, Beloved proceeds to consume her. "Dressed in Sethe's dresses, she stroked her skin with the palm of her hand. She imitated Sethe, talked the way she did, laughed her laugh and used her body the same way down to the walk, the way Sethe moved her hands, sighed through her nose, held her head. Sometimes coming upon them making men and women cookies or tacking scraps of cloth on Baby Suggs' old quilt, it was difficult for Denver to tell who was who" (p. 241). Sethe and Beloved become so exclusive with each other that they allow nothing to interfere with their relationship—not Paul D, not Denver, not the community, not even work.

The narcissistic stage, however, ends abruptly when Sethe discovers the scar on Beloved's neck that marks her crime. The irresolution of Sethe's act becomes a wedge between them. Sethe and Beloved begin to argue, Sethe attempting to impose parental restraints on the spoiled Beloved and Beloved rebelling against a mother she feels abdicated her responsibilities when she slit her throat. When Sethe eventually gives in to the enormity of the guilt, Beloved becomes her executioner, condemning her to a slow death in which redemption, no matter how earnest or feverish the repentance, is denied. Beloved is Sethe's own unforgiving memory, growing obese with Sethe's guilt while Sethe withers to an emaciated condition.

Since Sethe is locked into her self-imposed psychological terror she is incapable of extricating herself from the grip of her double. Denver takes it upon herself to save her mother, an ironic twist since, as Denver says, "the job she started out with, protecting Beloved from Sethe, changed to protecting her mother from Beloved. Now it was obvious that her mother could die and leave them both and what would Beloved do then?" (p. 243). Denver enlists the aid of the community, the women in particular, to intervene in a situation out of control. The ghost-turned-demon Beloved is exorcised by a community that knows too well the corrosive sin of guilt and who, like Ella, "didn't like the idea of past errors taking possession of the present" (p. 256).

While the double can explain Beloved in psychological terms, it cannot explain the fact that Beloved is visible and real to the other characters as well—Denver, Paul D, the women in the community. Her manifestation is a slow and careful process, Morrison purposely offering revelation in degrees. Though initially an invisible force only capable of the typical poltergeist activities—moving chairs, rattling cabinets, frightening dogs and children—Beloved eventually manifests herself as a ghostly apparition, then as a full-blooded human being. Finally, Beloved grows to obese proportions until she explodes under the collective gaze of an indignant gathering of women. Beloved can never be fully conceptualized because she is continually in a state of transition. But the fact that she can be seen at all is testimony to her power as a supernatural force, a semiotic haint.

Beloved represents not only the spirit of Sethe's daughter; she is also the projection of repressed collective memory of a violated people. The ghost of the murdered child, Beloved epitomizes the inconceivability not only of slavery but of the extent to which it dehumanized people. The real Sethe, Margaret Garner, killed her daughter so that she would not become a slave, a more frightening and terrifying prospect than death itself. Such a story plumbs the depths of human depravity, something that most people choose not to contemplate. Morrison says she wrote *Beloved* convinced that "this has got to be the least read of all the books I'd written because it is about something that the characters don't want to remember, I don't want to remember, black people don't want to remember, white people don't want to remember. I mean, it's national amnesia."[7]

The fact that Morrison did write the book and that it is such a success suggests that readers feel the same need as Morrison to purge themselves; once again, writer, audience, and text engage in a dynamic of identification. *Beloved*, then, functions as supernatural memory relived for the sake of psychic and spiritual rehabilitation. Only through memory can the past be integrated into the present providing meaning to what it means to be human.

Since Morrison's assumption in writing *Beloved* is that everyone wants to forget, she exerts considerable creative energy in making us remember. Her own characters live a daily struggle to ward off the ever-present past. When Sethe suggests to Baby Suggs that they could move from the haunted 124, Baby Suggs responds, "What'd be the point. . . ? Not a house in the country ain't packed to its rafters with some dead Negro's grief" (p. 5). Baby Suggs also suffers memory loss with regard to her eight children, all now gone. She says, "My first-born. All I can remember of her is how she loved the burned bottom of bread. Can you beat that? Eight children and that's all I remember." Sethe remarks, "That's all you let yourself remember" (p. 5). But Sethe, too, only remembers in snatches; her own children are distant memories: "As for the rest she worked hard to remember as close to nothing as was safe" (p. 6). When Stamp Paid approaches 124, he senses the history of incredible pain and suffering that "was the mumbling of the black and angry dead" (p. 198). The atmosphere created by this conglomeration of dead souls Stamp Paid likens to a jungle, but one implanted in blacks by whites: "And it grew. It spread. In, through and after life, it spread, until it invaded the whites who had made it. Touched them every one. Changed and altered them. Made them bloody, silly, worse than even they wanted to be, so scared were they of the jungle they had made" (pp. 198–99). And finally, on Paul D's return to Sethe, he attempts to put the past behind him: "Me and you, we got more yesterday than anybody. We need some kind of tomorrow" (p. 273).

While this chapter in Sethe's and Paul's life ends on a hopeful note—both having come to grips with their yesterdays—the novel does not end with any conciliatory remarks. Lest readers think they can read the book, feel cleansed, and then lay it down, Morrison provides an unsettling coda. "It was not a story to pass on," she says, though indeed that is what she has just done. After acknowledging the unsuitability of retelling this story, she then accuses her characters, and by implication, her readership and herself, of convenient memories: "They forgot her like a bad dream" (p. 274). By drawing attention to the literary production of her novel and to the casual nature in which it is ingested and then forgotten, Morrison has anticipated the inevitable and final reader response.

Despite the pessimism that marks the ending, *Beloved*—as well as her other works—endeavors to transcend the restrictive notion of time, invoking the supernatural as both a figurative and actual means to reunion with the past. The supernatural in Morrison's world may inevitably be historicity—the blind horsemen, the chevaliers, Circe, Ryna, Shalimar, the night women, Macon Dead, Beloved. Only by recovering that past, Morrison suggests, can individuals be provided with a total vision of their world and, hence, a foundation of truth without which there would be no hope for "some kind of tomorrow."

Notes

1. Schelling quoted in Allan Gardner Lloyd-Smith, *Uncanny American Fiction* (New York: St. Martin's Press, 1989), 1.
2. Toni Morrison quoted in Elizabeth Kastor, review of *Beloved,* in *Washington Post,* rpt. *Raleigh News and Observer,* 23 October 1987, D3.
3. Interview with Bonnie Angelo, "The Pain of Being Black," *Time,* 22 May 1989, 120.
4. Lloyd-Smith, *Uncanny American Fiction,* 10.
5. Ibid., 12.
6. Ibid., 8.
7. Angelo, *Time* interview, 120.

Giving Body to the Word:
The Maternal Symbolic
in Toni Morrison's *Beloved*

JEAN WYATT

In *Beloved* Toni Morrison puts into words three orders of experience that Western cultural narratives usually leave out: childbirth and nursing from a mother's perspective; the desires of a preverbal infant; and the sufferings of those destroyed by slavery, including the Africans who died on the slave ships. The project of incorporating into a text subjects previously excluded from language causes a breakdown and restructuring of linguistic forms; to make room for the articulation of alternative desires, Morrison's textual practice flouts basic rules of normative discourse.

Through the device of the ghost story, Morrison gives a voice to the preverbal infant killed by a mother desperate to save her child from slavery: the dead baby, Beloved, comes back in the body of a nineteen-year-old, able to articulate infantile feelings that ordinarily remain unspoken. Her desire to regain the maternal closeness of a nursing baby powers a dialogue that fuses pronoun positions and abolishes punctuation, undoing all the marks of separation that usually stabilize language. Beloved also has a collective identity: she represents a whole lineage of people obliterated by slavery, beginning with the Africans who died on the Middle Passage, the "Sixty Million and more" of the novel's epigraph. She describes conditions on the slave ships in fragmented images without connective syntax or punctuation, capturing the loss of demarcation and differentiation of those caught in an "oceanic" space between cultural identities, between Africa and an unknown destination (Spillers 72).

The mother figure, Sethe, defines herself as a maternal body. Her insistence on her own physical presence and connection to her children precludes an easy acceptance of the separations and substitutions that govern language: she will not, for example, use signifiers to represent her nursing baby, so she cannot tell the story of the baby's murder. The novel's discourse also tends to

Reprinted by permission of the Modern Language Association of America from *PMLA* 108, no. 3 (May 1993): 474–88.

resist substitution, "the very law of metaphoric operation" (Rose 38): when the narrative focuses on either the maternal body or the haunted house, metaphors abandon their symbolic dimension to adhere to a baseline of literal meaning. For instance, a figure of speech in which *weight* usually means "responsibility" turns out to describe only the physical weight of Sethe's breasts (18). A similar "literalization" of spatial metaphors mimics the materializations in the haunted house: the phrase "she moved him" indicates not that Beloved stirred Paul D's emotions but that she physically moved him, from one location to another (114).[1] The continual shift from the abstract to the concrete creates the illusion of words sliding back to a base in the material world, an effect congruent with Morrison's emphasis on embodiment—on both the physical processes of maternity and the concrete presence of the ghost: "Usually [slavery] is an abstract concept. . . . The purpose of making [the ghost] real is making history possible, making memory real—somebody walks in the door and sits down at the table, so you have to think about it" (qtd. in Darling 6).

Describing a child's entry into language as a move from maternal bodily connection to a register of abstract signifiers, Lacan inadvertently sums up the psychological prerequisites for belonging to a patriarchal symbolic order. I invoke his paradigm to point out Morrison's deviations from dominant language practices and from the psychological premises that underlie them; I use the term *maternal symbolic* to discuss not only an alternative language incorporating maternal and material values but also a system that, like Lacan's symbolic, locates subjects in relation to other subjects. While Sethe operates within her own "maternal symbolic" of presence and connection, it is Denver, Sethe's surviving daughter, who in the end finds a more inclusive replacement for Lacan's paternal symbolic: a social order that conflates oral and verbal pleasures, nurtures her with words, and teaches her that caring is "what language was made for" (252).[2]

THE MATERNAL BODY IN LANGUAGE: A DISCOURSE OF PRESENCE

The mother figure of *Beloved* occupies a contradictory position in discourse. On the one hand, Sethe's self-definition as maternal body enables Morrison to construct a new narrative form—a specifically female quest powered by the desire to get one's milk to one's baby—that features childbirth as high adventure. On the other hand, this same self-definition forecloses Sethe's full participation in language.

In presenting Sethe's journey from slavery in Kentucky to the free state of Ohio as a maternal quest, Morrison is elaborating the figure of the heroic slave mother that in many female slave narratives replaces the figure of the heroic male fugitive. Harriet Jacobs's *Incidents in the Life of a Slave Girl,* for example, turns the rhetoric of heroic resolve common to male slave narratives into a text of courage drawn from a mother's love for her children: "I was resolved that I would foil my master and save my children, or I would perish in the attempt"; "Every trial I endured, every sacrifice I made for [the children's] sakes, drew them closer to my heart, and gave me fresh courage" (84, 89–90). If Jacobs (and other female slave narrators, like Lucy Delaney) appropriates the conventions of male heroism for the celebration of motherhood,[3] Morrison in turn reconstructs the acts of maternal heroism as the reproductive feats of the maternal body. Both Sethe and Jacobs find the courage to escape because they want their children to be free—"It was more for my helpless children than for myself that I longed for freedom," writes Jacobs (89)—but Jacobs's spiritual and emotional commitment becomes in Sethe a physical connection to the nursing baby she has sent on ahead: "I had to get my milk to my baby girl" (16). Sethe, like Jacobs, experiences the wish to give up the fight for survival and die, but while Jacobs says she was "willing to bear on" "for the children's sakes" (127), the reason that Sethe gives for enduring is the physical presence of the baby in her womb: "[I]t didn't seem such a bad idea [to die], . . . but the thought of herself stretched out dead while the little antelope lived on . . . in her lifeless body grieved her so" that she persevered (31).

The central heroic feat of Sethe's journey is her giving birth in the face of seemingly insuperable obstacles. Alone in the wilderness in a sinking boat on the Ohio River, in a state of physical injury and exhaustion, Sethe has only Amy, a white runaway indentured servant, to help her. Breaking the silence that has surrounded birth in Western narrative, Morrison provides a physically detailed account of childbirth, and—also new in Western cultural discourse—she gives labor its due as good work: Sethe and Amy "did something together appropriately and well" (84).

When Sethe finally wins through to Ohio, the text celebrates not the achievement of freedom but togetherness; a confusion of prepositions reflects the multiplicity of connections between mother and children: "Sethe lay in bed under, around, over, among but especially with them all" (93). At the triumphant close of her maternal quest, Sethe reports, "I was big, Paul D, and deep and wide and when I stretched out my arms all my children could get in between. I was *that* wide"; "she had milk enough for all" (162, 100). Thus the "nurturing power of the slave mother" (Gates xxxi) celebrated in women's slave narratives becomes literal in Morrison's account: Sethe's monumental body and abundant milk give and sustain life. But in spite of its mythic dimensions, the maternal body seems to lack a subjective center. During the journey, Sethe experiences her own existence only in relation to her children's survival; she is "concerned" not for herself but "for the life of her children's mother." She thinks, "I believe this baby's ma'am is gonna die" and pictures herself as "a crawling graveyard for a six-month baby's last hours" (30, 31, 34).

Sethe maintains this roundabout self-definition through the many images of nursing that picture her as the sustaining ground of her children's existence; even after the children are weaned, her bond with them remains so strong that she continues to think of it as a nursing connection (100, 162, 200, 216). While celebrating the courage and determination that Sethe draws from this attachment, Morrison's narrative also dramatizes the problems of Sethe's maternal subjectivity, which is so embedded in her children that it both allows her to take the life of one of them and precludes putting that act into words.

When Sethe tries to explain her attempt to kill herself and her children to prevent their reenslavement, she finds speech blocked: "Sethe knew that the circle she was making around . . . the subject would remain one. That she could never close in, pin it down for anybody who had to ask."[4] A gap remains at the heart of her story, which the omniscient narrator subsequently fills in:

> [W]hen she saw [the slave owner] coming [to recapture them, she] collected every bit of life she had made, all the parts of her that were precious and fine and beautiful, and carried, pushed, dragged them through the veil, out, away, over there where no one could hurt them . . . where they would be safe. (163)

Sethe extends her rights over her own body—the right to use any means, including death, to protect herself from a return to slavery—to the "parts of her" that are her children, folding them back into the maternal body in order to enter death as a single unit (though she succeeded in killing only one of her daughters). The novel withholds judgment on Sethe's act and persuades the reader to do the same, presenting the infanticide as the ultimate contradiction of mothering under slavery. "It was absolutely the right thing to do, . . . but it's also the thing you have no right to do," Morrison commented in an interview (Rothstein).[5]

Sethe's sense of continuity with her children also makes it difficult for her to take the position of narrating subject and tell her story. Her troubled relation to language can be read as a carryover from a nursing mother's attitude toward separation. When she engineered her family's escape from slavery, Sethe had to send her nursing baby ahead of her to Ohio: "I told the women in the wagon . . . to put sugar water in cloth to suck from so when I got there in a few days [the baby] wouldn't have forgot me. The milk would be there and I would be there with it" (16). Sethe would not compromise with absence, overlooking the potentially life-threatening lack of food for her baby "for a few days" to insist on presence: the milk would be "there," and the mother would be "there with it." The standpoint of nursing mother precludes separation and the substitutions that any separation would require.

Sethe's embrace of a relational system of presence and connection, her reluctance to accept the principle of substitution, extends to her refusal to invest in words and helps explain the link between her failure to tell the story of her baby girl's death and that baby's embodiment in Beloved. Lacan's account of a child's entry into language opposes bodily connection and verbal exchange in a way that clarifies Sethe's choices. To move into a position in language and the social order, according to Lacan, an infant must sacrifice its imaginary sense of wholeness and continuity with the mother's body. (Sethe is of course in the mother's position rather than the child's, but her physical connection with her nursing baby resembles the infant's initial radical dependency on the mother's body.) Lacan later makes the repudiation of maternal continuity an oedipal event, when the social law of the father prohibits the child's access to the maternal body. In "The Function and Field of Speech and Language in Psychoanalysis," however, he borrows from Freud an unmediated mother-child anecdote, perhaps to focus more intensely on the either-or choice between bodily presence and abstract signifier. Freud's grandson Ernst becomes a speaking subject in the same moment that he acknowledges his mother's absence. Throwing a spool out of his crib and bringing it back to the accompaniment of sounds ("ooo! aaa!") that Freud interprets as "Fort! Da!" ("Gone! There!"), the baby assumes a symbolic mastery over what he cannot control in reality—his mother's presence and absence (Freud, *Pleasure* 8–10). Lacan adds that the child "thereby raises his desire to a second power," investing desire in language (103). By acknowledging that he must put a signifier there, where his mother's body used to be, the child both recognizes absence and accepts loss. The word "manifests itself first of all as the murder of the thing" (104), or in John Muller's gloss, "the word destroys the immediacy of objects and gives us distance from them" (29).[6] It is this distance, this loss, that Sethe rejects. Just as she declined any mediation between her body and her nursing baby, insisting on presence, she now refuses to replace that baby with a signifier, to accept the irrevocability of absence by putting the child's death into words. Her denial of loss is fundamentally antimetaphorical—that is, the refusal to displace libido onto words is a refusal to let one thing stand for another and so impedes the whole project of speech.[7] Sethe remains without a narrative but with the baby ghost—there, embodied, a concrete presence.

Through Sethe's reluctance to substitute words for things, not just Beloved but all the painful events of the past that Sethe has not transformed into narrative are left there, where those events first occurred. "[W]hat I did, or knew, or saw, is still out there. Right in the place where it happened," Sethe tells Denver (36). The plot reflects this spatialized time, as incidents from the past occupy the various rooms in which they originally took place. In the shed, the murder replays, at least for Beloved; in the keeping room, an injured and demoralized Sethe once more gets bathed "in sections" by loving hands; and a white man "coming into [Sethe's] yard" triggers a repeat of her murderous attack—with a saving difference (123–24, 272, 262). The plot—present time—cannot move forward because Sethe's space is crammed with the past:

> When she woke the house crowded in on her: there was the door where the soda crackers were lined up in a row; the white stairs her baby girl loved to climb; the corner where Baby Suggs mended shoes . . . the exact place on the stove where Denver burned her fingers. . . . There was no room for any other thing or body. . . . (39)

There are no gaps in Sethe's world, no absences to be filled in with signifiers; everything is there, an oppressive plenitude.

Language reinforces the sense that materializations clog the haunted house: spatial images that usually function as figures of speech take shape as actions. For example, when Paul D, a former slave from the same plantation as Sethe, finds her again after an absence of eighteen years, he feels out his chances for establishing a relationship with her by asking if "there was some space" for him (45). While his expression seems natural in the circumstances, the situation in the house causes Paul D to make a space for himself more literally than any suitor in literature: "[H]olding the table by two legs, he bashed it about, wrecking everything, screaming back at the screaming house" (18). Evidently Morrison wants the opening statement of the novel— that "124 was spiteful. Full of a baby's venom" (3)—to be taken quite literally. Before the dead baby takes the shape of Beloved, her amorphous spirit haunts the house, filling it so completely with her spite that "[t]here was no room for any other thing or body until Paul D . . . broke up the place, making room, . . . then standing in the place he had made" (39).

After Paul D exorcises the ghost from the house and it returns in the shape of Beloved, spatial metaphors continue to reflect the materialization of things that belong by rights in a spiritual realm. The sentence "She moved him," for example, opens a chapter about Beloved's domestic relations with Paul D (114). Because the grammatical object of *moved* is a human being— *him* rather than *it*—the phrase seems at first glance to operate figuratively, as in "she affected him emotionally." But the spiritual meaning quickly gives way to physical actuality as it becomes clear that Paul D "was being moved" literally (126)—out of Sethe's bed, out of the living room, finally out of the house altogether—by Beloved's jealous desire to expel her rival.

Textual practice similarly seconds Sethe's emphasis on presence by rejecting metaphorical substitutions for the maternal body. In the opening scene, after Sethe has told Paul D about her quest to get her milk to her baby in Ohio, he cups her breasts from behind in a display of tenderness: "What she knew was that the responsibility for her breasts, at last, was in somebody else's hands" (18). The reader does a double take: the phrase "in somebody else's hands" usually functions as a metaphor meaning "someone else's responsibility"; here the hands are literally there, and what rests in them is not an abstract concept but flesh. The same slippage occurs in the next sentence, as Sethe imagines being "relieved of the weight of her breasts" (18). Because *weight* appears within the usually figurative phrase "relieved of the weight of," readers assume that it is a metaphor for care or responsibility, but the modifying phrase "of her breasts" gives *weight* back its literal meaning. When the maternal body becomes the locus of discourse, the metaphorical becomes the actual, a move that reinforces Sethe's definition of motherhood as an embodied responsibility: there are no substitutes, metaphorical or otherwise, for her breasts.

In the same passage, Paul D "reads" the story of slavery engraved on Sethe's back by a final savage beating. Because the scar tissue is without sensation—"her back skin had been dead for years" (18)—Sethe's back is, in a sense, not her own; it has been appropriated and reified as a tablet on which the slave masters have inscribed their code. She cannot substitute for this discourse of violence her own version of the event, in spite of Paul D's insistence (over the space of three pages) that she tell him about it. Sethe refuses, repeating instead Amy Denver's description of the wound left by the whipping as "a whole tree . . . in bloom": "I got a tree on my back. . . . I've never seen it and never will. But that's what she said it looked like. A chokecherry tree. Trunk, branches, and even leaves" (79, 15–16). The metaphor masks suffering and puts it at the distance of a beautiful image—an act of poetic detachment appropriate, perhaps, to Amy's position of onlooker after the event but not to Sethe's subjective experience of pain.[8] Unable to seize the word and thus become master of her own experience, Sethe remains "a body whose flesh . . . bears . . . the marks of a cultural text" that inscribes her as slave (Spillers 67).[9] Sethe's problematic relation to language results from her position as body not only in a maternal order but also in a social order that systematically denied the subject position to those it defined as objects of exchange.[10]

In the absence of a speaking subject, Morrison makes the most of body language, as the passage I have been analyzing, quoted in full, shows:

> Behind her, bending down, his body an arc of kindness, he held her breasts in the palms of his hands. He rubbed his cheek on her back and learned that way her sorrow, the roots of it; its wide trunk and intricate branches. . . . [H]e would tolerate no peace until he had touched every ridge and leaf of it with his mouth, none of which Sethe could feel because her back skin had been dead for years. What she knew was that the responsibility for her breasts, at last, was in somebody else's hands.
>
> Would there be a little space, she wondered, a little time, some way to . . . just stand there a minute or two, . . . relieved of the weight of her breasts . . . and feel the hurt her back ought to. Trust things and remember things because the last of the Sweet Home men was there to catch her if she sank? (17–18)

On Sethe's back, the extreme of a patriarchal symbolic order "recast . . . in the terms of cultural domination" (Abel 187), a "hieroglyphics of the flesh" (Spillers 67); on her front, the locus of a maternal system of relations based on presence and connection: Paul D, flexible man, "reads" both stories through touch, quickly becoming a participant in Sethe's discourse of bodily connection. Implicit in the space Paul D's kind body protects is the possibility of yet a third relational system: Sethe thinks that with him there she might feel safe enough to "go inside," "feel the hurt her back ought to," and thus replace the outside language the slave owners imprinted on her body with an inner language of articulate memory; she might be able to tell her story (46, 18). But the potential for reclaiming her past along with its pain is not realized till Paul D re-creates this holding space in the last scene, enabling Sethe to move into the position of narrating subject from a base in physical intimacy. First she has to live out the unspeakable drama of the past that possesses the house—a symbiosis with her daughter that would only have been appropriate eighteen years before, when Beloved was a nursling in body as well as in spirit.

WHO IS BELOVED?

In part 2, Sethe lives out the dream of sustaining her ghostly daughter with her own substance—a nursing fantasy writ large. On the personal level, Beloved is the nursing baby that Sethe killed. But in the social dimension that always doubles the personal in *Beloved,* the ghost represents—as the generic name Beloved suggests—all the loved ones lost through slavery, beginning with the Africans who died on the slave ships. In one sense, then, the pain that haunts Sethe's house is nothing special: "Not a house in the country ain't packed to its rafters with some dead Negro's grief" (5). Accordingly, Beloved's message means one thing to those within the family circle and another thing altogether to those who listen from outside the house, from the vantage point of the community.[11] Morrison introduces the conversation of Sethe, Beloved, and Denver that takes up most of part 2 as "unspeakable thoughts, unspoken" (199): in its drive toward unity, the mother-daughter dialogue wipes out all the positions of separation necessary to language, and it is in this sense "unspeakable." But Stamp Paid, who listens from outside, from social ground, hears in Beloved's speech a whole chorus of "the black and angry dead," a communal "roaring" that is "unspeakable" because the accumulated sufferings under slavery overwhelm the expressive possibilities of ordinary discourse (198, 181, 199). What cannot be encompassed within the symbolic order continues to haunt it, hovering on the edge of language.

Beloved herself ends up outside social discourse, wandering, after the narrative's conclusion, in a limbo where she is "[d]isremembered and unaccounted for" (274). Her position in the epilogue is symmetrical with that of the "Sixty Million and more" of Morrison's epigraph. Having perished on the slave ships midway between a place in African history and a place in the history of American slavery, these lost souls never made it into any text. Lost still, they remain stranded in the epigraph, where their human features are erased beneath a number; they are quantified in death, as they had been in life by a property system that measured wealth in terms of a body count. Morrison's "and more" indicates the residue left over, left out, unaccounted for by any text—like Beloved at the end. Denver gestures toward the larger dimension of Beloved's identity when she responds to Paul D's question "You think [the ghost] sure 'nough your sister?" with an echo of the epigraph: "At times. At times I think she was—more" (266).

Morrison is unwilling, apparently, to leave the historical parallel at the level of suggestion. She links Beloved to the "Sixty Million and more" by joining her spirit to the body of a woman who died on one of the slave ships. But first, in a monologue that comes out of nowhere, Beloved gives an account of slave ship experience:

> I am always crouching   the man on my face is dead . . . in the beginning the women are away from the men and the men are away from the women storms rock us and mix the men into the women and the women into the men   that is when I begin to be on the back of the man   for a long time I see only his neck and his wide shoulders above me . . . he locks his eyes and dies on my face . . . the others do not know that he is dead. (211–12)

Since Morrison does not identify these scattered perceptions as observations of life on a slave ship or tell how Beloved came to be there or give any coordinates of time and place, readers are baffled: they have no idea where they are. Their confusion thus imitates the disorientation of the Africans who were thrown into the slave ships without explanation, suspended without boundaries in time and space, "in movement across the Atlantic but . . . also nowhere at all . . . inasmuch as . . . the captive[s] . . . did not know where [they were]." The fragmented syntax and absence of punctuation robs the reader of known demarcations, creating a linguistic equivalent of the Africans' loss of differentiation in an "oceanic" space that "unmade" cultural identities and erased even the lines between male and female, living and dead (Spillers 72).

Readers who try to understand these unsettling images as metaphors for Beloved's passage from death to life can find a basis for doing so in the African American narrative tradition, which pictures the Middle Passage as a journey toward a horrific rebirth. (Robert Hayden calls the Middle Passage a "voyage through death to life upon these shores" [48, 54]; Richard Wright remarks, "We millions of black folk who live in this land were born into Western civilization of a weird and paradoxical birth" [12].) The nightmare collage of bodies piled on bodies in the slave ship, where it is hard to tell the living from the dead, would then figure Beloved's difficulty in discerning, in her transitional state, whether she is alive or dead, traveling toward death or toward life. But

Morrison everywhere demands that readers confront the horrors of slavery "in the flesh" rather than at the comfortable distance of metaphor (qtd. in Darling 5). "I wanted that haunting not to be really a suggestion of being bedeviled by the past," she comments, "but to have it be incarnate" (qtd. in Rothstein). What at first appears symbolic becomes actual in a characteristic collapse of metaphor into literal reality—a slippage that accompanies the central material-ization of the novel, Beloved's embodiment. Scattered through Beloved's monologue are fragments that form the following sequence. Beloved becomes attached to the face of a woman actually on the slave ships, follows the woman's body into the sea after the sailors throw it overboard, and "joins" with it: the woman's "face comes through the water . . . her face is mine . . . I have to have my face . . . she knows I want to join   she chews and swallows me   I am gone   now I am her face" (211–13).[12] Beloved returns, then, in the body of one of the original "disappeared," and all her gestures are shadowed by a larger historical outline. Or, as she herself sees it, "All of it is now   it is always now": the unnumbered losses of slavery are collected in Beloved, in a temporal space outside the linear time of history (210).[13]

But Beloved is also the one-year-old baby that Sethe killed. Morrison skillfully exploits the parallels between a spirit in search of a body and a pre-oedipal child who desires a merger with her mother. To both, the boundaries between persons are permeable, permitting a "join," and both project this identity confusion as a dialectic of faces. As disembodied spirit, Beloved says, "I need to find a place to be," with the words "to be" taking on all the urgency of their literal meaning. Neither her language nor her need to find a support for her existence changes, however, when it is her mother's face that she needs: "I need to find a place to be . . . [Sethe's] smiling face is the place for me" (213). The ghost's insistence on becoming embodied blends, in Mor-rison's song of desire, with the preverbal child's dependence on the maternal face as a mirror of her own existence.[14]

Beloved wants from words the verbal equivalent of a face that reflects her exactly as she is, reassuring her of her own existence and of her identity with her mother. In the mother-daughter dialogue that follows her mono-logue, language bends to Beloved's desire. While a spoken dialogue (ideally) moves toward something new, with the difference voiced by one speaker moving the other speaker away from his or her original position, the dialogue among the three women imitates a mother-infant dialectic: it is motivated not by difference but by the desire to ascertain that the other is there and that the other is the same. It "moves" only toward the stasis of interreflecting mir-rors, ending in identical statements wherein like mirrors like:

> You are mine
> You are mine
> You are mine.
> (217)

What happens to language here reflects what happens in the female family circle, as Sethe (and Denver, for a time) is persuaded by Beloved's preoedipal understanding that the mother is an extension of the self: "I am not separate from her   there is no place where I stop" (210). Punctuation disappears, leaving the sentence of each participant open to the sentence of the next speaker, and the personal pronouns *I* and *you* move toward each other, losing their difference first to become interchangeable and then to mesh in the possessive *mine*. Initially, some difference remains. Sethe and Denver say:

> You are my sister
> You are my daughter

to which Beloved responds:

> You are my face; you are me.
> (216)

In Sethe's and Denver's lines, normative language reflects normative family life. Separate pronouns correspond to the separate positions of family members who are connected only in the circumscribed ways authorized by conventional kinship structures. Beloved's statement, though, overthrows the classifications that locate persons in cultural space, insisting on a closer relationship than either language or family law allows: "you are me."

"You are my face; I am you. Why did you leave me who am you?" With this line, Beloved completes the limited and stubborn logic of the preoedipal: if I am you, there is no leeway for separation; you *cannot* leave me. In the lines

> I have your milk . . .
> I brought your milk

the nursing connection erodes the distinctions of the symbolic by making the boundary between "you" and "me" soluble (216). Is the milk that the baby drinks part of the baby or part of the mother? Does the "I" in "I have your milk" refer to Sethe, who might be saying that she "has" (is carrying) Beloved's milk, or to Beloved, who could just as well be the "I" who speaks, saying that she "has" Sethe's milk inside her? The dedifferentiation of possessive pronouns dramatizes the impossibility of separating what belongs to the one body from what belongs to the other when the two are joined by the nipple or, rather, by the milk that flows between them, blurring borders.

Nursing serves as a figure for the totality and exclusivity of mother-daughter fusion: "Nobody will ever get my milk no more except my own children," says Sethe, turning inward, and Beloved completes the circle, "lapping devotion like cream" (200, 243). Since Beloved has moved Paul D out and thus demolished the shadowy oedipal triangle ("the three shadows [who]

held hands" [47, 49]) that threatened her hold on her mother, no father figure diverts Sethe's attention from her baby, and no "paternal signifier" points
Beloved toward a larger symbolic order. She gets to live out the preoedipal
wish "to be the exclusive desire of the mother" (Lacan, "Les formations" 14;
qtd. in Rose 38).

The nursing paradigm does not work as the governing principle of family life, though. "Beloved . . . never got enough of anything: lullabies, new
stitches, the bottom of the cake bowl, the top of the milk. . . . [W]hen Sethe
ran out of things to give her, Beloved invented desire" (240). As preverbal
infant, Beloved has not accepted the law of symbolic substitutions with which
Freud's grandson made his peace, so no partial gift will do. She wants a total
union with the mother, to have her and to be her. The text literalizes a nursing baby's fantasy of oral greed consuming the breast, the mother, and all
(Klein 200–01): Sethe wastes away while Beloved becomes "bigger, plumper
by the day" (239).[15] This drama of oral incorporation is also appropriate to
Beloved's role as the past that sucks up all Sethe's energies, leaving nothing
for "a life" with a present and future (46).

"You are mine" is of course what the slave owners said, and as in the
larger social order, the disregard of the other as subject, the appropriation of
the other to one's own desires, leads to violence. Although now Beloved's disregard of limits eats up Sethe's life, the logic of "You are mine" originally permitted Sethe to exercise life-or-death rights over the children she conceived as
"parts of her" (163).

A Maternal Symbolic

It is Denver, Sethe's surviving daughter, who in part 3 initiates the breakup
of this self-consuming mother-child circle. Impelled by the need to get food
for her starving mother, she moves into the larger community, but the search
for food is aligned with her own "hunger" for learning. Denver joins a social
order of language and exchange that both feeds her and teaches her to read.
Morrison thus rewrites the entry into the symbolic in terms that retain the
oral and maternal, challenging the orthodox psychoanalytic opposition
between a maternal order of nurturing and a paternal order of abstract signification.

From the beginning, Denver's development reverses Lacan's maturational sequence: what Morrison explicitly calls Denver's "original hunger" is
not for the mother's body but for words (118, 121). At the age of seven, after
a year of reading lessons, Denver abandons language to avoid learning the
truth about her mother's murder of her sister. She becomes deaf and dumb
for two years, "cut off by an answer she could not bear to hear." Since the
period of silence follows the period of verbal exchange, Denver's nostalgia

focuses not on a past of mute connection with the mother's body but on a time of verbal *jouissance*—delight in "the capital *w,* the little *i,* the beauty of the letters in her name, the deeply mournful sentences from the Bible Lady Jones used as a textbook" (103, 102). Not for Denver the normal progress from oral to verbal, from the breast that fills the baby's mouth to verbal substitutes that never quite do so and always leave something to be desired. Instead, words give Denver the pleasures of the mouth, as the conflation of learning with eating implies: "sentences roll[ed] out like pie dough"; Lady Jones "watched her eat up a page, a rule, a figure" (121, 247).

What causes Denver to give up nourishing words for the hunger of not speaking? As a young girl, she lives out the unspeakable, as if to keep her mother's silence intact by locking it up in her body. Her empty ear and empty mouth reproduce in a corporeal language the empty place at the center of the text where her mother's story of the infanticide should be. In Freud's model of hysterical conversion, the symptom enacts the content of a repressed desire; here the paralysis of ear and throat represents not Denver's desire—her own primal hunger is for words—but her mother's wish that the story remain unspoken, the act unnamed, the memory repressed. Denver in effect closes herself up in her mother's silence. At the same time, she gives up her initial indifference to the ghost and begins to "fix [her concentration] on the baby ghost" (103). The complement of her mother's silence is the concrete presence of Beloved, the literalization of what Sethe refuses to abstract into words. When Denver goes "deaf rather than hear the answer, and [keeps] watch for the baby and [withdraws] from everything else" (105), she is retreating into her mother's world, making the rejection of speech and the obsession with the unnamed her own.

The paralysis of Denver's development shows how urgent is the need for a story that will make sense of the baby's death, mark the baby's disappearance, and lay her and the past she represents to rest. Even after Denver returns to speech and hearing, she lacks the narrative context to deal with the baby's death on a conscious level, so she processes it unconsciously in "monstrous and unmanageable dreams" about her mother: "She cut my head off every night" (103, 206). The unconscious, notorious for repetition without resolution, endlessly plays out dream derivatives of the repressed signifier. Meanwhile, the nonsignifying word *thing* marks the gap left by the signifier repressed from conscious thought: "certain odd and terrifying feelings about her mother were collecting around the thing that leapt up inside her" in response to questions about her mother. Freud remarks that the unconscious operates by means of "thing presentation" rather than "word presentation" ("Unconscious" 201). In Denver's idiom the unconscious marker "thing" fills the gap where conscious significance fails. It represents something in her own unconscious: "the thing that leapt up *in her* . . . was a thing that had been lying there all along" (102; my emphasis). Sethe's inability to confront and articulate her action—she hears primary process noises rather than conscious sequential thought when she tries to tell Paul D about the baby's death—results in the unsignified "thing" being lodged like a lump, undigestible and unsignifiable, in her child's unconscious, where it generates the repeated dream of decapitation.[16]

When Denver tries to leave the haunted house to get food for her mother and Beloved, she finds herself imprisoned within her mother's time—a time that, clinging to places, is always happening again: "Out there . . . were places in which things so bad had happened that when you went near them it would happen again. . . . Denver stood on the porch . . . and couldn't leave it." She crosses the threshold into social discourse only when the voice of Baby Suggs, the ancestor, speaks out: "You mean I never told you . . . nothing about how come I walk the way I do and about your mother's feet, not to speak of her back? I never told you all that? Is that why you can't walk down the steps?" (243–44). To a child afraid to step out into the world, the particulars of how that world damaged her grandmother and mother are hardly comforting. It is the speech act itself, the voice of the grandmother putting the past where it belongs, into oral history, that frees Denver to enter the present.

After Denver leaves the closed family circle, she goes straight to the place of verbal nurturance, the house of Lady Jones, the woman who had taught her to read some ten years earlier. However belatedly (she is by now eighteen), she takes the crucial step from the imaginary of mother-daughter fusions to the symbolic order of language and society. But this step does not entail abandoning maternal intimacy. "Oh, baby," says Lady Jones when Denver tells her about her starving mother. "[I]t was the word 'baby,' said softly and with such kindness, that inaugurated her life in the world as a woman." Lady Jones's maternal language indicates that Denver is a child of the community, not just of her mother: "Everybody's child was in that face." She bakes raisin loaves for Denver while teaching her to read Bible verses, and "all through the spring, names appeared near or in gifts of food" (248, 246, 250, 249). Morrison thus confounds the distinction between words and good things to eat, between oral and verbal pleasures.

Denver moves into the symbolic by leaving one nurturing maternal circle for another, but there is a difference. The community, which operates as a network of mutual aid (originally, the network helped slaves escape), takes offense at Sethe's claim of maternal self-sufficiency—that "she had milk enough for all"—and demands instead a reciprocal nurturing. "To belong to a community of other free Negroes [is] to love and be loved by them, . . . [to] feed and be fed." Denver enters into this nurturing reciprocity, "pay[ing] a thank you for half a pie," "paying" for help by telling her story (100, 177, 252, 253).

Acts of maternal care also enable Sethe to move into an order of linguistic exchange. After the community of women intervenes and routs Beloved,[17] Sethe retreats into the keeping room in an imitation of Baby Suggs, who withdrew there to die. "I think I've lost my mother," Denver tells Paul D: the loss of Beloved entails the loss of Sethe, who is still attached to her baby (266). When Paul D offers to bathe her, taking the restorative maternal role once occupied by Baby Suggs (93, 98), Sethe can only protest that she is "nothing . . . now. . . . Nothing left to bathe." Then a consciousness of her body begins to emerge: "Will he [bathe her] in sections? First her face, then her hands, her thighs, her feet, her back? Ending with her exhausted breasts? And if he bathes her in sections, will the parts hold?" (272). Gone is her self-image as maternal life-giver (her breasts are "exhausted" now, after the ordeal of sustaining Beloved); she puts herself together anew, imitating in her fear of fragmentation the first infantile self-image, the body in pieces, that precedes the cohesion of the mirror stage and motor control (Lacan, "Mirror Stage" 4). After the body, the spirit revives. Suddenly freed from the "serious work of beating back the past," Sethe lets all the losses she has repressed flood into her mind: "that she called, but Howard and Buglar walked on down the railroad track and couldn't hear her; that Amy was scared to stay with her because her . . . back looked so bad; that her ma'am had hurt her feelings and she couldn't find her hat anywhere." Having confronted her grief consciously, Sethe quickly moves to put loss into words: "She left me" (73, 272). The act of acknowledging absence and saying "she" splits Beloved off, detaches her from the maternal body that has held the nursing connection static, entombed, and puts a signifier there, where the child's body had been.

In thus shifting from a subjectivity embedded in maternal connection to a subjectivity based on the separate positions of the linguistic register (*she* and *me*), Sethe indeed follows the Lacanian schema, in which taking the position of speaking subject requires a repudiation of continuity with the mother's body (or, for Sethe, with the nursing infant's body). But Morrison revises Lacan here, too, softening his opposition between bodily communion and the abstractions of verbal exchange: "She was my best thing," Sethe says of her lost daughter. Paul D "leans over and takes her hand. With the other he touches her face. 'You your best thing, Sethe. You are.' His holding fingers are holding hers." Sethe answers, "Me? Me?" expressing surprise and disbelief, perhaps, but also recognizing herself in the first-person singular (272–73).[18] Replacing Lacan's vision of the move into language—a move away from bodies touching to the compensations of abstract signifiers—Morrison makes physical contact the necessary support for Sethe's full acceptance of the separate subjectivity required by language systems.[19]

Though Paul D thus encircles Sethe physically, his intent is not to subsume her. The words "You are," standing alone, replace "You are mine," the hallmark of invasive identification in the mother-daughter dialogue. Paul D "wants to put his story next to hers"; the two stories may complement and complete each other (each person having lived out the missing fragment of the other's slave narrative), but they will lie "next to" each other—each whole, circumscribed, with its own beginning, middle, and end (273).[20] Difference can emerge within the space of relationship; a dialogue between self and other can replace the circular mother-daughter dialectic between same and same.

The hope at the end of the novel is that Sethe, having recognized herself as subject, will narrate the mother-daughter story and invent a language that can encompass the desperation of the slave mother who killed her daughter. Or will she? The heterosexual resolution, the enclosure of the mother in the symbolic, leaves out the preoedipal daughter, who wanders lost in the epilogue. She will not be remembered because "nobody anywhere knew her name"; she is "[d]isremembered and unaccounted for" because "they couldn't remember or repeat a single thing she said, and began to believe that . . . she hadn't said anything at all. So, in the end, they forgot her too." Outcast both as victim of slavery whose death is unspeakable and as preverbal infant who has not made her way into the symbolic order, Beloved remains outside language and therefore outside narrative memory. Her story is "not a story to pass on" (274–75). Of course, the sentence is ambiguous: Beloved's story, too terrible to find resolution in the logic of narrative, cannot be passed on from teller to teller, but it also cannot "pass on," or die (35). It continues to haunt the borders of a symbolic order that excludes it.[21]

Notes

1. Margaret Homans's notion of literalization enabled me to see how Morrison's metaphors work. "Literalization," which "occurs when some piece of overtly figurative language, a simile or an extended or conspicuous metaphor, is translated into an actual event or circumstance," is in Homans's opinion a characteristic of women's writing (30). Homans uses Nancy Chodorow's theory to challenge Lacan: because men and women develop differently, women might not polarize body and word, signifier and absent referent, to the extent that men do; thus women writers are less likely to privilege the figurative over the literal and more likely to conceive of presence as commensurate with representation (14).

2. As a white middle-class feminist who practices psychoanalytic theory, I come to this project burdened not only by the usual guilt about my own implication in the racist structures that Morrison uncovers but also by doubts about the suitability of psychoanalytic theory for analyzing an African American text. Psychoanalytic theory is, after all, based on assumptions about family and language grounded in Western European patriarchal culture, while Morrison's novel comes out of African and African American oral and written narrative traditions (see Christian, Holloway, Page, Sale, Sitter). Elizabeth Abel's essay "Race, Class, and Psychoanalysis?" performs an important service to feminist psychoanalysis by canvassing the difficulties of applying psychoanalysis to texts produced by other cultures and the possibilities for modifying object-relations theory and Lacanian theory to include "the roles of race and class in a diversified construction of subjectivity" (184). Reading Abel's essay both focused the limitations of my position as white middle-class female reader of an African American text and gave me the courage to "[k]now it, and go on out the yard" (Morrison 244)—to go on in spite of recognizing the hazards of venturing into a cultural space not my own.

3. Hazel Carby points out that "slave narratives by women, about women, could mobilize the narrative forms of adventure and heroism normally constituted within ideologies of male sexuality" (38). Lucy Delaney, for instance, describes her mother's struggle to free her

children in epic terms: "She had girded up her loins for the fight"; "others would have flinched before the obstacles which confronted her, but undauntedly she pursued her way, until my freedom was established" (35, 45). See also Claudia Tate's discussion of the idealized slave mother (the grandmother) in Jacobs's narrative (109–10).

4.   Sethe may hesitate to tell her story in part because the language available to her—a language structured by the logic of bipolar oppositions—cannot readily encompass the contradictions of motherhood under slavery. Had she access to it, Sethe would find in the discourse of actual slave mothers a language better suited to a world where "safe" from slavery can only mean "dead." Harriet Jacobs, writing from within the paradoxes of "the peculiar institution," indeed conflates maternal love and infanticide: "I would rather see [my children] killed than have them given up to [the slaveholder's] power"; "death is better than slavery" (80, 62).

Since Sethe cannot find a language of "motherlove" (132), her story remains in the rhetoric of the masters. As Mae Henderson points out, "the first [and, I would add, the only] full representation of the events surrounding the infanticide [is] figured from a collective white/male perspective, represented by schoolteacher and the sheriff" (78; see Morrison 149–51). Sethe's story is caught up in "the dominant metaphors of the master('s) narrative—wildness, cannibalism, animality, destructiveness" (Henderson 79).

5.   Readers learn about the infanticide a bit at a time from different perspectives, a technique that prevents them from making simple judgments. Maggie Sale shows that Morrison's narrative strategy forces readers to see the event from multiple perspectives and to recognize that each version depends as much on the needs of the narrator and the listener as on the historical "facts." The lack of a single definitive account "challenges readers to examine their own responses" both to Sethe's act and to the circumstances that force her to it (44).

Stephanie Demetrakopoulos, comparing Sethe and Beloved to mythic counterparts, remarks that "Sethe attempts to return the babies to perhaps a collective mother body, to devour them back into the security of womb/tomb death . . . as the ultimate act of protection" (52). Demetrakopoulos focuses on the destructive effects of Sethe's mothering, especially on her own growth as an individual.

6.   Lacan returns to the *fort-da* anecdote in *Four Fundamental Concepts* only to contradict his earlier reading. Focusing on the spool instead of the accompanying words, Lacan says that it represents an *objet petit a*—an object that is only ambiguously detached from the subject. Because Ernst holds the string that can pull back the spool, "it is a small part of the subject that detaches itself from him, while still remaining his, still retained" (62). In this later text, then, Lacan locates the *fort-da* episode in a zone intermediate between mother-child fusions and the clear-cut separations of the symbolic order instead of naming it, as he did earlier, "the moment . . . in which the child is born into language" ("Function" 104). Kaja Silverman and Elisabeth Bronfen read this second Lacanian interpretation as a parable for the eclipse the subject undergoes on entering language: in *Four Fundamental Concepts* the spool stands for Ernst himself, and the game rehearses his absence; he plays out the fading of the subject as, entering the order of representation, he is replaced by a signifier (Silverman 168–71; Bronfen 27). Bronfen gives a comprehensive and valuable account of various theorists' uses of the *fort-da* episode (15–38), and she adds a new dimension to standard interpretations by considering all the implications of the game's enactment of death (including Freud's use of the anecdote to compensate for the death of Sophie—his daughter and Ernst's mother—during the writing of *Beyond the Pleasure Principle*).

7.   Judith Butler helpfully summarizes the argument of Nicolas Abraham and Maria Torok, who distinguish between the work of mourning, which displaces libido onto words that "both signify and displace [the lost] object," and "incorporation," a refusal of loss in which one preserves the lost object as a (fantasized) part of one's own body (68). In *Black Sun* Julia Kristeva also identifies the melancholic's problem as a failure to transfer libido from the bodily connection with the mother to words; she or he maintains instead an undifferentiated sense of continuity with the maternal body.

8. Characteristically, Sethe can articulate only the part of the abuse connected with her maternal function: "[T]hey took my milk," she repeats (16, 17). In Anne Goldman's view, "schoolteacher orders [Sethe's milk] to be appropriated" because, as the one product of her labor that doesn't belong to the masters, it is the "signifier of an identity, a subjectivity, independent of white authorities" (324). Mae Henderson understands "the theft of her 'mother's milk' " as "the expropriation of [Sethe's] future—her ability to nurture and ensure the survival of the future embodied in the next generation. . . . Sethe must discover some way of regaining control of her story, her body, her progeny, her milk, her ability to nurture the future" (71). Barbara Christian points out that the nephews "milk" Sethe at the behest of schoolteacher, who wants to make the experiment as part of his "scientific observation" of slaves. Christian aligns schoolteacher, who measures slaves' body parts and observes their bodily functions with "apparently neutral" scientific curiosity, with the nineteenth-century white American intellectuals who buttressed slavery with various "scientific" treatises on the physiology of African Americans (337–38).

9. Hortense Spillers's essay helped me understand slavery as a system of domination that mandated slaves' "absence from a subject position" while imprinting the terms of their subjugation on their bodies (67).

By emphasizing the importance of language to a "used-to-be-slave woman," Morrison takes up a central theme of slave narratives (45). "[O]nly by grasping the word" could slaves, who were considered "silently laboring brutes," take part in speech acts that would help them achieve selfhood and give shape to their subjective reality (Baker 243, 245; see also Gates xxiii–xxxi).

Mae Henderson observes, "[B]ecause it is her back (symbolizing the *presence* of her *past*) that is marked, Sethe has only been able to read herself through the gaze of others. The challenge for Sethe is to learn to read herself—that is, to configure the history of her body's text. . . . Sethe must learn how to link these traces (marks of her passage through slavery) to the construction of a personal and historical discourse" (69).

10. Cathy Caruth summarizes theories of trauma and memory that can explain not only Sethe's inability to put the baby's death into narrative form but also the problems that other characters (notably Paul D and Baby Suggs) have in integrating the trauma of slavery. In the syndrome known as posttraumatic stress disorder, overwhelming events of the past "repeatedly possess, in intrusive images and thoughts, the one who has lived through them" (418). The original event escaped understanding even as it was happening because it could not "be placed within the schemes of prior knowledge. . . . Not having been fully integrated as it occurred, the event cannot become . . . a 'narrative memory' that is integrated into a completed story of the past" (418–19). Morrison's narrative form brilliantly recaptures traumatic memory: the past comes back in bits—a fragment here, a fragment there. Since the "truth" of the experience "may reside not only in its brutal facts, but also in the way that their occurrence defies simple comprehension," Morrison's text needs this pointillism, this fragmentation, to remain true both to the events and to "their affront to understanding" (Caruth 418–20). Philip Page shows how the circularity and fragmentation of Morrison's narrative structure parallels the indirect, piecemeal remembering of the characters. Gayle Greene also analyzes the way memory functions in *Beloved*.

11. For a summary of *Beloved*'s multiple relations to language and for a different view of the female family circle, see my *Reconstructing Desire* (195–200).

12. Deborah Horvitz thinks that it is Sethe's mother who speaks in these passages, wanting to "join" with the body of her own mother (162–63). Others have speculated that the face Beloved claims as her own is that of Sethe's mother, who indeed came over on the slave ships (though she, of course, survived the voyage). These interpretations are useful in suggesting the range of what Beloved may represent: a whole line of daughters desperately wanting to "join" with the mothers wrenched away from them by slavery.

13. Linda Anderson describes Morrison's "exploration of history's absences, of how what is unwritten and unremembered can come back to haunt us" (137). Karla Holloway

points out that these absences are not accidental, that "the victim's own chronicles of these events were systematically submerged, ignored, mistrusted, or superseded by 'historians' of the era. This novel positions the consequences of black invisibility in both the records of slavery and the record-keeping as a situation of primary spiritual significance" (516–17).

14. Morrison's account is true to a one-year-old's way of thinking, according to D. W. Winnicott. A baby looking into its mother's face imagines that it sees there the same thing its mother is looking at: its own face. The baby's still precarious sense of existence depends on the mother's mirroring face ("Mirror-Role" 112). Rebecca Ferguson also uses Winnicott's essay to explain Beloved's fixation on her mother's face (117–18). Barbara Mathieson cites Winnicott as support for her claim that Beloved's monologue mirrors the preoedipal child's conviction that its identity and its mother's identity "flow into one another as interchangeably as their faces" (2).

15. Barbara Schapiro discusses the novel's images of orality and the gaze in the context of slavery, pointing out that "the emotional hunger, the obsessive and terrifying narcissistic fantasies" are not Beloved's alone; instead, they belong to all those denied both mothers and selves by a slave system that "either separates [a mother] from her child or so enervates and depletes her that she has no self with which to confer recognition" (194). Thus when Sethe complains, "There was no nursing milk to call my own," she expresses her own emotional starvation in the absence of her mother, and that emptiness in turn prevents her from adequately reflecting her own daughter Denver (200, 198).

16. Nicolas Abraham cites similar cases, in which an unarticulated secret passes directly from a parent's unconscious to a child's unconscious. The child does not consciously know what the secret is but nevertheless acts it out, driven by a thing lodged in its unconscious that fits in with neither its conscious wishes nor its unconscious fantasies. "What haunts are not the dead, but the gaps left within us by the secrets of others" (75).

17. Missy Dehn Kubitschek identifies yet another maternal discourse in Beloved: she reads the women's roar that casts Beloved out as an imitation of "the sounds accompanying birth" (174). Morrison's text replaces the biblical verse, "In the beginning was the Word, . . . and the Word was God" (John 1.1), with the line, "In the beginning there were no words. In the beginning was the sound, and they all knew what that sound sounded like" (259). The women's communal groan recalls women's creation of life, not God's, and overthrows the male authority of the word. Kubitschek's chapter on Beloved addresses Sethe's need to change the static conception of motherhood she developed under slavery.

18. As Marianne Hirsch writes, Sethe's "subjectivity . . . can only emerge in and through human interconnection" (198). I differ with Hirsch because she ignores the hiatus in the middle of Sethe's narrative and regards Sethe as a mother who tells her story throughout (6). But Hirsch also says that Sethe's "maternal voice and subjectivity" emerge only in the concluding scene, where her "Me? Me?" implies that "she questions, at least for a moment, the hierarchy of motherhood over selfhood on which her life had rested until that moment" (7).

19. Morrison may have D. W. Winnicott's maternal "holding environment" in mind. Like Morrison, Winnicott pictures development as a joint project of self and other (mother) rather than as a movement toward increasing separation. Only in the presence of the mother can the infant be truly "alone," in Winnicott's terms. That is, the mother's protective presence releases the infant from survival needs and enables it to claim its impulses as authentically its own—hence to catch the first glimpse of an ongoing subjectivity ("Capacity" 34). Just so, Paul D's holding guarantees a space in which Sethe can safely think any thought, feel any feeling, and finally take the leap into a different subjectivity, one grounded in language. Morrison's ideal of heterosexual relations fits the "holding fantasy" that Jessica Benjamin claims women retain from experiencing that early maternal presence: "the wish for a holding other whose presence does not violate one's space but permits the experience of one's own desire, who recognizes it when it emerges of itself" (96).

20. Deborah Sitter describes the dialogic relation between Paul D's story and Sethe's story, showing how Paul D comes to a new definition of manhood. Kate Cummings also traces

Paul D's development from a definition of masculinity that enslaves him to the white slave master who named him to an identification with Sixo's different model of manhood—a shift that culminates in his "taking on the job of mothering" Sethe. Cummings lists mothering as one of three modes of resistance, along with menacing and naming: "Mothering provides the final and most fundamental opposition, for through it the subject is reconstituted and the body reborn in the flesh" (563, 564).

21.   I am grateful for the generous help of Elizabeth Abel in cutting this essay down to size; I also thank Frances Restuccia and John Swift for readings that enabled me to make new connections and Richard Yarborough for sharing his knowledge of Morrison's works.

Works Cited

Abel, Elizabeth. "Race, Class, and Psychoanalysis? Opening Questions." *Conflicts in Feminism.* Ed. Marianne Hirsch and Evelyn Fox Keller. New York: Routledge, 1990. 184–204.

Abraham, Nicolas. "Notes on the Phantom: A Complement to Freud's Metapsychology." *The Trial(s) of Psychoanalysis.* Ed. Françoise Meltzer. Chicago: U of Chicago P, 1987. 75–80.

Abraham, Nicolas, and Maria Torok. "Introjection—Incorporation: Mourning or Melancholia." *Psychoanalysis in France.* Ed. Serge Lebovici and Daniel Widlocher. New York: International UP, 1980. 3–16.

Anderson, Linda. "The Re-imagining of History in Contemporary Women's Fiction." *Plotting Change.* Ed. Anderson. London: Arnold, 1990. 129–41.

Baker, Houston A., Jr. "Autobiographical Acts and the Voice of the Southern Slave." Davis and Gates 242–61.

Benjamin, Jessica. "A Desire of One's Own: Psychoanalytic Feminism and Intersubjective Space." *Feminist Studies/Critical Studies.* Ed. Teresa de Lauretis. Bloomington: Indiana UP, 1986. 78–101.

Bronfen, Elisabeth. *Over Her Dead Body: Death, Femininity, and the Aesthetic.* New York: Routledge, 1992.

Butler, Judith. *Gender Trouble: Feminism and the Subversion of Identity.* London: Routledge, 1990.

Carby, Hazel. *Reconstructing Womanhood: The Emergence of the Afro-American Woman Novelist.* New York: Oxford UP, 1987.

Caruth, Cathy. Introduction. *Psychoanalysis, Culture and Trauma: II.* Spec. issue of *American Imago* 48 (1991): 417–24.

Christian, Barbara. " 'Somebody Forgot to Tell Somebody Something': African-American Women's Historical Novels." *Wild Women in the Whirlwind: Afra-American Culture and the Contemporary Literary Renaissance.* Ed. Joanne M. Braxton and Andrée Nicola McLaughlin. New Brunswick: Rutgers UP, 1990. 326–41.

Cummings, Kate. "Reclaiming the Mother('s) Tongue: *Beloved, Ceremony, Mothers and Shadows.*" *College English* 52 (1990): 552–69.

Darling, Marsha. "In the Realm of Responsibility: A Conversation with Toni Morrison." *Women's Review of Books* Mar. 1988: 5–6.

Davis, Charles T., and Henry Louis Gates, Jr., eds. *The Slave's Narrative.* New York: Oxford UP, 1985.

Delaney, Lucy. *From the Darkness Cometh the Light; or, Struggles for Freedom.* C. 1891. *Six Women's Slave Narratives.* Schomburg Library of Nineteenth-Century Black Women Writers. New York: Oxford UP, 1988. 1–64.

Demetrakopoulos, Stephanie. "Maternal Bonds as Devourers of Women's Individuation in Toni Morrison's *Beloved.*" *African American Review* 26.1 (1992): 51–60.

Ferguson, Rebecca. "History, Memory and Language in Toni Morrison's *Beloved.*" *Feminist Criticism: Theory and Practice.* Toronto: U of Toronto P, 1991. 109–27.

Freud, Sigmund. *Beyond the Pleasure Principle.* Trans. James Strachey. New York: Norton, 1961.

――――. "The Unconscious." 1915. *The Standard Edition of the Complete Psychological Works of Sigmund Freud.* Ed. and trans. James Strachey. Vol. 14. London: Hogarth, 1953–74. 159–215. 24 vols.

Gates, Henry Louis, Jr. "Introduction: The Language of Slavery." Davis and Gates xi–xxxiv.

Goldman, Anne. " 'I Made the Ink': (Literary) Production and Reproduction in *Dessa Rose* and *Beloved.*" *Feminist Studies* 16 (1990): 313–30.

Greene, Gayle. "Feminist Fictions and the Uses of Memory." *Signs* 16 (1990): 1–32.

Hayden, Robert. "Middle Passage." *Collected Works.* New York: Liveright, 1985. 48–54.

Henderson, Mae. "Toni Morrison's *Beloved:* Re-membering the Body as Historical Text." *Comparative American Identities: Race, Sex, and Nationality in the Modern Text.* Ed. Hortense Spillers. London: Routledge, 1991. 62–86.

Hirsch, Marianne. *The Mother-Daughter Plot: Narrative, Psychoanalysis, Feminism.* Bloomington: Indiana UP, 1989.

Holloway, Karla. "*Beloved:* A Spiritual." *Callaloo* 13 (1990): 516–25.

Homans, Margaret. *Bearing the Word: Language and Female Experience in Nineteenth-Century Women's Writing.* Chicago: U of Chicago P, 1986.

Horvitz, Deborah. "Nameless Ghosts: Possession and Dispossession in *Beloved.*" *Studies in American Fiction* 17 (1989): 157–67.

Jacobs, Harriet. *Incidents in the Life of a Slave Girl.* Cambridge: Harvard UP, 1987.

Klein, Melanie. "Some Theoretical Conclusions Regarding the Emotional Life of the Infant." *Developments in Psycho-analysis.* Ed. Klein et al. London: Hogarth, 1952. 198–236.

Kristeva, Julia. *Black Sun.* Trans. Leon Roudiez. New York: Columbia UP, 1989.

Kubitschek, Missy Dehn. *Claiming the Heritage: African-American Women Novelists and History.* Jackson: U of Mississippi P, 1991.

Lacan, Jacques. *Écrits: A Selection.* Trans. Alan Sheridan. New York: Norton, 1981.

――――. "Les formations de l'inconscient." *Bulletin de psychologie* 2 (1957–58): 1–15.

――――. *The Four Fundamental Concepts of Psychoanalysis.* 1973. Trans. Alan Sheridan. New York: Norton, 1981.

――――. "The Function and Field of Speech and Language in Psychoanalysis." 1953. Lacan, *Écrits* 30–113.

――――. "The Mirror Stage as Formative of the Function of the I." Lacan, *Écrits* 1–7.

Mathieson, Barbara O. "Memory and Mother Love in Morrison's *Beloved.*" *American Imago* 47 (1990): 1–21.

Morrison, Toni. *Beloved.* New York: Knopf, 1987.

Muller, John. "Language, Psychosis, and the Subject in Lacan." *Interpreting Lacan.* Ed. Joseph Smith and William Kerrigan. New Haven: Yale UP, 1983. 21–32.

Page, Philip. "Circularity in Toni Morrison's *Beloved.*" *African American Review* 26.1 (1992): 31–40.

Rose, Jacqueline. "Introduction II." *Feminine Sexuality: Jacques Lacan and the Ecole Freudienne.* Ed. Juliet Mitchell and Jacqueline Rose. New York: Norton, 1982. 27–57.

Rothstein, Mervyn. "Toni Morrison, in Her New Novel, Defends Women." *New York Times* 26 Aug. 1987: C17.

Sale, Maggie. "Call and Response as Critical Method: African-American Oral Traditions and *Beloved.*" *African American Review* 26.1 (1992): 41–50.

Schapiro, Barbara. "The Bonds of Love and the Boundaries of Self in Toni Morrison's *Beloved.*" *Contemporary Literature* 32 (1991): 194–210.

Silverman, Kaja. *The Subject of Semiotics.* New York: Oxford UP, 1983.

Sitter, Deborah Ayer. "The Making of a Man: Dialogic Meaning in *Beloved.*" *African American Review* 26.1 (1992): 17–30.

Spillers, Hortense. "Mama's Baby, Papa's Maybe: An American Grammar Book." *Diacritics* 17 (1987): 65–81.

Tate, Claudia. "Allegories of Black Female Desire; or, Rereading Nineteenth-Century Sentimental Narratives of Black Female Authority." *Changing Our Own Words.* Ed. Cheryl A.
Wall. New Brunswick: Rutgers UP, 1989. 98–126.

Winnicott, D. W. "The Capacity to Be Alone." *The Maturational Processes and the Facilitating
Environment.* New York: International UP, 1965. 29–36.

———. "Mirror-Role of Mother and Family in Child Development." *Playing and Reality.* London: Tavistock, 1971. 111–18.

Wright, Richard. *Twelve Million Black Voices.* New York: Thunder's Mouth, 1988.

Wyatt, Jean. *Reconstructing Desire: The Role of the Unconscious in Women's Reading and Writing.*
Chapel Hill: U of North Carolina P, 1990.

Reading at the Cultural Interface: The Corn Symbolism of *Beloved*

WENDY HARDING AND JACKY MARTIN

If the borders defining American literary studies have been redrawn over the past two decades to include works representative of a plurality of races, genders, classes, and ethnicities, the theoretical issues involved in reading the newly emergent texts are still in the process of being articulated.[1] The new American literature is being read in a variety of ways, not all of which do justice to its rich multiplicity. Critical methods developed in former years to demonstrate the homogeneity of American letters are still practiced, with the result that the differences of new texts are sometimes overlooked in the interest of emphasizing their universal features. More promising are alternative approaches that address not only the textual diversity of the revised American canon but also the multiplicity within individual texts.[2] Taking a passage from Toni Morrison's *Beloved* as our example, this essay will present a concept and a practice that endeavor to respond to the text's complexity.[3]

Morrison's novels have been characterized by both admirers and detractors as eccentric, enigmatic, mysterious, or indeterminate. While she admits in interviews to being fascinated by problems without resolutions (Tate 130), Morrison also expresses a longing for comprehension from her audience. In 1981 she complained, "I have yet to read criticism that understands my work or is prepared to understand it. I don't care if the critic likes or dislikes it. I would just like to feel less isolated" (LeClair 29). The writer's desire for comprehension and the perplexity of some readers indicate a block in the reading process which we intend to investigate. Some of *Beloved*'s early reviewers read Morrison from the dominant perspective, producing uncomprehending or hostile evaluations. In this view both the subject and style of the novel represent a serious lapse in taste.[4] These evaluations generally refuse close textual analysis and offer reductive summaries of events. Yet even by critics who read more attentively and sympathetically, Morrison's art is often mistaken for something more conventional. We will sketch out the problem empirically by

First published in *MELUS* 19 no. 2 (Summer 1994): 85–97. © 1994, The Society for the Study of the Multi-Ethnic Literature of the United States. Reprinted by permission.

examining the passage in which Sethe and Paul D, having just made love for the first time, think back to their earliest sexual experiences at Sweet Home. This passage, which we quote here in its entirety, centers on the cornfield where Sethe and Halle make love for the first time:

> Sethe made a dress on the sly and Halle hung his hitching rope from a nail on the wall of her cabin. And there on top of a mattress on top of the dirt floor of the cabin they coupled for the third time, the first two having been in the tiny cornfield Mr. Garner kept because it was a crop animals could use as well as humans. Both Halle and Sethe were under the impression that they were hidden. Scrunched down among the stalks they couldn't see anything, including the corn tops waving over their heads and visible to everyone else.
>
> Sethe smiled at her and Halle's stupidity. Even the crows knew and came to look. Uncrossing her ankles, she managed not to laugh aloud.
>
> The jump, thought Paul D, from a calf to a girl wasn't all that mighty. Not the leap Halle believed it would be. And taking her in the corn rather than her quarters, a yard away from the cabins of the others who had lost out, was a gesture of tenderness. Halle wanted privacy for her and got a public display. Who could miss a ripple in a cornfield on a quiet cloudless day? He, Sixo and both of the Pauls sat under Brother pouring water from a gourd over their heads, and through eyes streaming with well water, they watched the confusion of tassels in the field below. It had been hard, hard sitting there erect as dogs, watching corn stalks dance at noon. The water running over their heads made it worse.
>
> Paul D sighed and turned over. Sethe took the opportunity afforded by his movement to shift as well. Looking at Paul D's back, she remembered that some of the corn stalks broke, folded down over Halle's back, and among the things her fingers clutched were husk and cornsilk hair.
>
> How loose the silk. How jailed down the juice.
>
> The jealous admiration of the men watching melted with the feast of new corn they allowed themselves that night. Plucked from the broken stalks that Mr. Garner could not doubt was the fault of the racoon. Paul F wanted his roasted; Paul A wanted his boiled and now Paul D couldn't remember how finally they'd cooked those ears too young to eat. What he did remember was parting the hair to get to the tip, the edge of his fingernail just under, so as not to graze a single kernel.
>
> The pulling down of the tight sheath, the ripping sound always convinced her it hurt.
>
> As soon as one strip of husk was down, the rest obeyed and the ear yielded up to him its shy rows, exposed at last. How loose the silk. How quick the jailed-up flavor ran free.
>
> No matter what all your teeth and wet fingers anticipated, there was no accounting for the way that simple joy could shake you.
>
> How loose the silk. How fine and loose and free. (26–27)

At first reading, this passage seems to offer a satisfying conclusion to an unsatisfactory love scene. For the men rejected when Sethe chooses Halle, the feast of corn apparently assuages the frustration and exclusion they have experienced in observing the two lovers. For the couple lying in bed at 124 Bluestone Road, the interlaced recollection of the past seems to resolve differences, to bring them from rejection to mutual acceptance, from separation to togetherness. But while the phrases that conclude this section of the narrative suggest convergence, other elements reinforce the separateness and ambivalence of Paul D's and Sethe's past and present experience.

Our initial impression of harmonious resolution results from our sifting out signs that counter the positive values of some of the words and symbols. In fact, conventional models of interpretation encourage us to ignore or reconcile contradictory signs. As long as we construe the critic's role as the solution of problems raised in the text, we seek to unify our impressions and thereby reduce its complexity. To illustrate our point, we shall consider the ways in which various modes of criticism have accounted or might account for this passage, and, subsequently, we will offer an alternative critical approach that we define as criticism at the interface.

Most problematic among current critical approaches is the practice of judging a work according to conventional patterns derived from Western models. From this perspective literature of quality reasserts schemata held to be "universal"; consequently, departures from these patterns are treated as local and inessential variations on timeless themes. To be sure, few readers of Morrison apply this approach to her work deliberately; instead, they unwittingly misread Morrison's symbols as familiar tropes. For example, David Lawrence interprets the passage from *Beloved* as an example of "psychic union" between two people who are united sexually: "They silently recall, in tandem, the safe memory of love at Sweet Home. Morrison's narrator creates seamless transitions between their separate but simultaneous memories of Sethe and Halle's lovemaking in the cornfield. The recollection culminates in the shared trope for sexual arousal and fulfillment expressed in the husked corn" (Lawrence 194). Lawrence arrives at this interpretation by mistaking Morrison's narrative for a more conventional work. To be sure, the preliminary encounter between Sethe and Paul D seems to be building toward a satisfying climax. The narrator heightens expectations in representing Paul D's heated imagining of the long anticipated love-making: "Merely kissing the wrought iron on her back had shook the house, had made it necessary for him to beat it to pieces. Now he would do more" (20). Yet only by forgetting the subsequent disappointment and disjunction between the two characters can the corn be made into an emblem of sexual communion between Sethe and Paul D. The corn is obviously a highly erotic image, but it is made into a symbol of harmony and closure only through an extremely selective reading.[5]

As an alternative to traditional uniformizing habits of reading we could look to approaches based on the recognition of dichotomies in cultural productions. The more politically sympathetic view of classic Marxist criticism would still tend to reduce the complexity of the Morrisonian text. In this view, the resistance of dominated groups is pre-defined by the ruling class so that any expression of difference merely contributes to justifying the underdogs' subordinate status.[6] The minority writer has the possibility only of fictionalizing the very terms in which the dominant class wants minorities to see themselves. Maggie Sale offers a powerful reply to these kinds of approaches when she distinguishes in *Beloved* a distinctively Black aesthetics. Sale reads the passage we are studying as an example of repetition and improvisation characteristic of the blues. Morrison's novel represents a new form "in which a politically informed, multivocal discourse values innovation and difference rather than continuity and similarity" (Sale 49). Sale's approach illustrates that the African American writer is not doomed to replicate the forms of the dominant race, but her vision of call and response, of multivocality and difference, and of African American blues harmonies in *Beloved,* though extremely subtle, still tends to smooth over the disruptions and dissonances in the text. On closer inspection, the music of the passage we are studying is created from unreconciled differences between the characters that are not fully addressed in the call and response model.

In feminist criticism we find ways of reading designed to address divisions and conflicts within texts. Responsive to unconventional literature produced in a context of marginality, feminist readings constitute a significant part of the already quite substantial critical corpus on *Beloved.* Yet in privileging the female side of the gender division, the feminist perspective reveals blind spots of its own. Satya Mohanty's reading of this passage interprets the couple's "fused memory" of the corn silk and the juice as a shared "concern for the moral implications of being enslaved and being free" (Mohanty 58–59). Yet in Mohanty's reading the problems posed in the novel are resolved simply by the re-education of the male. Paul D must learn to understand "the historical achievement of black motherhood" and his "historical indebtedness" (Mohanty 65–66). Though this may be one of the obstacles to a harmonious resolution of conflict, it is by no means the only one.

In founding critical evaluation on a single code of reference, each of the critical paradigms outlined so far inevitably produces distortions and omissions. Determinants such as gender, race, class or ethnicity, although correctly explained in isolation, are not properly accounted for in situations when they interact with one another. Indeed, the place where cultural determinants overlap is a site of dense complexity, as Morrison has clearly demonstrated in her reading of *Moby Dick* as the "unspoken" response to the Black presence in American society, the moment "when whiteness became ideology" (Morrison "Unspeakable," 15). She discovers in this canonical text what she calls "the ghost in the machine" ("Unspeakable," 11), evidence of the shaping presence of Afro-Americans in American culture.[7] We intend to reverse this reading strategy and extend it to Morrison's work. In this perspective, Sethe's and Paul D's interlaced memory of the cornfield would respond both to the dehumanizing pressure of the institution of slavery and the necessity (for slave and ex-slave alike) to assert humanity. The resulting icon of the husk of corn is not a construction that masks contradiction like the white whale but one that emphasizes it. Rather than subsuming complexity in unity, Morrison's symbolism reveals ambivalence in multiplicity. In the cases of Melville's and Morrison's work, although in opposite ways, an ambivalent construction that we call an "interface" has been created between cultures in conflict.

The interface is the privileged site of observation for the critic for several reasons:

1) Divisions in culture are never simply dichotomous. Only through a reduction of their complexity can they be made to fit the dualistic categories of the dominant or the restricted political angle of the dominated. In fact culture's multiple divisions result in a complexity of intersections. Consequently, we want to eschew monistic approaches in order to discover a plurality of cultural references. From a binary perspective, corn is dichotomized into the edible and the non-edible, the cob and the husk. The cob is endowed with value and the husk is rejected. By contrast, in Morrison's text, both are given significance, and each is seen in association to the other. The corn symbol expresses a cluster of ambivalent positions:[8] freedom and confinement ("loose . . . silk" . . . "tight sheath" . . . "the jailed up flavor ran free"); up and down ("jailed down juice" . . . "jailed up flavor"); integrity and rupture ("corn stalks dance" . . . "corns stalks broke"); as well as a kind of polymorphous sexuality that goes beyond binary divisions ("the pulling down of the tight sheath, the ripping sound always convinced her it hurt" . . . "the ear yielded up to him its shy rows").

On consideration, we realize that for both Sethe and Paul D the corn symbol mediates not only satisfaction but also deprivation both in the remembered past and in the present act of remembering. In the remembered scene we discover contradictions in the couple's experience. Each of them is visible and yet not visible at the same time: Sethe is hiding yet watched by the men whose attention she wants to avoid; Paul D's desire is obvious (the men are "erect as dogs"), yet he is unnoticed by Sethe. Each is satisfied and yet deprived: Sethe enjoys the sex but not the corn; Paul D has the corn but not the sex. In the present, although Paul D and Sethe appear to achieve some kind of fusion, in fact their remembering of the experience is distinct. The apparent harmony of the passage results as much from the couple's shared ambivalence as from their shared experience. The parallel courses of the couple's remembering do not merge, as we might expect, with the "he" or "she" converging on the plural pronoun "we" or "they"; instead, in the last line of the passage the associative pronoun "you" invites the reader to participate in the ambivalence of the experience.

2) Resulting from interferences between social divisions and representing the consequent interactions, the interface is a place where signification is concentrated. Symbols have the importance accorded dreams or totems in Freud's analysis of dream and joke work, yet a vital distinction has to be made. This concentration of signification does not serve to conceal inadmissible evidences

accessible only through the process of analysis as in the Freudian system; on the contrary it juxtaposes glaring evidences to zones of mystery and complexity. The satisfactoriness of the corn is at the same time almost obscenely obvious and obscure: "No matter what all your teeth and wet fingers anticipated, there was no accounting for the way that simple joy could shake you" (27). On the one hand, the narrative gives the impression that consummation is fundamental to the scene, yet, on the other hand, we find that "now Paul D couldn't remember how finally they'd cooked those ears too young to eat" (27). Moreover, Paul D's memory block induces a feeling of satisfaction rather than malaise. Instead of signalling the Freudian process of secondary elaboration, it points to a temporary omission of disquieting elements present in the scene. This truncated memory is not a scrambled version of the underlying truth like the dream; rather it is the only truth Paul D can accommodate at this moment in the narrative. In contrast to Freudian symbolism, the corn is not a dissimulating symbol, but an intense source of signification in which both the lure and the reality it is supposed to conceal are to be considered simultaneously.

3) At the cultural interface groups are seen in an affronted state defending acquired ground and thus exposing their beliefs and their weaknesses. In mainstream literary productions the interface zone reveals the erasures and distortions which underpin the contradictions of dominant discourse. Conversely, at the interface minority cultures are revealed asserting their values in response to external pressures. In that perspective, Afro-American signifying answers white American claims to universality,[9] and the "double vision" attributed to Black Americans by Du Bois exactly matches the cultural monovision of the whites. In the minority text, the interface records transgressive or contaminative processes, one culture not just conflicting but overlapping with the other. Although the dominant symbolism is resorted to, it is reappropriated and displaced from its original context of exploitation. The reference to crows and to the racoon gives to this passage its particular double-edged humor, mocking at once the system and those submitted to the system. The reference to obvious racist stereotypes is at the same time interiorized and distanced when attributed to the whites ("that Mr. Garner could not doubt was the fault of the racoons") or used by the dominated in possible reference to themselves ("Even the crows knew and came to look").

The context of slavery has also been appropriated as an ambivalent symbol. Clearly, the cornfield in which Sethe and Halle make love remains the property of Mr. Garner, designated by him as "a crop animals could use as well as humans" (26). In their attempt to escape the cramped quarters allotted to them as slaves, the couple still cannot avoid the space of slavery or the pressure of its discourse. They find themselves in a similarly circumscribed situation, but they are, in addition, exposed to visibility expressed ambivalently as both integration in nature ("a ripple in a cornfield") and potential exposure to unwanted attention ("Even the crows knew and came to look"). The dichotomies of the whites have been reconverted and readdressed in a symbolism that straddles the contradictions of injustice and converts them into cultural complexity.

4) Finally, the interface does not coincide with boundaries between separate and opposed systems of values; it is the place where culture is produced in the friction between affronted groups. In her creation of the corn scene, far from simply evincing reversed, redressed, or marginal symbolism, Morrison both cites and challenges Western culture in order to propose new, surprisingly enriched cultural values such as the combination of contradictory qualities that we have already analyzed in the symbol of the corn. The restricted perspectives of the two groups of characters in the remembered scene and the two remembering characters are combined by the narrator who transforms the binarism of the dominant perspective into multivalent symbolism and thereby relays a new system of values. Morrison's artistic innovation is illustrated in the diagram that follows which attempts to demonstrate the multivalence of the corn symbol.

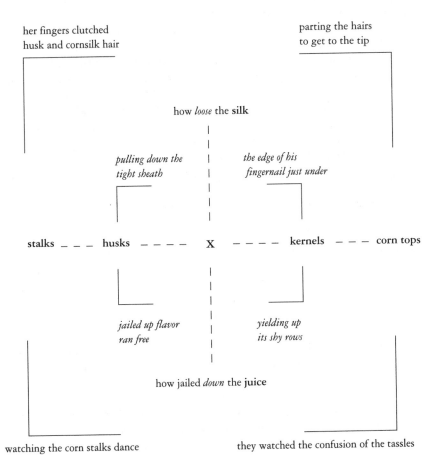

her fingers clutched
husk and cornsilk hair

parting the hairs
to get to the tip

how *loose* the **silk**

*pulling down the
tight sheath*

*the edge of his
fingernail just under*

stalks _ _ _ husks _ _ _ _ X _ _ _ _ kernels _ _ _ corn tops

*jailed up flavor
ran free*

*yielding up
its shy rows*

how jailed *down* the **juice**

watching the corn stalks dance

they watched the confusion of the tassles

What we saw earlier as a cluster of dualities now appears more as a complex of interconnected, overlapping positions expressed through the relationship of stalks, husk, silk, kernels, corn tops, and juice. The multiple desires of the subjects involved are projected onto an object that is characterized by its many-layered, imbricated structure.

Replete with a multi-layered signification as it is, the Morrisonian interface simulates the violence of conflicts and the forces of resistance which underpin it. Our contribution so far has been to reclaim that crypted seat of signification from partial recognition and to formulate principles to ensure its readability. We have shown that the narrative connects the slaves' distinctive experiences in the shared icon of the corn; the ambivalence of the symbol permits it to express both entrapment in the system and resistance to it. But the interfacial symbol should not be considered as merely an isolated or local site of meaning dealing with a particular moment of interference in the values of dominant and dominated. The symbolism of the interface also involves a form of narrative development unrecognized by the sequential, problem-solving model conventionally applied to texts.

In reading Morrison, we have also to take into account the syntagmatic dimension of her symbolism.[10] The narrative will return to the cornfield and to the corn symbol, multiplying and complexifying this initial ambivalence. So we discover at the end of *Beloved* that the Sweet Home slaves center their plan to run on the cornfield, agreeing to leave "when the corn is tall" (222) and to meet in the cornfield. For some of them the cornfield will be the place of escape, for others, the point where the whites redouble the repression. In this context, the corn image permits a stroke of double-edged irony as the white men attempt to roast the rebellious Sixo over a fire that is "only enough for cooking hominy" (226). When schoolteacher comes to claim Sethe and her children in Cincinnati, the narrative returns again to the cornfield, creating a further complexification in the development of the symbol. Although the potential strife caused by Sethe's marriage may have seemed resolved in the feast of corn at Sweet Home, discord returns the morning after the feast at Bluestone Road celebrating her escape from slavery. Where the first celebration takes place in the space circumscribed by slavery, the second is held in the supposedly free space of the North. Bluestone Road seems a place of miraculous plenty where ninety can be fed from the vegetable garden where Baby Suggs had planted corn and there is still some left over. "Much as they'd picked for the party, there were still ears ripening, which she could see from where she stood" (138). This spontaneous celebration of Sethe's freedom oversteps the balance of the earlier feast and in the associative logics of the narrative brings on the return of schoolteacher and the incursion of the bloody institution of slavery on the free side of the Ohio River. With the arrival of schoolteacher, we find a renewal of the problem of thinking one's actions in terms other than those of the dominant discourse. Schoolteacher predictably constructs a conventional narrative, explaining Sethe's actions in the logic of premise and conclusion, cause and effect: "Now she'd gone wild due to the mishandling of the nephew who'd overbeat her and made her cut and run" (149). Initially Stamp Paid (159) and Paul D (164) judge Sethe's actions in similar terms. Subsequently, they become reconciled to her through symbols which link Sethe's bloody act to their own histories: Stamp Paid's red ribbon, Vashti's black ribbon, and Paul D's Red Heart. The symbolism develops in an open-ended process that allows the possibility of further amplification through association, either in future narrative developments or in the contribution of experiences that readers bring to the text.

In fact Morrison's narrative develops according to two distinct dynamics. The symbolic dimension parallels, supplements and sometimes takes over from logical narrative progressions. Hence, according to the pattern of problem and resolution, Sethe is excluded from and finally reintegrated into the community, but her reacceptance is accomplished by symbolic "means" in the Shout. In a spiralling progressive-recessive movement characteristic of interfacial development, the Shout takes Sethe back to the Clearing "where the voices of women searched for the sound that broke the back of words" (261). Moreover, something is left over after the denouement, in the form of Beloved; something is unresolved, "disremembered and unaccounted for" (274) so that symbolism takes over at the point where narrativity leaves off. In this sense *Beloved* is not a story to pass on, that is, a story to be repeated, but an invitation to discard the story and espouse the values at stake in the novel's symbolism.

With the interface we seem to be dealing with what Deleuze and Guattari describe as rhizomatic "propagation" as opposed to traditional arborescent structures: while the former continues to grow and expand indefinitely, the latter only replicates an original structure (Deleuze and Guattari *Mille,* 11–37). According to Deleuze and Guattari's observations in connection with Kafka, the minority writer is "deterritorialized" and his act of creation, the construction of a "minor literature . . . within a major language" (Deleuze and Guattari *Kafka,* 16), becomes a means to reterritorialize his message and the community to which he belongs. Yet we feel that both the double system evoked in *Mille Plateaux* and the concept of "a minor literature" later developed in *Kafka: Toward a Minor Literature* contribute to replicating the dichotomies that we see systematically deconstructed and denounced by Toni Morrison, as well as other African American creative artists. We propose another tentative metaphor. Rather than being produced against or along with the dominant discourse, the dominated text filters or leaches through it by surcharging the oppressors' words, deriding them by subverting their most offensive strategies, building from them rather than ignoring or obliterating them. Hence symbols of oppression can be overprinted with the signs of liberation, the space of slavery can be rethought in terms of both the corn and the cornfield, and all the intermediary symbols that are often reduced to binary dualities can be reinstated in their full complexity.

Our analysis of Morrison suggests that what might initially be perceived as a rhizome is more fruitfully considered as an interaction which could be represented by the image of a parasitic vine, which like ivy supports itself on another plant that it devitalizes in order to thrive. Rather than identifying the interface with a dialectical process of confrontation or conciliation between two hostile and fundamentally distinct cultural systems, the "parasitic" principle would describe a process of mutual and conflicting occupation of *one* common cultural field going through constant cycles of flux and mutation. Thus, a clearcut distinction would be established between the political power game and the more fluid, more intricate and unaccountable world of ideological representations, restoring structural autonomy in complementarity to both planes. Although we are still very far from being able to articulate validly the two planes, it seems clear that we are shifting, at least as far as ideological representations are concerned, from dualistic structures like the Freudian or Marxist systems to more hybrid structures of mutual contamination in which already produced discourses serve as substrata for new discourses' proliferation. The general orientation would be toward increased complexification and expansion rather than toward harmonization and unification. The underlying dynamic principle would be synergetic rather than agonistic, interferential rather than dichotomous, multiplicative rather than reductive. The critic's function would have to be defined accordingly: instead of devising and revising hierarchies according to relatively immovable values, that is homogenizing the complexity of literary phenomena, we would be custodians of the literary complexity of our cultures, attentive to both continuities and discontinuities, to new departures and enduring conflicts.

Notes

1. See for example Newman's description of the changes that have occurred in the American literary canon during the past two decades (Newman 104–13).

2. An example of a theory responding to the plurality within texts is Gates's concept of Signifyin(g), which acknowledges both the repetition of Western rhetorical structures in Black literature and the transforming African American difference. In an extended theoretical development of W. E. B. Du Bois's memorable description of Negro identity, Gates speaks of the "two-toned" or "double voiced" black text (Gates 1984, 3).

3. For a further exploration of our intercultural approach, see our forthcoming study, *A World of Difference: An Intercultural Reading of Toni Morrison's Novels,* to be published by Greenwood Press.

4. Stanley Crouch's 1987 article is representative of this unsympathetic approach.

5. Even extremely subtle critics seek resolution in this scene. Deborah Sitter takes into account some of the differences between Sethe and Paul D but reads this particular passage as a prefigurement of the novel's conclusion where the couple will place their stories side by side: "The sexual frustration Sethe and Paul D experience at the outset of the bedroom scene is eventually transformed into sexual fulfillment. What prevents them at first and enables them at last is conveyed indirectly through the multivocal, multilayered, dense verbal texture of Morrison's style" (Sitter 27).

6. "Le minoritaire se trouve en fait intégré dans le système symbolique défini par le majoritaire quels que soient par ailleurs ses essais ou ses échecs à se constituer un système propre. Plus encore, ses efforts pour se définir un tel système sont orientés et canalisés par le majoritaire; il ne peut se définir sur des références internes et indépendantes, il doit le faire à partir des références que lui offre le système majoritaire" (Guillaumin 90). [Minorities are in fact part of the symbolic system defined by the majority in spite of their attempts or strategies to create their own system. Furthermore, their efforts to define such a system are directed and channeled by the majority; they cannot define themselves according to internal and independent references, they must do so on the basis of references available within the majority system (our translation).]

7. The approach to "mainstream" literature suggested in this 1989 article is developed at much greater length in Morrison's book *Playing in the Dark*.

8. In the absence of a positively connoted word expressing dual or multiple meaning we are forced to settle for the term ambivalent, although we are not completely satisfied with it. The English language betrays a bias against the possibility of a statement expressing more than one meaning at a time. To identify a statement as ambivalent, ambiguous, or equivocal is to judge it as a failed or devious attempt at communication.

9. Signifying—a concept whose complexity does not permit any more than a brief reference within the confines of this article—has been discussed as a linguistic practice (Kochman 336–45), as a literary typology (Ostendorf 158–60) and as a principle of Afro-American literary history (Gates).

10. We refer to this process in our article "Subjective Correlatives as Correlations of Subjection in Toni Morrison's Fiction" (Harding and Martin 109–10) and discuss it at greater length in our forthcoming book.

Works Cited

Crouch, Stanley. "Aunt Medea (Rev. of *Beloved*)." *The New Republic* (October 19, 1987): 38–43.

Deleuze, G., and Guattari, F. *Mille Plateaux*. Paris: Minuit, 1980. (English translation: *A Thousand Plateaux*. London: Athlone, 1987.)

———. *Kafka: Toward a Minor Literature*. Trans. by Dana Polan. *Theory and History of Literature*. Vol. 30. Minneapolis: U Minnesota P, 1986.

Gates, Henry Louis, Jr. "Criticism in the Jungle." In *Black Literature and Literary Theory*. Edited by Henry Louis Gates, Jr. New York: Methuen, 1984. 1–24.

———. *The Signifying Monkey: A Theory of Afro-American Literary Criticism*. New York: Oxford U P, 1988.

Guillaumin, Colette. *L'ideologie raciste: genese et langage actuel*. Paris: Mouton, 1972.

Harding, Wendy, and Martin, Jacky. "Subjective Correlatives as Correlations of Subjection in Toni Morrison's Fiction." *Profils Americains* 2 (1992): 103–11.

Kochman, Thomas. "Towards an Ethnography of Black American Speech Behavior." In *Afro-American Anthropology*. Ed. by Norman Whitten and John Szwed. New York, Free Press, 1970.

Lawrence, David. "Fleshly Ghosts and Ghostly Flesh: The Word and the Body in *Beloved*." *Studies in American Fiction* 19 (Autumn 1991): 189–201.

LeClair, Thomas. " 'The Language Must Not Sweat': A Conversation with Toni Morrison." *The New Republic* (21 March 1981): 25–29.

Mohanty, Satya P. "The Epistemic Status of Cultural Identity: On *Beloved* and the Postcolonial Condition." *Cultural Critique* (Spring 1993): 41–80.

Morrison, Toni. *Beloved*. New York: Alfred A. Knopf, 1987.

———. *Playing in the Dark: Whiteness and the Literary Imagination*. Cambridge: Harvard U P, 1992.

————. "Unspeakable Things Unspoken: The Afro-American Presence in American Literature." *Michigan Quarterly Review* 28 (Winter 1989): 1–34.

Newman, Katherine. "MELUS Invented: The Rest is History." *MELUS* 16.4 (Winter 1989-90): 99–113.

Ostendorf, Berndt. *Black Literature in White America. Studies in Contemporary Literature and Culture.* Brighton: Harvester P, 1982.

Sale, Maggie. "Call and Response as Critical Method: African-American Oral Traditions and *Beloved.*" *African American Review* 26 (Spring 1992): 41–50.

Sitter, Deborah Ayer. "The Making of a Man: Dialogic Meaning in *Beloved.*" *African American Review* 26 (Spring 1992): 17–29.

Tate, Claudia. "Toni Morrison." *Black Women Writers at Work.* New York: Continuum, 1983. 117–31.

ORIGINAL ESSAYS
◆

The Black English Oral Tradition in *Beloved:* "listen to the spaces"

Yvonne Atkinson

The oral tradition of Black English[1] plays an important part in the works of Toni Morrison. Morrison consciously writes a Black text, one that is centered in African American cultural traditions. Her novels come out of and utilize a tradition of storytelling from within Black culture.[2] Morrison has taken the spoken language of Black English and its systems of speech and written them into the discourse of the dominant culture without losing their essential Blackness.

Thomas Hamilton says Black people "must speak for themselves; no outside tongue, however gifted with eloquence, can tell their story."[3] In *Beloved,* Morrison uses the language of those who were oppressed to tell their story of oppression and survival. According to Geneva Smitherman, "Black Dialect is an Africanized form of English reflecting Black America's linguistic-cultural African heritage and the conditions of servitude, oppression and life in America. Black Language is Euro-American speech with an Afro-American meaning, nuance, tone, and gesture."[4]

Morrison, rather than trying to write an oral language, writes through the oral tradition. She uses in her written discourse systems from within the Black English oral tradition that facilitate the inclusion of nonverbal gestures and tonal inflections: Call/Response, Signifyin,[5] and Witness/Testify. Morrison masks the oral tradition within the written language of the dominant culture. Her texts become like Lewis Carroll's portmanteau words: the flexibility, improvisation, and tonality of the Black English oral tradition is "packed" within written language. She also reflects another aspect of the oral tradition of Black English: the stories that are told are not owned. They are not locked into a static position, but rather they have a flexibility that allows for, and validates, a number of tellings and retellings.[6]

Black English is used as a mark of identification in African American communities. It is spoken to those others who speak Black English. In situa-

This essay, based on a presentation at NEMLA in April 1996, was written specifically for this volume and is published here for the first time by permission of the author.

tions in which Common English is the dominant language, speakers of Black English will code-switch and speak Common English.[7] In other words, Black English is an in-group activity. Language is used to identify those who are in the group and those who are not. In African American culture, the use of Black English is an invitation, a formal request to participate in a unifying group activity. Participation in the discourse with the language systems and rituals of Black English identifies the speaker as part of the group. The invitation, initiating the discourse with Black English, identifies the initiator as part of the group. Thus by using Black English modes of discourse Morrison is identifying herself and her text as African American. She is also issuing an invitation to readers of *Beloved* to become members of the community she has created in her text by participation in the storytelling event.

In Black English, much of the meaning of the discourse is gained through the manner in which something is said. Tone of voice, facial expressions, and the body language of the speaker all give meaning to the discourse. These elements cannot be written into a text without a great deal of awkwardness; instead, implied meaning fills in the gaps caused by the limitations of written language. When the writer and the reader have a mutual understanding of language, then the nonverbal and tonal aspects of the language are already known and do not need to be identified or explained. Morrison brings the feel and sound of the oral tradition to her written text through the use of Black English modes of discourse.

Morrison's story in *Beloved* begins before the first word of the first chapter with the stark phrase "Sixty Million and more." This herald is a reminder of those who suffered and died because of slavery, and also a reminder of the strength required of those who survived. Morrison does not explain this statement within the novel, nor does she mention it again. The "Sixty Million and more" becomes the frame or the lens through which the rest of her narrative is viewed. These Sixty Million, who died without acknowledgment, are acknowledged in *Beloved*.

The opening line of the first chapter of *Beloved*, "124 was spiteful," is not indented, indicating that the story is already in progress before the first word of the first chapter is read.[8] This places the story's origin with Morrison's "Sixty Million and more" and the epigraph of the novel:

> I will call them my people
> which were not my people;
> and her beloved,
> which was not beloved.
> Romans 9:25[9]

The lack of an identifiable beginning also has its roots in the Black English oral tradition. Stories in the oral tradition are not owned; they are stories without beginning or endings. They are told and retold: revised and refigured as the circumstances of the tellers and hearers change and evolve. This telling and retelling is part of the oral tradition of improvisation. Like storytellers,

> Black singers felt absolutely free to take blues sung by others—friends, professional performers, singers of records—and alter them in any way they liked. Though blues became part of the commercial world of the entertainer and the recording industry, they remained communal property and were vehicles for individual and group expression. No single person "owned" a blues song. Ma Rainey expressed this well in her "Last Minute Blues": "If anybody ask you who wrote this lonesome song / Tell 'em you don't know the writer, but Ma Rainey put it on."[10]

Morrison does not own the story of *Beloved;* she is simply one teller of a tale that has been told and will be retold. The storytellers in *Beloved* do not own their stories, but tell their versions of the tales in their own way. The multiple tellings give a rich complexity to the individual stories and to the meaning of the overall story. These storytellers' memories of slavery are the foundations of their tales. Memory "[c]omes back whether we want [it] to or not" (14), Sethe says.

Both Sethe and Paul D, at the beginning of the story, "start the day's serious work of beating back the past" (73). They try to contain the past by not telling it, by not letting the stories of the past out. Paul D has locked his stories away "in that tobacco tin buried in his chest where a red heart used to be. Its lid rusted shut. He would not pry it loose . . ." (72–73). Sethe, when asked about her past, "gave short replies or rambling incomplete reveries" because "the hurt was always there—like a tender place in the corner of her mouth that the bit left" (58). Although both Sethe and Paul D try to contain their stories, they cannot. Their stories escape, his from the tobacco tin and hers from fragmented memories.

Telling and retelling is a way of remembering and honoring while it is also a release valve for those overwhelming feelings that are an elemental part of the residual effects of slavery. Morrison's layering of these harrowing tales allows readers the physical and mental space needed to assimilate the tales being told and to make a connection between the tellers, the tales, and themselves. Just as Sethe could not tell her story until Paul D could hear it ("her story was bearable because it was his as well—to tell, to refine and tell again. The things neither knew about the other—the things neither had word-shapes for"), the stories being told become bearable for readers through their telling and retelling (99).

Some characters have no way of knowing the whole story; rather, they must wait for others to fill in the gaps. Sethe knows only her own story of the tree on her back, while Paul D knows what happened to Halle. When Paul D asks Sethe about the tree, she answers by telling the story of how "[t]hem boys found out I told on em. Schoolteacher made one open up my back, and when it closed it made a tree. It grows there still" (17). Paul D has Halle's part of the story of that day in the barn: "The day I came in here. You said they stole your milk. I never knew what it was that messed him [Halle] up. That was it, I guess. All I knew was that something broke him. Not a one of them years of Saturdays and Sundays and nighttime extra never touched him. But whatever he saw go on in that barn that day broke him like a twig" (68).

Sethe and Paul D must tell their stories and learn to listen to the stories being told, their own and those of others. When Sethe tries to tell Paul D the story of the beating in the barn he cannot hear her tale:

"They used cowhide on you?"
"And they took my milk."
"They beat you and you was pregnant?"
"And they took my milk!" (17)

What he hears is that they beat her; what he cannot hear is that they milked her. It is not until much later in the story that her milking can find a way to settle into his mind. Then he can connect her milking to Halle's clabber-smeared face. Sethe cannot tell her story because it is "unspeakable" and Paul D cannot hear it because it is unhearable (58).

Morrison is teaching the reader how to hear these unspeakable stories. Just like Denver, the reader must "begin to see what [is being said] was saying and not just to hear it" (77). The ability to see what is being said requires active participation by the reader, who needs to make a connection with the story being told and the teller of the tale. This process moves the reader away from the role of passive observer into the role of meaning-maker within the text.

In the Black English oral tradition the storyteller and the audience are symbiotic: "Within Afro-American culture . . . the relationship of performers to their audience retained many of the traditional participatory elements, the give-and-take that was so familiar to nineteenth-century black storytellers and their audiences. The analogy is a particularly apt one since the performer and audience were frequently having an extended and complex conversation" (Levine, 234). In order to have such a conversation, the audience and the teller must have a shared knowledge about the language being used. John F. Callahan says, "Storytelling performances created a community of speech, interpretation, and response. . . . Ironically, the dehumanizing conditions of slavery, its prohibitions against literacy, against African language and ritual, reinforced the communal values of the oral tradition."[11] Morrison is using Black English oral traditions to tell her story, and she is also teaching the uninitiated reader how to hear this story. She is creating a community within the text and with the readers of the text.

One of the rhetorical tropes of the Black English oral tradition to facilitate this connection between the teller and the hearer is Call/Response.

Call/Response is the trigger for shared emotional events. It is, as Smitherman says, "stating and counter stating; acting and reacting." It is "spontaneous verbal and non-verbal interaction between the speaker and the listener in which all of the speaker's statements ('calls') are punctuated by expressions ('responses') from the listener" (119).

Call/Response is collaborative improvisation characterized by common content and shared experience. It improvises on known, shared material. As an outward expression of group, Call/Response signifies a connection, a shared history and culture, unifying the listener and the speaker. Call/Response is the catalyst that sets up the nonlinear style of storytelling that is part of the oral tradition of Black English: one person's story Calls to mind another story. These junctured stories have common foundations and their meaning can be enhanced by understanding the intersection of the stories.

When Stamp Paid tells Paul D the story of how Sethe killed her child, he "started with the party, the one Baby Suggs gave, but stopped and backed up a bit to tell about the berries—where they were and what was in the earth that made them grow like that" (*Beloved*, 156). Readers have already heard Baby Suggs's version of the party: "And then she knew. Her friends and neighbors were angry at her because she had overstepped, given too much, offended them by excess" (138). These two versions of one story are "circling the subject. Round and round, never changing direction. . . ." (161). Each story Calls to another story and when that other story is told, it is in Response.

The Response is immediate validation: "The process requires that one must give if one is to receive, and receiving is actively acknowledging another" (Smitherman, 108). It is a process that reestablishes and renews communal ties. When Sixo sings his death song, Paul D is Called on to Respond. Paul D "thinks he should have sung along. Loud, something loud and rolling to go with Sixo's tune, but the words put him off—he didn't understand the words. Although it shouldn't have mattered because he understood the sound: hatred so loose it was juba" (*Beloved*, 227).[12]

Call/Response is almost always triggered by a need to make an emotional connection. The Call is directed by an individual for the specific purpose of eliciting a Response. The reason the Response is given is because the Call generates an emotional summons that demands a Response. The emotional and verbal connections created by the Call/Response act is one of the elements that has facilitated communal and emotional survival of and within African American culture. Baby Suggs Calls the people to the Clearing when "she shouted, 'Let the children come' " (87). They Respond by "open[ing] their mouths and [giving] her the music. Long notes held until the four-part harmony was perfect enough for their deeply loved flesh" (89). Stamp Paid recalls Baby Suggs's "[p]owerful Call (she didn't deliver sermons or preach—insisting she was too ignorant for that—she *called* and the hearing heard)" (177).

Morrison's "Sixty Million and more" and the epigraph of *Beloved* are powerful, in part, because they Call forth an emotional Response from the reader, who has cultural, historical, and personal knowledge of the institution of slavery. Like Paul D and Sethe, many readers would be aware that the first two lines of the epigraph are referring to relationships destroyed by the institution of slavery when Morrison writes,

> I will call them my people
> which were not my people;
> and her beloved,
> which was not beloved.
> Romans 9:25

Sethe did not know her mother or her mother's language. Paul D became a brother to the other Alfred prisoners not because they were blood relatives, not because they were linked together with a chain, but because they, in their misery, had formed a community where their "eyes had to tell what there was to tell: 'Help me this morning; 's bad'; 'I'm a make it'; 'New man'; 'Steady now steady' " (107). Slavery re-marked boundary lines between people. It separated them by race and connected them through shared suffering. Readers are Called on to remember and Respond through understanding of the separation and reconnection, losses and gains that Blacks endured. The last two lines of the epigraph Calls on readers to understand that even though Sethe thought of her daughter as the "crawling-already? girl," "in the dark [her] name [was] Beloved" (75).

Readers are Called on to know that Sethe's "crawling-already? girl" was called Beloved. They are Called on to understand that "everybody knew what she was called, but nobody anywhere knew her name" (274). They are Called on to Respond by understanding that she who was called Beloved was not beloved.

Call/Response invites a close, intimate association between the speaker and the audience. It encourages a collaboration between the Caller and the Responder. When Paul D first meets Denver, she breaks the rules of her community's discourse when she sasses him: "How come everybody run off from Sweet Home can't stop talking about it? Look like if it was so sweet you would have stayed" (13). At the end of the story when Paul D and Denver meet, the Call/Response act that they participate in demonstrates their mutual membership in the community and a healing in their souls: "Paul D saw her the next morning when he was on his way to work and she was leaving hers. Thinner, steady in the eyes, she looked more like Halle than ever. She was the first to smile. 'Good morning, Mr. D' " (266).

Denver is the first to "Speak."[13] In the Black English oral tradition, Speaking is a ritualized form of the Call/Response act. When African Americans meet, they must Speak, which means to give some verbal or physical sign that they acknowledge the other's existence. Denver, by Speaking, is recognizing Paul D in a manner that is proper within her community's discourse. Because she speaks first, she is signaling that she has come of age. His Response acknowledges her adulthood, her membership in the community, and her correct use of the Call/Response ritual of Speaking. In the African American community, this back and forth exchange is essential and appropriate communal behavior.

Another appropriate mode of discourse from the oral tradition that Morrison incorporates in the written discourse of *Beloved* is Signifyin. Signifyin is a rhetorical trope from the Black English oral tradition that invites the audience to participate in the storytelling event.[14] It is the art of verbal battle that defines community and those who are in it. According to Claudia Mitchell-Kernan, "[W]hat pretends to be informative [in the Signifyin act] may intend to be persuasive. The hearer is thus constrained to attend to all potential meaning carrying symbolic systems in speech events—the total universe of discourse. The context embeddedness of meaning is attested to by both our reliance on the given context and, most importantly, by our inclination to construct additional context from our background knowledge of the world."[15] When Baby Suggs and Sethe have their Signifyin conversation, Baby Suggs is teaching a lesson to Sethe and the reader:

> Grandma Baby said there was no defense—they [White people] could prowl at will, change from one mind to another, and even when they thought they were behaving, it was a far cry from what real humans did.
> "They got me out of jail," Sethe once told Baby Suggs.
> "They also put you in it," she answered.
> "They drove you 'cross the river."
> "On my son's back."
> "They gave you this house."
> "Nobody *gave* me nothing."
> "I got a job from them."
> "He got a cook from them, girl."
> "Oh, some of them do all right by us."
> "And every time it's a surprise, ain't it?" (*Beloved*, 244)

Baby Suggs's Signifyin reminds Sethe of lessons she should already have learned and provides the reader with insight into the perceptions of oppression from one who has been oppressed: "[A]nybody white could take your whole self for anything that came to mind. Not just work, kill, or maim you, but dirty you. Dirty you so bad you couldn't like yourself any more. Dirty you so bad you forgot who you were and couldn't like yourself anymore" (251).

The denotative meanings of words are insufficient for understanding in the Signifyin act because it is an indirect discourse that relies on cultural context for meaning. Signifyin alludes to and implies ideas, feelings, and positions that may never be made explicit. Morrison's "Sixty Million and more" as an act of Signifyin carries with it implied censure. It indirectly asks: When was the last time you remembered or acknowledged those who came to America as slaves? What have you done to validate and honor those who died because of slavery? Morrison wants us to "[r]emember something [we] had forgotten [we] knew" (61).

Signifyin can be used as a way to release tensions. When Stamp Paid and Paul D Signify on Sethe, they are releasing the strain created by her murderous act and the appearance of Beloved:

> "Every time a whiteman come to the door she got to kill somebody."
> "For all she know, the man could be coming for the rent."
> "Good thing they don't deliver mail out that way."
> "Wouldn't nobody get no letter."
> "Except the postman."
> "Be a mighty hard message."
> When their laughter was spent, they took deep breaths and shook their heads. (265)

Stamp Paid and Paul D are engaged in a contest of wits and performance, and their weapons are words. Signifyin promotes audience participation because, as Mitchell-Kernan says, Signifyin is "a way of encoding messages or meanings which involves, in most cases, an element of indirection." The audience's interpretation of the meaning is through contextual and cultural knowledge (311). Indirectly, Stamp Paid and Paul D are empathizing with Sethe's need to defend her children and to strike out at those who are responsible for slavery and its consequences. They are also acknowledging the futility of her actions because one unempowered Black woman cannot put an end to a national system. She could not kill every White man she saw and if she did it would not change the situation. She would still be a Black woman trying to survive in a White man's world.

When Stamp Paid and Paul D Signify on Sethe, they are also participating in another mode of discourse taken from the Black English oral tradition: Witness/Testify. To Witness is to observe, affirm, attest, certify, and validate. Stamp Paid and Paul D are Witnesses to the consequences of slavery and the way that those consequences affected Sethe. In the oral tradition, Witness and Testify are inextricably linked experiences: one who Witnesses has an obligation to Testify. Smitherman defines Testifyin as a "concept referring to a ritualized form of black communication in which the speaker gives verbal witness to the efficacy, truth, and power of some experience in which all blacks have shared" (Smitherman, 58). The Signifyin that Stamp Paid and Paul D participate in is also an act of Testifyin. They are Witnesses to Sethe's act and by talking about it and Signifyin on it, they are Testifyin. In order to Witness one need not have seen or been present at a particular incident; one must simply have shared a similar experience, seen a similar incident, heard a similar story, and one must be willing and able to hold, share, and articulate someone else's memories. Witnessing is shared experience, emotional, physical, communal, historical. It is social empathy. Paul D and Stamp Paid had not been present when Sethe tried to attack Mr. Bodwin, but through the Testimony of those present they become Witnesses to the event: "As the scene neither one had witnessed took shape before them, its seriousness and its embarrassment made them shake with laughter" (*Beloved,* 265).

When Sethe gave "ten minutes for seven letters . . . rutting among the headstones with the engraver, his young son looking on, the anger in his face so old; the appetite in it quite new," she felt violated (5). Those readers who can and are willing to see, hear, and understand the violation are Sethe's Witnesses. As such they are obligated to Testify by articulating their own experiences that connect to Sethe's.

While the Call/Response act facilitates communication, the act of Witnessing freezes time for a split second. When people Witness, they momentarily step out of the present and relive the moment in their lives that connects them to the event they are Witnessing. They are transported to another place, to the emotions, the smell, the feel, the taste of a memory, and in that moment they relive the memory. Denver becomes a Witness to a "nineteen-year-old slave girl—a year older than herself—walking through the dark woods to get her children" when she can finally tell the story of her birth not just because "she loved it because it was all about herself" but because she "began to see what she was saying not just to hear it" (77). When Denver tells the story of her birth to Beloved, she is Testifyin. Denver becomes a Witness for Sethe's flight from slavery, she makes a connection with the woman that Sethe became and the girl that she was. Witness/Testify is personal and collective memory that is focused on the present, but framed in the past.

The group that hears Stamp Paid and Paul D's Signifyin on Sethe includes the readers. Those who are aware of the significance of Signifyin in the Black English oral tradition can choose to become Witnesses because they know why Sethe tried to kill her children. Aware readers know the context of Stamp Paid and Paul D's Signifyin and, therefore, can be Witnesses for Sethe, Stamp Paid, Paul D, and the situations that shaped them. Readers of *Beloved* learn about Halle's face smeared with clabber, know Paul D had to eat the iron bit, see Sixo burned and Sethe's mother hanged, and through discussion we, the readers, can Testify. The act of Witness/Testify is a reaffirmation of shared cultural experiences through individual participation in collective memory.

The Black English tradition of building and cementing community through language is mirrored in the modes of discourse of that tradition. Sethe and Denver are outside of their community until Denver walks out of her house and into the house of her former teacher, Mrs. Lady Jones. When the word is passed that there is trouble at 124 Bluestone, the women of the community unite and through their offers of food connect with Denver, and through her with Sethe. It is orality, word-of-mouth communication, that begins this reconnection with the community. And it is Denver's first "Thank you" (249) with the return of M. Lucille Williams's basket that cements the reuniting.

The communal help for Sethe combines the three modes of discourse: Call/Response, Signifyin, and Witness/Testify. The women come to Sethe's house to see "[t]he daughter? The killed one?" and deal with it (63). They can come because of Denver. She is the intersection between the women of the community and Sethe. They can also come because they have shared experiences with Sethe: Baby Suggs Called them to the Clearing, and they ate at the feast of excess. Ella decides to help Sethe because the reappearance of Sethe's dead daughter Calls to her to Respond: "There was also something very personal in her [Ella's] fury. Whatever Sethe has done, Ella didn't like the idea of past errors taking possession of the present. Sethe's crime was staggering and her pride outstripped even that; but she could not countenance the possibility of sin moving on in the house, unleashed and sassy" (256).

Ella is Called on to Witness Sethe's pain because "[s]he [Ella] had delivered, but would not nurse, a hairy white thing, fathered by 'the lowest yet.' It lived five days never making a sound. The idea of that pup coming back to whip her too set her jaw working, and then Ella hollered" (258–59). When the other women join her, they "step back to the beginning. In the beginning there were no words. In the beginning was the sound, and they all knew what that sound sounded like" (259). They are Witnesses to "the beginning" and their voices are their Testimony. They are Calling and Responding to each other and Witnessin of and Testifyin to their communal memory.

The prayer the women say when they first come into Baby Suggs's front yard is an act of Call/Response: "Denver saw lowered heads, but could not hear the lead prayer—only the earnest syllables of agreement that backed it: Yes. Yes. Yes, oh yes. Hear me. Hear me. Do it, Maker, do it. Yes" (258). The lead prayer Called and the rest of the women Respond. The reader is a Witness to this sacred act through the description of the event in the text. The reader's Testimony could be manifested as an understanding of the ritual, or through an understanding of the need to pray.

The women's voices Call on Sethe to Respond with memories of times and places she had Witnessed the power of the human voice: "[I]t was as though the Clearing had come to her with all its heat and simmering leaves, where the voices of women searched for the right combination, the key, the code, the sound that broke the back of words." Sethe "trembled like the baptized in its wash" (261). The women Respond, their voices purify, initiate, and re-call Sethe as a member of their community. In the midst of this moment is an act of Signifyin:

As long as a ghost showed out from its ghostly place—shaking stuff, crying, smashing and such—Ella respected it. But if it took flesh and came in her world, well, the shoe was on the other foot. She didn't mind a little communication between the two worlds, but this was an invasion.

"Shall we pray?" asked the women.

"Uh huh," said Ella. "First. Then we got to get down to business." (257)

Ella's Signification is a reminder that there are things older than prayer and that there are things that the Africans brought with them when they came to America, things that allow these women to understand that there is a close connection between this world and the next and that there are rules of conduct between the two.

The sound of Ella's statement is also part of the Signifyin. Readers who are cognizant of the Black English oral tradition will be able to hear Ella's tone and see her body language as she announces, "Uh huh, . . . First. Then we got to get down to business" (257). The aware reader knows that Ella's "Uh huh" is said low down in her throat while her facial expression says "Whatever you want." The initiated reader knows that when Ella says, "First" she emphasizes the word and then pauses that extra beat to let it sink in before she finishes her pronouncement.

Morrison's use of the aurality of the Black English oral tradition is a powerful tool that allows her to create meaning within her text and to create a community that can include both the readers and the characters of *Beloved*. Readers have to decide from what they know of Stamp Paid and through the stories he has told whether his "Uh uh" is a yes or a no (233). Stamp Paid begins his tale with his renaming, which leads to the story of his wife, Vashti, and how the master's son regularly used her sexually until he got tired of her:

> She sat by the window looking out of it, 'I'm back,' she said. 'I'm back, Josh.' I looked at the back of her neck. She had a real small neck. I decided to break it. You know, like a twig—just snap it. I been low but that was as low as I ever got.
>
> "Did you? Snap it?"
>
> "Uh uh. I changed my name." (233)

The sound the reader hears when Stamp Paid says, "Uh uh" is contextually based. The reader who has learned how to "listen for the holes—things [that were] not [said] . . . for the unnamed, unmentioned" has information needed to understand Stamp Paid's response through knowledge gained from the community within the text (92).

Morrison's use of the modes of speech taken from the oral tradition of Black English, Call/Response, Signifyin, and Witness/Testify, adds a richness to the narrative and allows the voices of African Americans to tell their stories. Frederick Douglass has said of his narrative, "My part has been to tell the story of the slave. The story the master never wanted for narrators. The masters, to tell their story, had at call all the talent and genius that wealth could command. They have had their full day in court. Literature, theology, philosophy, law, and learning have come willingly to their service, and, if condemned, they have not been condemned unheard."[16] Morrison's use of the oral tradition of Black English in *Beloved* assures that voices of Blacks will not go unheard. She commissions Black voices, using their language and language systems to tell their own stories of oppression from the point of view of the oppressed.

The last two pages of *Beloved* are a Call/Response that makes readers Witnesses to the story they have just heard, and to the oral tradition, because the readers' Response will depend upon the context they have gleaned from the stories they have just experienced and the way they interpret Morrison's phrase "This is not a story to pass on" (275). They might interpret this statement as meaning this story should not be retold, which is impossible after reading a tale that teaches that unspeakable things can and must be spoken. They might also interpret this statement as meaning this is a story that deserves everyone's full attention, it is not to be passed over. Either interpretation will, like the final full paragraph of *Beloved,* imprint this story on the mind: "By and by all trace is gone, and what is forgotten is not only the footprints but the water too and what is down there. The rest is weather. Not the breath of the disremembered and unaccounted for, but the wind in the eaves, or spring ice thawing too quickly. Just weather. Certainly no clamor for a kiss" (275). The very act of erasure insures memory. The act of setting a foot in a footprint reestablishes a connection. The acknowledgment of the disremembered and unaccounted is an act of memory and accountability.

Through the use of the oral tradition within her written text, Morrison has created a liminal zone where the usually oppositional orality and literacy meet and thrive. Within *Beloved,* the Black English oral tradition redefines the boundaries between the written text and readers. Call/Response, Signifyin, and Witness/Testify are modes of discourse that invite those who share a common language to participate in the storytelling event. Morrison's use of these modes invites readers into the community of Black English speakers.

Morrison's *Beloved,* because of its employment of the Black English oral tradition, becomes like a sacred rite, pulling readers in and engaging them as active participants of the storytelling event. The novel creates a place to explore and release the emotions evoked by the stories being told, and it can create a sense of community between the characters of *Beloved* and the novel's readers.

Notes

1.   I prefer to use the term "Black English" because of its historical use. Early scholars J. L. Dillard (*Black English* [New York: Vantage Books, 1972]) and William Labov (*Language in the Inner City* [Philadelphia: University of Pennsylvania Press, 1972]) use the term "Black English."

2.   African American culture is not a racially based classification; rather it is a category whose foundation is experiential—a cultural inheritance versus a genetic one. It must also be

understood that the culture that was developed by these people is not genetically based. African American or Black culture are terms used to identify people of African decent who share the same social experiences.

3. Thomas Hamilton, "Apology," *The Anglo-African Magazine* 1, no. 1 (January 1859): 1, quoted in Henry Louis Gates Jr., *Signifying Monkey* (New York: Oxford University Press, 1988), 173.

4. Geneva Smitherman, *Talking and Testifyin* (Detroit: Wayne State University Press, 1977), 2. Hereafter cited in the text.

5. "Language and culture are inseparable," according to Henry Louis Gates Jr. (*The Rhetorical Tradition,* ed. Patricia Bizzell and Bruce Herzberg [Boston: St. Martin's Press, 1990], 1186). Because the trope being discussed is from the Black English oral tradition, I will omit the "g" at the end of "Signifyin" because this is the name given to this trope in the oral tradition. It seems to me that Gates has, by bracketing the *g* in Signifyin(g) in his book *The Signifying Monkey,* tried to write himself into humanity by "demonstrat[ing] to white audiences that [he] is equal to them at least in [his] ability to use the language" (*Rhetorical Tradition,* 1185). The bracketed "g" identifies, implicitly and explicitly, the "otherness" of Black English that, in this study, is unnecessary and intrusive.

6. Maggie Sale examines the characteristic interactive, improvisational aspect of the oral tradition in "Call and Response as Critical Method: African-American Oral Traditions and *Beloved,*" *African American Review* 26, no. 1 (1992): 41–50.

7. The traditional name given to the "correct or proper" language used by the dominant culture of the United States is usually Standard English. The term "Standard" sets up a hierarchy. If there is a standard then anything else must be substandard. I know that the word Common can also be problematic, but in this instance I am referring to the discourse of the dominant community as a whole: the familiar, prevalent method of discourse that has been designated as the language of the people.

8. Subsequent chapters also begin with unindented paragraphs, which suggests a continuation of the stories being told. This lack of indentation is also an indication of cohesion within this nonlinear tale.

9. Toni Morrison, *Beloved* (New York: Plume, 1987), 3. Hereafter cited in the text.

10. Lawrence W. Levine, *Black Culture and Black Consciousness* (New York: Oxford University Press, 1977), 229. Hereafter cited in the text.

11. John F. Callahan, *In the African-American Grain* (Urbana: University of Illinois Press, 1988), 26.

12. "Juba" is a word from the Black English oral tradition. Juba means a holiday mood, a joyous occasion. Sixo's hatred was so unbound it was like a joyous occasion. According to Sterling Stucky, "Though the description of the "Juba" [dance] was based on its performance in the South, it was an African dance formation—one possibly named after Juba, the city in the Sudan—and rhythmic pattern." Sterling Stucky, *Going through the Storm* (New York: Oxford University Press, 1994), 70.

13. This is also an act of Signification. Denver is improvising on their first meeting when she mistakenly thinks D is Paul D's last name. Her Signifyin is a powerful demonstration of how much she has grown. When she and Paul D first meet she is awkward and shy, and she misuses the correct form of communal discourse. Now within the correct form of Call/Response, she is demonstrating that she understands her previous mistake and she is asking Paul D's pardon.

14. The definition of *Signifyin* in this study is taken from the Black English oral tradition. According to Henry Louis Gates Jr., his theory of Signifyin(g) is an "attempt to lift the discourse of Signifyin(g) from the vernacular to the discourse of literary criticism" (Henry Louis Gates Jr., *The Signifying Monkey* [New York: Oxford Press, 1988] xi). I attempt to examine the oral tradition within written discourse, not to lift it, which implies a predisposed hierarchy in which the vernacular of African Americans is less.

15.   Claudia Mitchell-Kernan, "Signifying," *Mother Wit from the Laughing Barrel,* ed. Alan Dundes (Englewood Cliffs, N.J.: Prentice-Hall, 1973), 310–328. Hereafter cited in the text.

16.   Frederick Douglass, *The Life and Times of Frederick Douglass* (1892; reprint, New York: Macmillan, 1962), 479.

Sethe's Re-memories:
The Covert Return of What Is Best Forgotten

JAN FURMAN

Near the beginning of *Beloved,* Sethe tells Denver that nothing ever dies. Speaking not just of biological life, Sethe explains that even events that have come and gone continue to exist as objectified memory. Unclear about her mother's meaning, Denver asks if other people can see these events. Yes, Sethe answers, and by way of explanation she gives an example: "Someday you be walking down the road and you hear something or see something going on. So clear. And you think it's you thinking it up. A thought picture. But no. It's when you bump into a rememory that belongs to somebody else."[1] This exchange between Sethe and Denver is obviously meant to foreshadow Beloved's return from the grave, since nothing ever dies. But the philosophical concept of externalized consciousness is so intriguing and so uncharacteristic of Sethe's otherwise unflinching pragmatism that Morrison must have intended it to do more than portend Beloved's coming; it apparently introduces an idea pertinent to the story in other contexts. After her explanation, Sethe warns Denver to "never go there. . . . Because even though it's over . . . it's going to always be there waiting for you. That's how come I had to get all of my children out. No matter what" (36). Sethe does not give "there" a name, but presumably she is referring to the Sweet Home of her memory. Yet in a broader reading "there" is not a specific place but a generalized abstraction encompassing Sethe's pervasive dread of the world; it is a universe of black grief: "what Baby Suggs died of, what Ella knew, what Stamp saw and what made Paul D tremble" (251). "There" is a world in which "anybody white could take your whole self for anything that came to mind" (251). This is schoolteacher's lesson. He had inspired Sethe's determination to die with her children before turning them out into that world, and he continues, she believes, to threaten her life: because of him she has lost all but one child, and she has no friends or community left. For Sethe, places and people of the past are not subject to the logic of chronological time; they are not relegated to history. As long as she can remember him, schoolteacher and

This essay was written specifically for this volume and is published here for the first time by permission of the author.

the tragedy he spawned exist; so do the dangers. Examining this implied tension between a conventional view of memory as a bridge from the present to the past and Sethe's re-memory, which reverses the maneuver by bringing the past forward into the present, is Morrison's concern in *Beloved*. One is the rightful province of memory; the other must be resisted because it resurrects buried anguish and disrupts peace of mind.

Sethe tries unsuccessfully to repress painful memories. Realizing the peril of keeping a past like hers alive, she tries "to remember as close to nothing" as is possible, but often, when she least expects it, an image from Sweet Home or other places, in South Carolina or Louisiana, emerges. In the midst of a routine chore, a sight, sound, or smell triggers memory, and "there was Sweet Home rolling, rolling, rolling out before her eyes" (6). Re-memories often displace existing life, making the past more authentic than the present: Halle, her wedding dress, Mrs. Garner's earrings, Baby Suggs's embrace, the hat worn by a woman who was said to be her mother; selected memories like these connected to another time evoke all the feelings and drama of human experience that are not available to Sethe in her current life. Significantly, she does not have memories of life after the death of Baby Suggs, who was a living link to Sweet Home. Almost nine years of Sethe's life at 124 Bluestone Road go unrecorded, as though any period not associated with the people and places of her former life are irrelevant. Sometimes these recollections nearly overwhelm Sethe, as when Paul D shares his memory (and thereafter Sethe makes it her own) of Halle squatting near the churn smearing butter over his face. Instead of closing out the image, Sethe works it in with the others and counts it as one more painful episode from the past. "No misery, no regret, no hateful picture too rotten to accept?" (70), she chides her brain. She has lived with the memory of being violated by schoolteacher's nephews as he stood nearby taking notes, and after Paul D's news she must add to that scene of the nephews the figure of her husband looking down and letting it happen. Her moment of self-pity over, Sethe concedes that "her brain was not interested in the future. Loaded with the past and hungry for more, it left her no room to imagine, let alone plan for, the next day" (70).

Remembering, involuntary and relentless though it may be for Sethe, is also necessary. Remembering constitutes her storytelling, the record of her life and what that life signifies. One of Sethe's two recurring and most meticulous memories is the flight from Kentucky to Ohio (the other is the flight to the woodshed), which chronicles her extraordinary rebellion against slavery. She had refused anyone's authority to define or abridge her. Schoolteacher had tried. At Sweet Home he had counted her a dumb creature, listing her animal characteristics in the records that he scrupulously kept, and his nephews had treated her as an animal, suckling Sethe as they would a cow. But Sethe contradicted their judgment of her deficiencies when she got herself and her children out of slavery and when she refused to let them be taken back. "I did it. I got us all out," Sethe tells Paul D. She remembers that "[u]p til then it was the only thing I ever did on my own. Decided. And it came off right, like it was supposed to. We was here. Each and every one of my babies and me too. I birthed them and I got em out and it wasn't no accident" (162). Sethe's courage and defiance distinguish who she is as a woman and mother and form a context for understanding every decision that she later makes.

Though savage, her escape was triumphant, and recalling it reinforces its achievement, not only for Sethe but for Denver. Sethe tells and retells Denver's birth, declaring her determination to keep herself and the unborn Denver alive, reviewing the desperate hours before delivery, which Sethe survived because of the offhanded compassion of a white girl named Amy. Certainly, Denver's attachment to events in which she took no part and therefore cannot remember for herself reflects and reinforces her impoverished emotional and social life. Like Sethe, she has no investment in a future, and at 18 she makes no effort to enter contemporary society, living instead in a closeted world constructed from Sethe's memories and the scraps of her own. Yet, rememories and the stories they spawn also attest to Denver's significance by recalling Sethe's sacrifice on her behalf.

Even Paul D relies upon Sethe's re-memories to help document and interpret his experiences. He arrives at 124 with a conflicting collection of memories about the early years at Sweet Home, about the final days of death and violence there, about prison in Georgia, and about life on the road. At Sweet Home with Garner he had believed himself to be a man. Schoolteacher and Alfred, Georgia, however, had broken him into a child, afraid to love, afraid to remain too long in one place, and like a child "thinking only about the next meal and night's sleep" (221). Looking back he wonders "how much difference there really was between before schoolteacher and after" (220). Was he ever really a man? "It troubled him that, concerning his own manhood, he could not satisfy himself. . . . Oh, he did manly things, but was that Garner's gift or his own will? What would he have been anyway—before Sweet Home—without Garner?" (220). All of these uncertainties are "packed tight in his chest" (224). Unable to settle down or stay with one woman for very long, he keeps the past buried. But in Sethe's familiar presence, Paul D's sufferings are moderated. "[T]he closed portion of his head [and heart are] opened" and the doubts silenced (41). He is reassured that Sethe is still the young girl "with iron eyes and backbone to match" whom he had known at Sweet Home (9). In her mind he, too, "looked the way he had in Kentucky. Peachstone skin; straight backed," treating her as he always had "to a mild flirtation, so subtle you had to scratch for it" (7). Together they recall the good and bad of Sweet Home, and Paul D begins to think that he can stop running from his past. When Sethe asks, "[Y]ou want to tell me about it?" (about having a bit put in his mouth by schoolteacher), Paul D admits, "I never have talked about it. Not to a soul" (71). Sethe's predictable reply is "Go ahead. I can hear it" (71). Later, he calls to mind the iron collar used to punish and restrain him after the failed escape and recollects that Sethe saw it and never made him "feel the shame of being collared like a beast. Only . . . Sethe could have left him his manhood like that" (273). Ironically, Sethe does for Paul D what she cannot do for herself, she makes him believe that a horrific past can be set aside and that something better is possible after all. For Paul D Sethe is like Sixo's Thirty-Mile Woman, "a friend of my mind," one who takes "[t]he pieces I am . . . gather[s] them and give[s] them back to me in all the right order" (273). With Sethe, who has preserved the best part of him through her memories, Paul D "wills himself into being" (221).

Everyone in this novel has a painful past and stories to chronicle it. Indeed, the point of Morrison's work here is to take overlapping personal histories and weave them together into a complete tapestry of a people's endurance. Every story is a distillate of the experience that shapes someone's life, and telling the story validates the life. Both Ella and Stamp Paid, like Sethe, remember a past life and tell the story of its significance. Because Ella survived a "puberty . . . spent in a house where she was shared by father and son, whom she called 'the lowest yet' " (256), she has come to the practical conclusion that she can survive anything. But unlike Sethe, Ella will not permit her memories of yesterday to undermine today and tomorrow. "The past," she believes, "is something to leave behind. And if it didn't stay behind, well, you might have to stamp it out [because] . . . freed life—everyday was a test and a trial" (256). Ella can never forget her suffering; its bitter lesson is her measure of life ("a killing, a kidnap, a rape—whatever, she listened and nodded. Nothing compared to 'the lowest yet' " [256]), but she would not dwell there. Stamp comes to an equivalent conclusion: The past is not forgotten; it is a foundation for building new life. As a younger man, he had considered killing his master's son for sleeping with his wife, and his wife because her helplessness emphasized his own. "That," Stamp tells Paul D, "was as low as I ever got" (233). Instead of murdering someone, he became reckless in other ways. Like someone who has reached the limits of endurance, he gave himself permission to do as he pleased because he had nothing more to lose. With that he contemptuously stamped his debt to slave society paid in full and committed himself to helping others do the same.

Even Baby Suggs, whose body and spirit are nearly broken, who bore eight children and lost them all, finds a way to be reconciled with her past. She creates what could be described as a ministry of rebuttal to the dehumanizing legacy of slavery. Summoning the community to a clearing in the woods, she urges men, women, and children to "cry for the living and the dead," to laugh and dance for each other, and to love themselves because in the world beyond the clearing they were not loved. Sethe, Baby Suggs believes, is lucky to have three children left. Of her "four taken [and] four chased," all Baby can remember is that the oldest, Ardella, "loved the burned bottom of bread." She advises Sethe to "[b]e thankful" (5).

In freedom, the community is reborn and the individual is transformed. Just as Baby hears her heart beat only after she crosses the Ohio River into freedom, life for Ella and Stamp, too, has a "before" and "after" quality. Before, Stamp was a husband with a timid presence in his wife's life, and Ella was innocent prey. Both recast themselves as independent agents, not only of the underground railroad but of their own lives. Both know the relation between past and present, in the words of Michel de Certeau here, "as one of succession (one after the other) . . . and disjunction (either one or the other, but not both at the same time)."[2] Stamp can look at Paul D, who has also struggled with this kind of self-willed metamorphosis from slave to free man, and say with certainty about his former life, "I didn't have the patience I got now . . ." (*Beloved*, 232), revealing a knowledge of self that comes from observing the past from an appropriate distance.

Sethe does not do this; to put slavery and schoolteacher behind her into history is to negate their perverseness and deny the moral necessity of her actions in the woodshed. Only such perverseness could provoke such a response. In order to insist upon a baby's death as a victory, in order to claim that she did what was right, Sethe must remember slavery's atrocities and see schoolteacher riding into the yard with his three companions as nothing less cataclysmic than coming face to face with the four apocalyptic horsemen. This is what Sethe attempts to explain when Paul D sits at her table with the newspaper clipping spread between them. Schoolteacher embodied the intolerable connection between her past and her children's future. To make this point Sethe weaves a long and seemingly convoluted narrative, going back to the beginning to, as she says, "recollect what I'd seen back where I was before Sweet Home" (160), describing a little-girl confusion about not knowing her own mother, cataloging the difficulties of trying to take care of her children and a profusion of other chores at Sweet Home, and culminating with the escape that ratified her power as a mother. In coming for her, schoolteacher was dismissing that power. Cutting her baby's throat is not a matter for Sethe's facile explanation. She can only hope that Paul D will understand her decision if he knows the entire story of her life as a woman and mother. Impatient for answers, Paul D wants Sethe to "get . . . to the point" instead of spinning around the room and circling the subject (162). But "Sethe knew that the circle she was making around the room, him, the subject, would remain one" because "pin[ing] it down" to a simplistic cause-and-effect explication must be left to the likes of newspapermen (163). To kill herself and her children was not merely to keep them all from being locked down in slavery, but it was to keep them from being dirtied "so bad you couldn't like yourself anymore" (251), as she and others had been. Sethe came to this instant understanding as soon as she saw schoolteacher in the yard. She knew that her children's future was her past and with the stroke of a saw she canceled that unthinkable future. By the time Sethe faced schoolteacher, "looked him dead in the eye, she had something in her arms that stopped him in his tracks" (164).

Sethe's "outrageous claims" of victory place her outside the community. Ella, and probably others, "understood Sethe's rage . . . , but not her reaction to it. Which Ella thought was prideful, misdirected . . ." (256). After the woodshed—following their initial spirit of meanness in not warning Sethe of schoolteacher's approach, feeling remorseful perhaps—the women who had been her friends gather in Baby Suggs's yard, ready to embrace Sethe and her sorrow, but when Sethe emerges from 124 self-sufficient, with her head high and back stiff, the group steps back. In refusing to show weakness or need, Sethe rejects any disapproval of her action. To break down would be to doubt. Left to herself, Sethe manages to keep body and soul together by working at the restaurant and taking care of Denver. But without friends, neighbors, a church, without involvement in a community, in other words, she has little potential of rehabilitating her life beyond the woodshed. "The twenty eight days [fertile with possibility] of having women friends, a mother-in-law, and all her children together; of being part of a neighborhood; of, in fact, having neighbors at all to call her own—all that was long gone and would never come back" (173).

For a short while Sethe does think seriously about consciously living in the present with Paul D. Briefly, she looks forward to "launch[ing] her newer stronger life with a tender man" (99). He had rid her of the constant ghostly reminder of the past, and she had helped to ease the burden of his troubles. Although she is tempted to "leave things the way they are" (45), she consents to do as Paul D asks and trust some of her life to him. The carnival day that he engineers is her literal and figurative journey back into contemporary black society. For too long Sethe has lived isolated and apart, and carnival day commences a reconnection of the severed ties to community. Along the road from the house to town, Paul D hails everyone within hearing distance, and in his presence people nod and smile as they look more kindly than usual upon Sethe and Denver. For the first time mother and daughter enjoy the frivolity of freedom. In her optimism, Sethe notices that in the last morning light going to town and in the last afternoon light returning home, her own, Denver's, and Paul D's shadows are holding hands. "She decided that was a good sign. A life. Could be" (47).

Shadows recede and so do Sethe's prospects for starting over. In order to move forward, Sethe must abandon her old rebellion and make peace with the past. But she cannot do that. As she tells Paul D, who asks why she does not leave 124 to make a better life for Denver, "I got a tree on my back and a haint in my house, and nothing in between but the daughter I am holding in my arms. No more running from nothing . . ." (15). When Paul D suggests that Sethe let Denver grow up, treat her as the woman she is, Sethe bristles again. "You can't protect her every minute," he warns, unaware of the extraordinary extent to which Sethe has already gone to protect her children. "What's going to happen when you die?" Sethe's unequivocal reply is "Nothing! I'll protect her while I'm live and I'll protect her when I ain't" (45), implying that there are no boundaries on her mothering. Past and present, life and death are the same. In her words, "It's so hard for me to believe in time" (35). Later, when Paul D learns about the woodshed and realizes that Sethe's remark is not just an idle pledge, like the others in her community he walks away and Sethe is "junkheaped for the third time . . ." (174).

Paul D's leaving coincides with Sethe's full recognition of Beloved as her daughter, and each event, in its way convinces Sethe of the futility of believing in real time as a measure of change. Paul D had argued for beginning anew—for giving up the timeless existence that Sethe has been tolerating at the edge of black life in Cincinnati. Together they could have a baby and a future. His abandonment hardens Sethe's isolation, but she is now comforted by the realization that her critics are wrong: Her baby did not die, and Beloved's return is the proof. With this knowledge "[s]he opened the door [to 124], walked in and locked it tight behind her" (198). Sethe aims to create a sanctuary for three in a place where dangers from the past can be forgotten. This self-contained, insular world will offer possibility, a future, all that Sethe has given up. As she says, to no one in particular, "[M]y love was tough and she back now. I knew she would be" (200). Finally, past and present are aligned as they should be—in succession and not collapsed into each other. Beloved gives back the 18 years that Sethe put on hold and Sethe is restored as a mother to "tend her [daughter] as no mother ever tended a child" (200). Now Sethe "can look at things again. After the shed [she] stopped" (201). She even makes plans for their future: planting in spring, watching the sun rise, noting the color of grass. She now believes that the three figures holding hands are mother and daughters moving forward. Sethe is relieved that she "ain't got to remember no more." She can "Do like Baby said: Think on it then lay it down—for good" (182).

Sethe of course is deluded: Beloved is not the future but Sethe's past incarnate. She will not give Sethe respite from memory. On the contrary, she will be a steadfast reminder of much that Sethe longs to forget. Tell me about the earrings, sing that song, tell me about your mother, tell about you and me and our time together, Beloved demands. Even Denver is pressed into service as chronicler, "step[ping] into the told story that lay before her eyes" as she recalls for Beloved the near mythic account of Denver's birth and Sethe's escape (29). And when Beloved asks Sethe the big question—Why did you leave; why did you take your face away?—Sethe, pathetically, must relate again and again her version of the woodshed. So completely is Sethe focused on satisfying Beloved's need to know what happened that she loses all links to real time and place: "Neither Beloved nor Sethe seemed to care what the next day might bring . . ." (243). Sethe is taken over by the past, trying to convince Beloved "that what she had done was right because it came from true love" (251).

Beloved cannot comprehend Sethe's logic. In fact, looking at Sethe's actions through Beloved's eyes, Morrison says, a little sarcastically and mostly in jest, that Beloved "didn't think it [having her throat cut] was all that tough. She thought it was lunacy. Or, more important, 'How do you know death is better for me. You've never died. How could you know?' "[3] Before Beloved appeared, Sethe had not consciously acknowledged the full truth of taking a life. She faced any opposition with the claim of motherlove, protection, and safety: "[A]ll the parts of her that were precious and fine and beautiful [she] . . . carried, pushed, dragged them through the veil, out, away, over there where no one could hurt them" (163). But despite Sethe's earnest declarations, Paul D is right in suggesting that she reconsider her triumph. Her sons have disappeared, Denver is afraid to leave the yard, Baby Suggs died of a broken heart, and more important than all of this, Sethe's plan for keeping her children inviolate did not work. Indeed, Beloved returns to her more damned than (be)loved. Having never lived as a member of a community, Sethe does not have its store of folk wisdom. She does not know, as Ella and Stamp know, "that people who die bad don't stay in the ground" (188); or what Baby Suggs knew, that "[n]ot a house in the country ain't packed to its rafters with some dead Negro's grief" (5); or what Paul D thinks, that Beloved is a witch; or, finally, that "clamoring around [Sethe's house] . . . was the mumbling of the black and angry dead" (198). Beloved's voice contributes to the clamor. She is not, as Sethe hopes, the regenerate daughter come home to forgive and forget, but a tormented and tormenting spirit.

Beloved does not actively seek revenge against Sethe, but she gets it nonetheless. Punishment for crimes, even righteous ones, is obligatory in Morrison's fiction. Terry Otten makes this point quite convincingly in his study of crime and innocence in *Beloved:* "Unable to avert choice, Sethe sacrifices her innocence, and even if it is 'the only thing to do,' Morrison grants her no reprieve from judgment. . . . Her deed carries the paradoxical qualities of an existential victory and a moral offense."[4] Beloved's return is Sethe's reckoning. Hungry for the life that she lost and with Sethe her only resource, "Beloved ate up [Sethe's] . . . life, took it, swelled up with it, grew taller on it" until Sethe is reduced to sitting in a corner "licking her lips like a chastened child . . ." (*Beloved,* 250). Both try feverishly to make up time, but what is gone is gone. Beloved has the bad manners of the unparented girl she is. And Sethe evinces the tentativeness of a doting mother feeling guilty of neglect. "When once or twice Sethe tried to assert herself—be the unquestioned mother whose word was law and who knew what was best—Beloved slammed things, wiped the table clean of plates, threw salt on the floor, broke a windowpane" (242). Each wears the distorted face of love: One gives too much; the other takes too much. Sethe embraces an idea of Beloved descended from a re-memory of the "crawling-already?" baby catching at her mother's earrings and playing on the white stairs (93). But the woman who returns in place of the child is not just older; she is not even of the same genealogy (if one can think of a ghost in biological terms). In a manner of speaking, Beloved is an aberration conceived during Sethe's extorted sex with the engraver as his resentful son looks on. An unnamed baby is buried, and 10 minutes of "rutting among the headstones" with a stranger gives that baby a name and its essence (5). Beloved inherits not only Sethe's bad feelings, but all of the ill will and misery related to her death, and these give power—first to the baby ghost and then to the fully-formed woman who takes the ghost's place.

Someone has to break the hateful link between Sethe and Beloved, and that job goes to Denver and the community. Denver understands that without her intervention, Sethe will perish. In Denver's view Sethe is "trying to make up for the handsaw" and Beloved is "making her pay for it" (251). Breaking out of the cocoon Sethe had created, where Denver fed off stories from the past, she "leave[s] the yard" and "step[s] off the edge of [her] world" (242), leaving Sethe and Beloved behind. At first she fears a landscape seeded with the frightening re-memories of schoolteacher, which Sethe had warned "would always be there waiting," but in seeking out Lady Jones Denver finds a new kind of schoolteacher and a community of women waiting to claim and "inaugurate her life in the world as a woman" (248). From these women she learns to be respectful and responsible, neither of which Sethe had had the opportunity or will to teach, so busy was she protecting Denver from anticipated assaults. With Sethe she had been willful and undisciplined, even rude when Paul D arrived and threatened her safe reclusion. But under the nurturing and tutelage of village women whose kindness Denver must repay with a word of thanks and a smile, she learns both self-reliance and gratitude. Her new life brings education, friendship, employment, and maybe even romance. When Paul D sees her on her own for the first time outside the yard of 124, he is struck by the transformation. "Steady in the eyes," without the old rancor or mistrust, Denver has achieved what Sethe could not: A future.

As Denver advances into a new life, Sethe regresses into a world of re-memory until, having completely exchanged re-memory for presence of mind, she charges Edward Bodwin with an ice pick in the deranged belief that he is schoolteacher come for her babies, her "best thing[s]" (272). Anticipating Sethe's attack, Denver and the 30 women gathered in Sethe's yard intercede and prevent Sethe from murdering the man who had kept her from hanging 18 years earlier. His death would have endangered the entire black community. "It'd be the worst thing in the world for us," Stamp explains to Paul D. The two men joke about Sethe's penchant for killing "[e]very time a whiteman come to the door" (265). But humor aside, this final episode of violence encompasses the tragic contradiction of Sethe's situation, what one critic describes as "the paradox of a past and present self and place."[5] Sethe's legendary escape from Sweet Home had given her the courage to enter the woodshed where she expected to escape once more, this time to freedom on the other side. Sethe does not die, but having taken that bold step, she is trapped, metaphorically, in the shed, consigned year after year to remember and relive. Beloved's return releases her and brings a second chance for motherhood, Sethe believes, but unfortunately Beloved will not allow her to forget and Sethe's new idea of family is sabotaged by old fears that have been kept alive over the years by re-memories of schoolteacher and slavery. The real world has changed but Sethe has not, as her rampage against Bodwin illustrates.

Sethe suffers pain and guilt, but in the end she is also redeemed by devotion. Loving her children more than herself and surviving all that she has makes Sethe her own "best thing" (273). Her fortitude is rewarded with the true possibility of a new life with Paul D in the here and now. Paul D knows what Sethe will learn—that with "more yesterday than anybody," they are entitled to "some kind of tomorrow" (273).

"This is not a story to pass on," Morrison writes repeatedly and enigmatically in the epilogue (274). She explains that "[r]emembering seems unwise," unsettling as it were. So those who could (and that was everyone eventually) forgot Beloved. And yet, Morrison hints, there is an awful sadness when "all trace is gone" (275). Thus the ambivalence for Morrison, her readers, and her characters: The millions of dead, casualties of slavery, whom Beloved represents, ought to be remembered and accounted for, but as Sethe's story proves, remembering takes its toll. Beloved had a strong claim on the living. Even Paul D, with all of his suspicions, found Beloved a familiar presence, a reminder of something he was "supposed to remember" (234), and nights with her "escorted [him] to some ocean-deep place he once belonged to" (265). These "memories within"[6] inspire Morrison's text, which in turn strums the reader's collective racial unconscious. But Paul D is also grateful for "Sifting daylight [that] dissolves the memory, turns it into dust motes floating in light" (264) because, as Morrison admits, this kind of story "sort of beats you up." She found that sometimes, while composing Beloved, she would "write a sentence and . . . jump up and run outside or something," so intense were her characters' lives (Morrison, "Site," 122). The remedy is to remember, but to build strength and not weakness from these unsettling recollections. This is the point Baby Suggs makes from the other side when Denver stands on the porch remembering long ago conversations between her mother and grandmother about evil turned loose in a world where black people were defenseless. In a chiding voice Baby admonishes Denver to remember her people's suffering. Remember the broken hips and scarred backs, she commands, "and go on out the yard" (244). Morrison no doubt is giving her readers the same advice.

Notes

1. Toni Morrison, *Beloved* (New York: Alfred A. Knopf, 1987), 36. Hereafter cited in the text.

2. Michel de Certeau, *Heterologies: Discourse on the Other* (Minneapolis: University of Minnesota Press, 1986), 4.

3. Elissa Schappell and Claudia Brodsky Lacour, "Toni Morrison: The Art of Fiction," *Paris Review* (Fall 1993): 107.

4. Terry Otten, *The Crime of Innocence in the Fiction of Toni Morrison* (Columbia: University of Missouri Press, 1989), 83.

5. This is the title of Patrick Bryce Bjork's chapter on *Beloved* in *The Novels of Toni Morrison: The Search for Self and Place within the Community* (New York: Peter Lang, 1992), 141.

6. Borrowing this phrase from Zora Neale Hurston, Morrison uses it to describe her own imaginative recollections which she says are the "subsoil of my work." See Toni Morrison, "The Site of Memory," *Inventing the Truth: The Art and Craft of Memoir,* ed. William Zinsser (Boston: Houghton Mifflin, 1987), 111. Hereafter cited in the text.

The Disruption of Formulaic Discourse: Writing Resistance and Truth in *Beloved*

LOVALERIE KING

He has come to believe that the domestication of the "inferior races" will come about by his conditioning of their reflexes. But in this he leaves out of account the human memory and the ineffaceable marks left upon it; and then, above all there is something which perhaps he has never known: we only become what we are by the radical and deep-seated refusal of that which others have made of us.
—Jean-Paul Sartre, "Preface" to *The Wretched of the Earth* by Franz Fanon

For blacks victimized by the Atlantic Slave Trade, resistance was constant, and it took many forms, such as killing, taking over slave ships, escaping from plantations, and engaging in alternative discourses. This last, more subtle, type of response has been passed on in various written forms, including autobiographical narratives and fiction. A neo-slave narrative that brings to light information subjugated by the privileging of certain narratives over others, Toni Morrison's *Beloved* exists as a form of alternative discourse and, thus, takes its place in a continuing tradition of resistance. A microanalytic approach to the text reveals certain narrative patterns that perform the work of resisting the "master" narrative—especially in a key exchange between Sixo and schoolteacher—which Morrison uses to demonstrate that truth is neither fixed nor absolute but is, instead, produced in discourse. In the case of Sixo and schoolteacher, the production of truth takes place while Sixo is engaged in resisting the power (or the master narrative) that schoolteacher represents.

Scholars in the field of early African American literature point to a number of constraints under which autobiographical narratives were produced.[1] For example, one scholar, discussing the evolution of white American sentiment toward blacks, writes that:

This essay, based on a presentation at NEMLA in April 1996, was written specifically for this volume and is published here for the first time by permission of the author.

The slave narrator was an alien whose assertions of common humanity and civil rights conflicted with some basic beliefs of that society that he was addressing. . . . Black men usually desired the same freedoms and responsibilities that white society reserved for itself. As a black, the narrator shared these desires. As a nonwhite, he knew these desires were socially unacceptable to white society.[2]

Robert Stepto adds dimension to this conversation by elaborating on the extent to which Henry Bibb had to relinquish control over his own narrative because of an elaborate authentication process (8). Hazel Carby's analysis of *Incidents in the Life of a Slave Girl* examines the fine line that Harriet Jacobs negotiated in relating her decision to choose a white lover so as to neutralize the sexual advances of her owner:

In order to retain narrative authority and to preserve a public voice acceptable to an ante-bellum readership, Jacobs carefully negotiated the tension between satisfying moral expectations and challenging an ideology that would condemn her as immoral. Jacobs's confession was at once both conventional and unconventional in form and tone. The narrator declared in a direct address to her readers that the remembrance of this period in her "unhappy life" filled her with "sorrow and shame" and made no reference to sexual satisfaction, love or passion, as such feelings were not meant to be experienced or encouraged outside of marriage and were rarely figured to exist within it.[3]

These critics (and others) point out in various ways the extent to which certain institutions and conventions shaped autobiographical narratives for public consumption.

Neo-slave narratives such as *Beloved* revisit and expand upon that earlier form. Morrison has explained that "in shaping the experience [slavery] to make it palatable to those who were in a position to alleviate it, they [ex-slave narrators] were silent about many things, and they forgot many other things.[4] The editor of Olaudah Equiano's narrative praised Equiano for putting "no emotional pressure on the reader other than that which the situation itself contains" (88). Morrison notes that "over and over the writers pull the narrative up short with a phrase such as, 'but let us drop a veil over these proceedings too terrible to relate' " (88). Her task in writing fictionalized accounts of slavery involves filling in gaps, finding a way to "rip that veil drawn over 'proceedings too terrible to relate' " (91). Morrison finds it even more troubling that some autobiographical narratives about slavery obscure the "interior life" of their black subjects; her work is designed to address this problem (91).

For autobiographical narrators, the act of writing countered the racist assumption that blacks were inherently inferior and, thus, incapable of producing coherent, well-reasoned discourse. Authors such as Equiano, Frederick Douglass, William Wells Brown, and Harriet Jacobs not only survived slavery, but also managed to achieve high levels of literacy. The autobiographical narratives they produced epitomize resistance merely by existing. In *Beloved,* Morrison harkens back to this tradition and carries it forward as a means of continuing the process of resistance and recovery—resistance to oppression in its multiple manifestations, and recovery from its restrictive and traumatizing effects.

As a neo-slave narrative, *Beloved* exemplifies the process of literary archeology.[5] Morrison describes her exercise this way:

> On the basis of some information and a little bit of guesswork you journey to a site to see what remains were left behind and to reconstruct the world that these remains imply. What makes it fiction is the nature of the imaginative act; my reliance on the image—on the remains—in addition to recollection, to yield up a kind of truth. (Morrison, "Site," 92)

The process at work in *Beloved* in particular resembles Foucault's "genealogy," or "a kind of attempt to emancipate historical knowledges from . . . subjugation, to render them . . . capable of opposition and of struggle against the coercion of a theoretical, unitary, formal and scientific discourse."[6] A genealogy is based "on a reactivation of local knowledges—of minor knowledges . . . in opposition to the scientific hierarchisation of knowledges and the effects intrinsic to their power." For Foucault, " 'archaeology' would be the appropriate methodology" of an "analysis of local discursivities," and " 'genealogy' would be the tactics whereby, on the basis of the descriptions of . . . local discursivities, the subjected knowledges which were thus released would be brought into play" (85). We see this phenomenon at work in *Beloved* through Morrison's use of memory, which she describes as the "subsoil" for her archeological work, and from which flows a treasure trove of local knowledges which are then put into play in the lives of her characters (Morrison, "Site," 92).

Truth is often associated with Baby Suggs in *Beloved,* but Sixo is Morrison's most dramatic symbol of resistance. Analysis of a key exchange between Sixo and schoolteacher, who personifies scientific discourse, reveals that Sixo is also associated with the production of knowledge, local knowledge that continues to be recalled and put into action long after his murder. The knowledge that Sixo produces in this exchange disrupts schoolteacher's discourse and, thus, represents a disruption of the dominant symbolic order.[7]

Prior to Sixo's central verbal confrontation with the coldly empirical schoolteacher, Morrison reveals him in small backward glimpses. The narrator first refers to "Sixo, the wild man" a few pages into the novel.[8] Next Paul D recollects that at Sweet Home he often sat with Sixo under a favorite tree that he called Brother. Sixo was "gentle then and still speaking English" (21). He had indigo skin and a flame-red tongue, and he "experimented with night-cooked potatoes" (21), which he never got right because he was out of synchronization with time in the New World. Nevertheless, Paul D recalls that Sixo walked 17 hours each way to visit a woman who was, Sixo said, a friend of his mind: "She gather me, man. The pieces I am, she gather them and give them back to me in all the right order. It's good, you know, when you got a woman who is a friend of your mind" (272–73). Sixo's excursions violate a Sweet Home rule (before and after schoolteacher's presence there), and he is so fatigued after his trips that his fellow workers must cover for him the following day.

Sethe remembers that Sixo never laughed until the end (23); and the narrator tells us that on one of Sixo's night excursions, he discovered a "deserted stone structure that Redmen used way back when they thought the land was theirs" (24). Sixo asked the structure for permission to enter and to bring Patsy, his woman, there. Feeling comfortable among trees, he danced alone there at night to "keep his bloodlines open" (25). While Sethe, Paul D, and the others laughed at schoolteacher's questions and thought him a fool for measuring their heads, Sixo recognized the harm in such invasions. Paul D remembers that Sixo learned about the "train" because he was the only one of them who crept away at night. Thus, they depended on Sixo to plan their escape from Sweet Home.

Following their escape attempt, Sixo, realizing that schoolteacher had discovered their hiding place, pushed Patsy—the Thirty-Mile Woman—away from him and, hopefully, toward safety. He and Paul D were subsequently captured, surrounded, and bound, but Sixo grabbed a rifle and began to sing. Swinging the gun, he was able to injure one of schoolteacher's accomplices but could do little more with bound hands. Schoolteacher at first instructed his men to take Sixo alive, but soon changed his mind and decided that "this one will never be suitable" (226). They tried to burn Sixo at the stake while he laughed and called out "Seven-O" even as his feet were cooking. Finally, his persecutors had to shoot him to "shut him up" (226). Later, as Paul D sat locked in a three-spoke collar, he thought that "he should have sung along" with Sixo, "loud, something loud and rolling to go with Sixo's tune, but the words put him off—he didn't understand the words. Although it shouldn't have mattered because he understood the sound: hatred so loose it was Juba" (227).[9] Toward the end of the novel, after he has survived physical slavery, Paul D looks at himself through Sixo's eyes and feels ashamed (267).

Thus constructed, Sixo stands apart from the other enslaved inhabitants of Sweet Home by refusing to speak the language of his oppressors; by deliberately ignoring certain rules that deny his humanity and that foster an unnatural sexual environment (bestiality); by adhering to certain behaviors, traditions, and customs that feel natural, right, or comfortable to him; and by planning an escape, resisting capture, and laughing in the face of physical death. In short, he is a highly disruptive presence in a system that defines him as less than human—especially under the terms of schoolteacher's scientific racism.

Sethe recalls that Sixo especially hated schoolteacher's questions (37), and in a verbal confrontation with schoolteacher, Sixo's ability to reason and to manipulate language subverts the objective of the formulaic discourse schoolteacher uses to justify punishing (whipping) Sixo for killing and cooking a shoat (190). The exchange is set up like a catechism, which, in its most basic format, is a tool for teaching "the principles of Christian dogma, discipline, and ethics" (*American Heritage Dictionary*). Used as a method of mind and language control popularized during slavery, especially in religious instruction, the catechism consisted of question-and-answer formulaic discourse such as the following:

Q. Who keeps the snakes and all bad things from hurting you?
A. God does.
Q. Who gave you a master and a mistress?
A. God gave them to me.
Q. Who says that you must obey them?
A. God says that I must.
Q. What book tells you these things?
A. The Bible.[10]

Subsequent questions in this particular formula attempt to inculcate a work ethic, describing workers in descending order from God, to angels, to Adam and Eve, and, finally, to the enslaved person. The point or objective is to enforce the notion that a reluctant slave is a lazy slave who is, therefore, wicked.

Q. What makes the crops so hard to grow now?
A. Sin makes it.
Q. What makes you lazy?
A. My wicked heart.
Q. How do you know your heart is wicked?
A. I feel it every day.
Q. Who teaches you so many wicked things?
A. The Devil.
Q. Must you let the Devil teach you?
A. No, I must not. (Fishel and Quarles, 114)

This distortion of religious doctrine supported the labor requirements of the institution of slavery, which served a capitalist system whose lifeblood has always been an abundant and easily exploitable source of cheap (or free, as during slavery) labor.

The catechism is designed to elicit specific prefigured responses, ultimately arriving at some overall, predetermined "truth" to be used in manipulating individual or group behavior. To control the mind is to control the physical body and its actions, and the bodies of enslaved persons serving as a docile and subservient—but eager to please—labor force represented a capitalistic utopia for the slaveocracy. William Wells Brown displayed another example of the catechism as capitalist tool in *Clotel*. Following a white-supervised religious service, blacks are required to respond in predetermined fashion to questioning by the white minister:

Q. Why may not the whites be slaves as the blacks?—

A. Because the Lord intended the Negroes for slaves.

Q. Are they better calculated for servants than the whites?—

A. Yes, their hands are large, the skin thick and tough, and they can stand the sun better than the whites.

Q. Why should servants not complain when they are whipped?—

A. Because the Lord has commanded that they should be whipped.

Q. Where has He commanded it?—

A. He says, "He that knoweth his master's will, and doeth it not, shall be beaten with many stripes."

Q. Then is the master to blame for whipping his servant?—

A. Oh, no! He is only doing his duty as a Christian.[11]

Georgiana, the "kind" plantation mistress, and a white man listen to the exchange and later overhear a black-only secret religious service led by the highly duplicitous Sam in his "true" voice. Sam sings a spiritual that reverses the sentiments of the earlier forced dialogue and thus signifies—repeats and revises—the catechism.

Like Brown's enslaved community, Morrison's characters demonstrate the ability to resist such attempts at mind control—especially when the attempts deny their humanity. In Sixo's confrontation with schoolteacher, the former's capacity for human reasoning, coupled with his power over language, reverses the objective of schoolteacher's formulaic discourse and thwarts the slaveholder's attempt to circumscribe Sixo's identity.

Morrison uses Sethe's memory and the question-and-answer format to render the exchange. Sethe recalls that after schoolteacher's arrival at Sweet Home, drastic changes took place: Schoolteacher effected and enforced more restrictive rules. Paul A was whipped for the first time. Sixo started watching the sky and "you could tell his mind was gone from Sweet Home" (*Beloved,* 197). Sethe also recalls that before schoolteacher took over, Sixo, the Pauls, and Halle used rifles to hunt game, but "schoolteacher took away the guns from the Sweet Home men and, deprived of game to round out their diet of bread, beans, hominy, vegetables and a little extra at slaughter time, they began to pilfer in earnest, and it became not only their right but their obligation" (190–91).[12]

When schoolteacher encounters Sixo eating meat from the shoat, he first asks and then answers his own question. Sethe remembers that schoolteacher acted "like he was just going through the motions—not expecting an answer that mattered":

> "You stole that shoat, didn't you?"
> "No. Sir." said Sixo, but he had the decency to keep his eyes on the meat.
> "You telling me you didn't steal it, and I'm looking right at you?"
> "No, sir. I didn't steal it."
> Schoolteacher smiled. "Did you kill it?"
> "Yes, sir. I killed it."
> "Did you butcher it?"
> "Yes, sir."
> "Did you cook it?"
> "Yes, sir."
> "Well, then. Did you eat it?"
> "Yes, sir. I sure did."
> "And you telling me that's not stealing?"
> "No, sir. It ain't."
> "What is it then?"
> "Improving your property, sir."
> "What?"
> "Sixo plant rye to give the high piece a better chance. Sixo take and feed the soil, give you more crop. Sixo take and feed Sixo give you more work." (190)

In "The Slave Narrators and the Picaresque Mode: Archetypes for Modern Black Personae," Charles H. Nichols calls attention to ways of responding to questioning by whites. One example involved the practice wherein the enslaved individual had to anticipate and supply the answer the slaveholder expected. The other involved the use of "subtle and ironic turns of speech" in which, for example, "the master exclaims angrily: 'You scoundrel, you ate my turkey,' " and the enslaved person replies, "Yes, sir, Massa, you got less turkey but you sho' got mo' nigger."[13] In the conflict with schoolteacher, Sixo chooses the latter type of response, though there is no indication that he effects a subservient stance. Indeed, his reasoning resembles that of Frederick Douglass, who claimed that taking meat that belonged to his owner did not deprive his owner of anything since he still owned the meat—as part of his human property.[14]

Sixo disrupts the flow of schoolteacher's supposedly empirical reasoning, and following the exchange, Sethe observes that Sixo's argument was clever, "but schoolteacher beat him anyway to show him that definitions belonged to the definers—not the defined" (*Beloved,* 191).

Two other passages that, taken together, achieve a similar objective of disrupting formulaic thought involve Baby Suggs, whose brand of spirituality makes her the appropriate vehicle through which to counter the effects of the catechism. In an effort to justify slavery to the abolitionist Bodwins, Garner asks Baby Suggs a series of questions as he delivers her to her new life in freedom. His questions are obviously designed to elicit a preconceived objective—to give credence to his claim that his "benevolent" form of slavery is not harmful:

> "Tell em Jenny.[15] You live any better on any place before mine?"
> "No, sir," she said. "No place."
> "How long was you at Sweet Home?"
> "Ten year, I believe."
> "Ever go hungry?"
> "No, sir."
> "Cold?"
> "No, sir."
> "Anybody lay a hand on you?"
> "No, sir."
> "Did I let Halle buy you or not?"
> "Yes, sir, you did," she said, thinking, But you got my boy and I'm all broke down. You be renting him out to pay for me way after I'm gone to Glory. (145–46)

Baby Suggs's answers satisfy Garner in the belief that she shares his distorted view of reality. She tells him what he expects to hear, but her true feelings are revealed in the thoughts she voices later during a discussion with Sethe about white people. Denver hears the discussion and recalls it at a crucial moment:

> "They [white people] got me out of jail," Sethe once told Baby Suggs.
> "They also put you in it," she answered.
> "They drove you 'cross the river."
> "On my son's back."
> "They gave you this house."
> "Nobody *gave* me nothing."
> "I got a job from them."
> "He got a cook from them, girl."
> "Oh, some of them do all right by us."
> "And every time it's a surprise, ain't it?"
> "You didn't used to talk this way."
> "Don't box with me. There's more of us they drowned than there is all of them ever lived from the start of time. Lay down your sword. This ain't a battle; it's a rout."[16] (244)

Baby Suggs revisits and revises her conversation with Garner by saying, essentially, that slavery is slavery, and there are no significant differences among white people. Denver, in her remembrance of Baby Suggs's truth, accesses what Foucault defines as "local knowledges"—in this case information about the oppressor as it is understood in the oppressed community. The memory of that truth invokes a paralyzing fear in Denver, but the spirit of Baby Suggs coaxes her into action even in the face of that fear—commanding her to "go on out the yard" to get help (244).

Obviously, Baby Suggs's spiritual presence serves as a site of resistance and functions also to disrupt and counteract certain types of indoctrination. Sixo, however, remains the novel's most dramatic personification of perpetual resistance. Like Denver, he takes deliberate action to avoid starvation, but in the dialogue with schoolteacher his reasoning contains multiple layers of complexity.

When Sixo killed the shoat, he had already made a conscious decision not to starve. Schoolteacher's task in the confrontation with Sixo is to establish that a challenge to the status quo has occurred, to identify the perpetrator, and to carry out the prescribed punishment; he is a prosecutor in the medieval sense of the word.[17] As a representative absolute ruler in the antebellum South, his control in defining truth is necessary to maintain his dominant position in the hierarchy of master and slave. Because Morrison demonstrates prior to the Sixo-schoolteacher confrontation that Sixo personifies resistance, Sixo's refusal to follow the formulaic discourse of the subsequent master-slave interaction is surprising only to schoolteacher because he has no access to Sixo's interior life or to local knowledges in the black community. Sixo's decision to speak the truth in the face of power disrupts schoolteacher's expectation of a routine exchange. Sixo demonstrates that he is capable of reason; he has aspirations extending beyond his immediate basic survival instincts. Sixo dares to claim the right to full humanity even while schoolteacher is engaging in the practice of distinguishing between his human and animal characteristics.[18]

Schoolteacher operates under the presumptions of the reigning racist theory of the day; he believes that blacks are lower on the chain of existence than whites. Sixo's refusal to accept less than his right to full humanity is a direct threat to the institution of slavery. In addition to desiring a life outside the boundaries of slavery, Sixo and Patsy are expecting a child, which suggests the possibility for grandchildren and extended family relations—an idea that neither Garner nor schoolteacher can envision.[19]

The encounter between Sixo and schoolteacher also provides an opportunity to examine the ideological implication that there is a natural correlation between "blackness" and theft. Morrison's narrator tells us that "after the conversation about the shoat, Sixo is tied up with the stock at night, and locks are put on bins, pens, sheds, coops, the tackroom and the barn door" (223). Laws dealing with the subject of "Negroes" and theft date back to colonial times. The association between the two became so commonplace that, as one historian notes, theft became associated with "race" or "blackness."[20] Harriet Beecher Stowe explores this idea in her creation of Topsy in the infamous *Uncle Tom's Cabin* by attempting to show how the institution of slavery leads to moral deterioration in blacks.[21] However, while demonstrating that Topsy is a thief who can be reformed, Stowe's narrative closes off at least two other possibilities: (1) Topsy's theft is insignificant in relation to the theft of millions of Africans, and (2) Morrison's solution relocates the site of truth, as exemplified by Sixo's line of reasoning.[22]

Sixo counters schoolteacher's definition of theft because his logic is based on a different set of syllogistic possibilities, beginning with a different premise and arriving at a different conclusion. Slavery, Sixo points out, is a closed economic system, and it is economically astute to maintain a healthy labor force. By improving himself, Sixo positively enhances Sweet Home's chances for prosperity. His reasoning is impeccable and Morrison underscores this fact by revealing the flaws of schoolteacher's reasoning and dramatizing its results: Schoolteacher's system of control leads ultimately to the loss of free labor that Sethe, her children, Halle, Sixo, and both Paul A and Paul D would have performed at Sweet Home.

By punishing Sixo, and later murdering him, schoolteacher asserts his right, under the auspices of American chattel slavery, to define truth, to exercise physical domination over the body of the enslaved individual, and, consequently, to subjugate the knowledge (or truth effects) produced by Sixo's system of reasoning; the knowledge produced serves as a different version of truth.

Morrison's recovery process throughout the text allows Sethe, Paul D, Denver, and other characters to recollect and appropriate these and other local knowledges and to put them into play as strengthening strategies. Sethe recalls Sixo's reasoning when guilt feelings arise as she prepares to pilfer from her employer in order to avoid an embarrassing and dehumanizing encounter with blatant racism at the local store—even though she feels guilty about doing so. Paul D's memory of Sixo's attraction to Patsy helps him to summon up the courage to return to Sethe near the end of the novel. In Morrison's hands, Sixo personifies resistance unto his death. Even as he is tied to a tree and set afire, he continues to call upon his inner reserves to resist. Paul D witnesses the scene and passes the story on to Sethe.

Sixo dares to assert his own version of truth and to claim ownership of himself. His presence in the memories of slavery's survivors symbolizes the slaveocracy's thwarted attempt to control and subjugate the mind and language of the enslaved individual along with her or his physical body. Through the memories of Sethe, Paul D, Denver, and other members of the recently emancipated black community in *Beloved*, Morrison exhibits her excavated local knowledges. She writes that "memories within" combined with "the act of the imagination" provide "access to the unwritten interior life" of people who lived under American chattel slavery (Morrison, "Site," 92). The murder of Sixo was inevitable in that time and place, but his presence in the collective memories of the survivors of slavery ensures that his spirit of resistance will endure and will, perhaps, be incarnate in Seven-O and others as long as there are numbers in the number line.[23]

Notes

1. Robert Stepto, *From Behind the Veil: A Study of Afro-American Narrative*, 2d. ed. (Urbana and Chicago: University of Illinois Press, 1979), 6. Hereafter cited in the text. Stepto distinguishes between autobiographical narratives and slave narratives.

2. Frances Smith Foster, *Witnessing Slavery: The Development of Ante-bellum Slave Narratives*, 2d. ed. (Westport, Conn.: Greenwood Press, 1979; Madison: University of Wisconsin Press, 1994), 6.

3. Hazel Carby, " 'Hear My Voice, Ye Careless Daughters': Narratives of Slave and Free Women Before Emancipation," in *African American Autobiography*, ed. William L. Andrews (Englewood Cliffs, N.J.: Prentice-Hall, 1967), 73–74.

4. Toni Morrison, "The Site of Memory," in *Inventing the Truth: The Art and Craft of Memoir*, ed. William Zinnser (Boston and New York: Houghton-Mifflin, 1987, 1995), 90–91. Hereafter cited in the text.

5. This is most apparent in her treatment of the sexual and reproductive exploitation of enslaved women such as Sethe and Ella, Baby Suggs, and Stamp Paid's wife, which goes far beyond what Jacobs could achieve in *Incidents* due to period and publication constraints.

6. Michel Foucault, "Two Lectures," in *Power/Knowledge: Selected Interviews and Other Writings 1972–1977*, ed. Colin Gordon, trans. Gordon et al. (New York: Pantheon, 1980), 85. Hereafter cited in the text.

7. Mae Gwendolyn Henderson, "Speaking in Tongues: Diologics, Dialectics, and the Black Women Writer's Literary Tradition," in *Changing Our Own Words*, ed. Cheryl Wall (New Brunswick, N.J., and London: Rutgers, 1989), 16–37. Henderson advances a model for reading black women's fiction that demonstrates how writers engage the dominant discourse in order to disrupt and revise it.

8. Toni Morrison, *Beloved* (New York: Knopf, 1987), 11. Hereafter cited in the text. "Wild" is an oft-used characterization in Morrison's body of fiction. It is usually associated with a character who is not easily subsumed under the normalizing tendencies of various societal institutions. In *Jazz* (1992), "Wild" becomes a full-blown character as well as a quality or force. Interestingly, the character who shows up as Wild in *Jazz* resembles the very black, "pregnant," naked woman who flees into the woods near the end of *Beloved*.

9. For examples and discussion of "Juba," see: "Secular Songs," in *Call and Response: The Riverside Anthology of the African American Literary Tradition*, ed. Patricia Liggins Hill et al. (Boston and New York: Houghton-Mifflin, 1997), 921–22 and Eugene Genovese, "De Big Times," in *Roll Jordan Roll: The World the Slaves Made* (New York: Random House, 1972, 1974), 573. Arna Bontemps also includes a black female character named Juba in his neo-slave narrative of the betrayed Prosser Rebellion, *Black Thunder* (1936).

10. Leslie H. Fishel Jr. and Benjamin Quarles, *The Black American: A Documentary History*, revised from *The Negro American* (Glenview, Ill.: Scott-Foresman and Company, 1967, 1970), 114. Hereafter cited in the text. (The authors note that this document is from *Frederick Douglass's Paper*, June 2, 1954, which reprinted it from *The Southern Episcopalian*, Charleston, S.C., April 1854). For another example, see Gilbert Osofsky, ed., *Puttin' on Ole Massa* (New York: Harper & Row, 1969).

11. William Wells Brown, *Clotel; or, The President's Daughter*, in *Three Classic African American Novels*, ed. Henry Louis Gates Jr. (New York: Random House, 1990), 86.

12. For a discussion of how enslaved persons distinguished between "stealing" and "taking," see Genovese, " 'Roast Pig is a Wonderful Delicacy, Especially When Stolen,' " 1974, (601–10).

13. Charles H. Nichols, "The Slave Narrators and the Picaresque Mode: Archetypes for Modern Black Personae," in *The Slave's Narrative*, ed. Charles T. Davis and Henry Louis Gates Jr. (Oxford and New York: Oxford University Press, 1985), 286–87.

14.   Frederick Douglass, *My Bondage and My Freedom* (New York: Miller, Orton, Mulligan, 1855), 189.

15.   Garner insists on calling Baby Suggs Jenny even after she explains that her husband's last name was Suggs, and he had called her Baby. Garner advises her that Jenny Whitlow is a safer name for a former slave (142). After he releases her from Sweet Home, Baby Suggs exercises the right to retain her name and identity. Other characters, such as Stamp Paid (Joshua) and Sethe—in selecting Denver's name—add dimension to the importance of naming in *Beloved.* Morrison highlights the importance of naming in even greater detail in *Song of Solomon* (1977). For an excellent discussion of naming and identity in African American literature, see Kimberly Benston, "I yam what I am: the topos of (un)naming in Afro-American literature," in *Black Literature and Literary Theory,* ed. Henry Louis Gates Jr. (New York: Metheun, 1984), 151–72.

16.   The final lines of the dialogue between Baby Suggs and Sethe seem to direct attention to Morrison's dedication of this novel to "Sixty Million and more."

17.   Michel Foucault, *Discipline & Punish,* trans. Alan Sheridan (New York: Random House, 1979), 19.

18.   Sethe recalls several times that her labor was used to make the ink that schoolteacher used to write about them (listing their animal and human characteristics in different columns) (271). Schoolteacher especially liked the way Sethe made the ink from Mrs. Garner's formula (37). For more on this subject, see Anne E. Goldman, "I Made the Ink": (Literary) Production and Reproduction in *Dessa Rose* and *Beloved,"* in *Feminist Studies* 16, no. 2 (Summer 1990): 313–30.

19.   For further insights on the significance of the relationship between Sixo and Patsy, see Trudier Harris, *Fiction and Folklore: The Novels of Toni Morrison* (Knoxville: University of Tennessee Press, 1991), 178–79.

20.   For examples of colonial charters, see Fishel and Quarles. For discussion of theft and race, see Genovese.

21.   Harriet Beecher Stowe, *Uncle Tom's Cabin* (1852; reprint, ed. Elizabeth Ammons, New York and London: W. W. Norton, 1994).

22.   One finds many examples of similar sentiments in African American literature. Indeed Genovese includes personal testimony reflecting this attitude among blacks, but he then goes on to echo Stowe's assessment by asserting that such an attitude was actually harmful in the long run—once blacks were no longer enslaved.

23.   See Harris, 178–79, for a discussion of the folkloric dimensions of the Sixo character.

Transfiguring the Narrative:
Beloved—from Melodrama to Tragedy

Terry Otten

Toni Morrison has repeatedly identified herself a black female author whose work should not be judged or interpreted by comparison to the established canon of European and American white literature. "It's very important to me that my work be African-American," she told Elisa Schappell in a 1993 interview. "[I]f it's assimilated into a different or larger pool, so much the better. But I shouldn't be *asked* to do that."[1] Yet Morrison's insistence on being perceived as an African-American woman writer is tempered by her disdain of literature that becomes "mere soapbox"—"or calculated or self-calculated or self-consciously black, because I recognize the artificial black writing some writers do. I feel them slumming among black people."[2] In contrast she attempts to "look at archetypes"[3], or, as she puts it, "to work with, to fret the cliche. . . . Most of the books that are about something—the books that mean something—treat old ideas, old situations."[4] By common consensus *Beloved* is one of those masterpieces that has entered the "larger pool," not despite its African-American roots but because of them. It remains a distinctly black, female novel of extraordinary power; but in Faulkner's memorable phrase, "it grieves on universal bones."

Like the work of other African-American authors, Morrison's writing echoes black oral and written traditions, especially that of the slave narrative, and the literary conventions of Western culture, which she subsumes, incorporates, reconstructs, and transfigures in her complex and multilayered texts. Most literary critics would concur with James Olney's claim that "the Afro-American literary tradition takes its start, in theme certainly but also in content and form, from the slave narratives."[5] Henry Louis Gates Jr. concludes that the slave narrative indeed provides "the very generic formulation which most subsequent African-American fictional and non-fictional narrative forms extended, refigured, and troped" and that the "self-consciousness of the ex-slaves" established "the formal basis upon which an entire narrative tradition has been constructed."[6] Morrison is of course fully aware of the pervasive

This essay was written specifically for this volume and is published here for the first time by permission of the author.

influence of the slave narrative, and she has discussed *Beloved* as a reconstructed narrative giving voice to what the slave narrative necessarily silenced. In a 1986 talk titled "The Site of Memory," she observed that the milieu of the slave narratives "dictated their purpose and style." Although they employed the traits of the popular sentimental novel, they attempted "to appear as objective as possible—not to offend the reader by being too angry, or by showing too much outrage, or by calling the reader names."[7] Freed from the restrictions yet building on the conventions of the narrative, Morrison extends the dimensions of the genre. Jan Furman has aptly written that *Beloved,* despite its inventive and revisionist traits, "is continuing an unfinished script of slavery begun over two centuries ago by the first slave narratives. . . . an act of recovering the past in narrative."[8]

Though sometimes disagreeing about the number or authenticity of slave narratives, literary historians generally agree that the genre follows a basic paradigm, the central plot depicting the "melodrama and romance of the perilous journey north to freedom."[9] But whereas the first-person slave narrative tends to recount the essential physical and spiritual quest for freedom in linear or chronological order, Morrison's postmodern tale weaves past and present in a series of shifting reenactments and points of view. Morrison employs the narrative structure even as she transforms it, moving the locus of the action inside the self, which she labels the "interior self." Given the intent to trigger the moral outrage of white readers, the slave narratives manipulated polemical and political devices, especially, as Francis Smith Foster notes, "the imaginary plights of many sentimental heroines" that would appeal to "the heightened sensibilities of romantic females or any other mass audience."[10] The "self" that emerged tended to be prototypical, creating in the first-person narrator a communal, universal figure that "is on the periphery instead of at the center of attention, looking outside not within, transcribing rather than interpreting a set of objective facts." This "self," William L. Andrews goes on to say, shifted the focus from the individual slave to the institution of slavery: "[S]peaking too revealingly of the individual self . . . risked alienating white sponsors and readers, too."[11] Henry Louis Gates Jr. adds that the slave narrative was consequently a "communal utterance, a collective tale, rather than merely an individual's biography."[12]

Morrison, however, explores the "interior" in order "to rip [the] veil drawn over 'proceedings too terrible to relate.' " This "task" of exposing "memories within . . . both distinguishes my fiction from autobiographical strategies" operating in slave narratives, she has written, and "also embraces certain autobiographical strategies" (Morrison, "Site," 91–92). In effect, *Beloved* presents not only reconstructed memory but deconstructed history. In it Morrison recreates a past, however painful, in order to shatter the ideological basis upon which it has been constructed by the dominant culture, employing the realism of the slave narrative but disengaging it from mere historical record and revitalizing it as lived experience. She has called her use of memory "willed creation . . . I wanted to translate the historical into the personal" (Schappell, 103).[13]

Although *Beloved* as an historical novel *is* "framed in purpose, thematics, and structure after the African-American slave narrative,"[14] it does not follow the narrowly prescriptive pattern of the genre. The novel shifts points of view from first- to third-person and from the external to the internal lives of its characters, relating historical events in multiple perspectives, revealing both the physical brutality of slavery and its devastating effects on the psychic development of characters, and avoiding the tendency toward melodrama and sentimentality typical in the slave narrative (depicting—in Robert Browning's phrase—"Action in Character, rather than Character in Action"). As Morrison and various critics have observed, *Beloved* articulates what the slave narratives could not speak, given their overtly polemical or propagandistic agendas. It explores not so much the communal disaster of slavery at large as its deepest personal consequences, converting powerful and meaningful melodrama into high tragedy, amalgamating and modifying the elements of seemingly contradictory genres.

Close reading of all of Morrison's fiction leaves "little doubt," Lillian Corti accurately concludes, "that she is quite conversant with the world of tragedy."[15] We can trace in her fiction the convergence of her knowledge of classical tragedy, possibly gained in large measure while completing a classics minor at Howard, and an insistent "black consciousness." Morrison noted in a 1981 interview with Bessie Jones that her intersecting interests were not encouraged when she was an undergraduate at Howard. She recalled that her desire to write a paper on black characters in Shakespeare "horrified" her professors because they "thought it was a sort of lesser topic." At the time, she noted, Howard was "very sort of middle class, sort of upwardly mobile and so on" (Jones, 131). Yet as early as her interview with Bessie Jones in 1981, she remarked that "Greek tragedy . . . seems to me extremely sympathetic to Black culture and in some ways to African culture" (142). Her own work is, in Gates's term, "double-voiced," reflecting both Western and African American traditions. Though decidedly committed to writing authentic African American literature, she acknowledges, "I write [in] what I suppose could be called the tragic mode in which there is some catharsis and revelation. There's a whole lot of space in between, but my inclination is in the tragic direction" (LeClair, 28).[16] When she left Howard to become "a naive teacher" at Texas Southern University, she apparently recognized the relevance of great tragedy to the black experience. Speaking of her commitment to teaching undergraduates, she reflected in the 1993 interview with Elissa Schappell, "I've always thought that the public schools needed to study the best literature. I always taught *Oedipus Rex* to all kinds of what they used to call remedial or developmental classes. . . . You have to give them the best there is to engage them" (Schappell, 122).[17] It is little wonder then that *Beloved,* while it defies simple generic labels, combines the features of tragedy with the rich tradition of slave literature. While inverting, qualifying, or violating the strict architectonic model of what Aristotle defined as high tragedy, *Beloved* maintains its essential vision and shaping characteristics, while at the same time tapping and modifying the resources of the slave narrative.

Clearly a "hybridized text—part ghost story, part historical novel, part slave narrative, part love story"—combining generic forms that "coexist uneasily, in a state of tension, if not antagonism," *Beloved* "can be seen both as tragedy, involving a mother's moment of choice, and as a love story" unified by the "thematic glue" of the slave narrative, Carl Malmgren contends.[18] In attempting to integrate the features of the slave narrative in her tragic vision, however, Morrison carefully avoids the tendency toward melodrama that characterizes most slave narratives. She writes, "My vulnerability would be in romanticizing blackness rather than demonizing it; villifying whiteness rather than reifying it."[19] Resisting the impulse to create what Robert Heilman calls "whole" characters in a melodrama, she projects in Sethe a classically "divided" heroine who, confronted with unresolvable opposites within, must choose against her "self."[20] The independent character who emerges achieves the authenticity and autonomy often denied the hero or heroine speaking autobiographically in the slave narrative. The teller of his or her story, as Houston Baker comments, can be totally obscured in the political and thematic qualities of the slave narrative genre. Once "subjected to the linguistic code, literary conventions, and audience expectations of a literate population," the voice of the "unwritten self," whose story the narrative tells, is often co-opted, "a self transformed by an autobiographical act into a sharer in the general public discourse about slavery."[21] In projecting the inner life of her heroine, Morrison rescues the authentic self, making Sethe the victim of her own divided nature and thereby making her capable of choice and, ultimately, of achieving tragic stature. Sethe's crossing the river into freedom marks the climactic victory of the slave narrative and the beginning of the potential for tragic action.

In her essay on *Medea* and *Beloved* Lillian Corti describes the similarities between the two works, the most obvious being the basic plots based on infanticide, the theme of hubris, and the use of the chorus. But in fact Morrison's novel is more essentially Sophoclean than Euripidean. To be sure, it is in some respects alien to Greek tragedy generally. It employs what Morrison calls "A-U-R-A-L" strategies, such as multivocal patterns, varying word rhythms, the blending of voices, and the subtle control of pauses and silences, rather than emphasizing the paradigmatic design of Greek tragedy, with its rigid trajectory of beginning-middle-end. Its postmodernism seems diametrically opposite the generic form of conventional tragedy. Nonetheless, the novel sustains tragic focus in its depiction of conflict within character, in its obsession with the presentness of the past, in its movement—however circuitous—toward reenactment, in its ritualistic elements, and in its ultimate ambiguity mirroring the "victory in defeat, defeat in victory" that ends high tragedy. Its extraordinary vision incorporates the seminal ingredients of tragedy without violating either its open-ended postmodern texture or its distinctiveness as an expression of African American literature.

Morrison has denied the Euripidean nature of *Beloved,* telling Amanda Smith in an interview published at the same time as the novel that "[t]his is not Medea who kills her children because she's mad at some dude, and she's going to get back at him. Here is something that is *huge* and *very* intimate."[22] The reality is that Sethe must confront the consequences of her *own* action 18 years before Beloved is reincarnated. Like Oedipus, who is obligated to resolve the plague he has himself generated, she must be reconciled to the Fury that visits her in the form of her grown dead daughter. As Amy tells Sethe, "Can't nothing heal without pain, you know."[23] And the most painful act of all is that which Sethe most struggles to evade, the act of "re-membering," of going back to the point of offense that defines her greatest act of love and her most unforgivable "crime."

In describing Sethe's profound confrontation with memory, Morrison in some respects combines the intentions of antebellum and post-war slave narratives. Whereas in early narratives "slavery was depicted as hell on earth, a perverse, obscene, and highly destructive force that threatened to annihilate the selfhood of slaves," post-war autobiographies attempted "to reconstruct the image of blacks who endured it and survived with their individual dignity intact."[24] By means of her frequently shifting narrative, Morrison both captures the horror of slavery and constructs an independent tragic figure. Instead of depicting Sethe as the slave narrator who perceives herself as victim of and finally victor over the debilitating powers of a degenerate system, Morrison describes a "freed" woman who sees herself as victim both of slavery *and* of herself, as one who must tragically destroy her own "best thing" in order to save it. Through multiple points of view, Morrison at once widens and deepens the narrative of emancipation by reversing its unwavering movement toward freedom in repeated retellings expressed by different narrators, finally culminating in the remarkable "unspeakable things unspoken" passage of the novel. Constantly interrupting the chronological record of the inexorable journey toward freedom through shifts in time and voice, Morrison centers on the unresolved present, invoking a pattern of tragic rhythm while maintaining a dualistic vision in which events that precede the crossing into freedom reflect the characterization of the slave narrative and those that occur after the crossing initiate a pattern of tragic action.

Central to Morrison's vision is the female protagonist. Accusing Morrison of designing the novel "to placate sentimental feminist ideology, and to make sure that the vision of black woman as the most scorned and rebuked of victims doesn't weaken," Stanley Crouch claims that the novel fails to achieve "a true sense of the tragic."[25] In fact it transforms first-person historical narrative into what Hazel V. Carby calls "a remarkable exploration or re-visioning of the conventional historical narrative for representing slavery."[26] The tradition of the female slave narrative undeniably surfaces in the work. Certainly one thinks of Harriet Jacobs's *Incidents in the Life of a Slave Girl*, especially in that text's freeing of the first-person narrator from the domination of the sentimental novel in what Valerie Smith describes as its "ironies and silences."[27] The important point to be made is that the female slave autobiography not only allowed women to achieve heroic roles assigned conventionally to males but also to act independently. This empowerment of women directly relates to the potential for their gaining status as tragic figures. As long as the women were seen as secondary in importance and were represented only as victims of abuse, they lacked the possibility of obtaining tragic stature. Although bound by the limitations of the genre, Jacobs frees herself from the more melodramatic features of the sentimental novel in her autobiography. As Linda Brent she portrays herself not as mere victim but as someone capable of choice, though she stops short of projecting herself as a fully tragic heroine. She lacks tragic dimension not because she lacks strength or the ability to act but because she suffers no internal division that leads her to act against herself. In tragedy, Heilman notes, the protagonist must choose between opposing impulses or imperatives in the self. In the slave narrative, the "enemy" is wholly evil and outside the self; in tragedy it is also within the self.

Beloved, though, is an intensely female work, structured in 28 minisections that parallel the female cycle. The ultimate "criminal" act in the novel is not only the singularly evil force of slavery but also the ambiguous act of infanticide committed by a mother driven by unrelenting love. The story of Margaret Garner as fictionalized by Morrison contrasts dramatically with another work based on the slave narratives, *Uncle Tom's Cabin,* in which infanticide also occurs. According to Eileen Bender, Stowe's work virtually created "the peculiar institution of American slavery that has entered American mythology" through the essential melodrama—"exhortative, lugubrious, part soap opera, bathetic, insufferably pious, peopled with racial stereotypes—white and black."[28] In portraying a similar world and placing infanticide at the matrix of the novel, however, Morrison evokes the realm of tragedy by illuminating the unredeemable opposites that compel Sethe to enact the deed. In *Uncle Tom's Cabin,* and generally in the slave narrative that inspired it, horrendous acts are committed by horrible people; in *Beloved* the horrific act of infanticide is attributable to a "free" woman who acts as a free agent.

Like a tragic figure doomed to confront the truth, Sethe wars with her past, attempting to bury the memory of her outrageous act: "[S]he worked hard to remember as close to nothing as was safe" (*Beloved,* 6). There was "[n]othing better than to start the day's serious work of beating back the past" (73); yet Sethe knows that memory "[c]omes back whether we want it to or not" (14), that "if you go and stand in place where it was, it will happen again; it will be there waiting for you . . . even though it's all over—over and done with—it's going to always be there waiting for you" (36). Once she hears "the click," when Beloved sings the song Sethe made up to sing her, Sethe ironically assumes that Beloved's return signals the defeat of the past, that she can "[t]hink about all I ain't got to remember no more" (182). "Thank God," she naively thinks, "I don't have to rememory or say a thing because you know it all" (191). But there is no escape from the past. In tragic rhythm every step forward is a step backward to the defining moment of the "crime."

As in *Oedipus Rex* the plague is already present in *Beloved* when the story begins some 18 years after the infamous event. The house anguishes as a person that "wept, suffered, trembled and fell into fits" (29). Driven by the ghost, Buglar and Howard have long-since fled, Baby Suggs is eight years dead, and Denver is 18 when Paul D arrives in 1873. Chased out by Paul D, the ghost returns as the reincarnated Beloved, whose appearance is described as a rebirth. Sethe sees her when she reenacts the birth process in the form of "voiding" on the way to the outhouse, recalling how Amy told her to "[h]old on" at Denver's birth: "But there was no stopping water breaking from a womb and there was no stopping now" (51). Beloved's "new skin, lineless and smooth," and "soft and new" hands signal her emergence "out of the water" (50). And as several critics have noted, the novel marks her aging as the tale unfolds. She is, as Denise Heinze comments, Sethe's alter ego, "nothing more or less than a memory come to life that has too conveniently been forgotten."[29] As Sethe discovers when she feels Beloved's hands choking her in the Clearing, "[T]he fingers that had soothed her before they strangled her had reminded her of something that now slipped her mind" (*Beloved,* 98). In her folk wisdom Ella tells Stamp Paid, "You know as well as I do that people who die bad don't stay in the ground" (188), and when Paul D catalyzes the action by triggering the ghost's transformation into the now 18- or 20-year-old Beloved, the past surfaces inexorably in the present and thrusts the action forward to the past in tragic irony.

Sethe's motherhood constitutes the nexus of the tragic vision in *Beloved;* it marks the essential difference between the melodrama that underlies the slave narrative and the possibility of tragic choice that transfigures melodrama into tragedy in Morrison's novel. In the slave community "motherhood" often became a bitterly ironic term because slave mothers did not own their children. They were breeders, like the cows and goats with which schoolteacher compares Sethe. Although historians observe that infanticide is infrequently recorded in official documents, it was likely more common than the written records show.[30] The attitude toward children expressed by slave mothers and the references to infanticide in *Beloved* indicate the prevailing irony of "motherhood." When Sethe is eight, Nan tells her that her mother "threw them all away but you. . . . You she gave the name of a black man. She put her arms around him" (62). Of Baby Suggs's eight children, she could only mother Halle, "the last of her children, who was barely glanced at when he was born because it wasn't worth the trouble to try to learn features you could never see change into adulthood anyway" (139). Locked in a room for more than a year, Ella was sexually abused by her master and his son, and she refused to nurse the "hairy white thing, fathered by 'the lowest yet'" until it died after five days "never making a sound" (258–59). For all these women motherhood is indeed a bitter irony. Yet, as Jan Furman writes, Morrison renders Sethe "almost completely as a mother." So long as she lives under the illusion that she *can* be a "mother" at Sweet Home, Sethe remains incapable of tragic action. Her escape, Furman concludes, "is Sethe's emphatic rejection of slavery's power to circumscribe her motherhood" (Furman, 70). But not until she crosses into freedom, thus completing the passage that serves as climax in slave narratives, can Sethe claim ownership of her children and acquire the capacity for choice that distinguishes high tragedy. Sethe tells Paul D, "Look like I loved em more after I got here. Or maybe I couldn't love em proper in Kentucky because they wasn't mine to love. But when I got here, when I jumped down off the wagon—there wasn't nobody in the world I couldn't love if I wanted to" (*Beloved*, 162). Sethe, Morrison told Marsha Darling in an interview, "*became* a mother" in consequence of being free; and she could then "claim responsibility for her children."[31] That ability and obligation to choose is the dividing line between melodrama and tragedy.

Paul D's reaction to Sethe's assertion of freedom as a woman-mother indicates his "slave" mentality. To put it another way, he still lives in the world of the slave narrative where characters are victims rather than free agents. Conditioned by the brutality of slavery, he fears risking such boundless assertions of love. Thinking as an imprisoned slave back in Alfred, Georgia, he knows that "[y]ou protected yourself and loved small." And he sees in Sethe's unqualified love the freedom he does not dare to risk, even though "[h]e knows exactly what she meant: to get to a place where you could love anything you choose . . . well now, *that* was freedom" (162). Psychologically speaking, he cannot "cross over" and sees danger in "a used-to-be-slave woman" loving "anything that much . . . especially if it were her own children she had settled on to love" (45).

Paul D cannot escape the compromising power of slavery that forces him to hold love in reserve in the "tobacco tin" at his heart; but Sethe's "rough choice" is a consummate if paradoxical act of love. Morrison pointed out in a television interview with Bill Moyers that Margaret Garner's case became a cause célèbre for abolitionists because they thought if she were tried for murder, "[I]t would have been assumed she had some responsibility over those children because she owned the rights of a free person."[32] In the novel Mr. Bodwin remembers how the abolitionists vainly attempted "to turn infanticide and the cry of savagery around, and build a further case for abolishing slavery" (260), only to see Sethe charged under the Fugitive Slave Act for the "real crime" of stealing property. In Morrison's adaptation of the story, infanticide is paradoxically a conscious act of murder . . . and of love. Sethe acts freely of her own will, and, as Carol E. Schmudde concludes, she is "morally responsible for her act." Schmudde perceptively adds that it is only the white characters of schoolteacher and Mr. Bodwin who deny Sethe's "choice" and diminish her as a character. Schoolteacher demeans her as incapable of choice and Bodwin excuses her as a helpless victim; "neither judgment assumes that Sethe herself is a fully responsible moral agent" (Schmudde, 124).[33] To acquire tragic stature, Sethe must be saved from innocence, from victimization that disallows choice or the ability to take on the full responsibility and consequences of choice.

It is her classical sin of pride that from the first alienates Sethe from the community of ex-slaves, a pride Baby Suggs first detects when she smells "the scent of disapproval" of the "uncalled-for pride" at the feast to celebrate the coming of Sethe and the children. Even then she wonders, "Why didn't Sethe get on board too?" along with the her children. "Nobody could make it alone" (135). Sethe does indeed exert "outrageous claims" of her "self-sufficiency" that extend to the end of the narrative, when she steals items from Sawyer's restaurant because "the pride made pilfering better than standing in line at the window of the general store with all the other Negroes" (191). At the scene of the infanticide, when the women look at Sethe carrying baby Denver out of the barn, the child sucking her sister's blood along with the milk at Sethe's breast, they ask, "Was her head a bit too high? Her back a little too straight? Probably" (152). As Stamp Paid tells Paul D, "Pride, well, bothers em a bit. They can get messy when they think somebody's too proud" (232).

Nonetheless, Sethe's hubris is akin to that of Oedipus, whose ego defines both his heroism and his villainy. His pride is at once the source of his victory and defeat. It makes him a magnificent king and a magnificent criminal. Even to the very end when he gouges out his eyes, he goes the gods one better. Sethe, too, gains tragic stature not despite her commanding selfhood but because of it—it both magnifies and diminishes her. In the free North, "Bit by bit . . . she had claimed herself" (75). The 28 days of freedom, also symbolic of the female cycle, prove enough time to acquire the tragic ability to enact her will: "All taught her how it felt to wake at dawn and *decide* what to do with the day" (95). To be sure, this is no Medea whose pride as lover is pricked by her lover's indifference and demands revenge. Sethe is catalyzed into action by the riotous love of a *freed* mother who acts as daringly as any man in the male slave narratives and who, in so doing, is self destructive. As Paul D unwittingly recognizes, such possessive motherlove is indeed a killer. Sethe proudly proclaims her free choice: "I birthed them and I got em out and it wasn't no accident. I did that" (162). She keeps repeating to Paul D that "it was me doing it. . . . Me using my own head. But it was more than that. It was a kind of selfishness I never knew nothing about before" (162). Without Halle, she boasts, she saved the children: "Up till then it was the only thing I ever did on my own. Decided" (162). What frightens Paul D is not "what Sethe had done" but "what she claimed" (164), the total possession of a freed woman-mother who "talked about safety with a handsaw" (164). Sethe first intended to kill everyone, including herself, but her "response—homicide rather than suicide—belongs to freedom, not to slavery," Missy Kubitschek writes insightfully (Kubitschek, 168). However regretful Medea may be to sacrifice her children, we never see her as truly divided within herself; and once she acts, she accepts no blame, welcoming the *deus ex machina* that rescues her from the consequences of judgment, and especially self-judgment, as a just recompense for her suffering. But Sethe, far more like Oedipus, accepts full responsibility for her actions and suffers the full consequences of her willful act. There is complicity on Sethe's part that Medea never entertains and that the heroine in the conventional female slave narrative lacks. It is this dimension in *Beloved* that makes it more than a melodrama. No mere chronicle of good and evil, *Beloved* exceeds the dualism of schoolteacher, who divides "reality" into neat opposing columns. As Baby Suggs understands, good and evil cannot be simplistically defined, and she herself cannot "approve or condemn Sethe's rough choice" (*Beloved,* 180). Infanticide was "absolutely the right thing to do," Morrison has remarked, "but she had no right to do it."[34]

Stanley Crouch argues that *Beloved* does not achieve "a true sense of the tragic" because Morrison lacks "the courage to face the ambiguities of the human soul, which transcend race" (Crouch, 43). Nothing could be further from the truth. At one point Paul D alludes to Sethe's face as "a mask with mercifully punched-out eyes" (*Beloved,* 9), an oblique reference to Oedipus suggesting that Sethe *fully* participates in "ambiguities of the human soul." As with other Morrison characters who commit outrageous acts of love, Sethe must pay a price. Like Eva Peace who must watch her beloved Hannah die in a fire after she embraces, anoints, and burns her hapless son Plum, Sethe too must endure the consequences of a loving act of infanticide. In Jan Furman's words, "[E]ven righteous crimes such as Sethe's have a reckoning" (Furman, 82). Ironically, Sethe insists she does not *have* to justify her act, and yet she keeps trying to explain that "if I hadn't killed her she would have died" (*Beloved,* 200). She is consumed by guilt, yet she cannot confess to a crime. She seeks forgiveness, yet Denver senses her "luxuriating" in *not* being forgiven: "Sethe didn't really want forgiveness, she wanted it refused" (252). Even in the magnificent "unspeakable things unspoken" section of the novel, when Sethe asks "Do you forgive me?" and "pleads for forgiveness, listing again and again her reasons" (241–42), she wants understanding rather than forgiveness. Her pride at possessing "what it took to drop the teeth of that saw under her chin" (251) will not allow a willful confession of murder. To be forgiven would be an admission of guilt for a transcendent act of love; and yet such destructive love—even motherlove—demands retribution. Sethe cannot escape the past or excuse it. Few modern works of literature convey the ambiguities of the human soul with such uncompromising authority.

It is Denver who understands the retribution that is occurring and who alone can move the action toward tragic resolution. As she witnesses the merger and reversal of mother and child in Sethe and Beloved until "it was difficult . . . to tell who was who" (241), she knows that Sethe is "trying to make up for the handsaw" and that Beloved is "making her pay for it" (251). In a desperate attempt "to be the two of us" (213) Beloved consumes Sethe, usurping the mother role as Sethe embodies "the teething child" (250), and Denver becomes the agent of reconciliation, as originally symbolized by her simultaneously sucking her mother's milk and Beloved's blood. Early on Baby Suggs recognizes the baby ghost as a supernatural force that has come, like a Greek Fury or a vengeful ghost in a Renaissance tragedy, to exact retribution. She assures Denver that there is nothing to fear. Denver knows "[i]t wouldn't harm me because I tasted its blood when Ma'am nursed me" (209). As the child born in freedom on the river, Denver discovers the ability to act. Just as Beloved represents all the suffering children of slavery as she speaks of the horror on the Middle Passage, Denver acquires mythic proportion. If Beloved is the daughter of history, the victim of slavery that can warp even motherlove, then Denver, as Ashraf Rushdy notes, "is the site of hope" (Rushdy, 571). According to Rushdy, Beloved and Denver are polar opposites, one the incarnation of Sethe's "guilt" and the perniciousness of slavery, and the other the symbol of transforming love, or, in Eusebio L. Rodrigues's words, "the child of the race . . . the seed 'in which the whole generation sleeps confident of the future.' "35

Even from the first, Denver realizes that she plays a role in a larger drama—"like a bill [were] owing somewhere and she, Denver, had to pay it" (Beloved, 77). At first fearing "there is something else terrible enough to make" her mother commit her "killer love" again, Denver exhausts her "outside self loving Ma'am" to keep her mother from killing her. Yet even in her fear she senses love in her mother's potential for violence. "I know she'll be good at it, careful. . . . it won't hurt," Denver thinks as she contemplates Sethe cutting off her head (206). Gradually, Rushdy concludes, Denver comes to understand "that because of a larger communal history, her mother's deed might not be so heinous as she first thought" (Rushdy, 583). As Beloved's presence drives Sethe back to the point of offense, it compels Denver toward the future. Finally realizing that "[i]t's all on me" (Beloved, 206), Denver must risk the ritual of death and rebirth so elemental in traditional tragedy: "[S]he has to step off the edge of the world and die because if she didn't they all would" (239). Baby Suggs had told her she must confront the truth even knowing "there was no defense . . . Know it, and go on out of the yard" (244). Part of the triad that comprises a composite tragic heroine, Denver leaves 124 Bluestone a dozen years later, armed with some awareness of her mother's unrestrained love and its frightful consequences, to seek the equilibrium that can only be restored when she has "told it all" and entrusted herself to the larger community to which the tragic figure always returns.

Freeing herself of her own pride, and not possessing the alienating pride of Sethe, Denver reestablishes the link with the community that takes form as the tragic chorus at the end of the novel. In her 1984 essay titled "Rootedness: The Ancestor as Foundation," Morrison says of her works, "[T]he chorus has changed but there has always been a choral note. . . . The real presence of a chorus. Meaning the community or the reader at large, commenting on the action as it goes ahead."[36]

Finally, in Denver's attempt to be restored to the community through dissolving "the personal pride, the arrogant claim staked out at 124," the chorus led by Ella finds its own culpability "for the years of their own disdain" (249). Resurrecting the communal services at the Clearing, the chorus cries, "Yes, yes, yes, oh yes. Hear me. Hear me. Do it, Maker, do it" (258), and steps back to the beginning, where no word is spoken. And when the women find "the right combination, the key, the code, the sound that broke the back of words . . . it was a wave of sound wide enough to sound deep water and knock the pods off chestnut trees. It broke over Sethe and she trembled like the baptized in its wash" (261).

The moment of catharsis culminates as Sethe symbolically returns like Oedipus "to the crossroads," the ending point of her "rememory" and the defining moment in her life. When Edward Bodwin arrives wearing a hat that for Sethe marks him as schoolteacher come to take "her best thing," she once again manifests her fierce will. As I have written elsewhere, she sees Bodwin as a "man without skin" looking at her "with a whip in his hand" (262), and identifies him with "the men without skin" Beloved recalls on the Middle Passage, with schoolteacher's sadistic nephews, and with the guards who brutalize Paul D in Alfred, Georgia; to her he is the embodiment of slavery. Acting this time to save Beloved rather than inflict her criminal love on her daughter, Sethe at last exorcises the vengeful ghost that has come seeking retribution. Linda Krumholz emphasizes the ritual power of the scene: "As a freed woman with a group of her peers surrounding her, Sethe can act on her motherlove as she would have chosen earlier." In trying to kill the white man rather than her children in order to "save" them from a slavery worse than death, Krumholz notes, Sethe assaults the symbolic representative of the system. "The reconstruction of the scene of the trauma completes the psychological cleansing of the ritual, and exorcizes Beloved from Sethe's life."[37] The communal nature of the scene, underscored by the ritual choral cries of the women, and Denver stopping Sethe before she stabs Bodwin restore the wholeness and equilibrium shattered some 18 years earlier.

In various interviews Morrison has used the classical terms "epiphany" and "catharsis" to describe the endings of her works—"the sense of a combination of the restoration of order . . . and the character having a glimmering of some knowledge." She has said of her novels that "something important has happened . . . some knowledge is there—the Greek knowledge—what is the epiphany in Greek tragedy" (Jones, 135–36).[38] She has related Greek tragedy to the open-endedness of African American folktales and, especially, jazz. Her books never reach total resolution, just as jazz "keeps you on edge. . . . There is no final chord. . . . There is something underneath that is incomplete."[39] Morrison also relates this element of her writing to "a strong influence of Greek tragedy."[40] Even though Sethe frees herself from the bonds of memory at the end and has come full circle in the traditional rhythm of tragedy, the ending remains uncertain. The novel ends not with completion but with the renewed possibility of choice as Sethe reaches a new dimension of freedom. "There is resolution of a sort," Morrison has commented in reference to her novels, "but there are always possibilities—choices." Self-recognition and the exorcising of the past do not resolve the suffering that "can't be undone. And in that sense [the ending] is Greek in the sense that the best thing you can hope for is some realization" and the awareness that "a certain amount of suffering is not just anxiety" (Jones, 136).[41] Unlike the heroine of the slave narrative whose story traces the painful but consummately victorious journey North, Sethe crosses into the ambiguous realm of tragedy, where she once again is free to choose and to bear the full weight of choice.

For all the reconstruction of history and inherent criticism of the prevailing myths of Western or American culture in *Beloved,* the novel places the community of African American characters in the larger context of classical tragedy. It weaves the themes and conventions of the slave narrative, particularly the female slave narrative, into the fabric of tragedy, expanding and deepening the narrative's universality and timelessness. The tragic understructure of the novel mirrors the achievement of the Thirty-Mile Woman, who, Sixo says, "gather[s] me, man. The pieces I am, she gather them and give them back to me in all the right order" (*Beloved,* 272–73).

Notes

1. Elissa Schappell, "Toni Morrison: The Art of Fiction CXXXIV," *The Paris Review* 128 (Fall 1993): 119. Hereafter cited in the text. In "Memory, Creation, and Writing," Morrison comments that she set out "to write literature that is irrevocably, undisputably Black" (*Thought* 59 [December 1984]: 389).

2. Claudia Tate, "Toni Morrison," in *Black Women Writers at Work,* ed. Claudia Tate (New York: Continuum, 1983), 118. Morrison told Jane Bakerman in a 1977 interview that she resents the way black writers seem "always to explain something to somebody else!" ("The Seams Can't Show: An Interview with Toni Morrison," *Black American Literature Forum* 12 [1978]: 59). Referring to *The Bluest Eye* in the *The Paris Review* interview of 1993, Morrison noted that the commercially successful model for black fiction at the time she wrote her first major work was the typical male novel based on " 'Let me tell you how powerful I am or how horrible you are,' or some version of that" (Schappell, 99).

3. Bessie W. Jones, "An Interview with Toni Morrison," in *The World of Toni Morrison,* ed. Bessie W. Jones and Audrey L. Vinson (Dubuque, Ia.: Kendall/Hunt, 1985), 138. Hereafter cited in the text.

4. Thomas LeClair, " 'The Language Must Not Sweat," *The New Republic,* 21 March 1981, 26. Hereafter cited in the text. Morrison also remarked to Claudia Tate that "[a] good cliché can never be overwritten; it's still mysterious. . . . the subjects that are important in the world are the same ones that have always been important" (Tate, 120–21).

5. James Olney, " 'I Was Born': Slave Narratives, Their Status as Autobiography and as Literature," *Callaloo* 7 (Winter 1984): 65. Reprinted in Charles T. Davis and Henry Louis Gates Jr., eds., *The Slave's Narrative* (New York: Oxford University Press, 1984), 148–75.

6. Davis and Gates, Introduction, xxxiii–xxxiv. Hereafter cited in the text.

7. Toni Morrison, "The Site of Memory," in *Inventing the Truth: The Art and Craft of Memoir,* 2d ed., ed. William Zinnser (Boston: Houghton-Mifflin, 1995), 87. Hereafter cited in the text.

8. Jan Furman, *Toni Morrison's Fiction* (Columbia: University of South Carolina Press, 1996), 80.

9. Bernard W. Bell, *The Afro-American Novel and Its Tradition* (Amherst: University of Massachusetts Press, 1987), 29. For a discussion of the correlation between the slave narrative and other paradigms of the spiritual journey, see Missy Dean Kubitschek, *Claiming the Heritage: African-American Women Novelists and History* (Jackson: University Press of Mississippi, 1991). Hereafter cited in the text.

10. Frances Smith Foster, *Witnessing Slavery: The Development of Ante-bellum Slave Narrative* (Westport, Conn.: Greenwood Press, 1979), 23.

11. William L. Anders, *To Tell a Free Story: The First Century of Afro-American Autobiography, 1760–1865* (Urbana: University of Illinois Press, 1988), 6.

12. Introduction to *The Classic Slave Narratives,* ed. Henry Louis Gates Jr. (New York: A Mentor Book, 1987), x. Foster also describes the narrator as "the community self," an attempt to combine the individual with "the counter desire to be a symbol" of the repressed slave (Foster, 5).

13. Ashraf H. A. Rushdy describes *Beloved* as "an introjection into the fields of revisionist historiography and fiction" and the expression of "a reconstructive—critical and hopeful—feminist voice within the fields of revisionist historiography and contemporary fiction." ("Daughters Signifyin(g) History: The Example of Toni Morrison's *Beloved,*" *American Literature* 63 [September 1992]: 568. Hereafter cited in the text.)

14. Wilfred D. Samuels and Clenora Hudson-Weems, *Toni Morrison* (Boston: Twayne Publishers, 1990), 95.

15. Lillian Corti, "*Medea* and *Beloved*: Self-Definition and Abortive Nurturing in Literary Treatments of Infanticidal Mothers," in *Disorderly Eaters: Texts in Self-Empowerment,* ed. Lilian R. Furst and Peter W. Graham (University Park: The Pennsylvania State University Press, 1992), 62.

16. Asked by Bessie Jones whether or not she detects the relationship between Greek tragedy and black experience in *Song of Solomon,* Morrison admitted simply, "Well, I do" (Jones, 134).

17. Interestingly, Gates argues that slave narratives perhaps most closely parallel the pattern and form of detective fiction; and *Oedipus Rex* is sometimes called the quintessential detective story in literature. As noted later, the going "back to the crossroads" in Sophocles's play mirrors the reenactment of the "crime" in *Beloved.* See Davis and Gates, xv.

18. Carl Malmgren, "Mixed Genres and the Logic of Slavery in Toni Morrison's *Beloved,*" *Critique* 36 (Winter 1995): 96. In addition to Malmgren and Corti's studies of *Beloved* as tragedy, see also Carol E. Schmudde, "Knowing When To Stop: A Reading of Toni Morrison's *Beloved,*" *CLA Journal* 37 (December 1993): 121–35. Hereafter cited in the text. I am also indebted to Erik Styles who, under my direction, completed an unpublished Senior Research Seminar paper at Wittenberg University in 1996 treating Morrison's use of the slave narrative and tragedy.

19. Toni Morrison, *Playing in the Dark: Whiteness and the Literary Imagination* (Cambridge, Mass.: Harvard University Press, 1992), xi.

20. Heilman fully describes and illustrates the distinctions between "whole" characters found in melodramas, or what he calls "disaster" plays, and the tragically divided hero in his often-cited study *Tragedy and Melodrama: Versions of Experience* (Seattle: University of Washington Press, 1968).

21. Houston A. Baker Jr., "Autobiographical Acts and the Voice of the Southern Slave," in Davis and Gates, 253.

22. Amanda Smith, "Toni Morrison (*PW* Interviews)," *Publisher's Weekly,* 21 August 1987, 51.

23. Toni Morrison, *Beloved* (New York: Alfred A. Knopf, 1987), 79. Hereafter cited in the text.

24. Deborah E. McDowell and Arnold Rampersad, eds., *Slavery and the Literary Imagination* (Baltimore: The Johns Hopkins University Press, 1989), xi–xii.

25. Stanley Crouch, "Aunt Medea," *The New Republic,* 19 October 1987, 40. Morrison has called the review not only "a misunderstanding, but . . . pernicious." (Cecil Brown, "Interview with Toni Morrison," *The Massachusetts Review* 36 [Autumn 1995]: 466). Various critics have attacked Crouch's now infamous review. See, for example, Roger Sale, "Toni Morrison's *Beloved,*" *The Massachusetts Review* 29 (Spring 1988): 81–86.

26. Hazel V. Carby, *Reconstructing Womanlove: The Emergence of the Afro-American Woman Novelist* (New York: Oxford University Press, 1987), 143, note 42. Bernard Bell describes *Beloved* as "a neo-slave narrative of double consciousness . . . that speaks in many compelling voices and on several time levels of the historical rape of black American women and of the resilient spirit of blacks in surviving as people" ("*Beloved:* A Womanist Neo-Slave Narrative; or Multivocal Remembrances of Things Past," *The African American Review* 26 [Spring 1992]: 9).

27. Valerie Smith, " 'Loopholes of Retreat': Architecture and Ideology in Harriet Jacobs's *Incidents in the Life of a Slave Girl,*" in *Reading Black, Reading Feminist,* ed. Henry Louis Gates Jr. (New York: Meridian, 1990), 225. As Gates observes, as early as Mary Prince's 1831 autobiography women began to speak "*for* themselves," celebrating "their self-transformation into subjects, subjects defined by those who have gained a voice" (*The Classic Slave Narratives,* xv). Hazel Carby also emphasizes that as narrators female slaves represented themselves "as acting their own vision" and as able to "take over their own lives" (Corby, 36). Valerie Smith differentiates female from male narratives in which males depicted "themselves as isolated heroic subjects" and described the journey North not only as that "from slavery to freedom but . . . from slavehood to manhood" (Valerie Smith, Introduction to *Incidents in the Life of a Slave Girl,* by Harriet A. Jacobs [New York: Oxford University Press, 1988] xxix).

28. Eileen Bender, "Repossessing *Uncle Tom's Cabin:* Toni Morrison's *Beloved,*" in *Cultural Power/Cultural Literacy,* ed. Bonnie Braendlin (Tallahassee: Florida State University Press, 1991), 130. In another comparison of *Beloved* and Stowe's novel, Cynthia Griffin Wolff offers a far more favorable view of *Uncle Tom's Cabin.* See " 'Margaret Garner': A Cincinnati Story," *The Massachusetts Review* 32 (Fall 1991): 417–40. In contrast Lori Askeland argues that *Beloved* "[s]ets itself up as a remodeling of *Uncle Tom's Cabin* that examines [conventional] ideology and revises it in a way that avoids reification of a patriarchal power structure" ("Dismantling the Model House in *Uncle Tom's Cabin* and *Beloved,*" *American Literature* 64 [December 1992]: 787).

29. Denise Heinze, *The Dilemma of "Double-Consciousness": Toni Morrison's Novels* (Athens: University of Georgia Press, 1993), 176.

30. See especially Elizabeth Fox-Genovese, *Within the Plantation Household: Black and White Women in the Old South* (Chapel Hill: University of North Carolina Press, 1985), 323–29, 456, note 58.

31. Marsha Darling, "In the Realm of Responsibility: A Conversation with Toni Morrison," *The Women's Review of Books* (March 1988): 6. In reference to Willa Cather's *Sapphira and the Slave Girl,* which she compares to the slave narratives that inspired it, Morrison explains in

Playing in the Dark that "slave mothers are not mothers; they are 'natally dead,' with no obligation to offspring or to their own parents" (20). Houston Baker Jr. notes that in Harriet Jacobs's *Incidents in the Life of a Slave Girl,* "A new bonding of Afro-American humanity consists, for Brent [Harriet Jacobs], in the reunion of mother and child in freedom" (*Blues, Ideology, and Afro-American Literature: A Vernacular Theory* [Chicago: The University of Chicago Press, 1984], 55).

32. Reprinted in *Conversations with Toni Morrison,* ed. Danielle Taylor-Guthrie (Jackson: University Press of Mississippi, 1994), 272.

33. In *Playing in the Dark* Morrison attacks the canonical American literary tradition that describes African Americans as "other." "We are choices," she insists, not simplistically the white culture's alter ego or shadow (9).

34. Marvyn Rothstein, "Morrison Discusses New Novel," *The New York Times,* 26 August 1987, Y19. Morrison repeated the remark in an interview on the *MacNeil-Lehrer Newshour* on PBS television on 29 September 1987.

35. Eusebio L. Rodrigues, "The Telling of *Beloved,*" *The Journal of Narrative Technique* 21 (Spring 1991): 84.

36. Toni Morrison, "Rootedness: The Ancestor as Foundation," in *Black Women Writers (1950–1980): A Critical Evaluation,* ed. Mari Evans (Garden City, N.Y.: Anchor Press/Doubleday, 1984), 341. Among others who comment on Morrison's use of the Greek chorus in *Beloved,* see especially Schmudde and Heinze. William R. Handley relates "the function and communal aspect of African art" with "the Greek chorus, antiquated in the West, [which] sings its lines and unites the audience and the actors in a communal performance of a culture's understanding of itself" ("The House a Ghost Built: *Nommo,* Allegory, and Ethics of Reading in Toni Morrison's *Beloved,*" *Contemporary Literature* 36 [Winter 1995]: 698).

37. Linda Krumholz, "The Ghosts of Slavery: Historical Recovery in Toni Morrison's *Beloved,*" *African American Review* 26 (1992): 403.

38. See also her remarks to Cecil Brown that her books end in recognition—"a note of epiphany in which somebody learns something about his or her situation" (Cecil Brown, "Interview with Toni Morrison," *The Massachusetts Review* 36 [1995]: 462). In an interview with Anne Koenen Morrison similarly observed that "at the end of every book there is an epiphany, discovery, somebody has learned something that they never would otherwise" (" 'The One Out of Sequence': An Interview with Toni Morrison [New York, April 1980]," in *History and Tradition in Afro-American Culture,* ed. Gunter H. Lentz [Frankfurt/New York: Campus Verlag, 1984], 213.)

39. Nellie McKay, "Interview with Toni Morrison," *Contemporary Literature* 24 (1983): 413–29.

40. Charles Ruas, "Toni Morrison," in *Conversations with American Writers* (New York: Knopf, 1995): 215–43.

41. Lillian Corti claims that the novel ends in "a mellow, comic quality that contrasts markedly with the stark outlines of the tragic denouement" and that "Sethe has a better chance of achieving the ancient ideal of moderation than the tragic heroine" (Corti, 73–74). But the novel concludes with a question mark and with Sethe bearing the devastating consequences of her action.

Index

◆

The Volume Editor

Barbara H. Solomon is a professor of English and women's studies at Iona College in New Rochelle, New York. She is also Director of Writing for the Department of English. Among the anthologies she has edited are *Bernice Bobs Her Hair and Other Stories of F. Scott Fitzgerald; Rediscoveries: American Short Stories by Women, 1832–1916; Herland and Selected Stories of Charlotte Perkins Gilman; Other Voices, Other Vistas: Twenty-Five Non-Western Stories; American Families; American Wives: Thirty Stories by Women, The Experience of the American Woman: Thirty Stories;* and the Signet edition of *The Awakening and Selected Stories of Kate Chopin.* Her current project is editing a collection of American short stories titled *The Have and Have Nots.*

The General Editor

Dr. James Nagel, J. O. Eidson Distinguished Professor of American Literature at the University of Georgia, founded the scholarly journal *Studies in American Fiction* and edited it for 20 years. He is the general editor of the Critical Essays on American Literature series published by Macmillan, which now contains over 130 volumes. He was one of the founders of the American Literature Association and serves as its executive coordinator. He is also a past president of the Ernest Hemingway Society. Among his 17 books are *Stephen Crane and Literary Impressionism; Critical Essays on* The Sun Also Rises; *Ernest Hemingway: The Writer in Context; Ernest Hemingway: The Oak Park Legacy,* and *Hemingway in Love and War,* which was selected by the *New York Times* as one of the outstanding books of 1989 and which has been made into a major motion picture. Dr. Nagel has published more than 50 articles in scholarly journals, and has lectured on American literature in 15 countries. His current project is a book on the contemporary short story cycle.